Aurea Vidyā Collection

17

* For a Complete List of Titles see page 533.

This book was originally published in Italian in 2005 as Bādarāyaṇa, *Brahamsūtra*, Edited by Raphael, by Associazione Ecoculturale Parmenides (formerly Edizioni Āśram Vidyā) – Revised Edition 2013.

First Published in English in 2014 by
Aurea Vidyā
39 West 88th Street
New York, NY 10024

ISBN 978-1-931406-17-8
Library of Congress Control Number 2014908614

On the cover

Guruparaṁparā, the "Uninterrupted chain of the *gurus*." According to Tradition, the lineage in the transmission of the Teaching of *Vedānta* is this: Nārayāṇa, Brahmā, Vāsiṣṭa, Śakti, Paraśara, Vyāsa, Śuka, Gauḍapāda, Govindapāda, Śaṅkara and his disciples Padmapāda, Hastāmalaka, Toṭaka and Sureśvara.

Bādarāyaṇa

BRAHMASŪTRA

with parallel Sanskrit Text

by Raphael

Aurea Vidyā

TABLE OF CONTENTS

Book Three
Spiritual Discipline

Book Four
The Fruit

NOTES TO THE TEXT

The English Text

1. Square brackets [ ] are ours. They enclose terms and phrases that are understood in the text, and also supplementary material that is considered helpful to a better understanding of the work.

2. Round brackets ( ) enclose the original Sanskrit of words and phrases which are under examination and which belong to the *sūtras* of the *Brahmasūtra*.

3. Single inverted commas ‘ ’ enclose quotations from particular scriptural sources.

4. Double inverted commas “ ” enclose single words or short phrases from the *sūtras* of the *Brahmasūtra* or the *Upaniṣads* or they indicate speech within quotations.

5. Italic type is always used for Sanskrit words (*Brahman*, *Ātman*, *Hiraṇyagarbha*, *māya*, etc.) and for the running heads.

6. The same noun will have an upper-case initial if it refers to a divine Form (*Vāyu*) and a lower-case initial if it refers to an element or form (*vāyu*).

7. Any discrepancies relating to scriptural references arise from the lack of uniformity in different editions and the different ways of dividing the texts from which they have been drawn.

The Sanskrit Text

1. The transliteration of the Sanskrit text from the original *devanāgarī* follows the currently accepted criteria and, apart from the few exceptions, does not separate the words.

2. Words are split into syllables. This practice also applies to Sanskrit words that appear in the English text.

The Notes

1. In the notes, Sanskrit nouns in parentheses are generally given in their dictionary form, except when it is preferable to give the declined forms or when they form parts of sentences. Sanskrit verbs are given in their root form, except when it is preferable to quote the conjugated forms.

2. References to verses in the *Brahamsūtra*, the *Upaniṣads*, and the other texts are given in accordance with the traditional numbering system used in the texts, such as *Brahmasūtra* I.I.1, or simply 'See I.1', or just the verse number, such as 1.

3. References to the Notes are given with the number relating to the *sūtra*.

The Phonetic Formation of the Letters

According to their mouthpositions

		gutturals	palatals	cerebrals	dentals	labials	
Simple breathing (formless sound)	h						
Release of breath	ḥ						
Vowels							
short		a	i	ṛ	ḷ	u	
long		ā	ī	ṝ	ḹ	ū	
		(a)					
Diphtongs			e-ai		o-au		
			(i)			(u)	
Semi-vowels			y	r	l	v	
Consonants							
unvoiced		k	c	ṭ	t	p	
aspirated unvoiced		kh	ch	ṭh	th	ph	
voiced		g	j	ḍ	d	b	
aspirated voiced		gh	jh	ḍh	dh	bh	
nasals		ṅ	ñ	ṇ	n	m	
Sibilants			ś	ṣ	s		
Pure nasal sound							ṁ
Nasal sound conformable to the consonant							ṃ

Guide to Pronunciation.

a	=	s**u**n	ḍ	=	or**d**er*
ā	=	f**a**ther	ḍh	=	har**d-h**eaded*
i	=	**i**f	ṇ	=	cor**n***
ī	=	f**ee**t	t	=	**t**able
u	=	p**u**t	th	=	an**t-h**ill
ū	=	m**oo**n	d	=	**d**ay
ṛ	=	**ri**ng	dh	=	go**d-h**ead
ḷ	=	reve**lry**	n	=	**n**o
e	=	**a**che	p	=	**p**ure
ai	=	m**i**ne	ph	=	**ph**oenix
o	=	h**o**me	b	=	**b**aby
au	=	l**ou**d	bh	=	a**bh**or
k	=	**k**ite	m	=	**m**other
kh	=	bloc**kh**ead	y	=	**y**ellow
g	=	**g**ate	r	=	**r**ed
gh	=	lo**g-h**ut	l	=	**l**ady
ṅ	=	si**ng**	v	=	**w**in
c	=	**ch**alk	ś	=	**sh**all
ch	=	coa**ch-h**ouse	ṣ	=	mar**sh***
j	=	**j**ug	s	=	**s**at
jh	=	he**dgeh**og	h	=	**h**eaven
ñ	=	fri**nge**	ṁ	=	b**on**b**on**
ṭ	=	dar**t***	ḥ	=	aa**h**
ṭh	=	car**th**orse*			

* With the tip of the tongue raised to the roof of the mouth.

List of Abbreviations

A. Ve.	*Atharva Veda*
Ai.	*Aitareya Upaniṣad*
Bha. Gī.	*Bhagavadgītā*
Bṛ.	*Bṛhadāraṇyaka Upaniṣad*
Bra. Sū.	*Brahmasūtra*
Chā.	*Chāndogya Upaniṣad*
Īśa.	*Īśa (vāsya) Upaniṣad*
Ka.	*Kaṭha Upaniṣad*
Kau.	*Kauṣītakī Upaniṣad*
Ke.	*Kena Upaniṣad*
Mā.	*Māṇḍūkya Upaniṣad*
Ma. Bhā.	*Mahābhārata*
Mā. Kā.	*Māṇḍūkyakārikā*
Mai.	*Maitry Upaniṣad*
Mu.	*Muṇḍaka Upaniṣad*
Pra.	*Praśna Upaniṣad*
Ṛ. Ve.	*Ṛg Veda*
Śa. Brā.	*Śatapatha Brāhmaṇa*
Sā. Kā.	*Sāṁkhyakārikā*
Śve.	*Śvetāśvatara Upaniṣad*
Tai.	*Taittirīya Upaniṣad*
Yo. Sū.	*Yogasūtra*

BIBLIOGRAPHICAL REFERENCES

Vedānta Explained, Śaṅkara's commentary on the *Brahma-Sūtras* translated by H. Date, Bombay, 1954-1959.

Brahma-Sūtra Śaṅkara-Bhāṣya, translated by V.M. Apte. Popular Book Depot, Bombay, 1960.

The Vedānta Sūtras of Bādarāyaṇa with the commentary by Śaṅkara, translated by G. Thibaut, in two parts. Dover Publications, Inc. New York 1962. [Reprint of Clarendon Press editions of "The Sacred books of the East" voll. 34, 38].

Die Sûtra's des Vedânta oder, die Çârîraka-Mîmâmsâ des Bâdarâyana, nebst dem vollständigen Kommentare des Çankara. Aus dem Sanskrit übersetzt von Paul Deussen. Hildesheim, Olms, 1966. [Nachdruck der Ausgabe Leipzig 1887].

The Brahma Sūtra. The Philosophy of Spiritual Life. Translated with an Introduction and Notes by S. Radakrishnan. Greenwood Press, Publishers, New York, 1968.

Brahma-Sūtra-Bhāṣya of Śrī Śaṅkarācārya. Translated by Swami Gambhirananda. Foreword by T.M.P Mahadevan. Advaita Ashrama, Calcutta 1972.

Vedānta Explained, Śaṅkara's commentary on the Brahma-sūtra by V.H. Date, 2 vols. Munshiram Manoharlal publishers Pvt. Ltd., Delhi 1973.

Brahma Sūtras. Translation and Commentary by Swami Sivananda. Motilal Banarsidass, Delhi 1977.

Brahma Sūtra. Testo sanscrito, con introduzione, traduzione, commento e lessico a cura di Icilio Vecchiotti. Ubaldini Editore, Roma 1979.

Brahmasūtrabhāṣya. Complete Works of Śrī Śaṅkarācārya in the Original Sanskrit, vol. VII. Sadanand Samata Books, Madras, 1983.

Brahma-Sutras. Traducíón del sanscrito, introducción y notas por Daniel de Palma. Etnos Indica, Varanasi 1997.

Brahmasūtra con il Commento di Śaṅkara, 2 volumi. Traduzione dal sanscrito e note a cura del Gruppo Kevala. Edizioni Āśram Vidyā, Roma 2000.

Brahma-Sutras con los comentarios advaita de Sankara. Editor Consuelo Martín. Editorial Trotta, Madrid 2000.

EDITORIAL NOTES

The *Brahmasūtra* contains 555 *sūtras*, arranged in four Books, each of which is divided into four Chapters.

The *Brahmasūtra* with Śaṅkara's *bhāṣya* and the other works published in Collezione Vidyā are prepared by the Associazione Ecoculturale Parmenides (formerly Edizioni Āśram Vidyā), a not-for-profit organization of Rome, Italy.

Commentaries and notes to the *sūtras* have been placed at the end of each Chapter, with the exception of those which do not impair the readability of the parallel Sanskrit text.

Unless otherwise specified, the quotations from the *Upaniṣads* are taken from the book, *Upaniṣad*, Edited by Raphael. Bompiani, Milan, 2010.

Heartfelt thanks go to Arthur and Phyllis Farndell for their valuable suggestions in the production of this work.

FOREWORD

Acknowledged as a work of vast importance, the *Brahmasūtra* has been commented upon by many realised Masters, by scholars, by students of culture, and by others. The commentators have interpreted the text from varying points of view, according to what they themselves have brought with them in terms of culture, spirituality, or mere erudition. It is also appreciated that some terms have been changed or modified in order to accommodate particular interpretative requirements.

One is thus faced with interpretations which may be based on theism, on ritualism, on *Advaita*, and so on. These have now become codified, and it is not easy to distance oneself from them.

We may give the names of some commentators worthy of note, among so many others that are equally valid: Rāmānuja, Madhva, Nimbārka, Vallabha, Śrīnivāsa, Bhāskara, Baladeva, and so on.

One of the most significant and profound commentators was undoubtedly Śaṅkarācārya, who provided, from the perspective of *nirguṇa Brahman,* a notable contribution based on a foundation of philosophy and metaphysics in accordance with the exposition given by the Master Bādarāyaṇa, who adopts the position of *Advaita Vedānta.*

At certain points, Raphael has referred to the Western tradition, to emphasise the fact that *the* metaphysical Truth is one, while *the* truths of the perceptible world are myriad.

At times he has also expatiated on certain aspects of the

Teaching, because they were already contained in embryonic form in the *Brahmasūtra*. On the other hand, the work is written in *sūtras* that are extremely compressed, so that some of them which are of particular importance can be expounded by remaining within the scope of Bādarāyaṇa's thought and therefore within the tradition of *Vedānta*; and this also makes it relevant for those Western inquirers who, for the first time, are meeting this fundamental work of *Vedānta*, also known as *Vedāntasūtra* or *Śārirakasūtra*.

Those who wish to go deeper into the subject in question may consult the extensive, deep, full *bhāṣya* (commentary) of Śaṅkarācārya, the codifier of *Advaita Vedānta*. The present volume may thus be seen as merely a preliminary study leading to that work.

Aurea Vidyā

atha prathamo 'dhyāyaḥ

jamanvayaḥ

BOOK ONE

Harmony

atha prathamo 'dhyāyaḥ

prathamaḥ khaṇḍaḥ

athāto brahma-jijñāsā //1//

atha: so, now, after this; *ataḥ*: hence; *brahma*: *Brahman*; *jijñāsā*: the research to know.

janmādyasya yataḥ //2//

janmādi: birth, origin, and so on; *asya*: of this; *yataḥ*: from which.

śāstra yonitvāt //3//

śāstra: the *Vedas*, the *Upaniṣads*, and all the other Scriptures; *yonitvāt*: on account of being the matrix, the source.

tat tu samanvayāt //4//

tat: that; *tu*: but, however; *samanvayāt*: on account of reciprocal connection, harmony, agreement.

īkṣaternāśabdam //5//

īkṣateḥ: with regard to seeing; *na*: not; *aśabdam*: non-evidence with reference to the Scriptures or word.

gauṇaś cen na-ātma śabdāt //6//

gauṇaḥ: secondary, figurative; *cet*: if; *na*: not; *ātma-śabdāt*: on account of the word '*Ātman*.'

Book One

Chapter One

1. *Now, hence the research to know the Brahman.*[1]

2. *From which the birth, and so on, of this.*[2]

3. *On account of being the source of the Śāstras.*

This *Brahman* is the source or the foundation of the *Śāstras*, the Scriptures in a broad sense. And in relation to this, if the Scriptures put forward variant views, what answer could be given?

4. *On That, however, [there is] agreement.*[3]

5. *The reference to seeing [is] not on evidence, [for which reason we shall say] no.*[4]

6. *If it is figurative, [it is] not [so] on account of the word 'Ātma.'*[5]

tanniṣṭhasya mokṣopadeśāt // 7 //

tan-niṣṭhasya: [for the one who is] established or resting in that; *mokṣopadeśāt*: the teaching on liberation.

heyatvāvacanāc ca // 8 //

heyatva: to be excluded, rejected; *avacanāt*: absence of affirmation; *ca*: but.

svāpyayāt // 9 //

sva: *Ātman*; *apyayāt*: on account of absorption, penetration.

gati-sāmānyāt // 10 //

gati: origin; *sāmānyāt*: through uniqueness.

śrutatvāc ca // 11 //

ca: and; *śrutatvāt*: the *Śruti* reveals it.

ānandamayo 'bhyāsāt // 12 //

ānandamayaḥ: full of bliss, made of bliss; *abhyāsāt*: through constant repetion.

7. *The teaching with a view to Liberation [is for the one who] rests in That.*

This would not be possible if the *Ātman* had to be related to *pradhāna*, because the teaching pertaining to liberation from the transmigrating ego, according to the Scriptures, points to *Brahman* and not to *pradhāna*.

> 'Having risen from this world through the wisdom of the *Ātman*... ' (*Ai*.III.4) does not allow one to consider *pradhāna* as the ultimate expression of realisation.

8. *But there is no affirmation for which it should be excluded.*[6]

9. *Through absorption into the Ātman.*

On account of the fact that the reflection of the *Ātman* (*jīva*) is re-absorbed into the *Ātman* and not into *pradhāna*.

10. *Through uniqueness of origin.*

Because there is uniqueness of the teaching and uniformity in the primary meaning of the Scriptures.

11. *And [because] the Śruti reveals it.*[7]

12. *Through the repetition of the fullness or bliss.*[8]

vikāra-śabdān-neti cen na prācuryāt // 13 //

vikāra-śabdāt (*t+n* = *n-n*): through modification of the word; *na iti* (*a+i* = *e*) *cet*: if it is not so; *prācuryāt*: abundance or fulness.

taddhetu vyapadeśāc ca // 14 //

tat: of that; *hetu*: cause; *vyapadeśāt*: because it is declared; *ca*: and also.

māntravarṇikam eva ca gīyate // 15 //

māntra-varṇikam: expressed or described in the *Mantras*; *eva*: also; *ca*: and; *gīyate*: is celebrated or sung.

netaro 'nupapatteḥ // 16 //

na: not; *itaraḥ*: other (*na+itaraḥ* = *netaro*); *anupapatteḥ*: on account of impossibility.

13. *If [one finds] not so, through modification of the word, this is not valid on account of fullness.*

If it is affirmed that the expression 'fullness' implies modification, and thus not plenitude of being, the response is that this is not so, on account of the fullness of the *Ātman*, which cannot contain anything that could become other than itself and therefore it does not need any attribute.

14. *And also through the declaration of that.*

Moreover, it is stated that the *Ātman*, or *Brahman*, being the primary cause of bliss itself, or fullness itself, cannot be conditioned by any modification.

15. *It is described in the Mantras and also celebrated [in the Brāhmaṇa].*

The *Brahman* that is described in the *Mantra* part is that which is also celebrated in the *Brāhmaṇa* part. For this reason one must accept that *Brahman* has the same significance in the *Mantra* part as in the *Brāhmaṇa* part, because these are not self-contradictory, and thus the *Ātman* or *Brahman* of fullness is indeed the supreme *Ātman* or *Brahman*.*

16. *Not the other, on account of impossibility.*

The *Ātman* described as full cannot refer to another, that is, it cannot refer to the being which transmigrates, which is characterised by time, for this is nothing but an effect; hence it is inadmissible and inappropriate to wish to refer the *Ātman* to the transmigrating being (*ahaṁkāra*).

---

* Cp. *Tai.* I.V.1-3.

bhedavyapadeśāc ca // 17 //

bheda: difference; *vyapadeśāt*: on account of the declaration or, affirmation; *ca*: and, besides; (*śāt+ca* = *śāc ca*).

kāmāc ca nānumānāpekṣā // 18 //

kāmāt: on account of an act of volition or desire; *ca*: and, again; *na*: not; *anumāna*: inference; *apekṣā*: consideration.

asmin asya ca tad-yogaṁ śāsti // 19 //

asmin: in this; *asya*: of this; *ca*: moreover; *tad-yogam*: union with that; *śāsti*: the teaching or instruction of the Scriptures.

antas tad dharmopadeśāt // 20 //

antaḥ: within, inside; *tat*: that; *dharma*: quality, fundamental property; *upadeśāt*: from the affirmation, spiritual instruction.

bheda vyapadeśāc cānyaḥ // 21 //

bheda: difference; *vyapadeśāt*: on account of the declaration; *ca*: and; *anyaḥ*: other.

ākāśas tallingāt // 22 //

ākāśaḥ: *ākāśa*, space, universal and all-pervading ether; *tat*: that; *liṅgāt*: on account of specific character or distinctive sign; (*tat+l* = *talliṅgāt*).

17. *And on account of the affirmation of difference.*[9]

18. *Again, [there is] no consideration of inference, on account of the act of volition.*[10]

19. *Moreover, what the Scriptures teach is the union of this with That.*[11]

20. *That is within, according to the declaration of [its] properties.*

What originates a phenomenon is a Principle which is inner and which transcends the phenomenon; it cannot be assimilated or identified with *pradhāna* because the traditional texts clearly state their difference.

21. *On account of the declaration of difference from other.*

The *Ātman* is distinct from every transmigrating being for the additional reason that there is a clear and concordant affirmation in the *Śruti*:

> 'He who dwells in the directions of space but is other than the directions of space, whom the directions of space know not, whose body is made up of the directions of space, and who rules the directions of space from within, he is the inner Ordainer, your immortal *Ātman*.'*

22. *Ākāśa [is] That on account of specific characteristic.*[12]

---

* *Bṛ.* III.VII.10 *et seqq.*

ata eva prāṇaḥ // 23 //

ataḥ eva: therefore, besides; *prāṇaḥ*: vital energy.

jyotiś caraṇābhidhānāt // 24 //

jyotiḥ: light; *caraṇa*: foot; *abhidhānāt*: on account of the mention or reference.

chando 'bhīdhānān neti cen na tathā ceto 'rpaṇa-nigadāt tathā hi darśanam // 25 //

chandaḥ: poetic meter; *abhidhānāt*: on account of the mention; *na*: not; *iti*: so, this; *cet*: if; *na*: not; *tathā*: so, this; *cetaḥ*: mind; *arpaṇa*: fixing; *nigadāt*: on account of the quotation or affirmation; *tathā*: like this, so; *hi*: moreover; *darśanam*: seeing, observing.

bhūtādi-pāda vyapadeśopapatteś caivam // 26 //

bhūtādi: beings, and so on; *pāda*: foot; *vyapadeśa*: indication; *upapatteḥ*: on account of reasoned demonstration; *ca*: and; *evam*: also, thus.

upadeśa bhedānneti cennobhayasminnapyavirodhāt // 27 //

upadeśa: teaching; *bhedāt*: on account of difference; *na*: not; *iti*: thus; *cet*: if; *na*: not; *ubhayasmin*: in both cases; *api*: also, still; *avirodhāt*: through lack of contradiction.

prāṇas tathānugamāt // 28 //

prāṇah: vital energy; *tathā*: in this way; *anugamāt*: on account of conformity or correlation.

23. *Therefore [also] the prāṇa.*

Prāṇa, like *ākāśa*, taken as an analogy, is also the *Brahman*.

24. *[It is] light on account of the reference to the feet [quarters].*[13]

25. *If [it is said that] it is not so because metre is mentioned, [the reply is that] it is so because there is a statement about fixing the mind; moreover, it is thus [that one needs] to see.*[14]

26. *The indication that beings, and so on, are the foot is also reasonable.*[15]

27. *If it is not so on account of difference in the teaching, [the answer is], once more, no, [because] in both cases [there is] no contradiction.*[16]

28. *In this way, prāṇa [is Brahman] on account of conformity.*

na vaktur ātmopadeśād iti ced adhyātma saṁbandhabhūmā-hy asmin // 29 //

na: not; *vaktuḥ*: of the speaker; *ātmopadeśāt*: on account of self-description or teaching; *iti*: so; *cet*: if; *adhyātma*: the inner *Ātman*; *saṁbandha*: reference, allusion; *bhūmā*: abundant; *hi*: because; *asmin*: in this.

śāstra-dṛṣṭyā tūpadeśo vāmadeva vat // 30 //

śāstra: Scriptures; *dṛṣṭyā*: through the vision; *tu*: but, however; *upadeśāḥ*: teaching; *vāmadeva-vat*: like Vāmadeva.

jīva-mukhya-prāṇa-liṅgān neti cen nopāsā traividhyād āśritat vād iha tadyogāt // 31 //

jīva: soul; *mukhya*: principal, fundamental; *prāṇa*: vital energy; *liṅgāt*: on account of specific sign; *na*: not; *iti*: thus; *cet*: if; *upāsā*: meditation (*na-upāsā*: *a+u* = *o*); *traividhyāt*: on account of the threefold form; *āśritatvāt*: on account of confirmation; *iha*: her; *yogāt*: on account of relation or union; *tad*: to that.

iti prathamaḥ khaṇḍaḥ

prathamo 'dhyāyaḥ

29. *If it is said that this is not so on account of the speaker's [reference] to himself, [the answer is that] this is not the case, because in this [passage] references to the inner Ātman are abundant.*[17]

30. *But the teaching [accords] with the vision of the Scriptures (Śāstras), as in the case of Vāmadeva.*

How can one understand the consideration of Indra as *Brahman*? According to the *Bṛhadāraṇyaka Upaniṣad* (I.IV.10) any being, from any level, which succeeds in *knowing Brahman* realises itself as *Brahman*.

Indra, knowing that 'his' *Ātman* is identical to the supreme *Ātman* or *Brahman*, instructs Pratardana on the infinite *Brahman* by availing himself of the words 'I am the breath... .' In the same way, Vāmadeva, having attained identity with That (the *Brahman*), expressed himself thus: 'I am Manu, I am Sūrya (the Sun).'

This teaching accords with the *Śāstras*.

31. *If it is not so on account of the specific signs of the jīva and the principal prāṇa, [the reply is that] this is not the case, on account of the three types of meditation, and [our thesis] is confirmed [elsewhere], and [also] here there is reference to That.*[18]

End of the Chapter One of Book One
of the Brahmasūtra

NOTES

[1] I.I.1 - 'Now, hence' indicates successiveness; it implies the acquired existence of something. What existence does it imply?

When there exist the requisite qualifications (*viveka*, *vairāgya*, and so on)[1], then one can investigate and know, or realise, the *Brahman*.

This work of the great Master, Bādarāyaṇa, who was subsequently identified with the mythical Vyāsa, may also be called *Vedāntamīmāṁsā* (reflection on the final parts of the *Vedas*), or *Brahmamīmāṁsā* (reflection on the *Brahman*), or even *Uttaramīmāṁsā* (reflection subsequent to *Pūrvamīmāṁsā*, 'prior reflection', which concerns the ritual aspect, from which it acquires its other name of *karmakāṇḍa* or 'ritual section') in relation to the *jñānakāṇḍa* or 'Knowledge section', the section which the text under examination represents.

The *Brahmasūtra*, like the *Vedas* and *Upaniṣads* themselves, is not a philosophical doctrinaire treatise in the manner of Western philosophical writings; and at times there are *sūtras* which are so obscure and concise, being composed of three or four words, that they are difficult to clarify and difficult to interpret. But this is typical of ways of expression that belong to the Eastern tradition. However, the text is interwoven with that culture and spirituality whose reference are the *Vedas* and the *Upaniṣads*, or, rather, the *Śruti* and the *Smṛti*. To

---

[1] For these qualifications see *sūtra* 19 in the *Vivekacūḍāmaṇi* of Śaṅkara, edited by Raphael. Aurea Vidyā, New York.

disentangle the *Brahmasūtra* from this fabric would be to divest it of meaning and make it impossible to decipher. The *darśanas* themselves, although varying in their philosophical framework, always have the Tradition of the *Vedas* and the *Upaniṣads* as their point of reference. The *Nyāya*, the *Vaiśeṣika*, the *Sāṁkhya*, and so on, are not the same thing, nor are they in conflict with one another, but complete each other mutually.

One may say, however, that the whole of the *Śruti*, the *darśanas*, and Brahmanical culture itself, all have a single aim: realisation, or the liberation of the being from *saṁsāra*. From this perspective, one can see that every *darśana* represents just one particular facet of a clearly defined principle expounded in the *Upaniṣads*; and on the other hand, one can see how the *Upaniṣads* themselves are derived from one or another of the four *Vedas*.

This diversification of perspectives can be understood to a large extent if one takes account of the fact that the *darśanas*, like the *Upaniṣads*, are not organic, self-contained 'philosophical systems', and they do not present dianoetic philosophy as it is understood in the West. If one wishes to speak of philosophy with reference to the *Upaniṣads* and the *darśanas*, one needs to view philosophy or traditional metaphysics as something quite different from the systematic demonstrative creation produced by an individual by means of his analytical mind. *Darśana* means 'vision', conception, maintaining or declaring a thesis, 'view', philosophical perspective.

It is frequently said that in the *Vedas* and *Upaniṣads* there is all that can be known: dualism, pluralism, monism, pragmatism, logic, psychology, pure metaphysics, and so on. But there is nothing akin to the philosophy of Aristotle, of Descartes, of Kant, and so on; and there cannot be, because the conclusion and the presuppositions are different. It is appropriate to clarify it from the very beginning.

The *Upaniṣads*, like the *Brahmasūtra*, are 'dialectical chunks', intended to stimulate the conscience of the inquirer into *waking up* from the 'sleep' into which the mind has enfolded him.

Like the *Upaniṣads*, the *Brahmasūtra* has been the subject of commentaries which are necessary, not to say indispensable, in shedding a little light on the darkness of the aphorisms; the interpretation thereof is in conformity with the level of consciousness from which the commentator himself speaks. Thus there are various Masters who, sometimes, may diverge among themselves. See Rāmānuja (theist), Jaimini (ritualist), Āśmarathya (assertor of the *bhedhābhedavāda* = difference-non difference), Auḍulomi, Śrīkantha, Baladeva, Bhāskara and so on. One should bear in mind, on the other hand, that the teaching was imparted orally, as was the teaching of Plato, so that writings acted solely as adjuncts to the teaching.

One of the greatest and most important commentators on the principal *Upaniṣads*, the *Brahmasūtra*, the *Bhagavadgītā*, the "triple science": *prasthānatraya*, in our view is Śaṅkara, with the depth of his teaching, his philosophical speculation, and the greater unity that he gave to the Tradition. But Śaṅkara himself had a precursor in the person of Gauḍapāda, the great Master of the Tradition, who made a commentary to the *Māṇḍūkya Upaniṣad* in his *Māṇḍūkyakārikā*. The first chapter of the *Māṇḍūkyakārikā*, on account of its depth of teaching, is considered to be an integral part of the *Upaniṣad* itself.

But, with reference to the *sūtra* under consideration, could not the term 'Now hence' relate to the study and performance of the *karmakāṇḍa*? This is equivalent to asking, 'Can the knowledge of *Brahman* be subsidiary to the performance of rites and to the Vedic injunctions?'

This point of view is irrelevant, because *Brahman*, being metaphysical by nature and hence beyond the sensible and the principial intelligible, cannot depend on acts or actions occurring in the world of contingent and transient phenomena. In other words, the Absolute does not depend on the relative. Besides, the two *Mīmāṁsās* have different aims. The *Pūrvamīmāṁsā* has as its aim the enjoyment of immortality, the attainment of the Gods or the reward of *Brahmaloka*; and so, by means of rites, one seeks to acquire, to have, to enjoy. The opening *sūtra* of the *Purvamīmāṁsasūtra* is *athāto dharma jijñāsā*: 'Now, hence the investigation of the Law' (I.I.1), which presupposes the recitation of thc *Vedas*; thus, only after effecting the recitation of Vedic *mantras* can one know the Law (*dharma*).

On the other hand, the *Uttaramīmāṁsā* has as its aim the realisation of identity with the *Brahman*, final liberation, and thus, rather than enjoying or acquiring something, one moves in the direction of Being. The requisite for Being is not so much *karman* or something external to the agent as an act of self-awareness (*anubhava*) of that which one already is, since:

> 'That which is infinitely subtle: all this has That as its foundation. That is the Reality. That is the *Ātman* and "You [*jīva*] are That", O Śvetaketu... .'[1]

> 'Certainly, he who, in truth, knows that supreme *Brahman* becomes *Brahman* itself.'[2]

If one is not qualified for the way of *jñāna* (*jñānamārga*), it is appropriate, indeed vital, for a correct *sādhanā*, to begin with

---

[1] *Chā*. VI.VIII.7.

[2] *Mu*. III.II.9.

the preliminary and preparatory stage of the *Pūrvamīmāṁsā*. In this way, when one has the right qualifications (which are inner and partake of the nature of the being, rather than outer and accidental), what should one investigate and *know*? One should know, realise the supreme Reality.

Jijñāsā is 'the requirement to know' the *Brahman*, which is the Highest Good, to use Plato's term.

The fact that the reference is to the *Brahman* and not to anything else is explained in the *sūtra* I.I.2.

[2] I.I.2 - That which is the pre-causal fount and which gives origin to the birth, development, preservation (*sthiti*) and dissolution (*bhaṅga* or *pralāya*) of the world (*asya* = of this world), and of all that these imply, is the *Brahman*. Since the world (name and form = *nāma-rūpa*) is born, grows, and dissolves, it cannot be the *Brahman*, the Eternal, the Unborn, the Unqualified, the Undetermined, because it is the foundation of all that exists.

> '... since the essence of the One is the generator of all things, it is none of these things. However, it is not "something"; it is not quality, not quantity, not spirit, not soul; it is not even "in movement", or conversely "in rest"; it is not "within a location" or "within a time"; it is, instead, the single Ideal, fully self-inclusive ["... it lies within itself (καθ' ἑαυτό τε κεῖται)", in the words of Parmenides fg. 8.30] or, rather, it is the Unformed, which exists prior to every ideal, prior to movement and prior to stillness, for these qualities are attached to Being and they make it manifold.'[1]

[1] Plotinus, *Enneads*, VI.9.III, translated by V. Cilento. Laterza, Bari, Italy.

> '... within It all things have their origin and dissolution'[1]

This is a reference to Being, or *Īśvara*; whereas the seventh *sūtra*, speaks of the *nirguṇa Brahman* as the supreme, unqualified Reality, which transcends time, space, and causality. In relation to the *sūtra Īśvara* can be understood as first cause of the development of manifestation

[3] I.I.4 - In the various texts of *Vedānta* there is agreement and harmony concerning That; in other words, the texts agree in establishing the same meaning and the same aim.

> 'In truth, as if there were duality, indeed there one smells another, one sees another, one hears another, one speaks to another, one thinks about another, one knows another. But when for him everything has become his own very *Ātman*, then what can be smelled and by what means? Then what can be seen, and by what means? Then what can be heard, and by what means? Then what can be spoken, and by what means? Then what can be thought, and by what means? Then what can be known, and by what means? By what means will it be possible to know That, through whom everything is known? By what means, my dear, will it be possible to know the knower?'[2]

> 'In the beginning, my dear, there was just Being, one only without a second. In this regard some say: "In the beginning this was just Non-being, one only without a second: from that Non-being is founded the Being."'[3]

---

[1] *Mā*. VI.

[2] *Bṛ*. II.IV.14.

[3] *Chā*. VI.II.1.

'In the beginning this was indeed the *Ātman*, one only... .'[1]

It was said earlier that this is not a philosophy devised by the analytical mind of an individual; the *Śāstras*, or the *Śruti*, arise from the receptivity or 'hearing' of the *Ṛṣis*, and thus they arise from universal planes. The word *Veda* derives from the root *vid*, which means to 'see' with the *eye* of the Heart which is responsive to the *buddhi*. The analytical mind plays no part in this. The *Ṛṣis* have *seen*; they have *heard* with the inner ear; and then they have propounded the Truth, using arguments that are sometimes obscure. Plato, too, declares that Knowledge is nothing but 'remembering' (*anámnesis*), and is therefore not a product of the dianoetic mind.

A further consideration needs to be made: for Plato, the terms ιδέα and εἶδος (Idea) are derived from the verb ἰδεῖν, which means 'to see.' The 'World of Ideas' (Being) is 'seen' by the soul; the Truth has not been 'revealed' to the soul, but the soul, of itself, has 'seen' the intelligible Reality or Truth, since the soul has an ontological constitution. The *Veda*, therefore, is not a Truth that has been revealed to someone who then assumes the mantle of the Messiah, or something similar, and subsequently founds a religion.

The Hindu *Sanātanadharma* is the eternal Law, the eternal Tradition, for *Truth* is not born and does not die; it is the 'Axis' of the world and of all worlds; it is the reference point around which all things revolve, and wherever this reference point is not acknowledged there is *adharma*, the absence of Order, of Law, and of Truth (*satya*); and hence there is a state of disorder, confusion, and subversion, in which every individual creates truth for himself, according to his own requirements (absolute relativism). Traditional Truth is not exclusive to the

---

[1] *Bṛ.* I.IV.17.

East, because the Western tradition has always had the same eternal Truth or Reality, though expressed in a different descriptive language, which at times is identical. Truth or Reality is one, and if it is one it cannot have limits.

[4] I.I.5 - With this *sūtra* Bādarāyaṇa starts his dialectic with the *Sāṁkhya darśana*. The first cause of the world cannot be *pradhāna* (substance) because this is not based on scriptural evidence.

[5] I.I.6 - If the term 'consider' can seem to be figurative or metaphorical, the answer is that this is not possible because of the explicit word '*Ātma*.'

The Scriptures speak of the original Source as of a luminous, intelligent Principle as Witness of all the causes or effects. *Pradhāna* cannot be assimilated metaphorically to an intelligent Being because when the Scriptures say: '*Om*. In the beginning the *Ātman* was this (*idam*), that is the One (*eka*). Nothing else existed other than this. He considered: "May I, now, create the worlds."'[1] they give to the term 'consider' a primary and explicit meaning and not a metaphorical or figurative one.

Pradhāna, which is characterised by the three *guṇas*, cannot be the *Ātman*, whose nature is that of the *Brahman*, beyond the three *guṇas*. And if the advocates of *Sāṁkhya* maintain that the *Ātman* is related to *pradhāna*, the author of the *Brahmasūtra* replies that *pradhāna* cannot stand for the *Ātman* because there is no statement declaring that the *Ātman* must be excluded.

[6] I.I.8 - If insentient *pradhāna* were the cause of existen-

---

[1] *Ai.* I.I.1.

tial movement, which is a mere object of perception, it would consequently exclude the knowledge of the ultimate Subject, that is pure essence.

> 'This is the inner Ordainer... the unseen observer, the unheard hearer, the unthought thinker, the unknown knower. There is no other seer distinct from Him; there is no other hearer distinct from Him; there is no other thinker distinct from Him; there is no other knower distinct from Him. This is the inner Ordainer, your immortal *Ātman*. Whatever is other than He is destined to perish.'[1]

The *Ātman* is He through whom mind thinks, hearing hears, and knowledge is able to reveal itself, being their foundation. What other reasons are there which show that the *Ātman* cannot be *pradhāna*? (See following note).

> [7] I.I.11 - 'For Him there is in the world neither ruler nor ordainer, nor That has any distinctive feature. That is the Cause, and the Patron of the patrons of the organs. He has no progenitor and no protector.'[2]
>
> '... When it is said that this individualised being sleeps, then, my dear, he is perfectly fused with Being, he is immersed into himself. This is why it is said of him that "he sleeps" because, in truth, he is absorbed into the *Ātman*.'[3]

The ultimate foundation of manifestation is thus the *Brahman*, and not *pradhāna*; it cannot be the *jīva*, because this is re-absorbed into the *Ātman*. One may say that *pradhāna* is an

---

[1] *Bṛ*. III.VII.23.

[2] *Śve*. VI.9.

[3] *Chā*. VI.VIII.1.

object of perception whose foundation is actually the *Brahman*. But to which *Ātman* or *Brahman* does the *Śruti* refer?

Bādarāyaṇa, the Teacher, gives an explanation in the *sūtras* that follow.

> [8] I.I.12 - '... In truth, beyond that, which is this [body or sheath] made of intellect, there is another [more] inward *ātmā* which is made of bliss. By this [body made of bliss] is filled that [body made of intellect].'[1] 3

The transcendent *Ātman*, through the *jīva*, expresses itself through the sheath of knowledge and that of fullness, in addition to the other sheaths; every sheath-body fulfils a specific function. Since there is the supreme *Ātman*, as well as that which is not supreme (*jīvātman*) and individual *ahaṁkāra*, to which *Ātman* does the *jīva*-body that is made of bliss refer? It refers to the supreme *Ātman* because it is repeated by the *Śruti* (*Mu*. III.I.1; *Mai*. VI.31) that this is the way.

The *Ātman* is that which gives being both to the *jīvā* and to all the vehicles of the *jīvā* itself.

> '... this body is as if endowed with consciousness, but it [the *Ātman*] is its vivifier.'[2]

[9] I.I.17 - Besides, the texts declare a difference between the *Ātman* that is full and birthless and the being which transmigrates.

> 'Two birds, which always go together and have similar names, sit on the same tree. One of them eats the fruit of

---

1 *Tai*. II.V.1.

2 *Mai*. II.6.

the *pippala* by the varied taste, [while] the other, without eating [any], watches detached.'[1]

[10] I.I.18 - Again, there cannot be identity of *pradhāna* with the supreme *Ātman* because *pradhāna*, being insentient and unintelligible, cannot express volition and intelligence. Any conceivable identity of *pradhāna* with the *Ātman* or *Brahman* would involve an inference, a deduction, by which *pradhāna* would be the origin of everything. And this is not in accordance with the *Śruti*.

[11] I.I.19 - Moreover, the *Śruti* teaches that the *jīva* merges into the supreme *Ātman* at the moment of liberation. It should be noted that the same *Śruti*, after enunciating the characteristics of *ānandamaya*: '... joy is its head, fulfilment is its right side, and so on.' (*Tai*. II.V.I), states that the *Brahman* is the foundation of all beings – particular, universal, and principial – together with their respective sheaths or bodies of expression. *Brahman* is thus the non-active [*akartṛ*] efficient cause, of everything, and *pradhāna* is the material cause.

[12] I.I.22 -The texts state that although *ākāśa* (space or ether) and *prāṇa* (the breath of life, the energy of life) are not the *Brahman*, they are by analogy related to the *Brahman* inasmuch as This is like the all-pervading ether and the breath which gives vitality to every formal expression of life.

'... [Eventually he becomes established] in the *Brahman* as *Mahā*. [Having become established in That] he attains independent sovereignty, he attains [the state of being] the lord of the mind. He becomes the lord of speech, the lord

---

[1] *Śve*. IV.6.

of vision, the lord of hearing, the lord of knowledge, and this which is beyond it: that which has space as body, the *Brahman*, whose essence is reality, that who has in *prāṇa* his own delight, that whose mind is bliss, that who is full of peace and immortal... .'[1]

'Fire, becoming speech, entered the mouth; wind, becoming *prāṇa*, entered the two nostrils... '[2]

[13] I.I.24 - 'Of such an immensity is his greatness, but compared to that, greater is the *Puruṣa*. All beings are [just] one of His feet. That of the three feet, immortal, is [established] in his own splendour.'

'So, that shining Light, which is above the sky, beyond the universe, beyond everything, in the supreme worlds which have no higher, it is certainly this light which is within the human being.'[3]

The *sūtra* under examination, together with the quotations from the *Śruti*, indicates that *Brahman* is both immanent and transcendent; being therefore all-pervasive, the substratum of everything or, to put it another way, the foundation of all that is sensible and intelligible, it cannot but be also in the 'heart of the human being.'

If it were obliged to be isolated or separated from the human being, an insurmountable duality would be created, as there would then be two mutually opposed natures.

[14] I.I.25 - 'The *Gāyatrī*, in truth, is all that there exists

---

[1] *Tai.* I.VI.2.

[2] *Ai.* I.II.4.

[3] *Chā.* III.XII.6; III.XIII.7.

and all that is. The word, in truth, is *Gāyatrī*. In truth the word is all that there exists, that sings and protects.'

> '*Gāyatrī* is truly the earth, because all that there exists is founded upon it, and does not transcend this very [earth].'
>
> 'This *Gāyatrī* has four feet and six forms. This is stated by [a *mantra* of the] *Ṛg* [*Veda*].'[1]

It may be thought that the *Śruti* is speaking of the *Gāyatrī*, and not of the *Brahman*, as the origin of the universe and of the four quarters. However, that would not reflect the truth, because the *Śruti* maintains that it is actually the *Brahman* that expresses itself through the *Gāyatrī* metre. An additional reason is that there is a reference to fixing the mind on the *Brahman*.

The *Brahman* is all that exists, as the *Chāndogya Upaniṣad* states (III.XIV.1); and the *Gāyatrī*, in this specific instance, is identified as the *Brahman* because, like the *Brahman*, it has four quarters or feet, each consisting of six syllables. The *Gāyatrī* and the light of the previous *sūtra* are simply portrayals of the *Brahman*. It is in this way, maintains the *sūtra*, that one should see and consider things.

[15] I.I.26 - It is thus reasonable to interpret the passage to mean that the *Gāyatrī* is the *Brahman* itself, with the consequent deduction that all beings, and so on, are the feet (*pādas*).

In the *Vedas* and *Upaniṣads* there is frequent use of analogies to indicate the supreme *Brahman* because it is only in this way that the empirical mind, that is based on relationship, can be made to understand something which cannot be conceptualised. The *Brahman* is therefore compared to the wind, to *prāṇa*, to the sun, to *ākāśa*, and so on. But this type

---

[1] *Ibid.* III.XII.1,2 and 5.

of expression belongs to all the Traditions. Plato himself has recourse to myth when he needs to indicate a metaphysical Principle that is beyond conceptualisation.

Regarding this problem see what will be said in the 'Appendix' to Chapter Two of Book Two of this work.

[16] I.I.27 - If it is objected that there is a difference of teaching in the two *Śruti* passages (*Brahman* is 'three quarters in heaven' and 'the light shines beyond heaven'), the answer is that there is no contradiction: it depends on the point of view from which one chooses to see things.

Brahman is 'in heaven' (qualified) and 'beyond heaven' (unqualified or undetermined), that is, *saguṇa* and *nirguṇa*. It is 'within and without'; *Brahman* is not exhausted through being 'within' (immanence), because it constitutes the substratum alone on which are interwoven the lights and shades of manifestation. The 'without' (transcendence) is not determined by the 'within'; just as the screen on which the frames of a film appear is not determined by the film.

The *Brahmasūtra* is not an immanentist, phenomenal teaching and hence naturalistic. This distinction is also made by Plato when he speaks of the One Good and the World of Ideas (or qualified Being). Plotinus is saying the same when he speaks of the transcendent One and the principial Intelligence or *Noûs*; the One is the founding factor of *Noûs*.

[17] I.I.29 - In the *Kauṣītakī Upaniṣad* (III.2 *et seqq.*) one reads that Indra, in his reply to Pratardana, said: 'I am the breath [*prāṇa*] and so on.'

Now, the god Indra is considered to be an aspect of the *Brahman*, a determined principle of the undetermined or unqualified *Brahman*. If everything is resolved into Indra, who in this specific case is identified with the vital energy, it follows that Indra, or *prāṇa*, is resolved into the *Brahman*. If it is supposed that Indra refers only to himself and not to the *Brahman* or the *Ātman*, it may be noted that in the same text from the *Upaniṣad* there is explicit mention of the inner *Ātman (adhyātmasaṁbandha),* and the *Ātman* is identified with the *Brahman*.

> '... this *Ātman*, is the Lord of all beings, the Ruler of all beings. As all the spokes of a wheel are fixed in the hub and the rim of the wheel, so in this *Ātman* are established all beings, all gods, all worlds... That is this *Brahman*, without antecedent or successor, without inside or outside... This is the teaching.'[1]

[18] I.I.31 - If it is objected that all these references are not relevant to the *Brahman* but are relevant to individual determinations such as the *jīva*, the *prāṇa*, and so on, the reply is that this is not (*na*) so, because this would lead to the supposition of three different types of meditation: on the *jīva*, on the *prāṇa* or breath, and on the *Brahman*.

The deduction from the *Śruti*, however, is that there is a single meditation, which is meditation on the *Brahman*, and when there is talk of meditation on the *jīva*, on *ākāśa*, on *prāṇa*, and so on, the implicit meaning is that these determinations are taken to refer to the *Brahman*; in other words, *Brahman* is seen with reference to its superimpositions (*upādhis*). Since *Brahman* is beyond the world of names and forms, the ability to refer to it must rely, at the level of discursive logic, on supports which clearly belong to the phenomenal and transient world.

---

[1] *Bṛ*. II.V.15,19.

According to the classic example, however, there is no need to mistake the rope for the snake.

Plotinus writes:

> 'In reality, everything – however beautiful and honourable it may be – is subsequent to Him, for the Principle of all this is He, (although, again, in another sense He, is not even the principle)... On the other hand, we should totally deny Him all relationship with things [*Vedānta* uses the word *asparśa*: non-contact, non-relationship] since He is That even before they exist, for it is true that we strip Him of even the verb "*is*", and consequently there is also the bare reference to beings, however that may be... The Principle of all things must have greater power and worth than that which is subsequent.'[1]

---

[1] Plotinus, *Enneads* VI.8.VIII and X. Op. cit.

Considerations on Chapter One of Book One

The First Book begins with a metaphysical affirmation.

What does one need to know or realise? Is it holiness, godliness, the soul's salvation, or empirical knowledge of things? It is none of these. What one needs to know is the *Brahman*, that uncaused Principle which underlies the appearance and disappearance of all manifested things: that Principle which represents the matrix, the root, or well-spring of all the *Śāstras* or holy Scriptures. And what is the aim of this knowledge? It is liberation from duality, from individual *avidyā* and from universal *māyā*. It is, therefore, supreme Realisation, and to attain this one needs to concentrate and *know* only That (*sat*). The goal towards which all beings tend, consciously or unconsciously, is absorption in *That*.

Vedāntasūtra offers a synthesis of a series of aphorisms which are in total conformity with the Tradition of the *Vedas* and *Upaniṣads*. The fundamental principles begin with these presuppositions:

1) There exists a Reality which is constant, eternal, and uncaused, the foundation of all existence, a foundation which is also present within us. This Reality unifies and therefore gives order to the multiplicity of becoming; without such foundation the all would go adrift.

2) How may one consider this Reality, this Constant, which depends on no external factor but rests upon

itself and for itself? According to *Vedāntasūtra*, this Reality, this Constant, is a state which the *Upaniṣads* call *Ātman* or *Brahman*.

3) Can this Reality, this *Ātman* or *Brahman*, be realised by a being, at whatever level of manifestation that being may find itself? According to *Vedāntasūtra*, this Reality can be realised. And why can it be realised? The answer can be given in the words of Plotinus, whose reply is identical to that given by *Vedānta*: 'We are thus not separate from Being, but we are within Being, and Being is not separate from us: all beings are therefore One.'[1]

4) What is the valid method or the specific means which allows the duality or *avidyā* to be resolved?
According to *Vedāntasūtra*, one must take into consideration cathartic Knowledge.

5) On what is this Knowledge based in order for it to be operative? It is based on intuitive discrimination, on *viveka*, on Platonic dialectic; Plotinus, with reference to Plato, writes: '[Dialectic], being our most precious faculty, is necessarily related to Being and to the most precious reality: as prudence [Dialectic] is related to Being, and as Intelligence it is related to that which transcends Being.'[2]

And that which transcends Being is the metaphysical

---

[1] Plotinus, *Enneads* VI.5.I, edited by G. Faggin, Bompiani, Milan, Italy.
[2] *Ibid*. I.3.V.

One, *nirguṇa Brahman*, the One Good of Plato.[1] These uncaused Principles are identical in the Eastern Tradition and the Western Tradition.

One should consider that the *jīva* does not receive knowledge from the sensible world, but from the intelligible world, from its participation with the *Ātman*. Therefore the *jīva* must not go out from itself, but it must enter into itself; the sensible plane, which remains as a mere object in becoming, can only offer changeable opinions, not science (ἐπιστήμη).

According to some schools of thought, such as the *darśana Sāṁkhya*, the origin of the appearance and disappearance of the worlds and of everything in them is *pradhāna*, that which has been put before everything: this is the first element. It is equivalent to *mūlaprakṛti*, or the primordial substance.

Manifestation takes its rise from an imbalance of the three *guṇas* (the constituents of *pradhāna*), which triggers the movement that gradually, by multiplying the elements, leads to the creation of forms and abilities such as mind, senses, subtle elements, gross elements, and so on (hence the name 'numeration' that is given to *Sāṁkhya*).

The phenomenal world of becoming, in its physical and subtle aspects, is nothing other than the effect of a particular 'evolution' (*pariṇāma* = the transformation of substance from one thing into another, the actual and real change of cause into effect); from which such system takes its other name of *pariṇāmavāda*, the doctrine of the real and substantial trans-

[1] With reference to the One it is interesting to note the *excursus* of G. Girgenti concerning the henological paradigm in Plato, Plotinus and Porphyry. G. Girgenti. *Il pensiero forte di Porfirio*, see chapter IV. Vita e Pensiero, Milan, Italy. Moreover see Porfiry, *Sentenze sugli intelligibili*, edited by G. Girgenti, and also G. Reale, *Per una nuova interpretazione di Platone*. Bompiani 2010, Milan, Italy.

formation of the original Principle, in contrast to *vivartavāda* or the doctrine of apparent change or transformation.

The first *sūtra* of *Sāṁkhyakārikā* begins with homage to Kapila, the codifier of the *darśana*:

> 'Let honour be given to Kapila, who, being moved by compassion for this world drowning in the sea of ignorance (*avidyā*), built *Sāṁkhya* as the ship of salvation. For the well-being of disciples I shall briefly and clearly expound this science, presenting its premises, its conclusions, and its proofs.'[1]

In contrast to *pradhāna*, *Sāṁkhya* posits a principle called *Puruṣa*, which does not take part in the movement of *pradhāna* but which can, nevertheless, be conditioned by the *guṇas*, so that Liberation occurs according to the degree to which *pradhāna*, being 'seen' by *Puruṣa*, stops the movement which produces the forms and faculties (*vikṛti*).

Pradhāna evolves into a multiplicity of states or principles, twenty-three in number. The first principle that is evolved is *buddhi*; then comes *ahaṁkāra*, the element which causes the distinction of 'mine and yours', egotism and egoism; next comes *manas*, the dualistic mind which makes distinctions, being filled with *ahaṁkāra*; next arise the senses (*buddhīndriya* and *karmendriya*); then come the subtle elements (*tanmātra*), and finally the five gross elements (*mahābhūta*).

The *Brahmasūtra*, however, proposes and explains that all the references to *pradhāna* – and to its various aspects, such as *prāṇa*, *ākāśa*, and *buddhi* – must, in the final analysis, be made to the *Brahman*. If *pradhāna* is insentient and not conscious or intelligent, and so on, how can it ever be that which

---

[1] Īśvarakṛṣṇa, *Sāṁkhyakārikā* "Invocation", edited by C. Pensa. Collezione Vidyā, Rome, Italy.

gives rise to the world and orders it? And then what meaning could there be in those passages in the *Śruti* which refer to *ākāśa*, *prāṇa*, the *Gāyatrī*, the *jīva*, and so on, as *Brahman*?

Such qualifications are nothing other than analogies superimposed on the supreme Principle. They are 'supports' which, taken in isolation, have no foundation, no independent reality, and no ipseity, since numerous passages in the *Śruti* declare that *Brahman* is the root of *ākāśa*, of *prāṇa*, and of everything else.

> 'In the beginning the *Ātman* was this (*idam*), that is the One (*eka*). Nothing else existed other than him.'
>
> '*Brahma* is intelligence.'[1]

Bādarāyaṇa has two things at the heart of his teaching:

1) To show, by means of the *Śruti*, the impossibility of considering *pradhāna* (*natura naturans*) as the supreme Principle of all that exists.

2) To keep the *Brahmasūtra* free from the possibility of being subject to an interpretation that is phenomenological, subjective, and thus naturalistic.

'Nature' (*pradhāna, prakṛti*), which is inert and insentient, cut off from its foundation, cannot be, as was indicated previously, the Principle from which everything arises, for *pradhāna* requires a source of intelligence and order; and it cannot be the ultimate object of meditation, in relation to which it is meaningless and irrelevant to speak of the liberation of the soul.

Again, the ultimate reality cannot be *prāṇa*, *Gāyatrī*, and so on, because, according to the *Śruti*, these are elements which have been produced. *Sāṁkhya*, however, considers that 'this

---

[1] *Ai.* I.I.3; III.3.

effort... made by nature [*pradhāna*], starting with the intellect and ending with the gross particular elements, takes place for the liberation of every single soul, that is, for the benefit of another, while apparently taking place for its own benefit.'[1]

But how is it that nature, devoid of sentience and intelligence, can produce an event which requires intelligence?

Here is the answer given by *Sāṁkhya*:

> 'Just as insentient milk acts with a view to the growth of the calf, so does nature act with a view to the liberation of the soul.'
>
> 'Nature, being generous, possessed of the constituent elements (*guṇas*) and having countless means at its disposal, accomplishes, without seeking any benefit for itself, what is useful for the soul, which is devoid of the constituent elements and does not give nature anything in return.'[2]

If nature, which is generous, has an aim, namely, the liberation of the soul (*Puruṣa*), and if it also possesses the means for the realisation of its aim and manages to stop its activity when it is 'seen' by the *Puruṣa*, this implies that *pradhāna* must necessarily have sensibility, consciousness, intelligence, and an intuitive capacity to react. And it is impossible for it to receive these elements from anything external to itself.

It cannot obtain them from the soul, because the soul is devoid of *guṇas* and isolated; and it cannot obtain them from itself because it is unintelligible.

On the other hand, *sūtra* 61 contains this statement: 'As soon as [nature, *pradhāna*] is conscious of having been seen, it no longer offers itself to the glance of the soul.'

---

[1] *Sā. Kā*, 56. Op. cit.

[2] *Ibid*. 57,60.

This implies that it possesses a reactive and intelligent capacity which is aware of an external stimulus.

The problem becomes more complicated if one goes on to consider that *Sāṁkhya* posits an eternal plurality of *Puruṣas* and, at the same time, an eternal unity of *prakṛti* or *pradhāna*.

According to the *Brahmasūtra*, only the supreme *Brahman* can be *sat*; *pradhāna* is only one of the infinite possibilities; of the unqualified *sat* or *Brahman*. There is no manifestation (qualified movement) in the absence of the underlying 'constant', and this constant is the *Ātman* or *Brahman*. The *Brahmasūtra* thus goes beyond the polarity of *Puruṣa* and *prakṛti* (*pradhāna*) by affirming a single Principle as the foundation of both, since Being and non-being (becoming) presuppose a Principle which embraces them both and at the same time, transcends them both.

> '[It follows that] only one discourse is left about the Way, that it is. On this way there are revealing signs in great numbers: that Being is not born, incorruptible, in fact it is in its entirety whole, immobile and without end.
> Nor was it ever, nor will it be, since it is now all together one, continuous. Which birth for it, in fact, will you be looking for?
> How and in what way would it have grown? From non-being I will not allow you either to affirm it or to think of it because it is impossible to affirm or to think of what is not. What necessity would ever have pressed it to be born, earlier or later, if it derives from no one?
> It is thus necessary for it to be altogether, or not at all.'[1]

To give the *Brahman* conceptual definitions such as

---

[1] Parmenides, *On the Order of Nature* fg. 8.1-11, edited by Raphael. Aurea Vidyā, New York.

'Reality undivided, single, undifferentiated, non born' is to fall into discursive thinking, because the *Brahman* or *Ātman* is ἕν, to use the Greek word; it transcends the Being which conceives itself (Aristotle), ὄν; and thus it can be indicated, as in Plotinus, by the terms ineffable, indefinable, and inconceivable, which show that it cannot be expressed in categories which are logical, empirical or dianoetic, for these belong to differentiation and to the polarity of subject and object: in other words, they belong to *pradhāna*.

Brahman can be indicated by the terms *neti neti* (not this, not this), that is, by negative terms. Both Plotinus and Plato have to resort to terms that imply negation. To realise Beauty, Plato rejects all that it is not, and all that it must not be, in order to make it impossible to alight upon Beauty conceived purely through dianoetic mind and not through dialectic.

'That is the *Ātman* indicated as: *neti neti*.'[1]

Nor can one say that the *Brahman* is 'positive', for this term is always used to express a category of logic. When Plotinus speaks of the positive nature of the metaphysical One, he explains that this term does not refer to the concept found in common parlance. Any statement that seeks to attribute something to something else cannot refer to the *Brahman* and cannot grasp the *Brahman*.

But how can one appreciate this Reality, of which nothing can be spoken or thought?

The *Brahmasūtra* posits what is normally known as Realisation. Realisation implies a dissociation from everything within us that obscures or veils, through the *guṇas*, that Reality, because our true essence is of the nature of the *Brahman*.

Plotinus speaks of philosophical, mystical 'experience.'

---

[1] *Bṛ.* IV.IV.22.

When referring to Beauty in the *Symposium*, Plato outlines a series of states of consciousness, ending with the attainment of 'Beauty in itself', not subject to birth or death, identical to the One Good, and transcending the 'World of Ideas' (Being).

As a final note, one may say that the *Vedāntasūtra* is not in complete opposition to *Sāṁkhya* or to the other schools of thought, because the six principal *darśanas*, as was indicated earlier, are only particular views, or visions, seen from the compilers' level of consciousness. Thus the orthodox *Sāṁkhya darśana* considers the question of causality, while *Vedānta* considers the question of non-causality: but in this there is no opposition because *Vedānta* does not exclude causality in absolute terms, or rather it does not consider it in terms of exclusivity. It may be said that they are two different, but not opposing, positions to see things and, therefore, they can integrate each other.

atha prathamo 'dhyāyaḥ

dvitīyaḥ khaṇḍaḥ

sarvatra prasiddhopadeśāt // 1 //

sarvatra: always; *prasiddha*: well-known; *upadeśāt*: on account of the teaching.

vivakṣita-guṇopapatteś ca // 2 //

vivakṣita: one desires to express; *guṇa*: quality; *upapatteḥ*: on account of being conformable; *ca*: and.

anupapattes tu na śārīraḥ // 3 //

an-upapatteḥ: on account of the sate of not belonging; *tu*: also; *na*: not; *sārīraḥ*: incarnate, embodied.

karma-kartṛ-vyapadeśāc-ca // 4 //

karma: acting, action; *kartṛ*: agent; *vyapadeśāt*: on account of the mention; *ca*: also.

śabda viśeṣāt // 5 //

śabda: word, sound; *viśeṣāt*: on account of variation or difference.

Book One

Chapter Two

1. *According to the teaching, always well-known.*[1]

2. *And [because] the qualities that one wants to express are conformable.*

Furthermore, the characteristics or qualities expounded by the Scriptures as a basis for meditation are always mentioned in a way that is conformable and appropriate to That; however, they are simple practical supports to assist the meditations of the neophyte.

3. *And [because] they do not belong to the embodied.*

An additional reason is that those properties cannot be referred to the individual mind or the individualised being.

4. *And [because] action and agent are mentioned.*[2]

5. *On account of the difference of the words.*

Although in some contexts the *Brahman* is indicated by the word *Puruṣa* and the individual by the word *Ātman*, two apparently different words being used, yet one should consider that this difference is not absolute, because from the perspective of 'Thou art That' there is no distinction. *Puruṣa* and *Ātman*, once the veiling superimpositions (*upādhis*) have been eliminated, are the same thing.

smṛteś ca // 6 //

smṛteḥ: from the *Smṛti*; *ca*: also.

arbhakaukastvāt tadvyapadeśāc ca neti cen na nicāyyatvād evam vyomavac ca // 7 //

arbhaka: restraint, limitedness; *okastvāt*: dwelling, location; *tat*: that; *vyapadeśāt*: from the indication or designation; *ca*: and; *na*: not; *neti*: not so; *cet*: if; *nicāyyatvāt*: from being reflected upon; *evam*: thus; *vyomavat*: like ether or space; *ca*: and.

saṁbhoga prāptir iti cen na vaiśeṣyāt // 8 //

saṁbhoga: enjoyment; *prāptiḥ*: attainment; *iti*: thus; *cet*: if; *na*: not; *vaiśeṣyāt*: difference.

attā carācara-grahaṇāt // 9 //

attā: eater; *carācara*: moving and unmoving; *grahaṇāt*: on account of grasping, taking.

prakaraṇācca // 10 //

prakaraṇāt: from the context; *ca*: also.

guhāṁ praviṣṭāvātmanau hi tad-darśanāt // 11 //

guhām: the cave or hollow; *praviṣṭāu*: penetrated, entered; *Ātmanau*: the two selves; *hi*: because; *tat*: that; *darśanāt*: on account of seeing [that].

viśeṣaṇāc ca // 12 //

viśeṣaṇāt: on account of distinctive specification; *ca*: and.

antara upapatteḥ // 13 //

antaraḥ: inner; *upapatteḥ*: on account of possibility or feasibility.

6. *And also from the Smṛti.*[3]

7. *If [one affirms] that it does not [refer] to That on account of the limited nature of the dwelling-place and on account of the indication [of its meaning, the reply is] no, because [That] is being reflected upon in this way [analogously] to ether or space.*[4]

8. *If [it is] thus, its enjoyment is attained. [On the contrary, the reply is] no, on account of difference.*[5]

9. *The eater takes within himself the moving and the unmoving.*

The reference is to the *Kaṭha Upaniṣad* (I.II.25):

> [That] for whom the [role of] *brāhmaṇa* and [the role] of the *kṣatra* are both [like] boiled rice, and for both of them Mṛtyu is [like] the seasoning: who can realise [That] in such a way, there where is [only] That?.'

Thus, does the devourer, the 'eater', represent fire or the manifest *jīva*, or does it, rather, represent the supreme *Ātman*?

10. *From the context, too.*[6]

11. *[The two] who have entered into the cave for the sake of seeing That are [aspects] of the Ātman.*[7]

12. *And on account of specification.*[8]

13. *Within [is That] because it is feasible.*

sthānādivyapadeśāc ca // 14 //

sthānādi: the seat or place, and so on; *vyapadeśāt*: on account of affirmation or declaration; *ca*: and.

sukha viśiṣṭābhidhānād eva ca // 15 //

sukha: bliss, fullness; *viśiṣṭa*: distinguished, characterized; *abhidhānāt*: on account of the mention, declaration; *eva*: also; *ca*: and.

śrutopaniṣatkagatyabhidhānāc ca // 16 //

śruta upaniṣatka: the one who has heard the *Upaniṣad*; *gati*: way, path; *abhidhānāt*: on account of the mention; *ca*: also, and.

anavasthiter asambhavāc ca netaraḥ // 17 //

anavasthiteḥ: on account of impermanence or transitoriness; *asambhavāt*: on account of the impossibility; *ca*: and; *na*: not; *itaraḥ*: other.

antaryāmyadhidaivādiṣu tad-dharmavyapadeśāt // 18 //

antaryāmi: the inner Ordainer; *adhidaivādiṣu*: within the universal gods, supernal and different; *tat*: That; *dharma*: characteristic; *vyapadeśāt*: on account of designation.

na ca smārtamatad dharmābhilāpāt // 19 //

na: not; *ca*: and; *smārtam*: the *Smṛti* scripture; *atat*: contrary to that; *dharma*: quality; *abhilāpāt*: on the account of the statement or mention.

śārīraścobhaye 'pi hi bhedenainam adhīyate // 20 //

śārīraḥ: the embodied or individualised being; *ca*: and; *ubhaye* (*a*+*u* = *o*) both, in the two cases; *api*: even; *hi*: for; *bhedena*: difference; *enam*: this; *adhīyate*: is stated.

14. *And on account of the declaration of place.*

15. *And also on account of the mention [of that which is] distinguished by fullness.*

16. *Also on account of the mention of the path of the one who has heard the Upaniṣads.*

17. *On account of impermanence and impossibility, not other.*

None other can be within the eye except the *Puruṣa*; all the quotations which refer to symbols or to something other are merely supports for meditation, being themselves impermanent and not identifiable with the absolute, unchanging *Ātman*.

18. *The inner Ordainer, of the supernal deities and of the others [is Brahman] because the characteristics of That are stated.*[9]

19. *And [the inner Ordainer] is not that which the Smṛti Scripture posits because the qualities mentioned there do not belong to it.*[10]

20. *And even this embodied being [it is not] because in the two cases the difference is stated.*[11]

adṛśyatvādiguṇako dharmokteḥ // 21 //

adṛśyatvādi: invisibility; *guṇakaḥ*: the one possessing qualities or nature; *dharmokteḥ*: from the mention of the characteristics.

viśeṣaṇabhedavyapadeśābhyāṁ ca netarau // 22 //

viśeṣaṇa: characteristics, distinctive attributes; *bheda*: difference; *vyapadeśābhyām*: on account of the twofold mention or affirmation; *ca*: and; *na*: not; *itarau*: both.

rūpopanyāsāc ca // 23 //

rūpa: body, form; *upanyāsāt*: on account of the affirmation or mention; *ca*: also.

vaiśvānaraḥ sādhāraṇa śabda viśeṣāt // 24 //

vaiśvānaraḥ: Vaiśvānara; *sādhāraṇa*: usual, normal; *śabda*: word, term; *viśeṣāt*: on account of the distinction.

smaryamāṇam anumānaṁ syād iti // 25 //

smaryamāṇam: that which is stated or declared by the *Smṛti*; *anumānam*: inference, deduction; *syāt*: may be; *iti*: thus.

śabdādibhyo 'ntaḥpratiṣṭhānācca neti cen na, tathā dṛṣṭyupadeśād asambhavād puruṣam api cainam adhīyate // 26 //

śabdādibhyaḥ: on account of the verb; *antaḥ*: within, inner; *pratiṣṭhānāt*: on account of the dwelling or existing; *ca*: and; *na*: not; *iti*: thus; *cet*: if; *na*: not; *tathā*: like this; *dṛṣṭi*: sight, vision; *upadeśāt*: on account of the teaching; *asambhavāt*: on account of being impossible; *puruṣam*: person, being; *api*: also; *ca*: and; *enam*: him; *adhīyate*: teaches, instructs.

21. *The one who possesses the nature of invisibility, is from the mention of its characteristics.*[12]

22. *And the other two [are] not, on account of the twofold affirmation of distinctive attributes and difference.*[13]

23. *And on account of the affirmation of the form.*

The relevant text is still the *Muṇḍaka Upaniṣad* (II.I.3 *et seqq.*; III.I.3). These references clearly point to the *Brahman* as the foundation of the wheel of becoming.

24. *Vaiśvānara, on account of the distinctions given by common terminology.*[14]

25. *What is stated by the Smṛti can thus be a logical deduction.*[15]

26. *If [it is said that it is] not [Vaiśvānara] on account of the term [in other words, that the term 'Lord' has a different meaning] or, [again], on account of the fact that it dwells within [a feature of the gastric fire; the reply is] this is not so, because the teaching conceives [of the supreme Lord as being metaphorically] like this [the gastric fire]; on the other hand, it is impossible [that the gastric fire should have a head, the sky, and so on] and also from the teaching about Him as a Person.*

In the *Śatapatha Brāhmaṇa* (X.VI.1.11) we find: 'This very fire is *Vaiśvānara*... .'

ata eva na devatābhūtaṁ ca // 27 //

ataḥ eva: for the same reason; *na*: not; *devatā*: divinity; *bhūtam*: element; *ca*: and.

sākṣād apyavirodhaṁ jaiminiḥ // 28 //

sākṣāt: directly; *api*: also; *avirodham*: non-contradiction; *jaiminiḥ*: Jaimini.

abhivyakteriti āśmarathyaḥ // 29 //

abhivyakteḥ: on account of manifestation; *iti*: thus; *āśmarathyaḥ*: Āśmarathya.

anusmṛter bādariḥ // 30 //

anusmṛteḥ: on account of remembering; *bādariḥ*: Bādari.

sampatter iti jaiminiḥ tathā hi darśayati // 31 //

sampatteḥ: on account of imagining the identification; *iti*: thus; *jaiminiḥ*: Jaimini; *tathā hi*: as such, thus; *darśayati*: expounds, states.

27. *For the same reason, [That] cannot be either the god [of fire] or the element [of fire].*[16]

28. *According to Jaimini, non-contradiction even by the direct [way].*[17]

29. *On the basis of manifestation, according to Āśmarathya.*

According to the teacher Āśmarathya, *Vaiśvānara* itself may be symbolically given a spatial location (such as the heart) in order to facilitate meditation for those who are not yet capable of raising themselves to the formless. Therefore, from the viewpoint of the manifest state, the scriptural passage (*Chāndogya Upaniṣad*, V.XVIII.1 *et seqq.*) which speaks of limitation in space may be accepted as Āśmarathya himself declares.

30. *According to Bādari, on account of remembering.*

The teacher *(ācārya)* Bādari also refers to spatial factors in connection with the *Brahman*, such as being located in the heart or in the mind, and so on, on account of ancient memories in which these symbolic representations were helpful in facilitating meditation on the Supreme.

31. *On account of imagining the identity: this is what Jaimini says and [what the Śruti] expounds.*

According to Jaimini, the use of a symbol can be extended to any human organ which helps to support meditation. This is also confirmed by the *Śruti*. As we saw earlier in the *Chāndogya Upaniṣad*, so it is also in the *Śatapatha Brāhmaṇa*.

āmananti cainam asmin || 32 ||

āmananti: they expound; *ca*: moreover; *enam*: this; *asmin*: in this.

iti dvitīyaḥ khaṇḍaḥ

prathamo 'dhyāyaḥ

32. *Moreover, [the Jābālas] expound That [as being] in this [space].*

The *Jābālas* refer to That which dwells in this space, that is, the space between the forehead and the chin. The reference is to the *Jābāla Upaniṣad*, which is part of the 'white' *Yajurveda*, (*sūtra* II):

> 'Where does he who is imprisoned reside? He resides between *varaṇā* and *nāśī*.'

End of Chapter Two of Book Two of the Brahmasūtra

NOTES

[1] I.II.1 - 'All this is truly the *Brahman*, [because the universe] draws its foundation on That. One should meditate [on That] by diving into peace. Since, certainly, the human being identifies with its own convictions, and as the human being has [conceived] his own determination in this world, so he becomes when he departs from here. [Hence] he must practise deliberation.'

> 'The *Ātmā*, whose [instrument is] the mind, whose body consists of *prāṇa*, whose essence is light, whose thought is *satya*, and of the nature of space, the agent of all actions and holder of all desires, possessing all fragrances, and tastes, pervading all this, devoid of speech, and free of all demands.'
>
> 'This *Ātman*, which is within my heart, which is smaller than a grain of rice or a grain of barley, or a seed of mustard and even the kernel of a seed of mustard. This *Ātman*, which is within my heart, which is greater than the earth, greater than the intermediate space, greater than the sky, greater than [all] these worlds.'[1]

In every scriptural context, the recommended meditations are always directed to the ultimate Essence, which is the *Brahman*, even where it seems that the object of meditation might be the *jīva*, or some other element.

---

[1] *Chā*. III.XIV.1-3.

At times a part may be used for the whole, but this is not to be taken literally, because the part is merely a symbol of a greater reality: 'All that exists is the *Brahman*', because without the *Brahman* nothing would be able to exist, manifest itself and find unity.

> '*Om*! That is fullness. This is fullness. Fullness is from fullness. Drawing fullness from Fullness, what is left is still Fullness. *Om śāntiḥ, śāntiḥ, śāntiḥ*.'[1]

This invocation from the *Īśa Upaniṣad* gives a clear demonstration that, ultimately, everything must be referred to that Reality which is supreme and without a second, because the Fullness of the *Brahman* permeates the totality of Being and of non-being, or, better, *Brahman* is the fount, the matrix, the foundation, by means of which the All has its *raison d'être*. All this is well known in the teaching given by the Scriptures.

[2] I.II.4 - The meditation cannot refer to the subject of the action and, at the same time, to the action towards which the meditation is directed.

The *Chāndogya Upaniṣad* (III.XIV.4) declares:

> '... This is the *Brahman*: with this I shall be in dentity after departing from here... .'

'The term "this", as considered here, clearly refers to the *Ātman*, on which one must meditate with the support of qualities such as the capacity to associate with the mind, and so on... On the other hand, the expression "I shall be in identity" refers to the embodied self as the one who is accomplishing the meditation, meaning by this the conscious being who as-

[1] *Īśa*. "Invocation".

sumes the role of subject with reference to the attainment of the aforesaid object.'[1]

[3] I.II.6 - This is also reinforced by the *Smṛti*. For example, one reads in the *Bhagavadgītā*:

> 'O Arjuna, because *Īśvara* resides in the region of the heart of all beings and, through the power of *māyā*, sets all creatures in movement as if each of them were nothing but a wheel in a vast machine.'[2]

The problem can be put in these terms: if one looks from the empirical point of view, that of mere *manas* and *ahaṁkāra*, one discovers a duality, that of *Brahman* and the manifest *jīva*; if one looks from the plane of *paramārtha*, one discovers that the *jīva* is a 'moment of consciousness' for the *Ātman*, for *Īśvara* itself, and that *Īśvara* is a 'moment of consciousness' for *Brahman*. *Brahman*, *jīva, Ātman* and *Īśvara* are the same thing. According to the level that they occupy within the context of manifestation, they may assume different names.

[4] I.II.7 - The ether or *jīva,* enclosed within a restricted location such as a human body or vehicle, is of the same nature as the universal *jīva* or ether.

For reasons related to particular occasions, there are frequent meditations which are directed to the *jīvātman* which is in manifestation; but this *jīva*, through contemplative realisation, is absorbed in the universal *Ātman*, being one of its rays of light or consciousness.

---

[1] *Brahmasūtra* I.II.4 with the *bhāṣya* of Śaṅkara, p.291. Collezione Vidyā, Rome, Italy.

[2] *Bhagavadgītā* XVIII.61, edited by Raphael. Aurea Vidyā, New York.

> 'This is the truth. Just as from a blazing and radiant [fire] sparks of [its] very same nature shoot out in their thousands, so, my beloved, innumerable existences originate from the Imperishable and precisely there they will return.'[1]
>
> 'This is the explanation on generation: the *Ātman* is considered as *jīva* (reflection of the *Ātman*) like the space enclosed in a vessel and also like compound things similar to vessels and so on.'
>
> 'Just as with the destruction of the vessel, [pots, jars and so on] the space enclosed in the vessel merges in the [universal] space, likewise the *jīvas* [merge] in the *Ātman*.'[2]

[5] I.II.8 - If the *jīva* is the *Ātman*, and if the *Ātman* is the *Brahman*, then the *Brahman* enjoys the pleasure and pain of the *jīva*. To this latest objection the reply is that this is not so, on account of their difference in location.

The reflection of the manifest *Ātman* (*jīva*), finding itself in relationship with instruments, or bodies, or pots, can be veiled by the vehicles or *guṇas* which undergo movement and dualistic experiences, but the *Ātman*, transcending limits and superimpositions, remains in its condition of fullness.

The *Ātman*, *Brahman*, is that by whose means the embodied being can exist, can be identified or not identified with the vehicles or *guṇas* and with the objects, and can become an object or return to its source. The *Ātman*, *Brahman*, is the essential foundation by means of which the light pours forth, without any need of the light on the part of the *Ātman* or *Brahman*. Again, It is that by which knowledge is born,

---

[1] *Mu*. II.I.1.

[2] *Mā*. *Kā*. III.3-4.

without any need of knowledge on the part of the *Ātman* or *Brahman*.

Moreover the embodied being, characterised by the *ahaṁkāra*, having *guṇas* which are different from those of other beings and being identified with one's own peculiar qualities or *guṇas* and its specific corresponding vehicle, stands out from other beings; therefore there are no interferences. In other words, the pain or joy of one being does not become the pain or joy of all the other beings. (*Mā. Kā.* III.5)

That which moves is *prakṛti* (which corresponds to the Platonic χώρα), the substance with which are made all bodies (quantity), from the mineral world to the bodies of the humans and to those of the gods; it contains the three *guṇas* (*sattva*, *rajas*, *tamas*), which manifest the multiplicity of qualities; the *jīva* may be limited by a particular instrument and bound by its specific quality. Liberation consists in liberating oneself from the bonds of the *guṇas* to find oneself *nirguṇa*, that is, devoid of the *guṇas*.

[6] I.II.10 - From the context of the same *Upaniṣad* one concludes that the devourer is the supreme *Ātman*, because it represents the foundation of the moving and the unmoving.

> 'This being is never born and never dies, it did not take its being from anything, nor anyone [came into being from It]. It is not born, eternal, always the same and ancient. It is not destroyed when the body is destroyed.'[1]
>
> 'This is the Lord of the Totality, (*sarveśvara*), the Omniscient, the inner Ordainer, this is the Source of all [that exists]; in It all things return?.'[2]

---

[1] *Ka.* I.II.18.

[2] *Mā.* VI.

[7] I.II.11 - In the *Kaṭha Upaniṣad* (I.III.1) we find:

'The two who pour as an offering the *ṛta* in the world of virtuous actions and who have penetrated into the cave [of the heart] which is the sublime abode of the Supreme (*parama*), these two are called shade and light by the knowers of *Brahman*, by the worshippers of the five fires and by those who perform the triple sacrifice of Nachiketas.'

It may be inferred that the two are the embodied *jīva* and the *buddhi*, which is the direct instrument of the *jīva*, but the *buddhi* would be merely an insentient tool if it were not that the *jīva* gave it life and expression. The luminosity belongs to the *jīva*, which is a reflection of the supreme *Ātman*. Thus when the physical body dies it is because the *jīva*, if it follows the "*devayāna* way", withdraws on the universal plane.

'That which you know as being beyond merit and demerit, beyond what is accomplished and not accomplished, and beyond the past and the future, That expound [to me].'[1]

[8] I.II.12 - There are, furthermore, precise specifications and distinctions between the two: the *jīva* can find itself on the universal plane, which is its natural dwelling place, and, by means of the *ahaṁkāra*, can reflect itself on the level of the gross physical plane (*viśva*).

The following *sūtras* (13-16) merely serve to confirm this truth.

We encountered earlier the symbol of the cave within the heart; reference is now made to the eye:

'This *Puruṣa*, which is perceived in the eye... is immortal

---

[1] *Ka.* I.II.14.

and devoid of fear. It is the *Brahman*. It is for this reason that, when on this [eye] are poured milk or water, they flow away.'[1]

The eye as the symbol of light is a reference to the universal Tradition. There is also the specification of the dwelling-place in which the supreme Being resides. The *Bṛhadāraṇyaka Upaniṣad* lists a series of dwelling-places, of which the *Brahman* or *Ātman* is the foundation:

> 'He who dwells in the earth but is other than the earth, whom the earth knows not, he whose body is the earth and who governs the earth from within, this is the inner Ordainer, your own immortal *Ātman*.'[2]

Then the *Upaniṣad* goes on to list fire, the atmosphere, the sky, the sun, the cardinal directions, and so on. As a reflection, the *Ātman* is immanent, but as essence it is transcendent.

[9] I.II.18 - In the *Bṛhadāraṇyaka Upaniṣad* (III.VII.1) we read:

> 'Hence Uddālaka Āruṇi questioned him. "Yājñavalkya", he then said "we were in Madras in the house of Patañcala Kāpya to study sacrifice. Over there was his wife possessed by a *Gandharva*. We asked him: who are you? He answered: Kabandha Ātharvaṇa. He addressed Patañcala Kāpya and us, who were learning about sacrifice [by saying]: Kāpya, do you know the *sūtra* by which this world, the subsequent world and all the beings are kept together? Patañcala Kāpya answered: Lord, I do not know it. He told Patañcala Kāpya and the students of sacrifice: O

---

[1] *Chā*. IV.XV.1.

[2] *Bṛ*. III.VII.3 *et seqq*.

Kāpya, he who knows this *sūtra* and the inner Ordainer, in truth, he knows the *Brahman*, he knows the worlds, he knows the *devas*, he knows the *Vedas*, he knows the beings, he knows the *Ātman*, he knows the all. Thus he spoke to them. I know this. If you, Yājñavalkya, know neither the *sūtra* nor the inner Ordainer and still intend to carry the brahmanic cows, your head could fall!." "In truth, O Gautama, I know both the *sūtra* and the inner Ordainer." "Anyone could affirm: I know it, I know it. Then reveal to us in which way you know it."'

Moreover, in the same *Upaniṣad* there are references to some distinctive aspects which make it clear that the subject being spoken of is the *Brahman*.

There has been an earlier allusion to the passage in which it is stated that 'He who dwells in the earth but is other than the earth... .'

This makes it clear that the *Brahman* transcends the world of quantity, quality, and causality; it is He who rules the universes but is unmanifest; He is not the inner Ordainer of the Gods themselves (who is *Īśvara*), but in fact He is the one who represents the ultimate substratum on which the very gods themselves can stand and be.

'Furthermore we see that this whole [universe] is transient and that, like these horseflies and flies, and so on, and like grass and trees, it grows and then comes to an end.'[1]

'This [*Ātman*] is the eternal splendour of the knower of the *Brahman*: it neither increases through action nor decreases.'[2]

---

[1] *Mai.* I.4.

[2] *Bṛ.* IV.IV.23.

[10] I.II.19 - In this context the *Smṛti* refers to *Sāṁkhya*. There is a *Śruti* passage (*Bṛ.* III.VII.23) in which it is explicitly stated that:

> 'There is no other seer but Him, there is no other hearer but Him, there is no other thinker but Him, there is no other knower but Him. This is the innermost Ordainer, your immortal *Ātman*. Whatever is other than He is destined to perish. Then also Uddālaka Āruṇi fell silent.'

The *Ātman* or *Brahman* cannot be identified with forms or with the *pradhāna* of *Sāṁkhya*, which is considered insentient, or with anything else which is a second.

[11] I.II.20 - Again, it is stated that the inner Ordainer is not the reflection of the *Ātman*, because the reflection remains limited by superimpositions (*upādhis*), although this reflection, as essence, does not differ from the *Ātman*.

> 'He who, residing in the intellect, but that is other than the intellect, he who the intellect knows not, he whose body is the intellect and rules the intellect from within, this is the innermost Ordainer, your own immortal *Ātman*.'[1]

Neither the one who dwells in knowledge nor the one who is embodied, whose empirical knowledge represents the body, is the inner Ordainer, for the difference is stated in both cases.

[12] I.II.21 - 'That which is imperceptible, ungraspable, without origin, beyond the social classes (*varṇa*), devoid of eyes and ears, That which is without hands and feet, but is eternal, all-pervading, omnipresent and infinitely subtle. That which is not subject to decay and which is

---

[1] *Bṛ.* III.VII.22.

the fount of all that exists, the determined sages realise it everywhere [through higher knowledge].'[1]

There are clear characteristics which show That to be imperishable, ungraspable, permanent, and so on, so that it cannot be seen or known through the empirical mind.

These specific properties cannot be attributed to *pradhāna*, because this has quite different characteristics: it is unconscious and in continual movement; it can be seen; it increases and diminishes; and it receives forms of life from the *Puruṣa*.

[13] I.II.22 - The other two, the manifest *jīva* and *pradhāna*, are not the source of all. In earlier *sūtras* it was stated that the source – and the well-spring of all that is – cannot be *pradhāna* or the *jīva*, on account of the distinctive features of each of these and on account of the difference of state characterising *pradhāna* and the same being or *jīva*.

In the *Muṇḍaka Upaniṣad* (II.I.2) it is stated that:

'The *Puruṣa* is luminous because, indeed, it is formless. It is at the same time both within and without [all] because, in truth, it is without birth. It is without *prāṇa* because, in truth, it is without mind. It is [wholly] clear because, in truth, it is [even] higher than the supreme indestructible.'

The 'indestructible' of the *Upaniṣad* is *Īśvara*, the supreme Lord, and '... in Him all things originate and dissolve.' (*Mā.* VI); this equates to *avyakta*, not to the supreme *Brahman*.

The term *Puruṣa* that is used here refers to the transcendent *Ātman*. It is therefore that Reality which transcends the principial entity. It is the Fourth of the *Māṇḍūkya Upaniṣad* (*sūtra* VII).

---

[1] *Mu.* I.I.6.

[14] I.II.24 - *Vaiśvānara* is the supreme Lord on account of the distinction made by terms which are in common use.

Certain expressions which are in common use allow us to infer that, by transference, they refer to that single, ever-existent Reality.

> '... "Which is our *Ātman*? Which is the *Brahman*?"... Then they took a decision. "O Venerable ones, at present there is a certain Uddālaka Āruṇi who indeed knows perfectly this *Ātman* which is *Vaiśvānara*. Let us go to him." So there they went.'
>
> 'He then said to them: "You who indeed, as such, certainly know this *Ātman,* which is *Vaiśvānara,* singularly [in its separate aspects], eat the food. But he who thus meditates on this *Ātman* which is *Vaiśvānara* and identifies it with one aspect alone, he eats the food in all the worlds, through all beings and through all the [vehicles of the] *Ātman*."'
>
> 'Indeed of that very *Ātman* which is *Vaiśvānara*, heaven itself is the head, *Viśvarūpa* [the sun] is the eye, *Pṛthagvartmā* [the air] is the vital *prāṇa*, pure space is the manifest body, water itself is the bladder, the earth itself is the two feet, the chest itself is the sacrificial altar, the hair is the *kuśa* grass, the [fire] *Gārhapatya* is the heart, the *Anvāhāryapacana* is the mind, the *Āhavanīya* is the mouth.'[1]

Although the terms *Ātman* and *vaiśvānara* are generally used with distinct meanings, these passages which have been cited (and there are, yet others) point unequivocally to the same thing, that is, they have identical meanings.

---

[1] *Chā*. V.XI.1-2; V.XVIII.1-2.

[15] I.II.25 A logical deduction may be drawn from the *Smṛti*, too, where it says:

> 'Homage to Him, the essence of the [triple] world, to Him who has fire in his mouth, the sky for his head, space for his navel, the earth for his feet, the sun for eye, the directions for his ears, this is the *lokātman*.' (*Ma. Bhā.* 12.47.68).[1]

[16] I.II.27 - Furthermore, *Vaiśvānara* cannot be considered as the element of fire as such, or the spirit of fire, for the same reason that fire, which is heat and light, cannot have paradise as its head, and so on; again, fire is merely an effect and cannot be the fundamental basis of all that exists: 'For the same reason [That] cannot be either the god [of fire] or the element [of fire].' (*sūtra* 27).

[17] I.II.28 - Jaimini, the codifier of the *Pūrvamīmāṁsā*, maintains that there is no contradiction even if *Vaiśvānara* is taken directly as a symbol, because meditation always results in being meditation on the *Brahman*.

---

[1] See also *Mu.* II.I.4 and *Chā.* V.XVIII.2.

atha prathamo 'dhyāyaḥ

tṛtīyaḥ khaṇḍaḥ

dyubhvādyāyatanaṁ svaśabdāt // 1 //

dyu: sky; *bhū*: earth; *ādi*: the rest, the remainder.; *āyatanam*: dwelling-place; *sva-śabdāt*: on account of the word 'own."

muktopaṣṛpya vyapadeśāt // 2 //

mukta: freed; *upaṣṛpya*: is to be attained; *vyapadeśāt*: designated.

nānumānam atacchabdāt // 3 //

na: not; *anumānam*: inference, deduction; *a-tat-śabdāt*: on account of not being mentioned in the texts.

prāṇabhṛc ca // 4 //

prāṇa-bhṛt: bearer of the vital energy; *ca*: and [not].

bheda vyapadeśāc ca // 5 //

bheda: difference; *vyapadeśāt*: on account of the declaration; *ca*: and.

prakaraṇāt // 6 //

prakaraṇāt: from the teaching context.

sthity adanābhyāṁ ca // 7 //

sthiti: on account of staying on; *adanābhyām*: on account of eating; *ca*: and.

Book One

Chapter Three

1. *The dwelling-place of the sky, the earth, and so on [is That] on account of the term 'own.'*[1]

2. *Because it is designated as that which is to be attained by one who is freed.*[2]

3. *It is not deduced because there is no text which mentions it.*[3]

4. *And [because] it is not the bearer of prāṇa.*

Nor can the *jīva*, which rules the *upādhis*, be considered as the supreme Being; the *jīva* is only a reflection of the Supreme, just as a ray of sunlight, as such, cannot be the totality of the sun. Nor, on the other hand, is the *jīva* spoken of by the *Śruti* as the metaphysical foundation of Being and non-being.

5. *And on account of the declaration of difference.*

Moreover, the *jīva* cannot be the foundation of everything because there is a declaration of the difference between it (the *jīva*), which needs to know, and the 'object' of knowledge (That).

6. *On account of the context.*[4]

7. *On account of staying on and eating.*[5]

bhūmā samprasādād adhyupadeśāt // 8 //

bhūmā: *Bhūman*; *samprasādāt*: the state of constant serenity; *adhi*: beyond, higher; *upadeśāt*: scriptural instruction or teaching.

dharmopapatteś ca // 9 //

dharma: attributes, qualities; *upapatteḥ*: on account of being appropriate; *ca*: and.

akṣaram ambarāntara dhṛteḥ // 10 //

akṣaram: unchangeable; *ambara*: space, sky; *anta*: end; *dhṛteḥ*: on account of being the foundation.

sā ca praśāsanāt // 11 //

sā: that; *ca*: and; *praśāsanāt*: on account of lordship or control.

anyabhāvavyāvṛtteś ca // 12 //

anya: other; *bhāva*: nature; *vyāvṛtteḥ*: on account of exclusion; *ca*: and.

īkṣati karma vyapadeśāt saḥ // 13 //

īkṣati: seeing; *karma*: object, act, action; *vyapadeśāt*: on account of the mention or description; *saḥ*: he, it.

dahara uttarebhyaḥ // 14 //

daharaḥ: small; *uttarebhyaḥ*: on account of the following or subsequent.

gati śabdābhyāṁ tathā hi dṛṣṭaṁ liṅgaṁ ca // 15 //

gati-śabdābhyām: on account of movement and the word; *tathā hi*: in this way indeed; *dṛṣṭam*: seen; *liṅgam*: inference; *ca*: and.

8. *The Bhūman [is That]; the teaching [puts it] above the state of constant serenity.*[6]

9. *And the qualities [are] appropriate.*

And also on account of the fact that exclusive properties, such as ultimate truth, non-duality, and bliss, pertain to the *Bhūman* and to no other condition of manifestation.*

10. *The Immutable is the foundation [of everything] as far as space.*[7]

11. *That, too, on account of lordship.*[8]

12. *And on account of the exclusion of any other nature.*[9]

13. *It [is] quoted as an object of seeing.*[10]

14. *Small, for the following [reasons].*[11]

15. *On account of movement and word, this is indeed how it is seen and inferred.*[12]

---

* Cp. *Chā* VII.XXIV.1-2.

dhṛteś ca mahimno 'syāsminn upalabdheḥ // 16 //

dhṛteḥ: on account of its being the foundation or support; *ca*: and, moreover; *mahimnaḥ*: greatness or magnitude; *asya*: its; *asmin*: within it; *upalabdheḥ*: on account of its being perceived or apprehended.

prasiddheś ca // 17 //

prasiddheḥ: through being well known; *ca*: and.

itara parāmarśāt sa iti cen nāsaṁbhavāt // 18 //

itara-parāmarśāt: other, on account of the reference; *saḥ*: suo; *iti*: thus, in such a way; *cet*: if; *nāsaṁbhavāt*: on account of impossibility.

uttarāc ced āvirbhūtasvarūpas tu // 19 //

uttarāt: on account of what follows, the subsequent text; *cet*: if; *āvirbhūta*: becoming, manifesting; *svarūpaḥ*: own nature; *tu*: instead.

anyārthaś ca parāmarśaḥ // 20 //

anya: other, different; *arthaḥ*: meaning; *ca*: and; *parāmarśaḥ*: reference.

16. *On account, furthermore, of its being the foundation and on account of the greatness perceived within it.*

Again, the 'small space' is a reference to the supreme Lord, because He is considered to be the greatness and the foundation of all that exists.

In the *Bṛhadāraṇyaka Upaniṣad* (III.VIII.9) it is said that heaven and earth, and all that exists and lives within them, have *Brahman*, the supreme Reality, as their foundation, authority, and support.

17. *And because it is well known.*[13]

18. *If [it is said that] the other [is the jīva] on account of a reference to it, [it is] not so, because [this is] impossible.*[14]

19. *If [it is still maintained that this is so] on account of the subsequent [text, the reply is that] on the contrary, its own nature is manifesting.*

20. *And the reference [to the jīva] has a different meaning.*[15]

alpaśruter iti cet tad uktam // 21 //

alpa: small; *śruteḥ*: on account of the *Śruti*; *iti*: thus; *cet*: if; *tat*: this, that; *uktam*: stated, quoted.

anu-kṛtes tasya ca // 22 //

anu-kṛteḥ: on account of subsequent action; *tasya*: sua; *ca*: and.

api ca smaryate // 23 //

api: moreover; *ca*: and; *smaryate*: [the *Smṛti*] confirms.

śabdād eva pramitaḥ // 24 //

śabdāt: on account of the word or term; *eva*: alone, also; *pramitaḥ*: measure.

hṛdyapekṣayā tu manuṣyādhikāratvāt // 25 //

hṛdi: in the heart, to the heart; *apekṣayā*: by reference; *tu*: but, however; *manuṣya*: man; *adhikāratvāt*: on account of specific or particular nature.

21. *If [it is declared that space, or ākāśa, cannot refer to the Supreme] on account of the smallness mentioned in the Śruti, [the answer is that] this has been stated.*

Once again, the *sūtra* wishes to make it clear that the passage in the *Chāndogya Upaniṣad* (VIII.I.1) which refers to the 'small space' has already been clarified (*Bra.Sū.* I.II.7-8). *Brahman* transcends the small and the great, although it pervades them both. Some meditations may be given which seem to picture the *Brahman* as being confined within a space, but this is a symbolic presentation to accommodate the neophyte who is still subject to space and time. (Compare also I.III.25).

22. *On account of subsequent action and its [light].*

23. *Moreover, [the Smṛti] confirms it.*[16]

24. *From the very word, it is measured.*[17]

25. *But the reference to the heart [is only] on account of the particular nature of human beings.*[18]

tadupary api bādarāyaṇaḥ sambhavāt // 26 //

tat: that; *upari*: above; *api*: also; *bādarāyaṇaḥ*: Bādarāyaṇa; *sambhavāt*: on account of the possibility.

virodhaḥ karmaṇīti cen nānekapratipatter darśanāt // 27 //

virodhaḥ: contradiction; *karmaṇi*: in ritual or sacrificial action; *iti*: on account of, by reason of; *cet*: if; *na*: not; *aneka*: many; *pratipatteḥ*: on account of assumption or acquisition; *darśanāt*: from observation.

śabda iti cen nātaḥ prabhavāt pratyakṣānumānābhyām // 28 //

śabde: in the word; *iti*: thus; *cet*: if; *na*: not; *ataḥ*: this; *prabhavāt*: on account of the origin; *pratyakṣa-anumānābhyām*: on account of direct perception and inference.

ata eva ca nityatvam // 29 //

ataḥ: for this reason, therefore; *eva*: indeed; *ca*: and; *nityatvam*: eternity.

samānanāmarūpatvāc cāvṛttāv apy avirodho darśanāt smṛteśca // 30 //

samāna-nāma-rūpatvāt: on account of similarity of name and form; *ca*: and; *āvṛttau*: in the revolution; *api*: also; *avirodhaḥ*: absence of contradiction; *darśanāt*: from revelation; *smṛteḥ*: from the *Smṛti*; *ca*: and.

26. *For those above it is also possible, according to Bādarāyaṇa.*

In fact, other beings, too, that are higher than man and of other worlds, are qualified to attain supreme Knowledge. Thus, even the 'gods', while retaining a body, admittedly of *sattva*, to express themselves and while dwelling in the world of manifestation, need to liberate themselves from those qualifications which are inherent in the *sattva guṇa*; and for this reason it is permissible, according to Bādarāyaṇa, to state that liberating knowledge is possible for them, too.

Liberation from *avidyā* does not depend upon time and space; in fact they speak of *krama-mukti*: 'deferred liberation' or liberation by degrees which may be carried out on the various existential planes.

27. *If [there is] contradiction in relation to sacrificial action, it is not valid, because it is seen that [they] assume many [forms].*[19]

28. *If [any contradiction is noted] in the words [of the Vedas], this is not so according to direct perception or inference, on account of the origin which comes from these [words].*[20]

29. *And, indeed, the eternity [of the Vedas follows] from this.*[21]

30. *And on account of the similarity of name and form [there is] no contradiction even in the revolution, as can be seen from [the Śruti and] the Smṛti.*[22]

madhvādiṣvasambhavād anadhikāraṁ jaiminiḥ // 31 //

madhvādiṣu: in honey or nectar, and so on; *asambhavāt*: on account of impossibility; *anadhikāraṁ*: non-qualification; *jaiminiḥ*: Jaimini.

jyotiṣi bhāvāc ca // 32 //

jyotiṣi: with reference to a sphere of light; *bhāvāt*: used; *ca*: and.

bhāvaṁ tu bādarāyaṇo'sti hi // 33 //

bhāvam: existence; *tu*: but; *bādarāyaṇaḥ*: Bādarāyaṇa; *asti*: is; *hi*: in fact.

śugasya tad anādara śravaṇāt tad ādravaṇāt sūcyate hi // 34 //

śuk: affliction, pain; *asya*: suo; *tad-anādara-śravaṇāt*: on account of hearing the irreverent words; *tat*: that; *ādravaṇāt*: causing him to run; *sūcyate*: is indicated or referred to; *hi*: indeed, for.

kṣatriyatvagateścottaratra caitrarathena liṅgāt // 35 //

kṣatriyatvagateḥ: on account of fame as a *kṣatriya*; *ca*: and; *uttaratra*: later, succeeding; *caitrarathena*: with Caitraratha; *liṅgāt*: on account of inference or deduction.

saṁskāraparāmarśāt tadabhāvābhilāpāc ca // 36 //

saṁskāra: purificatory rites; *parāmarśāt*: on account of the mention; *tat*: them; *abhāva*: absence; *abhilāpāt*: from the mention; *ca*: and.

tadabhāva nirdhāraṇe ca pravṛtteḥ // 37 //

tadabhāva: absence of that; *nirdhāraṇe*: on the ascertainment; *ca*: and; *pravṛtteḥ*: from the procedure.

31. *According to Jaimini [the* gods*] are not qualified for Madhu Vidyā: knowledge of the nectar, and so on.**

32. *And [the words which signify the gods are] used [in the sense of] spheres of light.*

33. *But, in fact, according to Bādarāyaṇa [the qualifications] exist [in accordance with the Śruti].*[23]

34. *The grief [of Jānaśruti arose] from hearing the irreverent words spoken by that man [Raikva], which caused him to run [towards] him. This is the reference.*

35. *And because [his] stature of kṣatriya is known from a later deduction [since he is mentioned together] with Caitraratha.*

36. *Because there is a reference to purificatory rites [for the higher orders], while there is no mention of them [for the śūdra order].*

37. *And from the procedure [of Gautama in initiating Jābāla] following the ascertainment of the absence of that [state of being a śūdra].*

---

* Cp. *Chā*. VI.III.3.

śravaṇādhyayanārthapratiṣedhāt smṛteś ca // 38 //

śravaṇa: hearing; *adhyayana*: study; *artha*: meaning; *pratiṣedhāt*: on account of prohibition; *smṛteḥ*: by the *Smṛti*; *ca*: and.

kampanāt // 39 //

kampanāt: on account of, or by reason of, vibration.

jyotir darśanāt // 40 //

jyotiḥ: light; *darśanāt*: on account of being mentioned.

ākāśo 'rthāntaratvādi-vyapadeśāt // 41 //

ākāśaḥ: space, ether; *artha*: reason; *antaratva*: different, diverse; *ādi*: and so on; *vyapadeśāt*: on account of being designated.

suṣuptyutkrāntyor bhedena // 42 //

suṣupti-utkrāntyoḥ: in deep sleep and the departure from the body (or death); *bhedena*: by means of difference.

patyādi śabdebhyaḥ // 43 //

patyādi: lord and so on.; *śabdebhyaḥ*: from the words.

iti tṛtīyaḥ khaṇḍaḥ
prathamo 'dhyāyaḥ

38. *And because the Smṛti forbids [śūdras] to hear or study the meaning [of the Vedas].*[24]

39. *On account of vibration.*[*]

40. *Light, on account of being mentioned.*

41. *Space (ākāśa) [is That] because it is designated as [something] different, and so on.*[25]

42. *And [because it is stated to be] different [from the jīva] in the states of deep sleep and the departure from the body.*

43. *From words such as 'Lord', and so on.*[26]

End of Chapter Three of Book One of the Brahmasūtra

---

[*] See *Ka.* II.II.5 and related commentary, and also *Bṛ.* IV.IV.18.

NOTES

[1] I.III.1 - In the *Muṇḍaka Upaniṣad* (II.II.5) we read:

'That on which are woven the heaven, together with the earth and the intermediate space, and also the mind, together with all the *prāṇas*, that very one is what one needs to know as the single *Ātman* and reject every other thought. It is the bridge to immortality.'

Sky, intermediate space and earth represent the three states of Being – *Īśvara, Hiraṇyagarbha, Virāṭ* – and these are woven on That (*Turīya*). The term 'own' (*sva*) implies the *Ātman* or *Brahman*, as is indicated by the text of the *Śruti*; thus it does not refer to *pradhāna* or any other being.

In the same *Upaniṣad* (II.II.6) there is frequent reference to Him in whom 'all the *nāḍīs* converge... just as spokes are fixed in the hub of the wheel', and the advice is to meditate solely on the *Ātman*, 'conceiving it as the syllable *Om*.'

[2] I.III.2 - Remaining with the *Muṇḍaka Upaniṣad* (III. II.8), we find the statement:

'As flowing rivers attain peace in the sea by losing name and form, likewise the sage, freed from name and form, realises the self-resplendent *Puruṣa*, which transcends even the highest [indestructible, *avyakta*].'

Which is the same as saying that the supreme *Puruṣa* is higher than Being or *Īśvara* (principial Being). There are other references in the *Bṛhadāraṇyaka Upaniṣad* (IV.IV.6-7.20.21), in which there is a clear indication that the aim of realisation is the *Ātman* or *Brahman*.

[3] I.III.3 - *Pradhāna* cannot be the *Brahman*, the supreme Being without a second, because it is insentient, unknowing, and not infinite in its possibilities, although it may be able to manifest indefinite numbers of complex forms. There is, in addition, no mention in the texts from where a specific deduction could be made that it represents the supreme Being, which is what occurs, on the other hand, with the *Brahman*. Thus the Platonic χώρα does not stand for the supreme One Good, but merely for the substance which is capable of creating multiple forms. The One Good of Plato and the *Brahman* of *Vedānta* transcend not only substance or *pradhāna*, which produces forms, but also that Being which is not supreme but which is the causal principle of manifestation.

[4] I.III.6 - In the *Muṇḍaka Upaniṣad* (I.I.3) we read:

> 'What is it, then, O Blessed one, which, once known, makes all that exists known?'

Manifest being directs its efforts to knowing that which, once known, realises the knowledge of That; and the *Upaniṣad* (III.II.9) continues:

> 'Undoubtedly he who knows, in truth, this supreme *Brahman* becomes the very *Brahman*. In his lineage there is no one who is not a knower of *Brahman*. He goes beyond suffering, goes beyond error and, freed from the knots [of the heart], he becomes immortal.'

There is thus a dialectical distinction between the one who needs to know and the one who *is* the 'object' of supreme Knowledge.

[5] I.III.7 - Again, in the *Muṇḍaka Upaniṣad* (III.I.1) we read:

'Two birds, which always go together and have similar names, sit on the same tree. One of them eats the fruit of the *pippala* by the varied taste, [while] the other, without eating [any], watches detached.'

The passage teaches that the *Ātman* dwells in its own immovability and contemplates its own reflection, which enjoys and feeds on the fruits of action.

[6] I.III.8 - The passage referred to is in the *Chāndogya Upaniṣad* (VII.XXIII.1 and XXIV.1):

'"In truth, That, which is Infinite, is bliss. There is no bliss in the finite. Only the Infinite is bliss. In truth, only the Infinite must be intensely searched for." "I intensely wish, O venerable one, to search for the Infinite."'

'"There where one sees no other, hears no other, knows no other, that is the *Bhūman* [= the Infinite, the Being]. But where one sees the other, hears the other, or knows the other, that is the finite. In truth, that which is *Bhūman*, or Infinite, is immortal, while that which is finite is mortal." "O venerable one, in what is That founded?" "In its own greatness, or not even in greatness."'

Greatness is infinite and not born, representing the essential foundation of all that exists.

The *Bhūman*, which is the supreme *Brahman*, is higher and transcends the state of *samprasāda*, the state of serenity which is represented in the Scriptures by the state of deep sleep, the state of *prājña*, where *prāṇa* gathers into itself all the sentient faculties and where the *jīva* experiences serenity.

[7] I.III.10 - The reference is to the *Bṛhadāraṇyaka Upaniṣad* (III.VIII.7-8), which declares:

> 'O Gārgī, that which is beyond the sky and below the earth; that which is between these two, sky and earth; and that which they call the past, the present, and the future: that is designed and woven purely on space. "And on what, surely, is space designed and woven?"'
>
> 'Then he answered: "O Gārgī, the knowers of *Brahman* affirm: in truth, this is the *Akṣara*. It is neither gross nor subtle, neither short nor long, neither red-hot nor liquid, it is not shade or darkness, it is not air and not even space, it is devoid of contact, it is without taste and without smell, it is devoid of eyes and devoid of ears, it is without word and without mind, it is without luminosity and devoid of vital energy, it is without mouth and without measure, it is devoid of within and devoid of without, it devours nothing and no one devours it."'

Past, present, future, earth, sky, ethereal space – in other words, the entire manifestation – is put below the Indefectible, the Immutable.

These factors can refer only to one who is beyond every dualistic and naturalistic expression.

[8] I.III.11 - Why is the *Brahman* the foundation of all? Because:

> '... Under the lordship of Him who is the *Akṣara*, O Gārgī, that the sun and moon keep their position, steadily held. In truth, under the lordship of Him who is the *Akṣara*, O Gārgī, the heaven and the earth keep their position, steadily held. In truth, under the lordship of Him who is the *Akṣara*, O Gārgī, instants, moments, days and nights,

fortnights, months, seasons and years keep their position, steadily held. In truth, under the lordship of Him who is the *Akṣara*, O Gārgī, some rivers flow towards east from the white mountains, while other rivers flow towards west, each in its own direction. In truth, under the lordship of is the *Akṣara*, O Gārgī, men pay homage to those who bestow gifts, the *devas* to him who performs a sacrifice and the Fathers wish that a free sacrifice be offered to them.'[1]

The *Brahman* sets Order, Unity, Meaning to the entire manifestation, giving it a *raison d'être*, while the principial Being develops the seeds or archetypes by bringing them into expression.

[9] I.III.12 - The reference is to the *Bṛhadāraṇyaka Upaniṣad* (III.VIII.11): 'That same, O Gārgī, is this Indestructible who sees but is not seen, hears but is not heard, thinks but is not thought, knows but is not known. Besides Him, no other seer exists, no other hearer exists, no other thinker exists, no other knower exists. And, in truth, it is on this Indestructible, O Gārgī, that the space is designed and woven.'

In many passages the *Śruti* clearly states that only the *Bhūman,* that is, the *Brahman* or *Ātman*, is the pre-causal foundation of the existence of essence and of substance, and thus of all beings. Hence, again, in the *Bṛhadāraṇyaka Upaniṣad* (II.V.15) we read:

'That very one, that is this *Ātman*, is the Lord of all beings, the Ruler of all beings. And just as all the spokes of a wheel are fixed in the hub and in the rim of the wheel,

---

[1] *Bṛ.* III.VIII.9.

so in this *Ātman* are established all beings, all Gods, all worlds, all organs and all these [individual] selves.'

[10] I.III.13 - The *Śruti* (*Pra.* V.2) states that:

'O Satyakāma, in truth, this very *Brahman*, who is [known as] both supreme and not supreme, is the syllable *Om*. For this reason, he who [thus] knows, through this support alone, attains one of the two.'

Does this meditation, in the passage quoted, refer to the supreme *Puruṣa* or to that which is not supreme? If we read V.5 in the same *Upaniṣad* we may have a better comprehension of the reference under consideration:

'Further, he who intensely meditates on this *Om* as the supreme *Puruṣa* through this same syllable as constituted by three measures [A+U+M] he is integrated in the sun as pure light. As that which crawls on its belly gets rid of its [old] skin, likewise, in truth, he frees himself from error. He is raised by the *mantras* of the *Sāma* [*Veda*] up to the world of *Brahmā*. From this unity of living beings [*Brahmā*] he recognises the supreme all-pervasive *Puruṣa*, which transcends also that.'

Again, for stronger confirmation we may read still from the same *Upaniṣad* (VI.7):

'Then [Pippālada] said to them: "This is precisely all I know of the supreme *Brahman*: there is nothing that transcends Him."'

This is a precise reference, by which the 'act of seeing' must be related to the supreme *Puruṣa*, which, in this context, may be understood as the supreme Reality.

[11] I.III.14 - The 'small space' located within the Heart

indicates the *Brahman*, for the following reasons. The small (space) which is spoken of is merely a symbol, an analogy, with a figurative meaning. In the *Chāndogya Upaniṣad* (VIII. I.1-3) we find this statement:

"'In this citadel of *Brahman*, there is this small receptacle in the form of a lotus flower. Within it there is a small space (*ākāśa*). That, which is within it, that is what must be enquired into. That, in truth, is what must be known." And if someone told him: "Now then, in this citadel of *Brahman*, there is this small receptacle in the form of a lotus flower. Within it there is a small space. What is to be found in that space, that must be the object of the search and that one would wish to know?'', he should answer: "In truth, as [vast] is this space [without] so is this space within the heart. Within it are to be found both heaven and earth, fire and air, sun and moon, lightning and stars. All that one owns here and that one owns not, all is to be found in this [space].'''

In the 'citadel of the Heart', in which resides the supreme *Ātmani* or *Brahman*, smaller than a mustard-seed and simultaneously greater than the whole universe, one should meditate.

[12] I.III.15 - Through entering the 'small space' and also by virtue of the word (*Brahmaloka*).

This is how it is seen in other parts of the *Śruti*. The next thing to demonstrate is how the 'small space' represents the *Brahman*.

In the *Chāndogya Upaniṣad* (VIII.III.2) we read:

'Then his *jīvas*, both those who are here and those who have departed, and whatever he has not achieved, though desiring it, he achieves all this by penetrating [within himself]. However, its true (*satya*) desires are covered by non-truth (*anṛta*). This is similar to those who, having no knowledge that a chest containing a treasure is hidden in a field, would not discover it even when walking repeatedly over it, so all these beings, even going from day to day into this *Brahmaloka*, have no knowledge of Him: in fact they are taken away by non-truth.'

All beings, though going day after day into deep sleep – the world of *Brahmā* or *Brahmaloka* – fail to know it, because they remain cut off from it on account of *māyā*. In this context, the 'small space' is called *Brahmaloka*, whose foundation is always the supreme *Brahman* and to whom one always needs to refer.

It is clear that the 'small space' is not intended to mean *pradhāna*, the *jīva*, the *prāṇa*, or anything derived from *pradhāna*, such as the coarse physical body.

[13] I.III.17 - Space, as *ākāśa*, is also likened to the *Brahman*. In the *Chāndogya Upaniṣad* (VIII.XIV.1) we find:

> 'In truth that is called space (*ākāśa*) which makes name and form manifest. That on which these are founded is *Brahma*. That is immortal. It is the *Ātmā*. May I attend the gathering [of the beings] at the dwelling of *Prajāpati*! May I become the splendour of the *brāhmaṇas*, the splendour of the *kṣatriyas*, the splendour of the *vaiśyas*! Splendour I will attain. Certainly I am That, the splendour of splendours! May I not enter into the rosy viscid [devourer], may I not enter into the rosy viscid [devourer!]'

[14] I.III.18 - If it should now be thought that the 'small space' could refer to the *jīva*, in absolute terms, the *sūtra* under consideration replies that this is not possible because, although in deep sleep the *jīva* is devoid of impurities and

seems completely at peace, the qualifications of the *jīva* are present in potentiality; and, furthermore, in deep sleep the *jīva* is still conditioned by the sheath of *ānandamaya*, which remains the final superimposition upon the realisation of the *Ātman* or *Brahman*. Now, a being that is conditioned by a sheath or body, even if the sheath is so elevated that it expresses *sattva*, is still unable to perceive itself in its own fullness.'

[15] I.III.20 - If it is maintained that further texts state that it is, nevertheless, the *jīva*, it can be said that there are passages in the *Śruti* where it is maintained that the *jīva* is potentially of the nature of the *Brahman* or *Ātman*, and there are other passages where the *jīva*, awakening, realises its identity with the *Ātman* or *Brahman*. This implies that it is necessary to understand the true meaning of the *Śruti* text.

The *jīvātman* is of the nature of the *Brahman* but some *Śruti* passages refer to the *jīva* as being conditioned by limited vehicles, bodies of manifestation, while other passages treat it as in identity with That: "*ahaṁ brahmāsmi*" (*Bṛ.* I.IV.10). See the preceding note.

[16] I.III.23 - The reference is to the *Kaṭha Upaniṣad* (II. II.15), with some slight variation, and the *Muṇḍaka Upaniṣad* (II.II.10), which make identical statements, affirming:

> 'There the sun shines not, the moon and stars shine not, lightning flashes not, nor does this fire. Because of the shining of That, all consequently shines; all this [universe] shines in different ways from the splendour of That.'

It can be understood from this passage that everything manifest shines because its splendour depends on a light which precedes it. Every happening and every action: everything is always subsequent to the source which inspires and motivates it. Manifest light is merely a reflection of the supreme Light.

This is also confirmed by the *Smṛti*. See the *Bhagavadgītā* (XV.6 and 12), where it is declared:

> 'It [the *Brahman*] is illuminated not by the sun, not by the moon, not by fire.'
>
> 'That effulgence of light proceeding from the sun and illumining this whole universe, that light within the moon and within fire: know it to be Mine.'

[17] I.III.24 - The reference is to the *Kaṭha Upaniṣad* (II.I.12-13):

> 'The *Puruṣa*, of the measure of a thumb, dwells within the individualised vehicle. [He who has realised the *Ātman*] as the Lord of past and future, because of this he does not try to safeguard [himself]. In truth he is That.'
>
> 'The *Puruṣa*, of the size of a thumb, is like a flame without smoke. It is the Lord of past and future. That very same is today, That, in truth, is tomorrow. In truth, it is That.'

'That' stands for the Lord, the ruler and the measure of past and future. If it is thought that the Lord spoken of in the *Upaniṣad* refers to the *jīva* and not to the *Brahman*, this is an impossible conclusion because the superimpositions (*adhyāropa*) upon the *jīva* prevent it temporarily from being the master of past and future.

[18] I.III.25 - The fact that there is a reference to a 'small space', which is the heart, or to an extremely small measure (a thumb), should not lead us to think that because these concepts are circumscribed they cannot refer to the *Brahman*. Such expressions are metaphorical and speak of the nature

and constitution of the human being. However, those who are qualified for *Vedānta* realisation will be able to discern the true import and convert it into metaphysical terms.

On the other hand, although realisation is offered to all the beings that manifest at the various levels of existence, many indications are given of the 'measure of man' as a seeker of supreme Truth at his own level of existence. See I.II.7 and I.III.21.

A simple consideration: space and time can be expanded up to the point of their annulment as happens on the level of *Īśvara* (the principial Being); talking about small and big is always a conventional indication. In the scriptures it is spoken of as *aṇu*: atom, infinitesimal, subtle, which has in itself the property of becoming big, large.

[19] I.III.27 - The *sūtra* answers a possible objection with regard to the gods, because, not having gross physical bodies such as the human body, they could not take part in the transmission of Knowledge through teaching or in the performance of ritual acts as suggested by the *Śruti*.

According to the teacher Bādarāyaṇa, this does not reflect the truth, because the gods can assume various forms through the powers that they exercise over *prakṛti*. But even a human being, by exercising the power of *yoga*, can assume different forms.

In the *Bṛhadāraṇyaka Upaniṣad* (III.IX.1) we read:

> "'How many *devas* are there, Yājñavalkya?'' Then the other replied with this liturgical formula: "According to the *Nivid* statements about the *Viśvadeva*, there are three hundred and three, and three thousand and three... ." "But how many *devas* are there really, Yājñavalkya?'' "Six... Three... Two... One and a half... One.''

A single Consciousness can assume different forms; for the gods, this is a natural power. For man, it comes through the practice of *yoga*, as is declared in the *Smṛti*:

> 'O thou that art the best of the Bharata race! The *yogi*, having gained power, is in a position to create numerous bodies for himself and to move through all of them... .'[1]

Moreover, the Gods, or beings dwelling in the intelligible plane, are characterised by the sheaths of the *buddhi* and of the *ānanda*, since they have already relinquished the sheaths of *manas*, of *kāma* and the sheath of the gross physical body which are presided over by the *ahaṁkāra* or ego sense.

[20] I.III.28 - If there is still talk of contradiction in relation to Scripture, Bādarāyaṇa replies that even in this case there can be no contradiction either by way of direct perception or by way of simple inference. The problem relates to language. Now, the Vedic language is eternal (see the *Pūrvamīmāṁsā*). For this reason, the very origin of the world arises from that Word (Logos) which is eternal. The Word has its own specific function within a form (the name and the object named), and hence there is no contradiction between the primordial Name and phenomenal existence, which is none other than the object named of that Name.

Phenomenal existence presents multiple forms which come to birth, grow, and vanish, but the Name remains constant. On the other hand, there could not be direct perception (*Śruti*) and deduction or inference (*Smṛti*) if behind this contingent multiplicity there were not a common denominator containing them both simultaneously.

---

[1] *Ma. Bhā.* XII.110.62.

[21] I.III.29 - The Truth contained in the *Vedas* is eternal because it arises, not from the human intellect, but from that source which transcends time and space; the *Ṛṣis*, the Seers, are the transmitters of that Truth which comes to be called Supreme, while that which is not supreme belongs to the world of contingencies and appearances. The supreme Truth reveals the absolute Reality, which represents the single motionless Centre around which rotate all the phenomenal representations, all the *manvantaras*, and all the beings latent within it.

In the *Ṛg Veda* (X.71.3) we read:

> 'By means of the sacrifice they came upon the tracks of the Word (*vāc*); they found it sheltering among the Seers (*Ṛṣis*); they took it and distributed it in many places. The seven cantors recite it.'

[22] I.III.30 - Between one *manvantara* (cyclical revolution) and the next there is no unbridgeable gulf, for there is a continuity of relationship such as happens with sleep, on waking from which the being continues with the next step of the waking state.

One world, one *manvantara*, is an unresolved *seed* from a previous world, as is attested by the *Śruti* and the *Smṛti*:

> 'It is possible to live devoid of speech, in fact we see the mutes; it is possible to live devoid of sight, in fact we see the blind; it is possible to live devoid of hearing, in fact we see the deaf; it is possible to live devoid of mind, in fact we see the fools; it is possible to live mutilated of arms, it is possible to live mutilated of legs: thus, in fact we see [them]. But certainly, the conscious *Ātman* is the *prāṇa*, which, on seizing this body thoroughly, keeps it upright [= in life]. For this reason on this very [*prāṇa*] one should meditate as *Ukta*. Precisely this is

the complete understanding regarding *prāṇa*: in truth, that which is *prāṇa*, that is consciousness (*prajñā*) and what is consciousness, that is *prāṇa*. This is the vision about it, this is the knowledge [about it]. When there is a human being who has fallen asleep [so deeply] that he does not perceive dreams, there [he] becomes unified in this very *prāṇa*. Then in it merge speech with all names, sight with all forms, hearing with all sounds, and mind with all thoughts. And when he awakens, as sparks from a blazing fire fly out in all directions, so from this *Ātman* the *prāṇas* go forth in different ways [each] to its [own] seat; [hence] from the *prāṇas* spring the *devas* (sensory faculties) and from the *devas* emerge the [relative] worlds (spheres of experience). For this reason on this very [*prāṇa*] one should meditate as *Ukta*. Precisely this is the complete understanding regarding *prāṇa*: in truth, that which is *prāṇa*, that is consciousness (*prajñā*) and what is consciousness, that is *prāṇa*. This only is the realisation about it, this is the knowledge [about it]. When there is a human being who is worn out by disease and is next to die, so that, having reached exhaustion, he faints, they say about him: "[his] mind has gone: he does not hear, does not see, does not utter word, does not think;" then he becomes unified in this very *prāṇa*. Then in it merge speech with all names, sight with all forms, hearing with all sounds, and mind with all thoughts. When he departs from this body, he departs with all these.'[1]

23 I.III.33 - If, in Jaimini's view, the gods are not qualified for the knowledge of the *Brahman* because they have

---

[1] *Kau.* III.3. Also *Ṛ.Ve.* X.190.3.

no qualification for *Madhu Vidyā* (knowledge of nectar), in Bādarāyaṇa's view they are so qualified, as has been previously maintained and as the Scriptures assert.

In the *Chāndogya Upaniṣad* (III.I.1) we read:

> '*Om*! In truth, the sun [the *saguṇa* Principle] above is the honey of the gods. Of that, the very sky is the cross of the bamboo canes; its intermediate heaven is the honeycomb, its rays are the procreation.'

Another passage in the same *Upaniṣad* (III.VI.1-2) says:

> 'Of a certainty the gods eat not, nor do they drink; they are satisfied merely by the sight of this nectar.'
>
> 'In this same aspect they immerse themselves and from it they emerge again.'

[24] I.III.38 - Earlier there was a consideration of whether Vedic Knowledge can be limited merely to particular categories of beings, such as human beings, or whether it is suitable also for superhuman or divine beings, because these, too, finding themselves at the level of manifestation, need to free themselves from all forms, even the lofty form which consists of *sattva*. The answer in the *Brahmasūtra* is that the realisation of Knowledge does not depend on time and space, and thus all beings may be fit to acquire Knowledge, provided that, in their respective time and space, they possess the necessary *qualifications*.

Now we come to a very important consideration, which requires going back to look at the social conditions of the times regulated by the *Vedas* and *Upaniṣads*; in other words, to look at the constitution of the social order (*varṇa*): *brāhmaṇa*, *kṣatriya*, *vaiśya*, and *śūdra*. This division is found in the *Ṛg*

Veda (X.XI.12) and in the *Bṛhadāraṇyaka Upaniṣad* (I.IV.15-16), where we read:

> '[This is how] these [four castes]: *Brahma*, *Kṣatra*, *Viṣ* and *Śūdra* [came into existence]. That [the *Brahman-Virāj*] came to be a [belonging to the caste or order] *Brahma*: as *Agni*, among Gods and as *brāhmaṇa*, among men. [That came to be] *kṣatriya* through the [divine caste] *Kṣatriya*, came to be *vaiśya* through the [divine caste] *Vaiśya* and *śūdra* through the [divine caste] *Śūdra*. Consequently the beings in the world (*lokam*) want [to attain the fruits of their rites] through fire or *Agni* among Gods and by means of the *brāhmaṇa* among men. In fact the *Brahman* was in these two forms. However, he who departs from this world without realising one's world [that is the *Ātman*], since he is unknown, That will not protect him, just like the unread *Veda* or any other action [to accomplish] which has not been accomplished. Or whoever, does not know Him thus may perform a great meritorious act here [in this existence]. Such an act will certainly exhaust itself and come to an end. One should meditate only on that world which is the *Ātman*. He who meditates only on that world which is the *Ātman* will not have his acts destroyed. In fact, he manifests whatever he wants from this very *Ātman*.'
>
> 'Therefore, in truth, this *Ātman* [of the one who does not know] is an object of fruition for all beings. He who offers oblations and performs sacrifices, he, by means of this, becomes an object of fruition for the Gods. Thus, he who instructs himself [with the *Vedas*], by means of this becomes [an object of fruition] for the *Ṛsis*. Thus he who makes offerings to the Fathers and wishes for an offspring, by means of this becomes [it] for the Fathers.

> Thus he who gives shelter to men and offers them food, by means of this becomes [it] for human beings. Thus he who gives food and water to animals, by means of this becomes [it] for animals. He, in whose dwellings dogs, birds and ants live, by means of this [becomes] an object of fruition for these [beings]. In truth, just as one wishes good health for one's own body, similarly all beings wish good health for one who knows thus. In truth this has been known and investigated.'

The word *varṇa* means 'colour', 'appearance', 'form', and so on; these are terms referring to external conditions of the being, to the vehicles, bodies of manifestation, together with their *guṇas*. Thus the four orders are 'seen' in relation to the qualifications of the *guṇas*, which make any being what it is at any particular moment.

Although the *essence* of all that exists is *one*, since That is behind name and form, at the level of manifestation there are distinctions of space and time (which are therefore not absolute) in accordance with the constitution of the *guṇas*. Now we may speak of *qualifications* inherent within beings in accordance with the 'colour' expressed by the *guṇas*.

In these *sūtras* 34-38 the question is raised as to whether the *śūdra* can qualify for the science of the *Vedas*. Śaṅkara the Teacher (*Ācārya),* for example, denies no order access to the knowledge, and so even *śūdras* can be qualified for the study of the *Vedas*, but by ways which may be different from the ways followed by *Brāhmaṇas*. In fact, *śūdras* may begin with the study of the *Purāṇas*, the *Ramāyāṇa*, and the *Mahābhārata*, which, of course, includes the *Bhagavadgītā*.

And so, in the *Brahmasūtra*, Bādarāyaṇa imposes a qualitative limit with regard to certain seekers, such as *śūdras*, because these, on account of their qualities or *guṇas*, would have to undertake some preliminary study before proceeding to the pure Knowledge for which they may not yet have the requisite qualifications. The episode of Jānaśruti and Raikva is related in the *Chāndogya Upaniṣad* (IV.II.3-4). King Jānaśruti asks Raikva to teach him, and Raikva, calling him *śūdra*, refuses, but subsequently gives him the Vedic teaching.

Bādarāyaṇa the Teacher lets it be understood that Jānaśruti is a *kṣatriya* rather than a *śūdra*, as is clear from *sūtra* 35, where Jānaśruti is related to Caitraratha, who is a *kṣatriya*. And so Raikva instructs Jānaśruti, considering him to be a *kṣatriya* and not a *śūdra*.

It may also be said that all teaching requires some preliminary qualifications to produce satisfactory results.

In fact, there are several types of *yoga* – from *Haṭha* to *Bhakti*, and ultimately to *Asparśayoga* at the metaphysical level – simply to accommodate the various kinds of temperament and the qualifications of the enquirers.

Thus we find in the Scriptures examples of *kṣatriyas* who impart the Vedic teaching, when such teaching would be the province of the *Brāhmaṇas* (See *Bṛ.* II.I.15).

Moreover, it is necessary to consider that the teaching of the *Vedas* and *Upaniṣads* does not represent a religion as this term is understood in the West. It is not a univocal, closed, absolute teaching but it is much differentiated; it has many open windows, therefore there is a way that is mainly ritual, devotional (*bhakti*), a volitional one (*darśanayoga*), a way of right action (*karmayoga*), of superior knowledge (*jñānamārga*) which correspond to the specific qualifications (*guṇas*) of the searcher. Also in the teaching of Plato there are different ways, according to the qualifications of the searcher: the way of dialectic, which corresponds to *jñānamārga*, the way of Eros which corresponds to *parabhakti*, the one of the guardians and so on. It can be said that the teaching of Plato is a complete teaching.

Thus for the *śūdra*, who acts on the manual plane, the teaching of the *Bhagavadgītā* is more suitable, but this does not mean that a *śūdra* might not have the qualifications for knowledge.

The four social orders of *Brāhmana*, *kṣatriya*, *vaiśya*, *śūdra*, are compared, by analogy, to the four legs of the elephant which form the elephant itself; thus the four orders, all together, form the institutional body of a society, by occupying each one its own right place. It is not the case to go further into this issue, however interesting. However, even in the West there are, in due proportions, these orders: from the judiciary, to the army, to the medical order and so on. (Compare *Bhagavadgītā* IV.13 and *Chāndogya Upaniṣad* IV.IV.1-5).

[25] I.III.41 - Now that the digression relating to the prerequisites for Vedic knowledge is at an end, the discussion about the correct interpretation of the *Śruti* is resumed.

The *Brahman* is the *prāṇa* on account of vibration; it is light because this is how it comes to be seen; it is *ākāśa* because it is designated as something different from the world of names and forms, since it is from the *Brahman* that these proceed, and so on.

The would-be objector strives instead to show that *prāṇa*, light (*jyoti*), and space (*ākāśa*) cannot, according to the texts, refer to the *Brahman*.

However, in the *Kaṭha Upaniṣad* (II.III.2) we read:

> 'All this world, and [all] which is, vibrates within *prāṇa*, having emerged [from That]. [That *Brahman*] is [the source] of great terror, [as] brandished lightning. Those who know this become immortal.'

In the *Chāndogya Upaniṣad* (VIII.XII.3) we read:

'In the same way, in perfect tranquillity, coming forth from this body and approaching the supreme light, he becomes established in his own nature. That is the supreme *Puruṣa*. There he moves, laughing, playing in the company of women, of carts, of relatives but he does not remember this body born from the contact [of a man with a woman]. Such [is the example]: like an animal bound to a means of transport, thus this *prāṇa* [the individual self] is bound to this body.'

One may presume that the last period of the *Chāndogya* must be altered because the supreme *Puruṣa*, which is established in the supreme Light and in its own nature, cannot find itself in the conditions proposed by the period under examination. This, on the other hand, may happen in the state of lower *taijasa*, which is an intermediate state between the gross physical state and the universal state. In lower *taijasa* the *ahaṁkāra*, with its vehicle of *kāma-manas*, still persists. Moreover, it is in contrast with the *sūtras* which follow.

Later in the *Chāndogya Upaniṣad* (VIII.XIV.1) we read:

'In truth that which makes name and form manifest is called space (*ākāśa*). That in which these are held is *Brahma*. That is immortal. It is the *ātmā*. May I attend the gathering [of the beings] at the dwelling of *Prajāpati*! May I become the splendour of the *brāhmaṇas*, the splendour of the *kṣatriyas*, the splendour of the *vaiśyas*! Splendour I will attain. Certainly I am That, the splendour of splendours! May I not enter into the rosy viscid [devourer], may I not enter into the rosy viscid [devourer]!'

Bādarāyaṇa maintains that these indications (*prāṇa*, *jyoti*, and *ākāśa*) are none other than symbols of the supreme Reality, which is *Brahman*. *Brahman* is that Source from which proceed *prāṇa*, light, and space or ether, so that these aspects are not sundered from the Source to create an insurmountable duality.

In fact, in the *Kaṭha Upaniṣad* (II.III.1) we read:

> 'Raising its roots on high and sending its branches downwards; this is the eternal *Aśvattha*. That very same is clear, That is the *Brahman*. Indeed, it is called immortal. In That are established all the worlds. Nothing, in truth, transcends That. It, [so described], is indeed That.'

In the *Chāndogya Upaniṣad* the 'supreme Light' is spoken of, that is, the *Brahman* 'is seen' (*darśanāt*) as supreme Light.

Thus, *ākāśa* itself, which manifests names and forms, finds its foundation in the *Brahman* which is not known; it is the *Ātman*. Although the *Brahman* is different from name and form because it is *not* name and form, it is, nevertheless, the well-spring, the root, the foundation of 'all the worlds. Nothing transcends it. It is indeed That.'

In company with Plato, one may say that the sensible world and the intelligible world partake of the reality of the supreme Being but are not Being, which is something more: the essential foundation of all that exists.

[26] I.III.43 - In the *Bṛhadāraṇyaka Upaniṣad* (IV.III.7 and IV.IV.22-23) we read:

> 'Which one, among all [the mentioned beings], is the *Ātman*? It is this *Puruṣa* with which knowledge is consubstantial, and which is intertwined with the vital functions and is the light within the heart. Becoming equal [to the intellect], it runs through both the worlds. It seems to think and to move; in truth, having become the dream, it transcends this world which consists of the forms of death.'

> 'That with which knowledge is consubstantial, and which is intertwined with the vital functions, in truth is this great non-born *Ātman*. It is that which dwells in that space within the heart. It is the Ruler of all, the Lord of all, the Governor of all. That does not become better by means of right action, nor worse because of non right action. That is the Lord of all; It is that which rules over the beings and which keeps the beings in existence. Just That rises as a barrier to separate these worlds, so that they do not get mixed up one with the other. The *brāhmaṇas* intend to know That through the study of the *Vedas*... .'
>
> '... I offer thee, O Lord, the lands of Videha and myself at thy service.'

One may think that this *Ātman* of which the *Upaniṣad* speaks is the *jīva* and not the supreme *Ātman*. According to Bādarāyaṇa, the correct interpretation of the passage, supported by other passages from the *Śruti*, is that it refers to the supreme *Ātman*, inasmuch as the *jīva*, the reflection of the *Ātman*, knows nothing, in deep sleep, of outer or inner; this potential state can be attributed to the *jīva* but not to the supreme *Ātman*.

> 'That, in truth, is its nature: beyond desire, released from error and without fear. Just like the one who, embraced by a beloved woman, sees nothing, either outer or inner, in the same way this *Puruṣa*, completely embraced by the self-aware *Ātman*, no longer sees anything either outer or inner. In truth this [is the condition], where desire is fulfilled and the *Ātman* is the only object of desire, devoid of any other desire, whose nature is free from pain.'

It is important to distinguish the two aspects of the *Ātman*, one being the reflection of the other. Thus the *jīva* is the reflection, or a ray of consciousness, of the *Ātman*, whose reality pervades the threefold world, while the other is the foundation, the source, of the *jīva*, and insofar as it is supreme and absolute it transcends time and space.

As we have seen earlier, they are the two birds on the tree, described in the *Śvetāśvatara Upaniṣad* (IV.6-7). One bird eats the sweet fruit of the *pippala* tree, while the other watches it without eating. One is manifest and grieves over its impotence, and the other remains motionless and transcendent.

The *Ātman* neither increases through action nor decreases (*Bṛ.* IV.IV.22-23).

atha prathamo 'dhyāyaḥ

caturthaḥ khaṇḍaḥ

ānumānikam apyekeṣām iti cen na śarīra rūpakavinyastagṛhīter darśayati ca // 1 //

ānumānikam: deduced; *api*: also; *ekeṣām*: by some [considerations of the text]; *iti cet*: if one [says]; *na*: not; *śarīra*: body; *rūpaka*: similar; *vinyasta*: reference; *gṛhīteḥ*: because; *darśayati*: demonstrates; *ca*: also.

sūkṣmaṁ tu tad arhatvāt // 2 //

sūkṣmam: subtle; *tu*: while; *tat*: that; *arhatvāt*: being appropriate [to that].

tad adhīnatvād arthavat // 3 //

tad-adhīnatvāt: on account of dependence on that; *arthavat*: significant.

Book One

Chapter Four

1. *If one [says] that it is also deduced by inference in certain [considerations], this is refuted, because [the word alluded to] is with reference to similarity with the body, as is also demonstrated [by the Śruti].*[1]

2. *While [avyakta] is subtle, being appropriate [to that].*

Given that, according to *Sāṁkhya*, the gross body cannot be considered to be at the 'subtle' level, the *Brahmasūtra* replies that, on the contrary, the gross body is none other than the expression of *avyakta*, inasmuch as the gross body (*rūpa*), not being a principle but a derivative and a compound, draws its *raison d'être* from its foundation, which is, of course, the *avyakta*. Thus the word 'subtle' is appropriate to the body that is under consideration.

3. *On account of dependence on That, [it can have] significance.*

Furthermore, even if the nature of *pradhāna* is of a subtle order, it still cannot refer to the first Cause. *Pradhāna* is not *causa sui*, but is a mere derivative, which means that it derives its existence from That. Only in this way can it acquire a justifiable meaning.

jñeyatvāvacanāc ca // 4 //

jñeyatva: knowable object; *a-vacanāt*: on account of not being mentioned; *ca*: moreover.

vadatīti cen na prājño hi prakaraṇāt // 5 //

vadati: one says; *iti*: thus; *cet*: if; *na*: not; *prājñaḥ*: intelligent endowed with knowledge; *hi*: because; *prakaraṇāt*: on account of the treatise, context.

trayāṇām eva caivam upanyāsaḥ praśnaś ca // 6 //

trayāṇām: of three; *eva*: only; *ca*: and; *evam*: moreover; *upanyāsaḥ*: statement; *praśnaḥ*: question; *ca*: and.

mahadvac ca // 7 //

mahadvat: like *mahat*; *ca*: and.

camasavad aviśeṣāt // 8 //

camasa-vat: like the bowl; *a-viśeṣāt*: on account of the absence of specific qualifications.

jyotir-upakramā tu tathā hyadhīyata eke // 9 //

jyotiḥ: light; *upakramā*: beginning, start; *tu*: however, on the other hand; *tathā*: in this way, thus; *hi*: because; *adhīyate*: interpret; *eke*: some.

kalpanopadeśāc ca madhvādivad avirodhaḥ // 10 //

kalpana-upadeśāt: on account of the mention of the image; *ca*: and; *madhu*: honey or the nectar from flowers; *ādi*: and so on; *vad* (*vat*): like; *a-virodhaḥ*: non-contradicion.

4. *Moreover, it is not mentioned as a knowable object.*

On the other hand, the *avyakta* spoken of by *Sāṁkhya* is not, according to the Scriptures, the true 'object' of knowledge, which is the *Ātman* or *Brahman*.

5. *If [it is alleged] that mention is made of this, [the allegation] is denied because [the ātman is] intelligence, according to the [scriptural] context.**

6. *And, moreover, there are statements and questions [inherent] in three [aspects] only.*[2]

7. *And like [the term] mahat.*[3]

8. *On account of the absence of specific qualifications, as [in the case of] the bowl.*[4]

9. *But there are [three], beginning with light, because some interpret [the text] in this way.*

The three elements of which the Scripture speaks are not the *guṇas* related to *pradhāna*, as *Sāṁkhya* understands, but they represent the three elements of which the first is fire or light (*jyoti*), followed by water and then food. This is how some interpret the Scripture.

10. *And on account of the mention of the image there is no contradiction, as [in the case of] honey and so on.*[5]

---

* *Ka.* I.III.15.

na sāṁkhyopasaṁgrahād api nānābhāvādatirekāc ca // 11 //

na: not; *sāṁkhya*: number; *upasaṁgrahāt*: on account of the quotation; *api*: also; *nānābhāvāt*: on account of diversity; *atirekāt*: on account of excess; *ca*: and.

prāṇādayo vākya-śeṣāt // 12 //

prāṇādayaḥ: vital energy.; *vākya*: statement, quotation from the *Vedas*; *śeṣāt*: complementary.

jyotiṣaikeṣām asatyanne // 13 //

jyotiṣā: by light; *ekeṣām*: according to some; *asatyanne*: in the absence of food.

kāraṇatvena cākāśādiṣu yathā vyapadiṣṭokteḥ // 14 //

kāraṇatvena: as the cause; *ca*: and; *ākāśa-ādiṣu*: *ākāśa* and the rest; *yathā*: as; *vyapadiṣṭokteḥ*: explained and described.

samākarṣāt // 15 //

samākarṣāt: on account of relationship or connection.

jagadvācitvāt // 16 //

jagat: world; *vācitvāt*: on account of the reference.

11. *Not even on account of the quotation of the number, its diversity, or its excess.*[6]

12. *[They are] the prāṇas, and so on, as in the complementary statement.*[7]

13. *In the absence of food some [as in the Kāṇva] by light.*

In the *Kāṇva* version some, in the absence of food, have recourse to the 'light' to reach the number five.

In the *Bṛhadāraṇyaka Upaniṣad* (IV, IV, 16) we read:

'On this side of That the year turns with its days. On That, which is the light of lights, the *devas* meditate as on life immortal.'

This passage from the *Śruti* precedes that mentioned in *sūtra* 11.

When there is lack of food (which would make the categories four in number), the followers of the *Kāṇva* version add the 'Light of lights' to make up five.

However, all this is totally irrelevant to the proposition put forward by *Sāṁkhya*, according to which such quotations must refer to *pradhāna*.

14. *Just as [Brahman] is described and expounded as the cause of ākāśa and the rest.*[8]

15. *On account of relationship.*[9]

16. *On account of the reference to the world.*[10]

jīva-mukhya-prāṇa-liṅgān neti (na-iti) cet tad vyākhyātam // 17 //

jīva: soul, person; *mukhya*: chief; *prāṇa*: vital energy; *liṅgāt*: on account of the sign or specific characteristic; *na*: not; *iti*: this; *cet*: thus; *tat*: that; *vyākhyātam*: already explained.

anyārthaṁ tu jaiminiḥ praśna vyākhyānābhyām api caivam eke // 18 //

anya: other; *artham*: aim, meaning; *tu*: but; *jaiminiḥ*: Jaimini; *praśna-vyākhyānābhyām*: on account of discussion and explanation; *api*: also; *ca*: and; *evam*: thus; *eke*: some.

vākyānvayāt // 19 //

vākya: sentence; *anvayāt*: on account of the correlation.

pratijñā-siddher liṅgam āśmarathyaḥ // 20 //

pratijñā: assertion; *siddher*: proof; *liṅgam*: indication; *āśmarathyaḥ*: Āśmarathya.

utkramiṣyata evam bhāvād ity auḍulomiḥ // 21 //

utkramiṣyataḥ: leaving or detaching oneself from (the body); *evam*: thus; *bhāvāt*: on account of being (what one is); *iti*: this, that; *auḍulomiḥ*: Auḍulomi.

avasthiter iti kāśakṛtsnaḥ // 22 //

avasthiteḥ: on account of being present or existence; *iti*: thus; *kāśakṛtsnaḥ*: Kāśakṛtsna.

prakṛtiś ca pratijñā dṛṣṭāntānuparodhāt // 23 //

prakṛtiḥ: material substance; *ca*: and; *pratijñā*: statement; *dṛṣṭānta*: illustration; *anuparodhāt*: on account of non-contradiction.

17. *If [it is said that] it is not so on account of the specific characteristic of the jīva and of the chief prāṇa, [the reply is that] this [has been] explained.*

This was explained in I.I.31, where it was stated that there is a single meditation on the *Brahman* and not numerous meditations related to the *jīva*, the *prāṇa*, the *ākāśa*, and so on.

18. *But Jaimini [maintains] that [the reference to the jīva has] a different meaning on account of the discussion and explanation, and there are some [others who think] the same.*[11]

19. *On account of the correlation of the sentences.*[12]

20. *The proof of the statement shows [this], according to Āśmarathya.*

21. *On account of being in identity after abandoning [the body]. This is Auḍulomi's [interpretation].*

22. *On account of the existence [of That as the jīva]. This is Kāśakṛtsna's [interpretation].*[13]

23. *[That is] the material cause [because] it is not in opposition to the statements and illustrations [of the Śruti].*

See the *Chāndogya Upaniṣad* (VI.I.4 *et seqq.*).

abhidhyopadeśāc ca //24//

abhidhyā: will; *upadeśāt*: on account of the declaration; *ca*: and, also.

sākṣāc cobhayāmnānāt //25//

sākṣāt: directly; *ca*: and; *ubhaya*: both, one and the other; *āmnānāt*: on account of the mention, mentioned directly.

ātmakṛteḥ pariṇāmāt //26//

ātma-kṛteḥ: on account of acting upon itself; *pariṇāmāt*: on account of change.

yoniś ca hi gīyate //27//

yoniḥ: origin, matrix; *ca*: and; *hi*: because; *gīyate*: it is celebrated.

etena sarve vyākhyātā vyākhyātāḥ //28//

etena: by means of this; *sarve*: all; *vyākhyātā vyākhyātāḥ*: expounded, presented.

iti caturthaḥ khaṇḍaḥ

prathamo 'dhyāyaḥ

24. *And also on account of the declaration of will.*

See the *Chāndogya Upaniṣad* (VI.II.1-4) and the *Taittirīya Upaniṣad* (II.VI.1).

25. *And also [because] both [birth and dissolution] are directly mentioned [by the Śruti].*

See the *Taittirīya Upaniṣad*: III.I.1 and the *Chāndogya Upaniṣad*: I.IX.1.

26. *On account of change [of form] through acting upon oneself.*

27. *And because it is celebrated [as] the matrix.*[14]

28. *In this way all [opposing points of view] have been expounded; they have been expounded.*[15]

End of Chapter Four of Book Four

of the Brahmasūtra

NOTES

[1] I.IV.I - We discussed earlier the question of the priority of the *Brahman* in relation to all that is manifest, limiting the aspect of *pradhāna* to the simple, material, and insentient substance of the world of names and forms.

Now we can ask whether the view of *pradhāna* as the original cause of manifestation can be inferred from the Scriptures.

The answer given by the *Brahmasūtra* is that there is no mention of this in the sacred Scriptures. In the *Kaṭha Upaniṣad* (I.III.3) there is the passage which declares:

> 'Know the *Ātman* as the master of a chariot and the body, in truth, as the chariot. Indeed know the *buddhi* as the charioteer, and the *manas* as the very reins.'
>
> 'The sense objects [*arthas*] are indeed higher than the senses and the *manas* is higher than the sense objects; indeed the *buddhi* is higher than *manas*, and higher than the intellect is the great *Ātman*.'
>
> 'Higher than the *Mahat* is the Unmanifest (*avyakta*), and higher than the Unmanifest is the *Puruṣa*. There is nothing higher than the *Puruṣa*: this is the ultimate goal and the supreme abode.'[1]

Now those who uphold *pradhāna* may think that *avyakta* refers to *pradhāna*; but the word 'Unmanifest, in its basic

---

[1] *Ka*. I.III.3,10-11.

meaning, refers to what is potential and hence to everything pertaining to the subtle level. Thus, in the case of the *Kaṭha Upaniṣad*, the reference is to the nature of the body (*śarīra-rūpa*), that is, to the nature of the 'chariot.'

In this Upaniṣadic phase, *Sāṁkhya* is still theistic, a characteristic which is lost in time but which will next be found in the *Yoga darśana* which is partly derived from *Sāṁkhya*. *Sāṁkhya* sees the beginning of the world as a concatenation of cosmic elements, proceeding from each other and starting with the principle of *Mahat*, where *pradhāna* stays in the potential state.

Since there are in the *Śruti* the sequential terms of *indriya*, *manas*, *buddhi*, *mahat* (the great Mind), *avyakta*, and *Puruṣa*, one is led to think of *Sāṁkhya*, which, having the same sequence of elements, can justify the beginning of the world from *avyakta*, which is likened to *pradhāna*.

But, according to Bādarāyaṇa, the word *avyakta* refers to the chariot or body mentioned in the *Upaniṣad*, and not to *pradhāna*.

In these first *sūtras*, the dialectic develops between *Vedānta* and *Sāṁkhya*, considered throughout as two orthodox *darśanas*, which therefore have the *Śruti* as their point of reference.

[2] I.IV.6 - If *Sāṁkhya* maintains that the Scriptures speak of *pradhāna* as an object of knowledge, the *Brahmasūtra* replies that in numerous scriptural contexts the words speak of knowing the *Ātman* or the *Brahman* as the true 'object' of knowledge or realisation. In other words, the *avyakta* of *Sāṁkhya* is not the *avyakta* of the Scriptures.

In the *Kaṭha Upaniṣad* (II.III.7-8) we read:

'The mind is higher than the senses; *sattva* [pure intellect]

> is higher than the mind, the great *Ātman* [individualized] is higher than *sattva*: the Unmanifest is higher than *Mahat*.'
>
> 'But higher than the Unmanifest (*avyakta*) is the *Puruṣa*, all-pervasive and devoid of qualities; on realising it, the living being becomes free and attains immortality.'

What must be known as the ultimate object of realisation is the *Ātman* or supreme *Puruṣa*, and not *pradhāna*.

In the *Kaṭha Upaniṣad* (I.I.9 *et seqq*.), Nachiketas asks Yama three questions regarding the sacrificial fire, the individualised *jīva*, and the supreme *Ātman*, but says nothing with reference to *pradhāna*.

[3] I.IV.7 - The word *mahat* (great) is used by *Sāṁkhya* to indicate the first aspect generated by *pradhāna*, although the Scriptures do not acknowledge any such meaning. On the contrary, the word *mahat* is also used in the *Śruti* to designate the *Ātman*.

> 'Meditating on the *Ātman*, as bodiless within the bodies, as constant within the inconstant, as great (*mahat*) and all-pervading, the sage ceases to experience suffering.'[1]
>
> 'I have realised this great Being, shining like the sun and beyond darkness. Only by knowing That death is transcended; there is no other way which leads there.'[2]

In the Scriptures, therefore, the word *avyakta* does not point to *pradhāna* as the principial cause of the manifestation of the worlds; *pradhāna* can be considered only as an elementary, substantial instrument for the construction of *nāma-rūpa*.

---

[1] *Ka*. I.II.22.

[2] *Śve*. III.8.

[4] I.IV.8 - In the *Śvetāśvatara Upaniṣad* (IV.5-6) we read:

'Indeed a he-goat having his pleasure with the sole red, white, and black she-goat, which has given birth to many other creatures like herself, identifies with her. Another he-goat, instead, is detached from her because he has had his pleasure with her.'

'Two birds, which are always united and have similar names, sit on the same tree. One of them eats the sweet fruit of the *pippala* by the varied taste, [while] the other watches detached without eating [any].'

The two passages from the *Śruti* have the same meaning: they both refer to the *jīva* as a reflection of the *Ātman*, experiencing the universal planes, and with its ray of consciousness the formal planes.

In the text, *ajā* (feminine) means 'she-goat', but also 'unborn'; *aja* (masculine) means 'he-goat', or the *jīva* which experiences. *Sāṁkhya* maintains that *ajā* refers to *pradhāna*, with its three *guṇas* (red, white, and black); while Bādarāyaṇa-Vyāsa justifies the text as a symbolic image without any definite or specific meaning.

Thus, in the *Bṛhadāraṇyaka Upaniṣad* (II.II.3) we read:

'There is a pot with its opening below and its base above.
Within it has been placed every type of knowledge.
On its rim sit seven sages.
The organ of speech, which has the knowledge of *Brahman*, is the eighth.'

In the subsequent passage, however, the term 'pot', 'jar', 'bowl', or similar, is specifically attributed to the head of the body.

'... This "pot with its opening below and its base above" is the head: it, in truth, is the pot with its opening below

> and its base above. [The sentence] "in it has been placed every type of knowledge" refers to the *prāṇas*: in truth it is said that the *prāṇas* represent any sort of knowledge. "On its rim sit seven sages" refers again to the *prāṇas*: in truth it is said that the *prāṇas* are the sages. "The organ of speech, which has the knowledge of *Brahman*, is the eighth" because, in truth, the organ of speech is the eighth and has the knowledge of *Brahman*.'

In contrast to the precise definition of the pot or body in the previous text, there is, in the use of the term *ajā*, no exact definition of the word and no specific reference. In fact: *jyotir-upakramā...* (*sūtra* 9).

[5] I.IV.10 - Thus, in the interpretation of the she-goat (*ajā*), as expounded in *sūtra* 8, there is no incongruity, because we also find in the *Chāndogya Upaniṣad* (VI.IV.1 *et seqq.*) that the colours white, red, and black are attributed to water, fire, and food.

> 'That which is the colour red of the sun is the colour of the [subtle] fire. That-which is the colour white [of the sun] is the colour of the [subtle] water. That which is the colour black [of the sun] is the colour of the food [the subtle earth]. [Thus] the radiant nature of the sun disappears. Every modification gives its origin only to the word and it is a mere denomination, while the three colours are the only reality.'

Thus the interpretation in the *Brahmasūtra* gives to the word *ajā* the connotation of elements which are not produced but which have the power to produce, and from which, in fact, things take their rise; indeed, the first factor is 'light.' Hence *sūtra* 8 is to be interpreted symbolically and not literally, just as when, in the *Chāndogya Upaniṣad* (III.I.1 *et seqq.*), the sun is spoken of as honey although it is not made of honey.

> '... In truth, the sun [the *saguṇa* Principle] above is the honey of the gods. Of that, the very sky is the cross of the bamboo canes; its intermediate heaven is the honeycomb, its rays are the procreation.'

It is clear that these images are symbols of truth of a different order and are not to be taken literally.

[6] I.IV.11 - That is, not even on account of the quotation of the number can *pradhāna* find confirmation in the *Śruti*, on account of the diversity of numbering, or on account of the excessive quantity.

In the *Bṛhadāraṇyaka Upaniṣad* (IV.IV.17) we read:

> 'That on which rest the five groups of five and the [subtle] space, that very *Ātman* I regard as the immortal *Brahman*. Realising [the *Ātman* as *Brahman*], I am immortal.'

The five groups of five (*pañcajanāḥ*) constitute twenty-five categories, which correspond to the exact number of the categories in *Sāṁkhya*.

In fact, the *Sāṁkhyakārikā* maintains:

> 'Nature or root is not produced; the seven successive principles – the intellect, and so on – are simultaneously producers and products, while the remaining sixteen are products only. The soul, in brief, is neither a producer nor a product.'[1]

From nature, the root, to the soul, *Puruṣa,* there are twenty-five categories; but do these categories correspond to those enunciated by the *Śruti*? Bādarāyaṇa answers in the

---

[1] *Sā. Kā.* 3.

negative. Why? Because the categories of *Sāṁkhya* cannot be differentiated into groups, as happens in the *Śruti*, both on account of the varied nature of the categories and on account of the excessive number mentioned in the *Bṛhadāraṇyaka Upaniṣad*, where, with the addition of the category of space or ether and the inclusion of the *Ātman*, the total reaches twenty-seven. In the enumeration given by *Sāṁkhya*, *Puruṣa* is already included in the twenty-five categories.

[7] I.IV.12 - The five beings that are mentioned are those that begin with *prāṇa*, as is confirmed by what follows in the *Upaniṣad* (IV.IV.18). In fact, the passage from the *Śruti* can be understood as referring to categories of higher beings, even if the reference is to the *prāṇas*.

In the *Chāndogya Upaniṣad* (VII.IX.1-2) we read:

> 'Food is certainly higher than strength. Therefore, if someone does not eat for ten nights, but despite it he goes on living, then he is not in the position of being an observer, a hearer, a thinker, someone who discriminates, an agent and someone who knows. But then, if food reaches him, then he becomes an observer, he becomes a hearer, he becomes a thinker, he becomes someone who discriminates, he becomes someone who knows. Meditate on food.'
>
> 'As for the man who meditates on food as *Brahman*, he attains worlds full of food and full of water; there he attains freedom of movement as far and wide as the realm of food. O venerable sir, is there anything higher than food?' 'Certainly there is something higher than food.' 'Tell me about it, O venerable sir.'

See further in the same *Upaniṣad* III.XIII.6 and VII.XII.1. In this way the *Śruti* often has recourse to analogies as a way of naming different beings.

[8] I.IV.14 - Because there are many passages in the *Śruti* which state that the cause of manifestation is, for example, *ākāśa* or *prāṇa* or Light and so on, *Sāṁkhya* maintains that, as there is no firm or definite point of reference, *pradhāna* also has a good right to be considered as the origin of the world.

The Teacher, Bādarāyaṇa, replies that there is no contradiction in the *Śruti* because all these factors, being merely concomitant causes, are linked to that single uncaused cause which is the *Brahman*, the basis of all that exists.

In fact, we can read several passages in the *Śruti* which demonstrate this:

> ‘In the beginning this [universe], in truth, was the *Brahman* alone. That knew only itself as “I am the *Brahman*.” Thus It became all. Whoever among the gods knows That becomes That. It is the same for the Sages and the same for [other] human beings. Realising That as this very [*Ātman*], Vāmadeva the sage acknowledged: “I myself became *Manu* and the sun.” Even now, whoever knows That thus, that is “I am *Brahman*”, he becomes all this [*Brahman*]. Not even the Gods may overpower him, because, in truth, he is their very *Ātman*. Therefore he who pays homage to another deity and thinks: “I am this and he is That”, indeed he does not know.’[1]

> ‘In the beginning, my dear, there was just Being, one only without a second. In this regard some say: “In the beginning this was just Non-being, one only without a second: from that Non-being is founded the Being.”’[2]

Another example is in the *Aitareya Upaniṣad*:

---

[1] *Bṛ.* I.IV.10

[2] *Chā.* VI.II.1.

> 'In the beginning the *Ātman* was this (*idam*), that is the One (*eka*). Nothing else existed other than him. He considered: "May I, now, create, the worlds."'[1]

These passages, like so many others, show that the *Śruti*, while mentioning *prāṇa* or something else as the cause of the production of the world, always posits, as the root and substratum of all that exists, that single Source which represents the primary Root of everything.

As we shall see later, the names that we read in these and other passages are there to indicate That which is beyond name; in relation to this, see the *Māṇḍūkyakārikā* (II.19 *et seqq.*).

> 'O Thou of so many names, how may I name Thee that art beyond name?... Thou art the One and the All, and yet art neither the One nor the All.'[2]

> '... Without the support of these ways of reasoning and of seeking direction, which are necessarily metaphorical, it would be impossible to indicate anything with regard to the Supreme Principles.'[3]

For Damascius, 'the Supreme Reality is Silence.' But the *Brahman*, too, is considered to be 'the Great Silence.'

[9] I.IV.15 - If the objection is raised – see *Sāṁkhya* – that some passages of the *Śruti* may contradict each other when they indicate that manifestation originated now from the *Brahman*, now from the *Ātman*, now from Non-Being, and so on, the answer given by the *Brahmasūtra* is that the truth can be deduced on the basis of the relationship that exists between one

---

[1] *Ai.* I.I.1.

[2] Proclus, *Hymn to the Godhead.*

[3] Damascius, *Questions on First Principles.*

passage and another. In fact, by comparing the various *Śruti* passages, one can deduce that, with a variety of names and indications, they always speak of the sole Reality. In addition, the contexts that follow give an explicit understanding that the references are to a single Reality, that supreme Reality.[1]

[10] I.IV.16 - This is a reference to the *Kauṣītakī Upaniṣad* (IV.19), where we read:

> 'At this point Bālāki fell silent. Then Ajātaśatru asked him, "Is this only, O Bālāki [that you intend to know]?" To this Bālāki replied, "Only this." Then Ajātaśatru told him: "Certainly, indeed, you made me speak in vain [when you said] 'I shall talk to you of *Brahman*.' In truth, O Bālāki, the acting subject (*kartṛ*) of these conscious beings [which beings we spoke of before], the One whose [all] this is the actual act (*karma*), only that must be known." Then Bālāki drew near with fuel in his hands [by saying]: "Take [me] as thy disciple." Ajātaśatru answered him: "I consider that it is not in accordance with the law for a *kṣatriya* to accept a *brāhmaṇa* as disciple. But come, I will allow you to comprehend." Thus, taking him by hand, they departed. Later, both of them fell in with a sleeping man. Then Ajātaśatru called him: "O you, great, white dressed king Soma!", but the man remained quite still. Hence he touched him with a stick and, because of this, the man stood up. Then Ajātaśatru told him: "O Bālāki, where was this man lying? Where has he gone afterwards? Whence has he come back?" To this Bālāki [answered]: "I do not know." Then Ajātaśatru told him: "O Bālāki, there, where this man was lying, there, where

---

[1] Cp. *Mā. Kā.* II.18 *et seqq.*

he actually was, there, from where he came back here, [those conditions] are the *nāḍīs* of the human being called *hitāḥ* which extend from the heart to the entire [subtle] body. They are as thin as could be an hair which has been split thousands of times. They consist of a subtle essence coloured golden brown, white, black, yellow and red. When [the human being] is [deeply] asleep he finds himself [diffused] in those: then he perceives no dream.'

Bālāki had pointed at times to the *jīvas* as *Brahman*, and at other times to the *prāṇas*, in his attempt to make it clear that it is not the *Brahman* that is the origin of everything. Ajātaśatru, on the other hand, who is instructing Bālāki, says explicitly and repeatedly in the passage quoted above:

'This *Ātman* is the guardian of the worlds, this is the sovereign of the worlds; this is the Lord of the universe... thus it must be known.'[1]

[11] I.IV.18 - With regard to the passage quoted from the *Kauṣītakī*, given that it refers to the *jīva*, Jaimini maintains that the reference to the *jīva* has a different purpose, on account of the subsequent discussion and explanation.

The supreme *Ātman* and the manifest *jīva* as a mere reflection may be distinct only apparently, for in deep sleep and at the causal level the *jīva* merges with its source; thus the reference always has as its ultimate end the supreme *Ātman* and not *pradhāna*.

Thus others, too, with reference to the *Vājasaneyins*, expound the text in a similar way.

The *Vājasaneyī Saṁhitā* is a collection of only *sūtras*

---

[1] *Kau*. III.8.

that belongs to the white *Yajur Veda* (*śukla*), which is paired with the black *Yajur Veda* (*kṛṣṇa*).

[12] I.IV.19 - The reference is to the *Bṛhadāraṇyaka Upaniṣad* where Yājñavalkya presents Maitreyī with the following:

> 'It is certainly not for love of the husband, my dear, that the husband is dear: but it is for love of the *Ātman* that he is dear; it is certainly not for love of the wife, my dear, that the wife is dear: but it is for love of the *Ātman* that the wife is dear; it is certainly not for love of children, my dear, that children are dear: it is for love of the *Ātman* that children are dear… "In truth, my dear Maitreyī, when the *Ātman* has been known thanks to hearing, reflecting and deep meditation, all this becomes known."'[1]

In this context one needs to understand whether Yājñavalkya is referring to the pure and supreme *Ātman* or, in accordance with some interpretations, to the embodied *jīvātman*. Bādarāyaṇa's answer is that the general context of the *Upaniṣad* justifies the deduction that the term '*Ātman*' means the supreme *Ātman*, even though the phrase 'for love of the *Ātman*' may apparently refer to the manifest *jīva*; in other words, there cannot be an absolute duality or an unbridgeable gulf between the *jīva* and the transcendent *Ātman*.

[13] I.IV.22 - These last three *sūtras* give the interpretations of Āśmarathya, Auḍulomi, and Kāśakṛtsna.

According to the first of these, there are simultaneously difference and non-difference (*bhedābheda*) between the *Ātman* and the *jīva*.

The difference exists when one is identified with the sensi-

---

[1] *Bṛ*. II.IV.5.

ble world and thus with physical manifestation; non-difference or non-distinction exists when the *jīva*, freed from the *guṇas*, understands that in the background there is the *Ātman* as the primal source of knowledge and of its own reality.

But in its contextual formulation the *Śruti* says that there is no difference or distinction, because the *jīva* is nothing but a state of consciousness superimposed on the state of consciousness of the *Ātman*, just as, in the classic example, a snake is erroneously superimposed on the rope.

According to the Teacher Auḍulomi, the *jīva* can re-integrate itself with its source, which is the *Ātman* or *Brahman*, only at death (*videhamukti*: liberation outside the body, because within the body knowledge remains virtual).

According to the Teacher Kāśakṛtsna, the supreme *Ātman* always remains what it is, so that only its apparent reflection can exist in objective manifestation. This interpretation may be considered to be consistent with the classical texts.

The interpretation given by Auḍulomi and that offered by Kāśakṛtsna may be taken into consideration because they follow the classical model; that given by Āśmarathya can be accepted as valid provided that non-difference, or non-distinction, is not viewed as absolute, because taking it as absolute would bring one face to face with an irreconcilable duality and a contradiction in terms; according to the proof given by Parmenides, another great Master, something either *is* or *is not*; thus, the *jīva* cannot be simultaneously different and non-different, because these terms cancel each other out and are mutually exclusive.

[14] I.IV.27 - In the *Taittirīya Upaniṣad* (II.VI.1) we read: 'After penetrating into it, it became the immanent and

> the transcendent, the expressible and the inexpressible, that which is support and that which is not support... .'

Brahman is the supreme support, hence all that exists finds its *raison d'être*. In the *sūtras* under consideration one can think that it is the *Brahman* to become, or to turn into (*pariṇāma*) the universe; this, on the other hand, pertains to the principial Cause that, though steady in itself, through *rajas*, which is the motive power, stirs to the multiplication and transformation of the forms.

> 'This is the Lord of Totality, the Omniscient, the inner Ordainer, this is the source (*yoniḥ*) of all [that exists]; 'in It all things originate and dissolve.'[1]

With reference to *rajas* it is possible to relate it to the *Eros* of Parmenides, there where the Daemon (Δίκη) through Eros, as motive power, stirs to the painful birth of the world.[2]

It is necessary to refer to what is the spirit of the scriptural context, hence of the *Upaniṣads*, where it is spoken both of the causal principle (see the above quoted *Māṇḍūkyakārikā* I.VI) and of the Foundation (*Māṇḍūkyakārikā* I.VII) where the non-born *Brahman* is posited, beyond the principial Lord.

In the *Kaṭha Upaniṣad* (II.II.15) we read:

> 'There the sun shines not, neither the moon, nor the heavenly bodies... .'

In the *Bṛhadāraṇyaka Upaniṣad* (IV.V.15) we read:

> '... That is the *Ātman* referred to as: not this, not this (*neti neti*). It is uncatchable because, in truth, it cannot be caught; it is indestructible because, in truth it is not

---

[1] *Mā*. I.VI.

[2] Parmenides, *On the Order of Nature* fg. 12-13 and related commentary. Op. cit.

subject to destruction, without contact (*ajati*) because, in truth, it has no contact with anything... .'

Further in the *Chāndogya Upaniṣad* (VI.XII.2-3) we read:

'Then [the father] told him: "My dear, you cannot perceive this subtle foundation; my dear, in truth, the great *nyagrodha* lives on this subtle foundation... ."'

'That which is infinitely subtle has That as foundation, That is the only Reality, it is the *Ātman* and "Thou art That" o Śvetaketu... .'

The word *yoni* (*sūtra* 27) can be interpreted as matrix, origin, source from which the movement of becoming proceeds. See *Māṇḍūkyakārikā* I.VI.

'When the seer sees the golden Form (*rukmavarṇa*), the *Puruṣa* who is the creator, the Lord and the source that is the *Brahman*, then the knower... reaches the supreme identity (*paramaṁ sāmyam*)'

'... from the Imperishable [*Īśvara*] multiple existences are generated... .'[1]

From these few quotations from the *Śruti* it can be inferred that the transformation cannot be ascribed to the *Brahman* or *Ātman*, nor can the *Brahman* be considered a mere substantial effect of the world.

It can be concluded that transformation or change, with regard to the *Brahman*, is only *apparent*, and not real or substantial. The *Brahman* through *māyā appears* as universe; but seen from the perspective of *avidyā* the *Brahman* is universe, it is the very manifestation. See further on Book II.I *sūtra* 7 and related note, and Book II.I.21-22.

---

[1] *Mu.* III.I.3; II.I.1.

[15] I.IV.28 - These final *sūtras* of Chapter Four in the First Book show how Being and non-being, the intelligible and the sensible, cannot have an intrinsic reality of their own, inasmuch as they are movement, and this presupposes an unmoved *cause*.

Power, according to Aristotle, is the power of the act, and the act is the norm and finality of power (*Metaphysics* Θ 8.1049-50). It was to give priority to act that Aristotle put *pure act* as the determinant, free of potentiality.

This pure act can also be reflected in movement, but it abides principally in the state of *immobility*, as happens with the Divine. Aristotle says:

> 'Divinity always enjoys a fullness that is single and simple. In fact, there is not only an activity of movement, but there is also an activity of immobility, and fullness consists more in stillness than in movement.'[1]

Brahman is the uncaused cause of both the intelligible and the sensible; it is the *root* of the tree, which, although outside formal objectivity, represents its metaphysical foundation. Thus, according to some schools of thought, it is neither *pradhāna*, with its determinations (the χώϱα of Plato) through which names and forms are expressed, nor the *jīvas* which are reflections of what stands behind them.

Sāṁkhya, which proposes what has already been said, is, anyway, one of the six Hindu *darśanas*, which are views, formulations, or visions related to the *Veda*s and *Upaniṣads*; they are thus interpretative aspects which are orthodox in nature. Now some commentators or codifiers of a *darśana* can take from the *Vedas* and *Upaniṣads* particular statements which, although valid and keeping to that particular aspect of

[1] Aristotle, *Nicomachean Ethics* H 15.1154b.26-28.

truth, cannot be considered as the absolute expression of what the *Śruti* declares in its all-embracing nature or universality.

Hence the differences between one *darśana* and another: differences which may be considered purely apparent if one has the ability to reach Unity or the ultimate Reality from which there may arise aspects, apparently diverse, of that single Reality or Truth.

It is the 'sameness within diversity' of which Plato speaks. Now the *Brahmasūtra* does not reject the *Sāṁkhya* teaching *in toto*, because it is an orthodox *darśana* and *Vedānta* itself has adopted some of the developments found in *Sāṁkhya*, but the *Brahmasūtra* seeks to clarify some aspects of *Sāṁkhya* with the help of other categories which the *Śruti* puts forward.

The codifier of a line of Vedic thought has 'seen' what the state of consciousness pertaining to that moment has been able to recognise in the vast complex vision of the *Vedas* and *Upaniṣads*.

In that Vision, therefore, some great Souls have 'seen' duality, unity or unity without a second, because, conversely, monistic, dualistic, or even non-dualistic formulations are found in the *Vedas* and *Upaniṣads*.

Hence it might be said today that the *Śruti* is characterised by a vision that is phenomenalistic, ontological, and decidedly metaphysical. In Platonic vein the *Śruti* posits the sensible world, the intelligible world, and even that ineffable world of pure non-duality (the world of the One Good). It is that last-mentioned world that is the world of *Advaita Vedānta*, as proposed by the *Brahmasūtra*.

Sāṁkhya has taken some points from the *Śruti* and has built an interesting and congenial structure, in such a way, however, as not to make absolute a truth which, compared with the total expression of the *Śruti*, is merely partial.

Sāṁkhya finds in insentient *pradhāna* the basis, the operational cause, of all that exists as becoming, both at the level of substance, form, and at the spiritual level; there is no other cause as the source and foundation of manifestation. *Pradhāna* is characterised by the three *guṇas* of *sattva*, *rajas*, and *tamas*, qualities which, in their intermingling, produce all the possible qualitative and quantitative factors of the sensible and intelligible existence.

Breaking the balance of the three *guṇas* generates manifestation, and when the balance is restored the manifestation of form disappears. There is thus an out-breathing and an in-breathing of the manifest. None of this is denied by the *Brahmasūtra*.

In addition to *prakṛti* or *pradhāna*, *Sāṁkhya* posits, as another factor, the *Puruṣa* in its state of stillness, in contrast to *pradhāna*, which is single and in movement. *Puruṣa* is the essence, *pradhāna* the substance.

The *Brahman*, according to the *Brahmasūtra*, is that by which both *pradhāna* and *Puruṣa* are enabled to exist and to be. The same demonstration will then be made with respect to other orthodox philosophies and even to heterodox philosophies such as Buddhism.

One may ask: why are the different *darśanas* and other interpretations, as will be seen along the text, confuted somewhat by Bādarāyaṇa?

This is because the codifier of the *Brahmasūtra* posits himself from the metaphysical perspective of the supreme *Brahman* as foundation of all that exists. It is clear that from this perspective the schools of thought which posit themselves only from the vision of the sensible or intelligible prove to be incomplete.

It is tantamount to saying that from the Platonic view

of the One Good some posit themselves solely from the perspective of the Demiurge and not from the perspective of the Being or, even better, of the One Good.

The repetition of the *sūtra* indicates that the First Book is completed.

atha dvitīyo ’dhyāyaḥ

avirodhaḥ

BOOK TWO

Absence of Contradiction

atha dvitīyo 'dhyāyaḥ

prathamaḥ khaṇḍaḥ

smṛtyanavakāśa doṣaprasaṅga iti cen nānyasmṛtyanavakāśa doṣa prasaṅgāt // 1 //

smṛti: teaching; *an*: not; *avakāśa*: position, space; *doṣa*: defect; *prasaṅgaḥ*: result; *iti*: thus, so; *cet*: if; *na*: not; *anya*: other; *smṛti*: text; *an*: not; *avakāśa*: position, space;; *doṣa*: defect; *prasaṅgāt*: on account of the result.

itareṣāṁ cānupalabdheḥ // 2 //

itareṣām: of others; *ca*: and; *anupalabdheḥ*: on account of non-perception.

etena yogaḥ pratyuktaḥ // 3 //

etena: on account of this; *yogaḥ*: *yogasmṛti*; *pratyuktaḥ*: refuted.

na vilakṣaṇatvād asya tathātvaṁ ca śabdāt // 4 //

na: not; *vilakṣaṇatvāt*: on account of difference of nature; *asya*: of this; *tathātvam*: that it is so; *ca*: and; *śabdāt*: according to the Scriptures.

abhimāni vyapadeśas tu viśeṣa anugatibhyām // 5 //

abhimāni: inclinations [of the deities]; *vyapadeśaḥ*: reference; *tu*: but; *viśeṣa*: difference; *anugatibhyām*: relation, correlation.

dṛśyate tu // 6 //

dṛśyate: it is seen; *tu*: but, however.

Book Two

Chapter One

1. *If [it is possible for] a defect to arise through denying space to certain Smṛti, it is not so because [one would then have] the subsequent defect of not [allowing] space for other Smṛti.*[1]

2. *And on account of the non-perception of the others.*

Aspects of *Sāṁkhya* such as *mahat* and other elements derived from *pradhāna* by means of particular transformations are not met with in the evidence given by the *Vedas*. When Bādarāyaṇa the Teacher designates *Sāṁkhya* as *Smṛti*, he merely wishes to point to the simple *Sāṁkhya* scripture and not to the whole of the *Smṛti*, which is much more complicated and extensive in its content.

3. *On account of this, yoga [Sāṁkhya] is refuted.*[2]

4. *[That is not] on account of the different nature of this [world], and the Scriptures [affirm] that it is so.*

5. *But the reference [is] to the inclinations [of the deities] who preside over difference and relationship.*

6. *However, it is seen.*[3]

asad iti cen na pratiṣedha mātratvāt // 7 //

asat: non existent; *iti cet*: thus, if; *na*: not; *pratiṣedha*: negation; *mātratvāt*: pure, simple.

apītau tadvat prasaṅgād asamañjasam // 8 //

apītau: in the dissolution; *tadvat*: same, the same nature; *prasaṅgāt*: on account of the connection or correlation; *asamañjasam*: unsatisfactory, inadequate.

na tu dṛṣṭānta bhāvāt // 9 //

na: not; *tu*: but, yet; *dṛṣṭānta bhāvāt*: on account of being examples.

sva pakṣa doṣāc ca // 10 //

sva: one's own; *pakṣa*: opinion, point of view; *doṣāt*: on account of the error; *ca*: and.

tarkāpratiṣṭhānād apy anyathānumeyam iti ced evam apy avimokṣa prasaṅgaḥ // 11 //

tarka: reasoning; *apratiṣṭhānāt*: lack of foundation; *api*: also; *anyathā*: otherwise; *anumeyam*: to reason; *iti*: thus; *cet*: if; *evam*: thus; *api*: also; *avimokṣa*: non-realization; *prasaṅgaḥ*: result, consequence.

etena śiṣṭāparigrahā api vyākhyātāḥ // 12 //

etena: by means of this; *śiṣṭā*: one who is well-versed in the Scriptures; *aparigrahå¢*: not accepted; *api*: also; *vyākhyātāḥ*: explained.

7. *If [the effect is said to be] non-existent, [the reply is that] this is not the case, because there is pure negation.*[4]

8. *In the dissolution [That is] of the same nature [as the effect or the world], on account of the fact that [the teaching that has been maintained so far is] not satisfying.*[5]

9. *Again, [it is] not [so], for there are examples [which support our thesis].*

On the other hand, by speaking in causal terms, the *sūtra* maintains that it is the effect which depends on the cause, and not *vice versa*: for example, an earthenware pot which breaks or crumbles returns to its elemental essence. In other words, it is the effect which is modified, and not the cause.

10. *And because the error [can also be attributed to] one's own point of view.*[6]

11. *Even if [it is said that], because the reasoning has no foundation, one must reason in a different way, [the response is that] even so, the result [is] non-liberation.*[7]

12. *In this way also the theories which are not accepted by the competent [the Sages] are explained (refuted).*

If some aspects of the *Sāṁkhya* teaching have been refuted even though in accord with the Vedic tradition, this is all the more reason to explain and refute with the same arguments all the theories of those who are not qualified to interpret the *Vedas* or who reject the *Śruti*.

bhoktrāpatter avibhāgaś cet syāt lokavat // 13 //

bhoktṛ: enloyer; *āpatteḥ*: on account of merging; *avibhāgaḥ*: non-distinction; *cet*: if; *syāt*: may be; *lokavat*: like ordinary experience.

tad ananyatvam ārambhaṇa śabdādibhyaḥ // 14 //

tat: of them, of those; *an-anyatvam*: non-difference; *ārambhaṇa*: origin; *śabdādibhyaḥ*: on account of words, terminology, and so on.

bhāve copalabdheḥ // 15 //

bhāve: on the existence; *ca*: and; *upalabdheḥ*: on account of perception.

sattvāccāvarasya // 16 //

sattvāt: on account of the existence; *ca*: and; *avarasya*: of that which follows.

asad vyapadeśān neti cen na dharmāntareṇa vākya śeṣāt // 17 //

asat: non-esistence; *vyapadeśāt*: on account of the reference or mention; *na*: not; *iti cet*: if thus; *na*: not; *dharma*: quality, characteristic; *antareṇa*: by a further, by another; *vākya*: declaration; *śeṣāt*: on account of the remaining part.

yukteḥ śabdāntarāc ca // 18 //

yukteḥ: from reasoning; *śabda*: Vedic text; *antarāt*: from another, from a further; *ca*: and.

13. *If there is no distinction [inasmuch as] the enjoying subject merges [into the object, the reply is that the distinction may show itself] in ordinary experience.*[8]

14. *The non-difference of those [cause and effect results] from terms such as 'origin' and so on.*

15. *And because perception [of the effect is based] on the existence [of the cause].*[9]

16. *And on account of the existence of that which follows.*[10]

17. *If [it is said that] on account of being denoted as non-existent, [the effect does] not [exist prior to the manifestation, the reply is that] this is not so, because according to the later declaration [of non-existence] another quality [is denoted].*[11]

18. *From reasoning and from another Scriptural text.*

From reasoning, because it is a logical assertion that there is no effect without a cause, and from further *Śruti* texts which occur in the various *Upaniṣads*, some of which have already been quoted.

paṭavac ca // 19 //

paṭavat: like material or cloth; *ca*: and.

yathā ca prāṇādi // 20 //

yathā: sa; *ca*: and; *prāṇādi*: the vital breath and so on.

itara vyapadeśāddhitākaraṇādi doṣa prasaktiḥ // 21 //

itara: other; *vyapadeśāt*: on account of being designated; *hita*: good; *akaraṇa*: absence, not doing; *ādi*: and so on; *doṣa*: defect; *prasaktiḥ*: applied, ascribed.

adhikaṁ tu bheda-nirdeśāt // 22 //

adhikam: something more, something higher; *tu*: but; *bheda*: difference; *nirdeśāt*: on account of the declaration.

19. *And like a piece of cloth.*

Śaṅkara comments: 'If a piece of cloth is rolled up, the quality of the cloth cannot be recognised and it cannot be known if it really is a piece of cloth or something else; but once it has been fully unrolled, it manifests itself perfectly in its own nature and it can then be recognised, thanks to this unfolding, that the object which had previously been rolled up is truly a piece of material.'

One may say that power passes into act.

20. *And as the vital breath, and so on.*

The five vital breaths – *apāna*, *vyāna*, *udāna*, and so on – proceed from the *prāṇa*, which contains them, and they are absorbed back into the *prāṇa*.

21. *Because the other [the jīva] is designated [as not different from Brahman], faults such as the absence of good would be ascribed [to the Brahman].*[12]

22. *But [Brahman] is something more [because] it is declared to be different.*

The *Brahman* spoken of by *Sāṁkhya* is not the *Brahman* spoken of by *Vedānta* which is something more precious and is above Being in dignity and higher power (Plato) and these are elements which may very well be referred to the supreme *Brahman*.

---

* *Bra. Sū*. II.I.19 with the *bhāṣya* of Śaṅkara. Op. cit.

aśmādivac ca tad anupapattiḥ // 23 //

aśma-ādi-vat: like stones and other things.; *ca*: and; *tat*: that; *anupapattiḥ*: nuntenability.

upasaṁhāra darśanān neti cen na kṣiravadd hi // 24 //

upasaṁhāra: collection; *darśanāt*: on account of observation; *na*: not; *iti cet*: if, così; *na*: not; *kṣiravat*: latte; *hi*: because.

devādivad api loke // 25 //

devādivat: like the gods and others; *api*: even, also; *loke*: in the world.

kṛtsna prasaktiḥ niravayavatva śabdakopovā // 26 //

kṛtsna: whole, entire; *prasaktiḥ*: consequence; *nir-avayavatva*: indivisible, having no parts; *śabda*: Scriptures; *kopaḥ*: non-observance; *vā*: or.

śrutes tu śabda-mūlatvāt // 27 //

śruteḥ: on account of the *Śruti*; *tu*: but; *śabda-mūlatvāt*: on account of its root in testimony.

ātmani caivam vicitrāś ca hi // 28 //

ātmani: in the *Ātman*; *ca-evam*: and so; *vicitrāḥ*: varied, manifold, variegated; *ca*: and; *hi*: because.

23. *[The objections raised are] untenable, on [the analogy of] stones and other things.*[13]

24. *If it is said that [the Brahman is] not the cause since it does not employ [instruments needed to produce something], this is not the case, precisely on account of its similarity to milk.*

25. *[It is] also like [the function] of the gods and other beings in the world.*[14]

26. *[If the world is caused by the Brahman] the consequence [is] the transformation of the entire [Brahman] or non-observance of the Scriptures [when they declare the Brahman to be] indivisible.*[15]

27. *But [there is no defect] on the basis of testimony and the Śruti.*[16]

28. *[Because] it is this way also within the Ātmā and in imaginary [creations].*

Thus it happens, for example, that from a single individual mind indefinite forms can manifest and be objectified; consider the content of dreams.

In the *Śruti* we read:

> 'In that place there are no carts, no draught animals, no roads; He therefore creates carts, draught animals, and roads... In that place there are no pools, no lakes, no rivers; He therefore creates pools, lakes, and rivers. He is in truth the creator.'*

* *Bṛ.* IV.III.10.

sva pakṣa doṣāc ca // 29 //

sva: one's own; *pakṣa*: opinion, point of view; *doṣāt*: on account of the error, vice, defect; *ca*: and.

sarvopetā ca tad darśanāt // 30 //

sarva: all; *upetā*: endowed; *ca*: and; *tat*: that; *darśanāt*: from observation (in the Scriptures).

vikaraṇatvān neti cet tad uktam // 31 //

vikaraṇatvāt: on account of the absence of organs; *na*: not; *iti cet*: if so; *tat*: that; *uktam*: explained, spoken.

na prayojanavattvāt // 32 //

na: not; *prayojanavattvāt*: on account of having an aim.

lokavat tu līlā kaivalyam // 33 //

lokavat: as in ordinary experience; *tu*: but, however; *līlā*: innocent game; *kaivalyam*: simple, mere.

vaiṣamya-nairghṛṇye na sāpekṣatvāt tathā hi darśayati // 34 //

vaiṣamya: partiality; *nairghṛṇye*: lack of compassion; *na*: not; *sāpekṣatvāt*: from consideration [of other factors]; *tathā*: so; *hi*: because; *darśayati*: declares.

na karmāvibhāgād iti cen nānāditvāt // 35 //

na: not; *karma*: action, activity; *avibhāgāt*: on account of non-distinction; *iti cet*: if thus; *na*: not; *anāditvāt* (= *an* + *ādi* + *tvāt*): on account of beginninglessness.

29. *And because the particular viewpoint [of the objector] is flawed.*

The same objection which is made against *Vedānta* can also be made against *Sāṁkhya*, which clearly maintains that *pradhāna* is one and indivisible and yet produces innumerable forms and occurrences. But the position of *Sāṁkhya*, in relation to *pradhāna*, ends, for reasons already given, by being problematic and untenable. It suffices to think that for *Sāṁkhya* the division of *pradhāna* is real, substantial and non-apparent; hence we are faced with a pluralistic realism.

30. *And [Brahman is] endowed with all [power]; this is observed (in the Scriptures).*

31. *If through the lack of organs [one can] not [act, the answer is that] this has been explained already.*[17]

32. *[Brahman can] not [be the originator, for this requires] having an aim.*

33. *But it is merely an innocent game, as in ordinary experience.*[18]

34. *[It is not subject to] partiality and lack of compassion; [on the contrary, there are other factors] to take into consideration, for [the Scripture] declares.*[19]

35. *If [it is said that it is] not [possible] on account of non-distinction, this is not the case, on account of beginninglessness.*[20]

upapadyate cāpyupalabhyate ca // 36 //

upapadyate (*upa* + *pad*): (is) proved (by reasoning); *ca*: and; *api*: also; *upalabhyate*: is acknowledged; *ca*: and.

sarva dharmopapatteś ca // 37 //

sarva: all; *dharma*: properties; *upapatteḥ*: on account of the possibility; *ca*: and.

iti prathamaḥ khaṇḍaḥ

dvitīyo 'dhyāyaḥ

36. *[It is] proved [by reasoning] and is also acknowledged.*

The evidence given in the previous *sūtra* is confirmed by reason and also acknowledged by the *Śruti*.

37. *And all the properties [are] possible.*[21]

End of the Chapter One of Book Two of the Brahmasūtra

NOTES

[1] II.I.1 - In the First Book and in the passages of the *Śruti* it was shown that the *Brahman* is the uncaused cause of the origin of all that exists. It is the metaphysical root of essence (*puruṣa*) and substance (*pradhāna*). It follows from this that *pradhāna* is not *causa sui*.

In the Second Book is shown the non-contradictory nature of the standpoint that has been taken and that the vision of the *Brahmasūtra* is not in opposition to the *Smṛti*. It is thus consistent with both the *Śruti* and the *Smṛti*.

It may be maintained that, since *Sāṁkhya* is consistent with the *Smṛti*, and since the *Smṛti* is held in high regard by those who are qualified to interpret it correctly, the compiler of the *Brahmasūtra* seems to refute the *Smṛti*; however, in this context the purpose is to affirm that *Sāṁkhya* does not consider the whole of the *Smṛti* but only one particular interpretative aspect of it; and thus the philosophy of *Vedānta* is not opposed *in toto* to the *Smṛti*.

The second aphorism confirms this.

[2] II.I.3 - As far as both *Sāṁkhya* and *Yoga* are concerned, that part is refuted which refers to *Sāṁkhya* and contradicts the *Śruti*. *Yoga*, in its meditative aspect, is indicated by the *Śruti*, but when it takes its rise from *Sāṁkhya* it supports the same view of *pradhāna* (even if the figure of *Īśvara* which governs *pradhāna* is inserted into a few *sūtras*).

Śaṅkara maintains: ‘On the other hand it is granted that

the *Smṛtis* referring to *Sāṁkhya* and *Yoga* benefit from actual applicability insofar as they do not contradict it [*Veda*].'[1]

It may be said that all *Smṛtis* are valid insofar as they are not in contrast with the *Śruti*. Where one meets with contradictions, of any kind, one must refer to the *Vedas* or *Upaniṣads* as ultimate authority.

[3] II.I.6 - It may be maintained (*sūtra* 4) that the *Brahman* is not the efficient cause of the world because That (which is insubstantial) is different in nature from this world (which is material and substantial). Although this proposal may seem logical, it is not in fact consistent with a stricter method of metaphysical reasoning. It can be said, however, that *Brahman* is the source of supreme Intelligence, and this allows the possibility of Fullness or bliss, while the world *has* intelligence or participates in the intelligence which belongs to That.

If it is further maintained (*sūtra* 5) that the actual bodily organs are not material or substantial, the reply is that this is not the case because those organs are presided over by the divinities which are of non-substantial orders.

Here is how Plato expresses this view:

> 'Say, therefore, that that which transmits the truth to cognisable objects and the power of knowing them to those who know them is the Idea of the Good. And while you should think of it as the cause of knowledge and truth, insofar as this is known, being both knowledge and truth, two beautiful things, you will not be deceiving yourself in any way if you believe that the Idea of the Good is distinct from them and is even more beautiful. And just as in the sensible world light and sight resemble the sun, although

---

[1] *Bra. Sū*. II.I.3 with the *bhāṣya* of Śaṅkara. Op. cit.

it is not right to put them in place of the sun, so in the intelligible world it is right to consider that knowledge and truth are both similar to the Good, but it is not right to consider that either of them is the Good, whose nature, in fact, is to be regarded as of much greater value.'[1]

On the other hand (*sūtra* 6), all this is seen and confirmed at the empirical level.

Śaṅkara, in his commentary, says: 'The term "however" [*tu*: but, however] is used with the aim of refuting the thesis [which has just been expounded]. 'Thus it has been asserted [by the *Tārkikas*] that, on account of a difference in intrinsic nature, the universe cannot have its substantial cause in the *Brahman*. This is not quite true. In fact, at the empirical level it is possible to ascertain the growth of such things as hair and nails, and so on, [which are not conscious beings and are] quite different in nature from the human being, and so on, which is well known as a being of conscious nature.'[2]

Thus the insubstantial can endow the substantial with *being*.

[4] II.I.7 - If it is maintained that the qualified effect – manifestation – cannot take its rise from the not qualified *Brahman* because in the beginning this was 'alone and without a second', one may conclude that, from this viewpoint, manifestation, the effect, is non-existent (*a-sat*) in absolute terms, so that there is pure negation. But this does not reflect the formulation put forward by the *Brahmasūtra*.

An effect cannot be negated before it comes into existence. Nothing can be negated which does not yet exist.

---

[1] Plato, *Republic*, VI.508-509. *Tutte le Opere*, edited by G. Pugliese Carratelli. Sansoni Editore, Florence, Italy.

[2] *Bra. Sū.* II.I.6 with the *bhāṣya* of Śaṅkara. Op. cit.

Śaṅkara, though adopting the viewpoint of *nirguṇa* (and conforming to the *Brahmasūtra*), maintains that the world of becoming is not like the 'horns of a hare' or the 'child of a barren woman', that is, it is not an absolute nothingness. This implies that a positive evaluation is given to the manifestation and to all the beings (not only human beings, therefore) which live and exist within it.

Śaṅkara accepts *Sāṁkhya* within the limits within which it is accepted by the *Brahmasūtra*, according to which the 'snake' (manifestation) exists as long as our sensory organs perceive it; however, within the world of sensible experience it is not possible for there to be no 'rope', because the world of names and forms, having no reason of its own to be, no ipseity, must depend on something which transcends its appearance.

Plato, too, as a result of his 'second voyage', proposed the 'different' to enable the world of becoming to be deciphered. According to this great Greek teacher, becoming is not absolutely nothing[1] but represents a point midway between Being (insofar as it exists and is not becoming) and absolute non-being. Plato describes becoming as participation in Being or the World of Ideas, by means of which there is a point of contact between the sensible and the intelligible.

> 'But this is what we have already found! It seems right that the things that people generally consider to be beautiful or possessed of some other quality – things which are innumerable – all somehow wander in an *intermediate*

---

[1] Parmenides agrees with this view because he regards the world of phenomena as 'appearance', being in this respect near to Gauḍapāda. Moreover, the Goddess tells him how the world of opinions or world of becoming (typical of the mortals) must be understood. Since he tries to explain it, this means he gives it a certain degree of truth; one cannot talk of what does not exist.

world between the world of non-being and the world of Being in its absolute purity.'[1]

Individual things are thus merely *appearances* of that which is *Beautiful* in itself.

Vedānta puts *māyā* midway between Being, which is and does not become, and absolute non-being. And, in epistemological terms, Plato puts *opinion* midway between true Knowledge and absolute non-knowledge (*Republic* V.478d-c), while *Vedānta* puts *avidyā* between *paramārtha* (supreme knowledge) and *ajñāna* (non-knowledge in absolute terms). It may be inferred that, according to Plato, Parmenides, and *Vedānta*, the mistake consists in taking as real and absolute that which is not real and absolute.

[5] II.I.8 - *Sūtra* 8 puts forward a thesis (*pūrvapakṣa*) by the speaker which is refuted by *sūtra* 9 (*uttarapakṣa*).

If, at the time of cosmic dissolution, the effect, or the world, returns to the *Brahman* or is absorbed into the *Brahman*, then the *Brahman* must remain conditioned by the qualified effect, which means that we cannot speak of the immaculate, pure, and unqualified *Brahman*.

[6] II.I.10 - The objections to *Vedānta* which have been put forward previously by *Sāṁkhya* can likewise be made against accepting *pradhāna* as the original cause of creation; and it is from this perspective that difficulties accumulate on account of the failure to understand how the categories or determinants, such as sound, form, and taste, not being within *pradhāna*, can still exist at the empirical level.

---

[1] Plato, *Republic*, V.479d, translation by E. Turolla. Rizzoli, Milan, Italy. Italics by the editor of the dialogue.

Sāṁkhya maintains that *prakṛti*, or *pradhāna*, is itself transformed; the cause is transformed into the effect (*pariṇāma*) in opposition to the *Vedānta vivarta* of Śaṅkara, in which the effect is nothing but a mere 'appearance' superimposed on the *Brahman*: the classic example of the snake superimposed on the rope.

[7] II.I.11 - Now evidence is put forward to show how all empirical reasonings, or reasonings of the dualistic mind, represent mere opinions which are endless, so that, at the point where they could diverge or come into conflict, one has to go back to the Vedic tradition. Thus, even if, from the empirical and logical point of view, the unestablished nature of Bādarāyaṇa's reasoning is maintained, the result remains unchanged.

We should always hold in mind that both *Sāṁkhya* and *Vedānta* have the Vedic tradition as their point of reference, and whatever speculations may be entertained by the empirical mind, the Tradition always remains the ultimate authority.

[8] II.I.13 - According to empirical logic, one may say that, if the subject and the object have an identical nature and thus there is no difference between them, the enjoyer can be that which is being enjoyed, and *vice versa*. If the *Brahman* (the subject) is of the same nature as the world (the object), then the enjoyer merges into the object of enjoyment, and *vice versa*. On the other hand, if it is acknowledged, within the empirical experience, that the subject and the object are two different things, then the experience of perception is more valid and real than that of the *Śruti*, inasmuch as the subject perceives and knows the object directly.

The objector is seeking to show two things:

1) *Brahman* is identical with the world, and *vice versa*, and thus we have pantheism.

2) Empirical knowledge is valid, direct, and real, which means that it can contradict the *Śruti*.

These two theses are confuted by the *Vedānta* Tradition. In fact, the *sūtra* under consideration provides the explanation by maintaining that there can be differences within things which of themselves are not different. Thus the enjoyer may be a person named Devadatta, and what he is enjoying may be food; the difference between these two factors is evident, but the *essence* of each is identical with the *Brahman*.

Sāṁkhya and *Vedānta* start from perspectives which are different yet not contrary. One of them, the *Vedānta* of the *Brahmasūtra*, rises to the decidedly metaphysical dimension by positing the ungenerated cause as the absolute Reality to which all things are related. It corresponds, it is said, to the One Good of Plato, the One of Plotinus, the Being of Parmenides, the *Ain soph* of the *Qabbālāh*, and so on. The other, *Sāṁkhya*, takes as its starting-point the polarity of *puruṣa* and *prakṛti*, or *pradhāna*, and, once it has established the *puruṣa*, beyond any attribute, but conditioned by *pradhāna*, is constrained to consider manifestation as an effect of *pradhāna*, which represents the efficient and material cause of all that exists *(pariṇāma)*. The cause transforms itself into the effect.

And from this position flow consequences which are logical and, we might say, unexceptionable. Thus arise all those lines of reasoning which originate from the different viewpoints. *Vedānta* includes *Sāṁkhya* but goes further and so cannot accept some of the incomplete aspects of *Sāṁkhya* which are untenable from the perspective of Unity, which is transcendent and without a second and which is conditioned by nothing.

[9] II.I.15 - It was said earlier (*sūtra* 13) that, from the empirical point of view, there is a difference between cause and effect. Now (*sūtra*s 14-20) this difference is being explained more closely by viewing it as apparent rather than as absolute, and this is on account of the word 'origin.' Thus, in the *Brahmasūtra*, 'appearance' (*vivarta*) is spoken of, therefore every modification that can be attributed to the *Brahman* is merely apparent and not real.

The view of *vivarta* is taken up and supported with greater depth and breadth and with exhaustive dialectic in the commentaries of Śaṅkara.

Hence, from the perspective of absolute Reality, this difference (of subject and object or cause and effect) cannot be admitted because between cause and effect there cannot be a difference in nature, which means that the manifestation cannot have – as was said earlier – an ontological status: it cannot exist without being related to the cause (the 'origin' mentioned in the *sūtra*) on which it depends.

Furthermore, the very knowledge of multiplicity could have no reality if it were not related to the one cause which permeates the multiplicity (*sūtra* 15). Thus, in the expression 'Thou art That', 'thou' (the *jīva*) knows itself because there is That which makes the knowledge manifest, although That is beyond knowledge.

These ideas may be clarified by emphasising certain essential points:

1) The world of names and forms (movement) is unable to exist unless there is behind it a 'substratum', an unmoved Being which unifies multiplicity so that multiplicity may be perceived and known (if there were an absolute distinction of the various beings, then they could not

even know each another) and at the same time provides the multiple with the possibility of perpetuating itself.

2) On the other hand, if the world of names and forms (the world of multiplicity) and the unity, or substratum, were both real, the very problem of realisation could not exist, and nor could the knowledge necessary for resolving the multiplicity (*sūtra* 13).

3) But that which is the same is that "substratum" or Essence, that unmoved Being, which permeates the whole of multiplicity. The diversity of names and forms constitutes an 'accident', to use an Aristotelian term, which appears and disappears on the horizon of Essence. 'For it [Being], will be names all of those things that the mortals decided, convinced that they were true... ,'[1] and hence absolute.

4) From the perspective of the supreme Reality, names and forms, according to *Vedānta*, can be considered, when compared to that Reality, mere phenomenon or appearance (*māyā*).

In the *Śruti* we read:

'Venerable One, in what way, then, is this teaching bestowed?' 'My dear, from a single lump of clay all that is made of clay is known, while any of its modifications is none other than mere denomination of name; hence the sole reality is the clay.'[2]

If this example, taken from empirical experience, is transposed to the realm of metaphysics it is seen that the origin is

---

[1] Parmenides, *On the Order of Nature*, fg. 8. Op. cit.

[2] *Chā*. VI.I.3-4.

one and the determinations are many, but while these appear and disappear from the metaphysical horizon (so that it may even be said that they appear but are not), the origin ever remains in its pure and absolute nature.

To the term 'Real' is ascribed the meaning of Being that which is, beyond time, beyond space, and beyond causality.

> '... This [*Ātman*] is the eternal splendour of the knower of the *Brahman*: it is neither increased by any action nor decreased... .'
>
> '... That is the *Ātman* referred to as: not this, not this. It is uncatchable because, in truth, it cannot be caught; it is indestructible because, in truth, it is not subject to destruction... .'[1]
>
> 'Which birth (γέννα) for it, in fact, will you be looking for? How and in what way would it have grown?'[2]

And so the *sūtra*s which follow speak of an interweaving of threads which form a tapestry and there is reference to the vital breath (*prāṇādi*).

[10] II.I.16 The absence of separation between cause and effect leads us to the conclusion that *Brahman*, as the substratum underlying the world of names and forms, abides even in the effect, which is the universe.

Thus the *jīva*, as an effect, is of the same nature as the cause, the *Ātman*: the effect is not separate from its cause. Yet, as we have seen before, the cause does not change into the effect, although this is the view typically held by *Sāṁkhya*. From the empirical or phenomenalist point of view, the cause

---

[1] *Bṛ.* IV.IV.23; IV.V.15.

[2] Parmenides, *On the Order of Nature*, fg. 8. Op. cit.

and the effect are not identical or absolute; from the standpoint of the *Brahman*, they are relative states because they merge into the principial Being. On the other hand, *Brahman* is not the world of names and forms, and hence there is no relationship of identity, but the relationship is one in which the world (cause and effect) depends on That, and not *vice versa*.

Words from the *Bṛhadāraṇyaka Upaniṣad* were given earlier: 'That is the *Ātman*... because, in truth, it is not subject to destruction', and thus its effect, which is the *jīva*, will be indestructible, for it is re-absorbed into the *Ātman* at the moment of Liberation, since it is a mere determination of That.

In the *Śruti* we read:

> 'This is the *Brahman*: with this I shall become identified after departing from here. Whoever cherishes this conviction and entertains no doubt [will realise the *Brahman*].'[1]

[11] II.I.17 - When we read in the *Śruti*: '... in the beginning this was just non-being (*asat*)... ,'[2] or 'In the beginning, here, there was really nothing... ,'[3] these statements concerning non-being and the non-existent cannot be taken in an absolute sense. In the same *Śruti* we read: 'In the beginning this [universe of objects of experience] was indeed the *Ātman*, one only;'[4] which implies that without the *Ātman* not even the universe or this dialectical debate would be suggested.

[12] II.I.21 - The *sūtra* posits the question of the dualism good and evil which is taken into consideration both from

---

[1] *Chā*. III.XIV.4.

[2] *Ibid*. III.XIX.1.

[3] *Bṛ*. I.II.1.

[4] *Ibid*. I.IV.17.

the religious point of view and from the philosophical point of view.

The thesis of the follower of *Sāṁkhya* is this: if the *Brahman* is the creator of the world, and of all beings, It has also created evil. This implies that in its nature there are qualities, attributes, attachments, movement and so on. This is why the human being, as 'subject', can do nothing to intervene on these attachments, since his destiny is that of submitting relentlessly to the God as the 'object' which, like a mighty cloud, towers above him.

It is an important question and of weighty consequences. However, in the following (22) *sūtra* Bādarāyaṇa answers that the *Brahman* which is spoken of is something more than and different from the *Brahman* proposed by the follower of the *Sāṁkhya*.

Now in the *Upaniṣads* there are *ślokas* where it is expressly said:

> 'This being is never born and never dies, it did not take its being from anything, nor anyone [came into being from It]. It is not born, eternal, always the same and permanent. it is not destroyed when the body is destroyed.'[1]

In the *Upaniṣads* there are many of these indications. The one quoted above is sufficient for us. In other contexts there are statements where it is said that the *Brahman*, since it is alone, wanted to become many.

> 'In truth this [universe] was then That (*Tat*) in [its] undifferentiated [state]. Then That differentiated by means of

[1] *Ka*. I.II.18.

name and form (*nāma-rūpa*) so that now it has this name and this form... .'[1]

By human expressions is indicated the One-many or the principial causal Body, whence the world arose. It is the ontological aspect.

There are a number of such quotations, faced with which the *Sāṁkhya*, as was mentioned above, rightly finds the starting-point to conclude that evil, time, space, and all the maculations which ensue, belong to the *Brahman* or *Ātman*.

It is now appropriate to refer to the *Sāṁkhya* doctrine which puts forward three principles which are inherent in *pradhāna* or *prakṛti*: *sattva*, *rajas* and *tamas*.

'*Sattva* is enlightening, light; *rajas* is mobile and stimulating; *tamas* is obstructive and heavy.'[2]

These three principles have been picked up by *Vedānta*. *Rajas*, activity, can move towards *tamas* or towards *sattva*. It depends on the *will* and *intelligence* of the being to orientate itself towards one or the other principle, called by *Sāṁkhya*, *guṇa*. Thus, if the human being directs *rajas* towards *sattva* he follows the road called Devayāna, if he directs it towards *tamas* he follows the road called *pitṛyāna*, the return way on the plane of *viśvaloka*. This brief synthesis has been given because it is indispensable for what will be said later on.

It is important to keep in mind that the *guṇas* belong to *pradhāna* and not to the *jīvātman* or, clearly, to the *Brahman* and that originally *pradhāna* is undifferentiated with possibilities of being shaped along different lines of expression, and

---

[1] *Bṛ*. I.IV.7.

[2] *Sā*. *Kā*. 13. Op. cit

moreover it is insentient. Now the question may be raised. Where and when is evil born?

In the *Maitry Upaniṣad* we read:

> 'With reference to this, some (*sāṁkhyas*) say that it is the attribute or quality (*guṇa*) which, because of the differentiation of nature (*prakṛti*) causes the bondage [of the reflection] of the *Ātman* by means of the determination [and the other mental faculties]; and from the destruction of faults, such as determination [and the other ones], in truth liberation is attained.'[1]

This is tantamount to saying that, if the being, in his free will, directs *rajas* towards *tamas*, he creates a *cleft* with the intelligible where *sattva* is predominant. Thus the being is left 'orphaned', isolated from the vital context; this condition, well expressed by the Hermetic Tradition, represents the 'tomb of Osiris', the 'sepulchre of the one who lives.' At this stage we can ask again: Where and when is evil born?

From what has been said, considering also *kārikā* 15 of *Sāṁkhya* itself, evil is born when there is an identification with the *guṇa tamas,* which has the possibility of *obscuring* the reason of the being who can commit acts which are not responsible.

Good and evil are only free *possibilities*; they are not a *necessity* imposed by some being, however high it may be, even to the point of touching the principial Cause.

The human being is endowed with intelligence, will and freedom, but these qualities and faculties, which are characteristics of the human being, produce great responsibility for the acts which are performed both towards one's fellow-men and towards the surrounding environment, as well as towards the

---

[1] *Mai.* VI.30.

divine Principle as 'inner Ordainer', creator of the *ṛta* which gives unity and *raison d'être* to multiplicity.

All teachings, both Eastern and Western, consist in *awakening* the being who lies in the 'sepulchre of Osiris', or in the 'dark cave', where only simulacra and appearances are seen, to bring him back to the light of the intelligible Sun, and even further for the one who is ready.

[13] II.I.23 - In *sūtra* 21 there is a hypothesis that if the *jīva* (the other) is identical to the *Brahman*, then the *Brahman*, too, must be sullied and must be the producer of good and evil. In *sūtra* 22 and *sūtra* 23 the previous thesis is refuted.

These considerations and the replies have been expounded in earlier *sūtras*.

The *jīva* and the *Ātman* are the two birds described in the *Upaniṣads*; there was also a reference to 'the same within the different', and so on.

The element of earth is not plant or animal and so on, although these owe their existence to this element.

On the other hand, from the metaphysical perspective of the *Ātman* or *Brahman*, which is devoid of *guṇas* (because *akartṛ*), there is no duality whatever, and the problem of good and evil as conceived in the individual dualistic state does not even arise.

[14] II.I.25 - In *sūtra* 24 it is maintained that the *Brahman* cannot be the foundation of all that exists because to be this foundation it would have to look outside itself for the means necessary for manifestation, just as a potter has to look outside himself for clay, ropes, wheels, and so on.

In *sūtra* 25 the reply is that the *Brahman* has no need

to gather contingent means from outside himself because the *Brahman* encompasses absolute fullness.

The gods, too, draw from themselves the potential for production and self expression; and the *yogi*, being endowed with special powers (*siddhis*) finds within himself the possibility of bringing forth many objective phenomena. In dream the individual finds within himself material for the creation of things innumerable.

Moreover, the supreme *Brahman* directs everything with its sole *presence*. Presence on which is founded every quality and quantity pertaining to a 'second.'

[15] II.I.26 - Other objections to the *sūtras* of Bādarāyaṇa are put forward by the adherents of *sāṁkhya*. Under different forms of expression the same lines of reasoning are propounded (See II.I.6-7).

If the *Brahman* is considered to be 'devoid of parts, without activity, pacified, free from imperfection, devoid of defects... .'[1] 'There the sun shines not, nor the moon, neither the stars, nor these thunderbolts flash. Whence [does the being draw] this fire? That very same shining, everything consequently shines; all this shines in different ways from the splendour of That.'[2] then how, being devoid of parts, formless, and so on, is it able, at the same time, to become manifold?

If the One, through its own nature, is thus, how can it become many? This is the fundamental philosophical question, as much for the West as for the East.

Dianoetic philosophy is unable to resolve this question, and it is unable to do so because the dialectical apparatus is

---

[1] *Śve*. VI.19.

[2] *Mu*. II.II.10.

not designed for this purpose. Being unable to resolve it, the non-traditional West has reverted to agnosticism and, consequently, to nihilism.

Pythagoras, Parmenides, Plato, Plotinus, Gauḍapāda, Śaṅkara, Rāmānuja, and others have taken this problem and have developed it with the assistance of the traditional Teaching (the 'ancient word' of which Plato speaks).

> How is it that the dreamer (in the waking state and in the dream state), while manifesting ideal and substantial multiplicity, yet remains one and indivisible?[1]

How is it that the One Good which Plato speaks of, while being the origin, or rather the root, of the many, is and ever remains the One Good?

Non-dual Being cannot be demonstrated theoretically, because the mind can only *conceptualise* Being: it cannot *comprehend* it. The one Being has to be *realised*. But Western philosophers, too, have spoken in relatively recent times of the 'expérience de l'Être' (Lavelle), 'ontological experience' (Albert), and 'experience of Being' (Heidegger).

Aristotle, too, maintains that whoever loves *myth* in its true essence is a philosopher and is thus inclined towards the experience of spiritual Being.

> 'Now whoever experiences a sense of doubt and wonder acknowledges that he does not know; and it is for this reason that anyone who loves *myth* is, in some way, a philosopher: *myth*, in fact, is constituted of an assemblage of things which arouse wonder. The result is that if men have practised philosophy in order to *free themselves from ignorance*, it is evident that they are seeking knowledge

[1] Cp. *Bṛhadāraṇyaka Upaniṣad* V.III.10 with the *bhāṣya* of Śaṅkara. Colezione Vidyā, Rome, Italy.

with the sole aim of knowing and not to achieve some practical usefulness.' 'And the highest of the sciences, the one which more than the others has to rule over the dependent sciences, is the science which knows the aim for which everything is done; and the aim in everything is the good, and, in general, in the whole of nature, the aim is the highest good.'[1]

In this there is identity with the *Vedānta* vision which equally states that the aim of philosophical knowledge is to free oneself from ignorance (*avidyā*). There is no other purpose.

Moreover, according to Albert, metaphysics, for Aristotle, is nothing other than 'the conceptual interpretation and the scientific representation of what is realised in metaphysical experience.'[2]

It may be said that the *unio mystica is* the end which the Philosopher attains through Dialectic.

And in the Plotinian view, the situation is that contemplation, at its highest, enjoys the unity of the being with the metaphysical One: contemplation which is a Knowing without a dianoetic knowing, that is, a knowing without thought.

The metaphysical experience, according to Plotinus, represents the re-union of the human being with the Divine. And this ultimate 'experience' Plato, making use of an expression from the Mysteries, calls *epopteía* (ἐποπτεία).[3]

From the view afforded by the *Brahmasūtra* we may call Bādarāyaṇa an Eastern metaphysician with methodologies,

---

[1] Aristotle, *Metaphysics* A 2.982 b, edited by Giovanni Reale. Bompiani, Milan, Italy.

[2] K. Albert, *Griechische Religion und Platonische Philosophie*. Mainer, Hamburg, Germany.

[3] Cp. Plato, *Phaedrus* 250 c, 251 a; *Symposium* 210 a - 212 b.

ideations, and panoramas which differ from Western dialectic, but what he propounds may be defined as the traditional metaphysics of realisation.

Thus the One-many (according to Plato and the *sūtra* in question) is a state of Being, a state of consciousness which may be solely and exclusively realised through an act of 'self-sameness' (on which see Plotinus). The Tradition of *para-vidyā*, or supreme Knowledge, has considered that subject and object rest on a substratum which gives them being.

In the *Muṇḍaka Upaniṣad* (II.I.1) there is a passage which allows us to understand the identity of metaphysics Eastern and Western: '... innumerable existences originate from the Imperishable... .'

This Imperishable is *Īśvara*, the supreme Person, the *Mahāpuruṣa*. Thus we have the *Brahman* as the absolute foundation, and the Imperishable as the Being which re-unites multiplicity within itself; It is the Unity which gives multiplicity the possibility of comprehending itself because there cannot be absolute duality. Two beings may understand each other, comprehend each other, and have the possibility of dialogue because there exists that Imperishable which unifies them, which gives them the possibility of meeting each other. The greater the relationship with Being, with Unity, the more closely do beings find themselves in perfect accord, harmony, and reconciliation. The further they move away from unity, the more they express the sense of separateness, exclusivity, and disorder, where everyone is opposed to everyone else. A society which presents itself as a 'daughter' of Unity is a traditional society and represents the perfect *polis*, where Order and Justice thrive. From this arises that universal Brotherhood and all-embracing universal Love which transcends the senses, and which all beings - not human beings only - can enjoy.

The Imperishable, to be what it is, must be immutable and thus immobile, in order to grant perfect equilibrium and continuity to the manifestation which is coming into being. It is the transcendent Unity, that which holds the world of names and forms together in stability, and it is in this way that the 'many' are maintained and unified within Being. Thus, the sun holds the diverse planets together by forming the unity of a solar system. Furthermore, the principial Unity finds its *raison d'être* from the *nirguṇa Brahman*; without This, unity itself could not exist.

The empirical view of what exists is not, however, utterly erroneous: it is merely partial, because to know and to define reality it uses the only means, or instruments, of the five senses, together with the *conceptualising mind*, and so it is a sense-based knowledge, concrete and tangible.

16 II.I.27 - In the *Śruti* we read:

'Such is its greatness; but in comparison to that the *Puruṣa* is higher. All beings are one foot [only] of it. That, by the three feet, immortal, is [established] in its own splendour. In truth, that, which is the *Brahman*, is certainly this space (*ākāśa*) which is outside man. In truth, that, which is the space outside man... this is certainly the space which is within man. In truth, that, which is the space within man... this is certainly the space which is within the heart.'[1]

In the view of the objector, one may think that the *Brahman* has 'transformed' itself into manifestation in such a way as to take on the qualities of sentient beings. In earlier *sūtras* it has been shown that such a thesis is untenable.

---

[1] *Chā*. III.XII.6-9.

The *Brahman* is immanent and transcendent, even if these terms are ontologically inadequate; it has been said that the *Brahman* is the metaphysical foundation of all that is and of all that exists. It is that by which light exists, but That beyond light and so on, according to the indications given by the *Śruti*. The *Brahman* with its quarters, which is a purely conceptual expression, embraces the mortal and the immortal, the world of men and the world of the gods, and more besides. There is no contradiction between the inner and the outer, between one quarter and another, between the higher and the lower. The *Brahman* according to the *Śruti* is indivisible, beyond time and space factors. 'The *Om* without measure is the Fourth, beyond any development of manifestation, beneficial, non-dual... .'[1]

The *Brahman* integrates and resolves all the dualities of the sensible and the intelligible worlds. This non-dual vision represents authentic and traditional metaphysics.

'The subtle *Puruṣa* was before the Sun and the Moon.'[2]

'Whatever is other than That is perishable.'[3]

[17] II.I.31 - The objection is that power is always expressed by *prakṛti*, by bodies, and by the *gūnas*; if the *Brahman* has no form and is without bodies and so on, how can the *Brahman* be thought to be endowed with power? *Brahman* is that by means of which the power of *prakṛti* can manifest itself, that by means of which knowledge can reveal itself, that by means of which light can shine; but It itself is beyond power,

---

[1] *Mā*. XII.

[2] *Atharvaśīra Upaniṣad* III. In *Cinque Upaniṣad*. Collezione Vidyā, Rome, Italy.

[3] *Bṛ*. III.IV.2.

beyond knowledge, and beyond light. *Brahman*, moreover, is given very clear expression by the *Śruti*.

> 'It is neither gross nor subtle, neither short nor long, neither red-hot nor liquid... it has no inner and no outer.'[1]

> 'It is not conscious-knower of the internal [world], it is not conscious of the external world; nor it is conscious of both of them, it is not a homogeneous unity of consciousness-knowledge, it is not either conscious or non-conscious; it is invisible, not agent, incomprehensible [to the senses], indefinable, inconceivable, indescribable; it is the sole essence of consciousness as *Ātman*; without any trace of manifestation; it is pacified, beneficial, non-dual. [The Wise] consider it the Fourth. That is the *Ātman* and as such must be known.'[2]

[18] II.I.33 - *Sūtra* 32 poses the same problem in order to demonstrate the impossibility of action on the part of the *Brahman*.

If the *Brahman* is beyond the *guṇas*, beyond action at all levels, and so on, it cannot be the cause of the universe because in ordinary experience it is found that every activity presupposes an aim or motivation, and, of course, the *Brahman* cannot have an aim.

Sūtra 33 refutes such a thesis. It is not stated that every deed must have a definite request for action or a conscious predetermined aim to attain. In fact, in common experience itself there can be innocent activity which is not motivated by clearly defined purposes because there is no *desire* to obtain anything. It is the 'actionless action' of which the *Bhagavadgītā*

---

[1] *Bṛ.* III.VIII.8.

[2] *Mā.* VII.

speaks. One could even say that it is *Īśvara* (*saguṇa*) which promotes actionless action or innocent action.

The causal Seeds, under the impulse of the *rajas gūṇa*, innocently develop and find expression, just as the seeds of plants, through contact with the rays of the sun, naturally find their own expression.

Even the realised and liberated man, putting himself beyond time and space, takes care that only certain events occur in the phenomenal world; he is not attached to the different levels of existence, and he is not attached to action, as if it were something of his, or to the fruits which may accrue from action. He has no acquaintance with that obsession of self-assertion which characterises the childish ego, and he holds of no account the diverse and contradictory opinions of human beings. His action is similar to a 'flight of swallows', which, while not moving their wings, slice through the space in which they move.

It is clear that a certain state of being is impossible to describe just as, and even more so, it is impossible to describe the Being which, while remaining motionless, causes the 'cosmic wheel' to rotate.

Moreover the sole *Presence* of the *Brahman* acts in such a way that everything finds its development and conclusion, just as the sun, in its transcendent centrality, allows each planet of its system to find its development and conclusion.

[19] II.I.34 - There is another objection. It cannot be admitted that the *Brahman*, as founding factor of all that exists, works iniquitously in terms of conduct and retribution of *karma*, so that some human beings suffer and others do not. This would create the understanding that inherent in the *Brahman* is the aspect or faculty of attraction and repulsion.

The answer given by the *Brahmasūtra* is that it is not possible for the *Brahman* to be the cause of the psychological duality which besets beings, because It is beyond all duality, and thus there may be other factors to take into consideration.

Now what are these factors? They are the merit and demerit of each being, according to its own state of consciousness and the degree of freedom from the *guṇas* that it is able to achieve. The being is free by its own nature, but an act which it freely commits may produce merit and demerit according to the degree of its freedom from *avidyā*.

The being is completely free to be or not to be on any of the indefinite levels of Being: it may rise or fall, act or refrain from acting, just as it may think and identify itself with the thought or refrain from identifying itself.

The *Brahman* is that through which everything can manifest itself (including the action of merit and demerit), without the necessity for the *Brahman* to transform itself into movement or manifestation or produce merit and demerit. This has been shown by some of the numerous passages which have been quoted from the *Upaniṣads*. See commentary to *sūtra* 21 (II.I.21) which may clarify the question posited by *Sāṁkhya*.

[20] II.I.35 - This *sūtra* raises the question of whether the polarity of merit and demerit is inherently present before manifestation comes into act; that is to say, inherent in the *Brahmā* itself.

According to the *Brahmasūtra*, the problem does not arise, because with reference to manifestation there cannot be a first and a later, and it cannot be said when manifestation has had its beginning, because proceeding from timelessness it cannot have a temporal relationship.

The *śruti* speaks of *mahāpralaya* and of the birth of

manifestation, that is to say the end of a cosmic cycle or of a *mahāyuga*, in which the entire *manvantara* goes into the potential state and the birth of a new cosmic cycle when the entire life comes out from the "sleep of *Īśvara*." It is the sleep and eventually the waking of *Īśvara*.

In the *Gītā* we read: 'In this world there is no perception of its form, its beginning, or its end.'[1]

The movement from one cosmic cycle to the next cannot be determined, because between the two there is an interruption of time. A temporal relationship can exist only between two factors which are both within time. Moreover, there is no certainty about what still has to come into manifestation.

[21] II.I.37 - For this reason the properties needed to reveal the world are possible within the *Brahman*. The objector maintains that, because the *Brahman* has no qualities or quantitative attributes, it cannot be the material cause of manifestation, which involves attributes, qualities, and quantities.

The reply given by the *Brahmasūtra* is that it is possible, inasmuch as the *Brahman* is the foundation of every property, and that, in fact, this property can exist only if there is behind everything that which makes it what it is, since of its own nature it is not aseity. Moreover, properties belong to *saṁsāra*, the phenomenal appearance, and not to the *substratum* or to substance considered as that which underlies all accidents.

> 'This being is never born and never dies, it did not take its being from anything, nor anyone [came into being

---

[1] *Bha. Gī.* XV.3. Op. cit. Also Cp. *Bṛ.* I.IV.7 with the *bhāṣya* of Śaṅkara. Op. cit.

from It]. It is not born, eternal, always the same and permanent. It is not destroyed when the body is destroyed.'[1]

It is because the *Brahman* holds this state without birth, eternal, that the *manvantara* can enter into sleep and awake; nor, on the other hand, can the *manvantara* do it by itself, since it is a mere effect, and does not have an absolute reality of itself.

[1] *Ka*. I.II.18.

atha dvitīyo 'dhyāyaḥ

dvitīyaḥ khaṇḍaḥ

racanānupapatteś ca nānumānam // 1 //

racanā: ordered design; *anupapatteḥ*: on account of the impossibility; *ca*: and; *na*: not; *anumānam*: that which is inferred.

pravṛtteś ca // 2 //

pravṛtteḥ: on account of creative activity; *ca*: and.

payo 'mbuvac cet tatra-api // 3 //

payaḥ: milk; *ambu*: water; *vat*: like; *cet*: if; *tatra*: there, then; *api*: even, too.

vyatirekānavasthiteś cānapekṣatvāt // 4 //

vyatireka: nothing other or separate; *anavasthiteḥ*: on account of the non-existence; *ca*: and; *anapekṣatvāt*: on account of non-relationship.

anyatrābhāvāc ca na tṛṇādivat // 5 //

anyatra: elsewhere, in another place; *abhāvāt*: on account of the non-existence, not being present; *ca*: and; *na*: not, not even; *tṛṇa*: grass; *ādi*: and so on; *vat*: like, as.

abhyupagame 'pyarthābhāvāt // 6 //

abhyupagame: in admitting; *api*: even; *artha*: purpose; *abhāvāt*: on account of the absence.

Book Two

Chapter Two

1. *That which is inferred [by Sāṁkhya is that pradhāna] is not [the cause of the world] because ordered design [is] not possible.*[1]

2. *And on account of the [non-] creative tendency [of pradhāna].*

Since *pradhāna* is inert and lacks creative impulse, it cannot produce anything manifest.

3. *If [it is said that pradhāna modifies itself] like milk and water, [the reply is that] even then [the modification is brought about through an intelligent principle].*

If one wishes to affirm that even water modifies itself and flows spontaneously, just as milk, too, issues forth by itself from the teats of the cow, the reply is that these occurrences presuppose an intelligence that is inherent in nature.

4. *And [there is] no other existence [outside pradhāna] because there is no relationship.*

5. *[Pradhāna does] not [modify itself] like grass, and so on, there being no other place.*

6. *Even admitting [this, it is not possible] on account of the absence of a purpose.*[2]

puruṣāśmavad iti cet tathāpi // 7 //

puruṣa: person, being; *aśma-vat*: like a stone (a lode-stone); *iti cet*: so, if; *tathā*: thus; *api*: even.

aṅgitvānupapatteś ca // 8 //

aṅgitva: relationship; *anupapatteḥ*: on account of impossibility; *ca*: and.

anyathānumitau ca jñaśaktiviyogāt // 9 //

anyathā: in another way; *anumitau*: from inference; *ca*: and; *jña-śakti*: power of knowledge; *viyogāt*: on account of absence of something.

vipratiṣedhāc cāsamañjasam // 10 //

vipratiṣedhāt: on account of contradiction; *ca*: and; *a-samañjasam*: untenable.

mahad dīrghavad vā hrasva parimaṇḍalābhyām // 11 //

mahat: great; *dīrgha*: long (in space and time), of long duration; *vat*: like; *vā*: or; *hrasva*: short; *parimaṇḍalābhyām*: spherical.

ubhayathāpi na karmātas tad abhāvaḥ // 12 //

ubhayatha: in both cases; *api*: also; *na*: not; *karma*: activity; *ataḥ*: hence; *tat-abhāvaḥ*: its absence.

7. *If [it is said to be] like a person [lame and blind] or like a stone, even this [is untenable].*

If it is stated that the *Puruṣa*, the being related to *pradhāna*, is able to guide *pradhāna* in its activity, even this is not admissible, because there is no substantial relationship between *Puruṣa* and *prakṛti* (or *pradhāna*). It may be said that they represent a duality.

Again, it cannot be maintained that the *Puruṣa* is able to influence *pradhāna* in the way that a lame man, by speaking, can guide a blind man, because the *Puruṣa*, attributeless and inactive, is said to transcend *pradhāna*.

8. *And on account of the impossibility of dominant relationship between principal [and subordinate].*[3]

9. *Even if through inference [one were to admit] another way [in pradhāna, this would not resolve the problem because] the power of knowledge is not present [in pradhāna].*[4]

10. *And on account of self-contradiction it is untenable.*[5]

11. *[The world may originate from That] as the great and the long [originate] from the short and the spherical [infinitesimally small].*[6]

12. *In both cases, too, activity [of the atoms is] not [possible]; hence its absence.*[7]

samavāyābhyupagamāc-ca sāmyād-anavasthiteḥ // 13 //

samavāya: relationship of inherence; *abhyupagamāt*: if it is admitted; *ca*: and; *sāmyāt*: by analogy; *anavasthiteḥ*: on account of infinite regression.

nityam eva ca bhāvāt // 14 //

nityam: permanent; *eva*: furthermore; *ca*: and; *bhāvāt*: on account of existence.

rūpādimattvāc ca viparyayo darśanāt // 15 //

rūpādimattvāt: on account of possessing colour, and so on (*rūpa*: colour; *ādi*: and so on); *ca*: and; *viparyayaḥ*: opposite, contrary; *darśanāt*: on account of seeing.

ubhayathā ca doṣāt // 16 //

ubhayathā: in both cases; *ca*: and; *doṣāt*: on account of error or defect.

aparigrahāc cātyantam anapekṣā // 17 //

a-parigrahāt: on account of non-approval; *ca*: and; *atyantam*: completely; *anapekṣā*: on account of non-consideration.

13. *And if one admits the relationship of inherence on the basis of analogy, the result is an infinite regression.*

Samavāya is the intimate relationship which exists between a substance and its qualities, and it is the seventh category of *Vaiśeṣika*. According to Bādarāyaṇa, this category cannot produce any relationship. Why is this? It is because the dyad and the other atoms related to it are of different qualities, and even if one admitted, as *Vaiśeṣika* does, that there is another *samavāya* which connects the dyad to the atoms, this would lead to an infinite regression.

14. *And, furthermore, existence [will be] on the basis of the permanent.*[8]

15. *And [atoms] possess colour, and so on; [they have an appearance which is] opposite [to that propounded by Vaiśeṣika], as can be seen.*

According to *Vaiśeṣika*, atoms are everlasting and indivisible by nature, composed of attributes such as colour and other qualities (*Vaiśeṣikasūtra* IV.I.1 *et seqq.*). Now even at the level of objective experience it is observable that all the qualitative attributes of a substance are impermanent and of material nature, while according to this theory a given event of any nature and level must be eternal; but this does not accord with the experience of everyday living. Every quantity and quality, inherent in a substance, is born, grows and dies.

16. *And in both cases [there is] error.*[9]

17. *On account of non-approval and complete non-consideration.*[10]

samudāya ubhaya hetuke'pi tad aprāptiḥ // 18 //

samudāyaḥ: constituent factors; *ubhaya*: two, both; *hetuke*: causes; *api*: even if; *tat*: that; *a-prāptiḥ*: not within the realm of experience.

itaretara pratyayatvād iti cen notpattimātra nimittatvāt // 19 //

itaretara: combined; *pratyayatvāt*: on account of the cause; *iti cet*: if [it is said to be] so; *na*: not; *utpatti*: origin; *mātra*: alone; *nimittatvāt*: on account of causality.

uttarotpāde ca pūrva nirodhāt // 20 //

uttara: subsequent; *utpāde*: in rising; *ca*: and; *pūrva*: preceding; *nirodhāt*: on account of ceasing to be.

asati pratijñoparodho yaugapadyam anyathā // 21 //

asati: in being absent, in the absence; *pratijñā*: the acknowledged principle; *uparodhaḥ*: contradiction; *yauga-padyam*: simultaneity; *anyathā*: otherwise.

pratisaṁkhyā 'pratisaṁkhyā nirodhāprāptir avicchedāt // 22 //

pratisaṁkhyā: voluntary; *a-pratisaṁkhyā*: involuntary; *nirodha*: cessation; *a-prāptiḥ*: impossibility; *a-vicchedāt*: on account of uninterruptedness.

ubhayathā ca doṣāt // 23 //

ubhayathā: in both ways or cases; *ca*: and; *doṣāt*: on account of the difficulty.

ākāśe cāviśeṣāt // 24 //

ākāśa: in *ākāśa*; *ca*: and, even; *aviśeṣāt*: on account of non-difference.

18. *Even if the constituent factors [proceed] from both [causes], this is not within the realm of experience.*[11]

19. *If [it is said that the formation of the constituent factors is possible] through the combined causality [of avidyā, and so on], [the answer is that] this is not the case [because they are only] the cause of the origin [and not of the constituent factors].*[12]

20. *And because in the arising of the subsequent the preceding ceases to be.*[13]

21. *[If the effect is admitted] in the absence [of the cause, there is] contradiction of the acknowledged principle; otherwise [there is] simultaneity [of cause and effect].*[14]

22. *Voluntary cessation and involuntary cessation [are] impossible because there is no interruption [in the series].*[15]

23. *And on account of the difficulty [which occurs] in both cases.*[16]

24. *Even for ākāśa [there is] no difference.*

Apart from the two types of extinction referred to in *sūtra* 22, there is also that of *ākāśa*, which is included in the same demonstrative perspective covered by *sūtra* 22.

anusmṛteś ca // 25 //

anusmṛteḥ: on account of memory; *ca*: also.

nāsato 'dṛṣṭatvāt // 26 //

na: not; *asataḥ*: from non-being; *adṛṣṭatvāt*: on account of non-agreement with experience.

udāsīnānām api caivaṁ siddhiḥ // 27 //

udāsīnānām: [for] indifferent [beings]; *api*: even; *ca*: and; *evam*: in this way; *siddhiḥ*: fulfilment.

nābhāva upalabdheḥ // 28 //

na: not; *abhāvaḥ*: non-existence; *upalabdheḥ*: on account of perception.

vaidharmyāc ca na svapnādivat // 29 //

vaidharmyāt: on account of different nature; *ca*: and; *na*: not; *svapnādivat* (*vat*: like): as in a dream, similar to dream, and so on.

na bhāvo 'nupalabdheḥ // 30 //

na: not; *bhāvaḥ*: existence; *an-upalabdheḥ*: on account of non-perception.

kṣaṇikatvāc ca // 31 //

kṣaṇikatvāt: on account of instantaneity (*kṣaṇa*: instant, moment); *ca*: and, again.

sarvathānupapatteś ca // 32 //

sarvathā: in all respects; *an-upapatteḥ*: on account of non-acceptability; *ca*: and

25. *And also on account of memory.*[17]

26. *[Being arises] not from non-being, [for this] does not accord with experience.*

Being cannot take its rise from non-being because this does not tally and is not acceptable, and it is not encountered within the empirical condition.

27. *And in this way even indifferent [beings] would find fulfilment.*[18]

28. *Non-existence [is] not [acceptable] on account of perception.*[19]

29. *And on account of a difference in nature [the waking state] is not like the dream state.*[20]

30. *The existence [of mental impressions is] not [possible] because of the non-perception [of external objects].*

31. *Again, on account of the instantaneity [of consciousness itself, so that it cannot be the substratum of impressions].*

32. *And because [such a proposition] is unacceptable in all respects.*[21]

naikasminnasambhavāt // 33 //

na: not; *ekasmin*: in the same, in one; *a-sambhavāt*: non on account of impossibility.

evaṁ cātmākārtsnyam // 34 //

evam: thus; *ca*: and; *ātmā*: *Ātman*; *a-kārtsnyam*: not all-pervading.

na ca paryāyād apyavirodho vikārādibhyaḥ // 35 //

na: not; *ca*: and; *paryāyāt*: on account of modification; *api*: even if; *a-virodhaḥ*: non- contradiction; *vikārādibyaḥ*: on account of change, and so on.

antyāvasthiteś cobhayanityatvād aviśeṣaḥ // 36 //

antya-avasthiteḥ: on account of final permanence; *ca*: and; *ubhaya-nityatvāt*: on account of the permanence of both; *aviśeṣaḥ*: non-distinction.

patyur asāmañjasyāt // 37 //

patyuḥ: of the Lord; *a-sāmañjasyāt*: on account of untenability.

sambandhānupapatteś ca // 38 //

sambandha: connection; *anupapatteḥ*: on account of the impossibility; *ca*: and.

33. *On account of the impossibility [of opposing qualities] within one and the same thing, [the Jain point of view is] not [tenable].*

34. *And in this way the Ātman [is] not all-pervading.*[22]

35. *And [it is] not [possible to avoid] contradiction, even if [there is] successive modification on account of change and so on.*

Even if the soul undergoes an increase or decrease in its parts through successive modifications, this does not solve the problem, because the soul itself is of the nature of change, and hence there is a contradiction in affirming both bondage and liberation. These two categories cannot exist simultaneously where there persists a continuous fluidity in what one is.

36. *And on account of the final permanence [of the soul] and on account of the permanence of the two [preceding aspects: the beginning and the intermediate phase, there is] no distinction.*[23]

37. *The Lord [as the efficient cause of the manifestation is] untenable.*[24]

38. *And on account of the impossibility of connection.*

It may be thought that once the reality of the Lord has been admitted this must act directly in the production of causes and would thus act directly on *pradhāna* and on the *puruṣas*. There would therefore be a relationship of continuity between the Lord, the souls (*puruṣas*) and *pradhāna*, but this is not possible, because the Lord is distinct from both *pradhāna* and *puruṣas*.

adhiṣṭhānānupapatteś ca // 39 //

adhiṣṭhāna: foundation, support, base; *a-nupapatteḥ*: on account of the impossibility; *ca*: and.

karaṇavac cen na bhogādibhyaḥ // 40 //

karaṇa-vat: like the sense organs; *cet*: if; *na*: not; *bhoga*: on account of enjoyment; *ādibhyaḥ*: and so on.

antavattvam asarvajñatā vā // 41 //

antavattvam: limitation; *a-sarvajñatā*: *a-sarva*: not all; *jñatā*: knowledge; *vā*: or.

utpattyasambhavāt // 42 //

utpatti: origin; *a-sambhavāt*: on account of the impossibility.

na ca kartuḥ karaṇam // 43 //

na: not; *ca*: and; *kartuḥ*: from the operator; *karaṇam*: instrument.

39. *And on account of the impossibility of a support [on which to operate].*

Some schools of thought admit that the Lord causes *pradhāna* to be set in motion by giving direction to the action, just as the potter sets the clay in motion by also imparting a direction to it; this implies an absolute immanentism. But this is not possible, because *pradhāna*, being insentient, is not capable of perception. The analogy cannot be correct. The Lord is then completely different from both the clay and the pot, and from the 'I' or *ahaṁkāra* as these are elements that have been produced.

40. *If [it is said to be] like the sense organs, [it is] not [so], because of enjoyment and so on.*[25]

41. *[He would have] limits or non-omniscience.*

Moreover, if this thesis were admitted, the Lord would have a limited and contingent nature and be deprived of omniscience.

42. *On account of the impossibility of origin.*[26]

43. *Moreover, the instrument is not [produced] from the operator.*

At the time of the *Brahmasūtra* the craftsman's tools were not produced by the craftsman himself. This is an example to show that the *Bhāgavata* thesis is not valid when it maintains that from the individual self, as agent (*saṁkarṣaṇa*), there arises the mind (*pradyumna*), and that from the mind there arises the sense of 'I' (*aniruddha*).

vijñānādibhāve vā tad apratiṣedhaḥ //44//

vijñāna-ādibhāve: in the possession of knowledge, and so on; *vā*: or, oppure; *tat*: that; *a-pratiṣedhaḥ*: the non-removal.

vipratiṣedhācca //45//

vipratiṣedhāt: on account of contradiction; *ca*: and.

iti dvitīyaḥ khaṇḍaḥ
dvitīyo 'dhyāyaḥ

44. *Or, even if [Vāsudeva, Saṁkarṣaṇa, and others] possessed the knowledge [there would still be] the non-removal of that [the impossibility of self-origination].*

To the objection expressed earlier (*sūtra* 43), the supporter of the thesis in the previous *sūtra* (42) admits that beings such as *Saṁkarṣaṇa* and so on could be considered as divine principles endowed with those properties inherent in *Vāsudeva* which would prevent them from being subject to birth and death.

Bādarāyaṇa replies that even this thesis has no foundation because if these principles have the same properties as *Vāsudeva* it is impossible to understand why there have to be four distinct principles when there is in fact only one being, which is *Vāsudeva*; moreover, to admit four principles, or Lords, is against the *Bhāgavata* teaching itself, according to which there is only one Lord.

45. *And on account of contradiction.*

Once more, there is a contradiction, because at times the four principles are mentioned as qualities, at times as aspects of the agent (*Saṁkarṣaṇa*), and at other times as being identical with the agent.

End of Chapter Two of Book Two
of the Brahmasūtra

NOTES

[1] II.II.1 - The aim of all the previous *sūtras* has been to show that the *Brahman* alone is the root or foundation of all that exists; the attempt is now made to show the mistaken nature of the formulations made by other lines of thought, even if once again, up to *sūtra* 10, there is renewed confrontation with *Sāṁkhya* from the point of view of logic.

The *sūtra* puts forward the following thesis: once *pradhāna* is held to be insentient, devoid of consciousness, and inert, it cannot be the origin of the world in which an ordered, intelligent, and rational production is apparent.

What is more, discovering an inert tendency within *pradhāna* implies that it is quite impossible for *pradhāna* to produce anything. For an active condition to exist, there must be an intelligent dynamism inherent in the productive subject.

[2] II.II.6 - *Pradhāna* has no relationship with *Puruṣa* because:

1) *Puruṣa* is equidistant from *pradhāna*, in addition to being inactive.

2) All the other factors expressed by *Sāṁkhya* are products and not producers. Therefore, since *pradhāna* is the only reality enunciated, it cannot be simultaneously active and at rest without an intelligent reality that is able to preside over such acts, acts which are mere

> effects. 'In fact, a single reality will not be able, in its entirety and simultaneously, to exercise the twofold function of being passive and active, for if it could do this, it would be no longer one, but two.'[1]

On the other hand, it cannot be considered to be like grass, which is changed into milk, because grass, of itself, does not have the capacity to produce milk except by means of the cow, which functions as the transforming cause. Even admitting the above (in relation to the declaration of *Sāṁkhya*), it would still be impossible, in the absence of an intelligent purpose.

[3] II.II.8 - The *sūtra* refers to the three *guṇas*, which are elements inherent in *pradhāna*. These are initially in a state of equilibrium (*pralaya*), and the breaking of this equilibrium gives life to manifestation. Now, without an agent that is external to *pradhāna* this breaking cannot occur; the *guṇa* which becomes dominant on account of the breaking of the stillness has no relationship with the other *guṇas* and has no hierarchical dependence. Even if one admits that the beginning of the primordial movement is an aspect which is seated in the very nature of *pradhāna*, through *rajas*, still one has to acknowledge that within the same *pradhāna* there is a determinative nature and there is an intelligent tendency towards an aim that is to be attained. None of this seems to belong to *pradhāna*.

[4] II.II.9 - The interlocutor puts forward other hypotheses to show that within *pradhāna* abides the cause of the generation of the universe.

---

[1] Plato, *Parmenides* 138 b, in *Tutti gli scritti*, edited by G. Reale, Bompiani, Milan, Italy.

Even with the absence of intelligence and knowledge in *pradhāna*, however, the interlocutor maintains that the *guṇas* - attributes of *pradhāna* - can have, within their very instability, the inherent power to produce equilibrium and also to break it. In other words, *pradhāna* itself can convey manifestation from power to act. But even if, through inference, one were to admit this operational possibility or modality, the problem would not be resolved, for since *pradhāna* has the nature of instability it could not return to the stability of *pralaya*. Whether *pradhāna* has the nature of instability or the nature of stillness, there is always a need for a prior external agent which can act as a stimulus either to produce or to come to rest.

Movement presupposes an unmoved reality. Moreover, the thesis of *Vedānta*, as previously expounded, is ever valid: since *pradhāna* lacks intelligence and knowledge, it is unable, of itself, to manifest an ordered world governed by laws.

[5] II.II.10 - Because *Sāṁkhya* is a source of contradictions, *pradhāna*, as the sole cause of manifestation, cannot be the beginning and the end of the universe. In fact, it contradicts itself when it states that within *pradhāna* there are rest and instability simultaneously. There is further contradiction when, with reference to the production of the elements, it says at times that the senses are seven and at other times that they are eleven, and when it says on occasions that the subtle elements (*tanmātras*) are produced by the first determination of *pradhāna* (*mahat*), and on other occasions that they are created by the sense of 'I' or *ahaṁkāra*.

Pradhāna, in its different gross and subtle aspects, lacks a single principle which contains within itself those archetypes which will develop as time goes by, and which will form the world of names and forms. In other words, it lacks an ontological factor, unifying and proposing, which would give *raison d'être* to multiplicity.

[6] II.II.11 - Now that the reasoning in relation to *Sāṁkhya* has ended, the next step is to address the atomistic *Vaiśeṣika* of Kaṇāda.

The objector begins by refuting the view of *Vedānta*, maintaining that if the quality of the first cause is found in the effect, then the intelligent cause, the *Brahman*, must be found in the effect, which is to say that the cause is transformed into the effect. If the *Brahman* is pure intelligence, this should be the predominant quality of the manifestation, and this is not evident in *pradhāna*, or *prakṛti*.

The answer given by the *Brahmasūtra* is on the same demonstrative basis as that employed by *Vaiśeṣika*: if the dyad (the combination of two atoms) comes from the single atom [of *Vaiśeṣika*], to be followed in turn by the triad, the tetrad, and so on, the simple nature of the atom becomes vitiated by the nature of multiplicity; a dyad is small and short, while the triad and the tetrad, being compounds, are big and long. From this viewpoint the simple *nature* of the atom is lost.

Thus the atom becomes transformed into the dyad and then into the triad, and so on. If the atom is therefore divisible, then there will be an infinite extension with no possibility of completely forming a particular being.

If it is still maintained that it is the nature of the atom, the causal and primary element, to produce different effects, one may say in the same vein that the *Brahman*, the supreme plenitude, can produce different effects from itself.

[7] II.II.12 - If it is still postulated that there is a progression from non-being to being (from the single unmanifest atom

to atomic multiplicity), following the impulse of a thrust of disturbance by which the atom creates the cosmos, the answer given by the *Brahmasūtra* is that this is not possible because no positive or formative action can occur within a state in which everything is static and formless. If, moreover, it is supposed that this causal impulse can reside in an invisible principle, that is to say *adṛṣṭa*, even then this is not possible because, according to *Vaiśeṣika*, *adṛṣṭa* is nothing other than that unseen power which responds to the cohesive formation of atoms, this being the result of a past association with actions both meritorious and non-meritorious. This implies a *karma* or action which is unintelligible and unconscious of a past experienced by manifested beings. This point of view posits manifest effects which give rise to the primordial unmanifest cause, and since this is impossible there is 'absence of that', that is, absence of the cosmos.

[8] II.II.14 - There is another contradiction in the philosophy of *Vaiśeṣika*, according to which atoms may be active (agents and producers) or inactive (non-agents), or active and inactive simultaneously. If atoms had the nature of activity, there would be a permanent maṇifestation with no possibility of coming to an end; if, on the other hand, atoms were by nature permanently inactive (non-agents), there would be no production and on account of providing a beginning to manifestation, necessarily inactivity must cease. Again, if activity and non-activity occur simultaneously, this cannot happen on account of the law of the principle of non-contradiction, that is, the impossibility of opposites co-existing at the same time.

[9] II.II.16 - There is an error in maintaining the *Vaiśeṣika* point of view. The two aspects that were previously presented -

the indivisible eternality of atoms and the qualitative attributes inherent in their very nature - cannot stand up to a carefully reasoned approach. If atoms have no qualitative attribute, it means that there is no mention of qualities; if they have qualitative attributes, they cannot be permanent or eternal by nature, that is, they cannot have an absolute nature. According to Aristotle, 'accident' (or attribute) is that which belongs to something, not for ever and not for the most part, but only at times and hence in a chance manner; or alternatively, it is whatever belongs of itself to something but does not pertain to its very essence (*Metaphysics* E.2-3). Hence attributes are not inherent in atoms themselves.

[10] II.II.17 - Once the premises of the previous *sūtras* have been considered, the view of atoms as the first cause of creation is to be fully rejected.

Bādarāyaṇa, in the *Brahmasūtra*, develops a very convincing thesis on the impossibility of maintaining as valid the theory of the atomists. And Śaṅkarācārya reinforces this impossibility with metaphysical arguments. However, both the *Sāṁkhya* of Īśvarakṛṣṇa[1] and the *Vaiśeṣika* attributed to Kaṇāda are two *darśanas* (particular views of the complex teaching of the *Vedas* and *Upaniṣads*) which are orthodox in nature. What Bādarāyaṇa seeks to show is the *relative* nature of the thesis which maintains that *pradhāna* is the first and only cause or the foundation of the world of names and forms; and in a similar way he seeks to show how the atoms

---

[1] Tradition attributes the codification of the *darśana* to Kapila. The *Sāṁkhyakārikā* of Īśvarakṛṣṇa is the oldest and best known treatise of this school.

of *Vaiśeṣika* cannot, of themselves, be the primordial cause of formal and informal existence.

Bādarāyaṇa the Teacher is not attacking the entire thesis of either *darśana*, but he is revealing their partial nature and incompleteness. An all-inclusive, non-partial and therefore *advaita* teaching must take account of the whole question existing in the *Vedas* and *Upaniṣads*. This implies making use of true Science (according to the view of the Greeks), that is, of that ultimate knowledge which attains the supreme Reality beyond time, space, and causality. This is not to deny that mutual exchanges, sometimes quite substantial ones, occur among the various *darśanas*. *Yogadarśana* accepts *Sāṁkhya*; *Vaiśeṣika* acknowledges both *Nyāya* and *Sāṁkhya*; *Nyāya* refers to *Vedānta* and *Sāṁkhya*; and *Vedānta* itself does not exclude any of the others.

When studying and contemplating the *Brahmasūtra* it must be borne in mind that Bādarāyaṇa considers *nirguṇa Brahman* to be the foundation of (ontological) Being or *Īśvara* and, therefore, of the world of names and forms (*nāma-rūpa*) which is evolutionary or cosmological by nature, which implies that his position is metaphysical and therefore supra-intelligible; and since it is such, all conceivable dualisms (such as that of *Sāṁkhya*, of *Nyāya*, or of the very God-Person-Being) becomes integrated within that One without a second which represents the Infinite to which all possible references must ultimately be made.

[11] II.II.18 - If the atomist theory, according to *Śaṅkara*, can reach a partial nihilism which is opposed to the *Vedas*

and on account of which some parts of it must be rejected as invalid, there is even more reason to reject the completely nihilistic theory found in some systems of thought.

For example, pluralistic realism (*Sarvāstivāda*)[1] posits two kinds of aggregates: those which are objective or material (*bāhya*) and those which are subjective or psychological (*abhyantara*). Even if the factors which constitute the multiple aggregates (beings) had to take their rise from both causes (internal, or subjective, and external, or objective), this could not be considered to be a convincing or valid thesis.

The inner or subjective aspects consist of the five *skandhas* or constituents of being: *rūpa*, *vijñāna*, *vedanā*, *saṁjñā*, and *saṁskāra*. The outer or objective aspects consist of atoms which have the nature of solidity, fluidity, heat, and movement (earth, water, fire, and air). This objective classification posits two kinds of objects: the *asaṁskṛta dharmas*, which are not compounds, and the *saṁskṛta dharmas*, which are compounds.

These *skandhas*, characterised by the inner and outer aspects, are determined by immediacy (the momentary existence of the *dharmas* or beings); the combination of these factors and the inter-relationship or linking together of all these determinations cause the contingent experience or perception to take place and to manifest.

With such premises, it is necessary to ask whether or not there is a conscious principle which produces the determinations. If there is, then the conscious principle to which all the *dharmas* relate must constitute a stable governing element, which is denied by such a teaching, apart from the fact that it would contradict the condition of the simple immediacy

---

[1] The *Sarvāstivāda* is divided into two streams: *Sautrāntika* and *Vaibhāṣika*. They show some differences in their vision of what is real. However, both of them belong to the pluralistic realism.

of acts. If there is no such principle, it could be asked how there can be an inter-relationship or linking together of the *dharmas* when these exist only for a moment and they are independent of each other (as indicated by the *sūtra* in question). Moreover, who would be able to perceive the aggregate, which exists for an instant, if there were no primal element, intelligent and steadfast, which could cause the awareness of the moments to be continuous? Hence, the result of all this is a succession of mechanical acts which necessitate an unmoving principle to affirm the appearance and disappearance of the *dharmas*. According to Aristotle, identity is necessary for any change to occur. And Kant, too, states: 'Without the permanent no relationship in time is possible' (First analogy of experience). Thus, if the objective aspect, in its relativity, becomes real in the act of perception, and if both (subject and object) are factors in an uninterrupted series of instants, which are nevertheless separated from each other, then we find ourselves in a total void or nothingness, unless this 'void' indicates the one absolute Reality of which the *Vedas* and the *Upaniṣads* speak.

[12] II.II.19 - Again, if it is stated that the constitution of the aggregates is made in the same way as the cause which gives rise to the effect or *avidyā* which produces fruit, so that there is no need for an intelligent principle, Bādarāyaṇa replies that this is not possible because causality could eventually explain the simple sequence of one atom (effect) from a preceding atom (cause), but it is unable to explain the combination of inert and unconscious atoms within a complex aggregate in such a way that an intelligent being is created. It is only by having recourse to a conscious, ordaining and intelligent principle that we can explain the combination of acts which

produce complex phenomena that are governed by definite laws. Without a primordial archetype that is steadfast and everlasting there cannot be a formal prototype, not even for the duration of an instant.

The *sautrāntikas* maintain that all the *dharmas*[1] are instantaneous, come unexpectedly into existence, living for a moment, and vanish into non-existence. This represents the teaching of instantaneousness (*kṣaṇikajñānavāda*). It implies that the *dharmas* are mere names without any foundation to which a reason for existence can be attributed.

Even the individual self (*pudgala* = sensory vehicle) is a mere concept to indicate aspects which are simply psychical and momentary. It is necessary to consider that if dialectic which is quite to the point (see the commentaries of Śaṅkara) is developed by the various commentators, it is also true that the presuppositions and the substance are already in the *Brahmasūtra*.

On the other hand, the commentary's proper function is to develop the theme which is put forward synthetically in a treatise (and this is especially true in the Vedic Tradition). Moreover, successive commentators have availed themselves of a wide range of more comprehensive language and of a more mature dialectical development which has been created in the passage of time, in addition to having greater parallels extending beyond the ambit of a single culture.

[13] II.II.20 - It was said earlier that the cause could eventually explain the simple succession of one atom from a preceding atom. This *sūtra* goes even further in showing that if

---

[1] The word *dharma* stands for quite a number of things: rule, religion, the phenomena of life, the objects of various nature, and so on.

the preceding atom, in its instantaneousness, has gone out of existence it cannot be the cause of anything:[1] the absolutely non-existent cannot produce the existent. Merely by admitting a continuous flux of momentary phenomena which determines cause and effect, another factor is needed to execute the creation of compound and complex aggregates; and although it may be stated that atoms have within themselves the intelligence or consciousness to effect the aggregation, yet this very consciousness or intelligence, according to this school of thought (*Sautrāntika*), is part of the moment which appears and disappears. On the other hand, if the various instants are absolute, there would be an infinite number of absolutes which are unable to relate to each other, for the instant has within itself its own inevitable reason for existing and its own ontological state, which is and cannot become other than itself.

If the various instants are relative, then they have a definite duration (an instant) which time devours, causing these instants to be born and to die. But if all the *dharmas* are relative, this view is also relative, going back to the viewpoint of mere opinion and not having any foundation at all on which to support itself. According to this view, one cannot even speak of realisation, liberation, or illumination with their potential for dispelling *avidyā*.

On the other hand, for there to be inter-relationship and mutual understanding and knowledge amongst beings, a common denominator is necessary, with the power to create a relationship of reciprocity and communion. Beings may be many, but they are joined and bound together by something

---

[1] According to the logic of this school a datum can determine another datum without having its own intrinsic persistence.

which is common to all manifest beings so that they may be able to recognise each other.

According to the *Sautrāntika*, there are no beings as such, but only beings in process of becoming; and these beings in process of becoming do not have an independent reality of their own, their own aseity.

As far as knowledge is concerned, the *Sarvāstivādins* posit two instruments: perception and concept or cognition. Perception (*grahaṇa*) gives us direct reception, free of cognition (*kalpanā*), but this reception is indeterminate and indefinite; and so it is the function of cognition to give definition to things, but this definition of *dharmas* is only an ideal cognition by means of which there is, on the one hand, perception that is imprecise and untrue because it does not have within it any possibility of knowledge; and there is, on the other hand, cognition that is clearly defined but devoid of real substance because it represents mere imagination. Wishing to explain everything in terms of subject (perception, in this context) and object (external *dharma*) leaves the phenomenal world without an explanation, and there cannot be any kind of knowledge which does not have at least some degree of truth. Everything is relative to the very relativity of the mind that is making the proposition.

In any case, although this teaching may be dialectically acceptable, it cannot explain the becoming of the things.

In the *Abhidharmakośabhāṣya* we find the statement:

> 'Are we obliged to think that wood perishes from its contact with fire?
>
> '*Yes*, because we no longer see the wood when it is burnt, and no argument is as forceful as the evidence of our senses.'
>
> '*No*, it is a question of reasoning, since even if we no longer

see the wood, this could be because the wood perishes of itself and stops renewing itself. The non-existence of the wood, which you say is caused by the fire, is a pure nothingness, a non-entity, and a non-entity cannot be an effect and cannot be caused.

'Moreover, if the destruction or non-existence which follows existence had a cause at some time, then, as is the case with births, it would always have a cause. And, of course, you would willingly concede that flame, sound, and thought are momentary by nature.

'If things perish without a cause but through their own nature, just as objects thrown into the air fall down, then they must perish the moment they are born, and they cannot exist beyond the moment in which they effectively receive their being, for if destruction, which has no cause, does not take place at the very moment of birth, it will not take place later, since the thing remains what it is.'[1]

Thus we cannot destroy that which is, nor can we destroy that which is not. A flame dies out because it is momentary and not because it is put out.

[14] II.II.21 - If it is admitted that the effect exists in the absence of the cause, this would lead to the invalidation of this school of thought; if it is then affirmed that the cause persists until the manifestation of the object, this produces, on the one hand, the contradiction of instantaneousness and, on the other hand, the contemporaneity of cause and effect, which cancel each other out.

---

[1] Quoted from S. Radhakrishnan in *La filosofia indiana* Vol. 1: p. 683. Collezione Vidyā, Rome, Italy. See this volume to go deeper into these Buddhist doctrines.

If it is still postulated that the transition of one atom to another, in order to provide continuity of being, happens through mere induction, so that the succeeding atom is qualified in an exclusively mechanistic way, this still does not solve the problem, because everything that is produced lacks sufficient reason to be what it is.

Moreover, if the transmitted qualities are the same, there would be a permanent continuity of qualities for the same species and nature. If they are not the same, in which way can the second element, to which these qualities have been transmitted, become other than itself or change its nature, being precisely a factor which does not depend on an *ante* element or a *post* element? If, according to some *Sarvāstivādins*, the cause is then transformed into the effect (*pariṇāma*), and the primary elements are thus transformed, each giving rise to something else, the problem remains unresolved, even if it were possible to consider the primary elements as temporarily eternal. In this way there is nothing but a continuous transformation of *dharmas* in mechanical succession (the mechanical becoming of things and events).

[15] II.II.22 - Neither voluntary cessation nor involuntary cessation can be admitted on account of the lack of extinction or uninterruptedness of perception. According to the theory under examination, an event, whatever its nature, exists through the function of perception. But perception itself, as we have seen earlier, is a being and a non-being simultaneously, besides being untrue. A being's perception either persists during its appearance and then disappearance, in which case there is something constant underlying or it vanishes, in its

instantaneousness, with the being itself, without being reproduced; and this is the thesis or line of thought propounded by nihilistic materialism.[1]

It should be remembered that, according to this school (*Sarvāstivāda*), there are three uncompounded elements:

1) *Ākāśa*, which is devoid of form (*a-rūpa*) and is not anything material (*vastu*).

2) *Apratisaṁkhyā*, which is the non-perception of *dharmas* that is produced by the absence of any *pratyaya* whatsoever, and is not the product of knowledge.

3) *Pratisaṁkhyā*, which is the fruition of knowledge.

These three categories are refuted by the compiler of the *Brahmasūtra*.

[16] II.II.23 - When confronted by these difficulties, the thesis of the school under examination is, according to the *Brahmasūtra*, unacceptable.

They are, however, two different conceptions, or, rather, two points of view, which start from opposite positions in relation to consciousness; and while *Vedānta* accepts the contingent aspect of manifestation as far as form is concerned, such as *ahaṁkāra* itself, this school accepts only the thesis of nothingness, according to which everything returns to nothing, for there is nothing permanent, not even the person who is affirming being or non-being.

But it is precisely this contradiction which the *Brahmasūtra* seeks to demonstrate: if the person making the affirmation *is not*, then he cannot affirm anything, least of all the *absolute nature* of non-being.

---

[1] See commentary to *sūtra* 20.

Empirical relativism uses thought only to affirm or to deny: 'I think, therefore I am.' Being exists as thought, and this thought, the product of brain cells, is destined to vanish, and consequently the thought-being disappears with it. On the other hand, he who puts himself beyond thought (a sensory and dualistic expression), either by way of an intellection made by *noûs* or *buddhi* or by way of direct experience, clearly changes the perspective so as to overturn the postulates of empirical relativism. A metaphysical way of realisation, such as that propounded by the *Brahmasūtra*, considers the polarity of spirit and matter, of intellect and thought, and so on, as an aspect which is resolved in the One, beyond the second, or in the One without a second. Yet this Way is not only Eastern: in the Western tradition, too, the same Way has been propounded since remote antiquity and illuminated, in times less remote, by Orphism, Pythagoras, Parmenides, Plato, Plotinus, Proclus, and others.

This last-mentioned traditional school reverses that relativistic assertion 'I think, therefore I am' into 'I am, therefore I think', and thought, which is movement, can be extinguished in the state of 'I am', which *is* and does not become.

[17] II.II.25 - Even the very emptiness of space or ether or *ākāśa* cannot be maintained, on account of the memory which the being possesses at different moments of existence, something that is unverifiable when the very knower or experiencer, according to the teaching of *Vaibhāṣika*, has the nature of instantaneousness. And it is not possible to postulate a momentary being which transmits the memory to the next momentary being by means of simple induction, without admitting also, as has been said, an identical substratum for

them both which acts as an agent of continuity, stability, and connection.

Nothing like this is found in nature: even a particle of light (a photon), being separated from another particle, has within it the continuity of being, because this continuity is transmitted by its source, the sun, which represents the foundational stable principle with regard to the particle that appears and disappears, and this principle transmits to it the reality of its own being.

[18] II.II.27 - The thinking of the *Sarvāstivāda* that has been examined so far does not admit the existence of the effect within the cause or the continuity of the cause within the effect, which would allow the perceived existent to arise from the non-existent.

Thus if something can take its rise from nothing, then even indifferent beings would find the fulfilment of their aims. The birth of an effect is the death of the pre-existent cause; a shoot is born from the seed when the seed perishes. But from pure and simple non-existence or absolute nothingness nothing can come into being. Without a shoot there can be no seed, and without a seed there can be no tree. If the cause is destroyed and no longer exists, no effect can come forth.

If the cause does not have within it the nature of being, it has no possibility of producing anything; thus it is impossible to support the realisation of *nirvāṇa* or liberation for anything or anyone. Moreover, from their own reasoning, since the cause is the product of others that do not have their own nature within themselves (*śūnya*), it can be deduced that their theory is unreal, untrue. Then, considering the arising of being from non-being or from emptiness, it could be admitted that even beings that are totally indifferent to any type of action could obtain real effects by simply fantasising. Moreover, since the manifestation has no being as its archetype, all the *dharmas* would be able to create whatever they desire, which would result in *adharma*, licence, and total chaos as the foundation for being and living.

[19] II.II.28 - *Sūtra* 27 brings to an end the discussion with the train of thought found in the *Sarvāstivāda*; now we begin to consider the thesis of *Vijñānavāda*, absolute idealism.

Non-existence of effects or of objective beings cannot be acceptable, because not only do we perceive events and objects but we also have direct experience of external data. To maintain that the world is non-existent, like 'the horns of a hare', declares Śaṅkara, is not conformable to reason because the very inadmissibility of the world makes it admissible. Moreover, such a point of view leads to nihilism.

Absolute idealism may be considered in two ways: either the external world is absolutely unreal or it is nothing but a mere reflection of *my* subjective world; in other words, the objective world is *my* ideation. Schopenhauer begins his work 'The World as Will and Representation' with the statement 'The world is my representation', intending thereby to express the very essence of Kantism. Other thinkers, too, such as Renouvier, Rickert, and E. Hartmann, start from an essential epistemological presupposition: the state of the object of knowledge as a mere representation or idea.

Bradley's idealism, in 'Appearance and Reality', leads to the conclusion that the world is unreal or that it is an *appearance* when compared to Reality. The *Vedānta* of Bādarāyaṇa refutes both the thesis of the objective pluralistic realism of *Sarvāstivāda* and the thesis of the absolute idealism propounded by *Vijñānavāda* or *Yogācāra*: *Yogācāra* insofar as it is a practical way, and *Vijñānavāda* insofar as it constitutes a way of knowledge.

[20] II.II.29 - The *sūtra* states how the waking state differs from the dream state, as regards both learning and experience.

In Gauḍapāda's *kārikās* to the *Māṇḍūkya Upaniṣad* there is, apparently, the same theory of idealism; we say 'apparently' because, in fact, there are substantial differences in what is taught.

According to *Vijñānavāda*, the world is a mental representation of *mine*, and reality is merely the product of thought. There is no external reality except in the thought of the one who is thinking it. According to Gauḍapāda's *Asparśavāda*, the world is an effect of the Lord, in whom 'all things have their origin and dissolution.'

> 'Indeed, one should know the *praṇava* as *Īśvara* [the principial Lord] seated in the heart of everyone. Having known the syllable Om as all-pervading, the determined sage grieves no more.'[1]

According to Gauḍapāda, the mind itself (which, according to *Vijñānavāda*, creates the world) has no real birth (*ajāti*) and is not the cause of the world.

> 'Those who perceive the birth of that [mind], indeed, are similar to those who see [birds'] footprints impressed in the sky.'[2]

Thus it is not *my* particular 'dream' which gives life to the reality of existence. According to absolute idealism, 'I

---

[1] *Mā. Kā.* I.28.

[2] *Ibid.* IV.28 and related commentary.

exist insofar as *I think* I exist. And 'you' exist, have reality, insofar as 'I' think you (solipsism).

If Gauḍapāda the Teacher considers waking and dreaming to be on a par with each other, this is because he is taking a decidedly metaphysical viewpoint, according to which not only the waking state and the dreaming state but also the state of dreamless sleep (the three states of Being) form part of the great cosmic Dream of the principial Lord. Hence this 'dream' is not the product of a single and empirical subject: it is not *my* exclusive dream. If, as Gauḍapāda says, Reality remains as the birthless *Brahman* alone, then the mind is seen to be a mere phenomenon which is unable to create the world or the other beings. This excludes the idealistic factor.

Adopting this perspective, Gauḍapāda approached the question in two ways: that of traditional orthodoxy, which is necessarily in conformity with the *Vedas* and *Upaniṣads*, and that which, accepting the *Brahman* as the final sole Reality, excludes any kind of 'second', sensible or intelligible. If the One is the absolute and supreme Reality, then the 'second' *is not* and cannot be, because two absolutes cannot co-exist. Similarly, it cannot be admitted that the *Brahman* is the world and hence a mere phenomenon in becoming.

Thus, according to Gauḍapāda, manifestation can be considered as a dream or phenomenon only if compared to the supreme Reality, which is and does not become. An 'accident', according to Scholasticism, can change or disappear, while Essence or Substance remains always the same. *Kārikā* III.19 states: 'It is by virtue of *māyā* that this [*ātman*] unborn is able to differentiate itself.'[1]

---

[1] 'If the objective world is considered *māyā*, appearance or phenomenon, by *Vedānta*, then both logics and the original assumption are completely different from the school under consideration.

Gauḍapāda asks (II.11): 'If one grants the non-reality of the various perceived objects in both states, who knows these various objects? And who, in truth is the one who projects them?' And then he supplies the answer (II.12): 'The self-resplendent *Ātmā*... .'

Śaṅkara the Teacher, then, accords a certain degree of reality (*vyāvahārika*: reality that is empirical, phenomenal, or relative) to the waking state and hence to manifestation (Śaṅkara says that the world is not like 'the horns of a hare', a pure illusion, or a nothing). By thus adopting a different cognitive viewpoint, Śaṅkara is seeking to connect with the understanding of those who are beginning *sādhanā* from the dianoetic level [of the *manas*] rather than that of *noesis* [of the *buddhi*].

Step by step, however, he takes the seeker to the realm of pure knowledge known as *pāramārthika* (ultimate supreme truth), where the two great Masters meet and find each other in identity. In this context, where the teaching of *Vijñānavāda* is being discussed, Śaṅkara is careful to distinguish the teaching of the *Brahmasūtra* from that of *Yogācāra*, in order to obviate the possibility of the former being looked upon as similar or equivalent to the latter.

It may be said that *Śaṅkara* begins with the *vyāvahārika*[1] knowledge while the Teacher Gauḍapāda places himself exclusively at the *pāramārthika* perspective.

Thus between the two vantage-points there is neither opposition nor contradiction: there are two ways that can be adopted, both leading equally to the supreme *nirguṇa* Truth. *Vedānta*, and hence Gauḍapāda, do not disregard external objects or make them merely nothing (even a dream has its own

---

[1] See the *Vivekacūḍāmaṇi* of Śaṅkara. Op. cit.

relative reality), but such objects, in their intrinsic appearance and disappearance, reveal the foundation of the *Brahman*, which is the absolute constant.

According to Plato, the 'World of Ideas' is not *my* ideation, not my subjective or psychological world: it is a world that holds within it that reality by means of which the 'World of Ideas' is real and not ideal or subjective insofar as Being, in its turn, draws its reason for existence from the One Good.

[21] II.II.32 - According to the Teacher Bādarāyaṇa, and later according to Gauḍapāda and Śaṅkara, the universe or manifestation (*nāma-rūpa*) can be considered as a mere appearance, as if it had been projected by the 'magic' of a magician; but, it has been said, it is an appearance in comparison with the supreme Reality, the *Brahman*, which is not recognised by the *Vijñānavāda* teaching.

> 'Just as the rope, whose nature has not been well ascertained, is imagined in the half-light to be a snake, a trickle of water, and so on, so the *Ātman* is imagined in various ways.'
>
> 'When the true nature of the rope is ascertained, all the imaginings that have been superimposed [on the rope] vanish and there remains only the rope and nothing but the rope. This also happens with the *Ātman*.'[1]

In other words, one exchanges the *Ātman* or *Brahman* for the 'snake' universe or appearance. Liberation actually consists of freeing oneself from this false knowledge or perception and *seeing* what one really is. As was mentioned earlier, it is a mistake to say that the universe is *Brahman*, but it is also a mistake to define the universe as aseity, because a phenom-

---

[1] *Mā. Kā.* II.17-18.

enon, such as a dream, presupposes an efficient Principle on account of which the phenomenon is able to be and to exist.

To affirm that everything is relative, including the subject making the affirmation, is to maintain that a relative is affirming an absolute (which is then always relative), and this is a contradiction in terms.

If there is extinction of the consciousness or of the being, identity (because it is relative), there must be another consciousness, identity, which is aware of that extinction.

> 'If nothing eternal existed, not even becoming could exist.'[1]

> 'For it [absolute Being] will be *names*, all of those things that the mortals decided, convinced that they were true.'[2]

If the world of objects is not accepted, one may ask what kind of latent impressions (the fruit of experience with objects) there can be.

On the other hand, if there is no stable principle which allows the possible connection of the impressions, there can be no memory or conscious experience that is referable to time or space, especially since, according to *Sarvāstivāda*, consciousness itself is momentary by nature.

Thus both the doctrine of an objective pluralistic relativism which is always relative and contingent (*Sarvāstivāda*) and the doctrine of subjective idealism considered to be absolute or even a dream of the subject himself (*Vijñānavāda*), as well as the doctrine of absolute emptiness (*Sarvaśūnyavāda*), are all to be viewed as imperfect and without logical foundation, apart from the fact that they are not within the perspective of the *Vedas*, which instead, according to the *Brahmasūtra*,

---

[1] Aristotle, *Metaphysics* B 4.999 b. Op. cit.

[2] Parmenides, *On the Order of Nature*, fg. 8. Op. cit. Italics are ours.

constitutes the essential reference point. The Appendix to the present chapter contains a synthesis of these three currents of thought that have been looked at.

[22] II.II.34 - With this *sūtra* there begins the refutation of certain aspects of the Jain teaching. According to those who support this teaching, there are seven categories of *dharma*: the *jīva* as the experiencing subject; that which is not the *jīva* (*a-jīva*), or the world of experience; the sensory stimulus which is directed towards objects (*āsrava*); self-mastery (*saṁvara*); asceticism, in the form of withdrawal from objects (*nirjarā*); slavery born of activity (*bandha*); liberation (*mokṣa*). In other words, one is faced with the I and the non-I, the subject and the object. Now, the *jīva* has a physical aspect because it co-exists, throughout its whole extent, with the body; it is the integrating part of the body inasmuch as it endows it with life and the reason for existing. In this way the soul, having opposing qualities, cannot be eternal; and as it undergoes the polarised changes of the body, it cannot have a knowledge that is determined and stable and it cannot preserve the principle of universality (as the *sūtra* says, it is not-pervading).

[23] II.II.36 - According to the Jains, the soul becomes stable at the end of bondage, that is, when it is liberated from the *a-jīva*; however, if it is permanent and stable in the final phase, it cannot be something changeable in the initial and intermediate phases, and it cannot be in any sense a product, because whatever is produced is impermanent, and impermanence cannot give rise to anything permanent. Moreover, there is no distinction between the beginning, the middle, and the end of the soul's journey. And this does not provide clarity for the aims of liberation.

The teaching of the Jains (from the root *ji*: be victorious) appears between the definitive edition of the *Vedas* and the composition of the *Āraṇyakas* and the earliest *Upaniṣads*. It may be said that this teaching acknowledges a substantial and ethical dualism.

The universe is composed of two uncreated aspects which co-exist: the soul (*jīva*) and the non-soul (*ajīva*), the organic and the inorganic. The soul is bound to the body, giving life to a psycho-physical unity. *Karma* (cause and effect), which represents a residue of merit and demerit, binds the soul to the body. The organic element (*jīva*) has the ability to grow by itself and to develop (movement) and it resides in all living organisms; the inorganic is incapable of growth unless it is supported by external assistance. The Jain ideal is epitomised by the jewel with three facets (*triratna*): faith, right knowledge, and right conduct. Observance of these three factors leads to the liberation of the soul from the bondage of the senses, thus providing stability and freedom.

Vardhamāna, who is also known as Mahāvira, is the principal historical figure in Jainism. It also needs to be understood that Buddhism and Jainism are two heterodox threads, in contradistinction to *Vaiśeṣika*, *Nyāya*, *Sāṁkhya*, and *Yoga*, which are all orthodox, and thus these two systems do not accept the authority of the Vedic Tradition. This leads to the consideration that certain words, such as *Ātman*, *jīva*, *buddhi*, and *manas* can acquire different meanings for these systems.

However, objective unilateral relativism, absolute idealism, and the non-existence even of the subject, which predicates both being and non-being, as in any dualistic system, cannot bear an attentive and deep dialectical development.

This *sūtra* ends the comparison which Bādārayaṇa makes with regard to the Jain line of thought.

[24] II.II.37 - This *sūtra* poses the problem of the manifestation of the world.

The theses against which this discussion is directed are those of *Nyāya*, *Vaiśeṣika*, *Yoga* and so on.

The fact that within the manifest world there are polarities such as merit and demerit, attraction and repulsion, and good and evil is not attributable to the Lord (*Īśvara*) because it is not He who directs the behaviour of beings, but they determine themselves in their varied expressive possibilities; the Lord does not operate within the psychological causes of beings but is simply their foundation, with the result that such aspects may have, or not have, the possibility of manifestation. This has been spoken of earlier.

[25] II.II.40 - The opponent continues to maintain that if his theses are not acceptable, then another explanation can be given: just as a person presides over the sensory functions, such as visual perception, in the same way the Lord presides over the manifestation and directs it. If this analogy were true, then just as the being who perceives also enjoys and suffers in relation to the actions that he performs, so the Lord, too, would be subjected to and conditioned by the experience of pain and suffering or pleasure and enjoyment; he would, moreover, necessarily be in ceaseless movement and would experience polarity, including the polarity of birth and death. A manifest body is produced after the principial Existence, and in the absence of a body this Existence cannot be subjected to the polarity of pleasure and pain.

[26] II.II.42 - *Sūtras* 42-44 refute the aspects of the *Bhāgavata* teaching which has been inserted into the current thought of the *Vaiṣṇavas*. The preceding *sūtras* have refuted the thesis held

by those who maintain that the Lord is only the efficient cause and not the substantial cause as well; now the *Brahmasūtra* addresses the thesis of those who affirm that the Lord is both the efficient cause and the substantial cause. They believe that the Lord, being identified with *Vāsudeva*, has created the soul of the being, the soul known as *Saṁkarṣaṇa*.

Bādarāyaṇa the Teacher, on the other hand, maintains that this is not possible because every created thing must have an end, so that there is no sense in speaking of liberation, and also because the *Śruti* declares that the soul is eternal and not something produced. The soul, or *jīva*, is only a ray of the Sun or *Ātman*.

Appendix

A very brief outline may be given of the three streams of thought that have been examined in Chapter Two of Book Two of the *Brahmasūtra*.

The followers of *vijñānavāda* (or *yogācāra*), who maintain that there is only consciousness or intellect (absolute subjective idealism), argue against the followers of *sarvāstivāda* by denying the truthfulness of their pluralistic realism formed from elements which, although momentary, are considered real, thus siding with the *mādhyamikas* or *śūnyavādin* in maintaining, to the contrary, the essential relativity and interdependence characteristic of all external reality. However, according to the followers of *yogācāra*, even the teaching of the *mādhyamika* in considering each existence as relative and hence, in the final analysis, unreal or devoid of independent reality, cannot be viewed as valid because the conclusion would be that even consciousness would ultimately be unreal.

The followers of *yogācāra* have distanced themselves from this perspective of thought by declaring that everything can be considered illusory except consciousness (*vijñāna*); hence, for the followers of *vijñānavāda* consciousness alone has independent reality. The world, viewed from the *yogācāra* standpoint, turns out to be an effect projected by the consciousness of the various *dharmas* or beings. But this formulation, conceived as 'everything is merely mind or consciousness' is rejected not only by the *Brahmasūtra* but also by other followers of Buddhism, according to whom it could lead to the belief that this exclusive consciousness, being the sole reality, could come close to the idea of the *Brahman* which is found in the *Upaniṣads* and which Buddhism rejects.

On the other hand, even some followers of *advaita* have maintained that a consideration of the *Brahman* as wholly and solely consciousness could give the impression of approaching the views of those who follow *vijñānavāda* (note the charges levelled against Gauḍapāda and Śaṅkara himself although their pre-suppositions and conclusions are very far removed from the three currents of thought that have been mentioned). In any case, several passages in the *Upaniṣads* and other parts of the teaching speak of the *Brahman* as 'unqualified' and therefore *nirguṇa*. This implies that *nirguṇa Brahman* is that by means of which consciousness and everything else can be and exist, while It is beyond all definition. However, it needs to be considered that some followers of *advaita* who were later than Śaṅkara came close to the kind of conception held by the followers of *yogācāra*, just as others approached objective realism even though naturally pre-supposing the reality of the *Brahman*.

Considering the three threads of thought spoken of by Bādarāyaṇa, we have the following:

— The followers of *sarvāstivāda* consider the basic elements to be absolute truth and hence external reality, while every other being - and consciousness itself - is real only in relation to these primary and fundamental elements (objective realism, objective materialism).

— The followers of *yogācāra*, on the contrary, maintain that consciousness alone exists and that external objects or beings are relative to consciousness (absolute subjective realism); every experience and every reality which are not of *vijñāna* order are denied.

— The followers of *śūnyavāda*, as if to complete the circle, maintain that both external data and internal subjective data are essentially 'void'; no *dharma* or being has its own independent and self-existent nature, and thus the *Ātman* itself can have no level of reality (theory of the *anātman*). The non-reality of one's own identity (quiddity) is also put forward with the famous dialogue between King Milinda and Nāgasena, the Buddhist monk. When the king asks him his name, the monk replies that 'Nāgasena' is a mere word without substance. And to support this statement he gives the example of the cart. The cart is an assemblage of elements which cannot be taken as a real entity. The same is true of 'Nāgasena', which is an assemblage of impermanent elements[1] which are considered as a living being.

Since relationships are the substance of all that exists, both the soul and the objective world are nothing but an assemblage of contingent relationships (absolute relativism).

In considering this school of thought, one may say that if *śūnya* can refer to the essence which permeates the forms of manifestation, which are empty, then it can be deemed equivalent to the *Brahman*. If *śūnya* is an empty word, with no reference to a positive, negative, or neutral *dharma*, it can be reckoned as nothing, a mere word without meaning, although predicating "nothingness" presupposes an active subject who actually predicates it.

If *śūnya* means something real to which no name of any nature can be attributed, then it corresponds to what is declared by *sūtra* VII of the *Māṇḍūkya Upaniṣad* and what is taught by all the spiritual Traditions.

---

[1] The five indivisible elements (*skandha*: aggregates) which constitute any being or *dharma*.

Śaṅkara in his *bhāṣya* to the *Bṛhadāraṇyaka Upaniṣad* (II.III.6) states: 'Now then, in what way, by means of these two expressions: "not this, not this", are the "truths of the Truth" meant to be described?'

It is said: by eliminating all the qualifications due to the limiting superimpositions... , so That [*Brahman*] cannot be defined as: "this", like in common language one may indicate: "over there a cow with white horns is grazing" [therefore in positive terms].

The *Brahman* can be indicated [indirectly] only through the name, the form and the activity which are superimposed on it by means of expressions such as: "*Brahman* is knowledge and bliss" (*Bṛhadāraṇyaka Upaniṣad* III.IX.28). "... it consists indeed of a unity of pure consciousness" (*Bṛhadāraṇyaka Upaniṣad* II.IV.12) and so on or [directly] by means of terms such as *Brahman* or *Ātman*. If, on the other hand, the intention were to describe its very own nature, which transcends all the identifications determined by the superimpositions, it cannot be indicated in any way. In such a case there is only this method, that is the designation with the terms: "not this, not this" *neti neti* (*neti* = *na*+*iti*), through which all the qualifications that could be attributed to it are gradually eliminated... "there is no other better" description. Therefore only this is the [possible] description of the *Brahman*.'

When Śaṅkara indicates *Brahman* both directly: *Brahman* is consciousness and bliss, and so on, that is when the being attributes to it names of various nature, and indirectly: *Brahman* is not this, not this (*neti neti*) which annuls the previous statement, he gives us an indication of extreme importance: that is, he leads us into the heart of metaphysics which goes beyond *ratio*.

Again, if the word *śūnya* is used to mean that absolute

formulations are to be eschewed, we need to go back again to what Śaṅkara said earlier.

To say that everything is relative and only relative is, in fact, always an absolute statement, and such a pronouncement, being itself relative, is bereft of truth. A relative truth can always be contradicted by another relative truth, and so on *ad infinitum*.

As a consequence, these currents of thought have occasioned many dialectical discussions, but they are theoretical discussions which have, by all means, promoted the cultural heritage of Buddhism.

The Enlightened One, in truth, posed only the essential problem of the universality of suffering as the effect of *avidyā* and of the desire (*tṛṣṇā*) to live exclusively at the level of forms, when he enunciated, in the well-known sermon at Varanasi, the 'Four Noble Truths' and offered the practical means, outlined in the 'Eightfold Path', which led to the suppression and elimination of suffering.

In the course of time, however, the Enlightened One has been, for the most part, replaced by various threads, admittedly spun out of deep dialectic, which have moved away from the simplicity of an undisputed fundamental truth: the origin of suffering, of conflict, and of the dichotomy in which the being of *saṁsāra* has placed itself in helping to create the greatest tragedies of this world.

The *Brahmasūtra*, however, does not stand against the various currents of thought: it merely reveals their limits and integral lack of Knowledge. In this way, it has been seen that it does not oppose the various *darśanas* but points out the relative nature of their affirmations, which can become even dogmatic when compared to the infinite possibilities of the supreme *Brahman*.

See also note 9 relating to II.I.15.

To conclude these brief considerations we would like to quote a significant extract from an interview[1] with the Dalai Lama given in 1998.

The interviewer asks:

'There is a quote in the Pali *sūtras*, in which one of Gautama the Buddha's monks asks him whether there is something or "nothing at all" that exists. This question - whether there is "something" or "nothing" - is an interesting one, because the notion that "nothing at all exists" could easily lead to nihilism. The Buddha responded definitively to this monk by declaring that there is what he called the *unborn*, and it is because of this that the possibility exists of an escape from the suffering of worldly existence. I have heard that some Tibetan currents also describe the existence of "something." Could you explain to us what you think the Buddha meant when he said:

> 'There is that which is not born, not become, not created, not conditioned. If there were not that which is not born, not become, not created, not conditioned, there could be no escape from that which is born, become, created, conditioned here. But since there is that which is not born, not become, not created, not conditioned, therefore the escape from that which is born, become, created, conditioned, is made known.'[2]

The Dalai Lama replies: 'This points to exactly what was said earlier. If there was inherent existence and inherent causation, then we couldn't escape from *saṁsāra*. So therefore

---

[1] The interview is by Amy Edelstein for the semesterly Review "What is Enlightenment?", founded by Andrew Cohen and published in the Autumn - Winter 1998 issue.

[2] *Suttapiṭaka*, *Udana* VIII.1-3.

what we say is that on the conventional level there is a path, there is causation and so forth. But because of the fact that the causation has no *inherent* existence is equivalent to ignorance (*avidyā*). And to be able to perceive that lack of causation in the nature of inherent existence is wisdom.

If there were independent existence, then the perception of that existence would be valid. If there were independent existence, then when we investigate to find out whether an object exists *independently*, we would have to be able to find it. But when we analyse carefully, we can't find these objects existing independently.

This is how we can see that the perception of independent existence is wrong, is *ignorance*, and that the perception of *non-independent* existence is valid, is wisdom. These two possibilities are in opposition, and when you have two things like this in direct opposition they cannot go together; only one can have a valid foundation... .

When you experience the *ultimate reality* [the italics are ours], it is so powerful that the understanding of a conventional, objective reality is very different. For example, if the absorption of one's mind in emptiness *(śūnya)* is really powerful - *totally* absorbed in the state of *ultimate reality* or *emptiness* [the italics are ours] - the influence and appearance of conventional reality will be almost negligible.'

From the two statements of the Buddha and of the Dalai Lama we have the following:

There is a "subject" in the world of the born, to whom the aforesaid indications are directed. Indications with which, by means of knowledge, it is comprehended that there is the other world of the not born, not formed, not created and so on. By realizing it that "subject" can find its salvation.

Or else if there were not that which is not born, not become and so on, the "subject", fallen into the born, could have no escape, so it would have to perpetuate its *avidyā* forever.

If to the "subject", fallen into error, for mere communication's sake, we give a name, whatever it may be, we can close the circle.

Thus, as extreme synthesis, everything is impermanent except for the *unborn* (*śūnya*); thus everything is impermanent[1] except for the *unborn* (*ajāti* or *Brahman*).

From the viewpoint indicated by the Dalai Lama the two expressions, *śūnya* and *Brahman* or *Ātman*, can also be equivalent. They are the ultimate reality. But then it is futile to pose the problem of the *anātman*, that is the non-existence of the *Ātman* (*Subject*), because this is none other than the *Brahman* seen from a particular viewpoint. Just as the space within the pot (*skandhakośa*) is of the same nature as the space outside the pot.[2] What is impermanent is the *ahaṁkāra*, the ego sense or empirical ego, with its attributes (*nāma-rūpa*), not the *Ātman* or *Brahman* (*śūnya*), who gives *raison d'être* to the impermanent, although the impermanent, for *Vedānta*, is not absolute "nothingness" but a phenomenon in becoming.

---

[1] In the *Maitry Upaniṣad* (I.4) we read: 'We see, furthermore, that this whole [universe] is transient and that, like these insects and flies, and so on, and like the grass and the trees, it grows and then comes to an end.'

[2] Cp. *Mā. Kā.* III.3 *et seqq.*

atha dvitīyo 'dhyāyaḥ

tṛtīyaḥ khaṇḍaḥ

na viyad aśruteḥ // 1 //

na: not; *viyat*: *ākāśa*, ether, space; *a-śruteḥ*: on account of not being in the *Śruti*.

asti tu // 2 //

asti: there is; *tu*: but, however.

gauṇyasambhavāt // 3 //

gauṇī: secondary; *a-sambhavāt*: on account of the impossibility.

śabdāc ca // 4 //

śabdāt: because of the Vedic sound or word; *ca*: and, also.

Book Two

Chapter Three[*]

1. *Space is not [originated], and the Śruti does not [mention it].*

2. *However, there is [one mention in the Śruti].*

The *Śruti* speaks of fire, water, and food (the gross element), but not of space or ether (*Chā*. VI.II.3-4). On the other hand, the *Taittirīya Upaniṣad* (II.I.3) says:

> 'From That, that is from this very *Ātman*, space takes its origin, from space air, from air fire... .'

In the development of manifestation it seems that at some point in the *Śruti* there are times when fire is mentioned and there are other times when space or ether is mentioned, which might lead to the thought that there must be a contradiction.

3. *[The mention is] secondary on account of the impossibility [of the origin of ākāśa].*[1]

4. *And also in the [Vedic] Word.*

---

[*] The last two Chapters of Book Two clarify the apparent contradictions which could emerge about some statements of the *Śruti*

syācchaikasya brahma śabdavat // 5 //

syāt: it is possible; *ca*: and; *ekasya*: of the one; *brahma-śabdavat*: like the word '*Brahman*.'

pratijñā'hānir avyatirekāc chabdebhyaḥ // 6 //

pratijñā: statement; *a-hāniḥ*: non-renunciation; *a-vyatirekāt*: on account of the non-distinction; *śabdebhyaḥ*: according to the words of the Scriptures, of the *Vedas*.

yāvad vikāraṁ tu vibhāgo lokavat // 7 //

yāvat: as much as; *vikāram*: effect; *tu*: but, però; *vibhāgaḥ*: distinction; *loka-vat*: as in the world.

etena mātariśvā vyākhyātaḥ // 8 //

etena: by means of this; *mātariśvā*: air; *vyākhyātaḥ*: is explained.

asambhavas-tu sato'nupapatteḥ // 9 //

a-sambhavaḥ: non-origin; *tu*: but; *sataḥ*: of that which is; *anupapatteḥ*: on account of the impossibility.

tejo 'tas tathā hyāha // 10 //

tejaḥ: fire; *ataḥ*: from this; *tathā*: thus; *hi*: in truth; *āha*: declares.

5. *It is possible [to interpret] the same [word 'origin' both in its primary or absolute sense and in its secondary or relative sense], like the word 'Brahman.'*[2]

6. *The non-renunciation of the [initial] statement [results from] the non-distinction [of the world from the Brahman], according to the words of the Vedas.*

To understand that *ākāśa* is not produced, it is necessary to consider that the *Brahmasūtra* examines this element from the empirical point of view; it is indeed considered to be effected, or produced, but not in contradistinction or opposition to the *Brahman*.

It is always useful to remember that *That* represents the foundation of *ākāśa* itself. Nothing can exist without That; in other words, there is no contradiction. The initial statement which declared, 'Once That is known, everything else is known' remains valid for all time.

7. *But wherever [there is] effect [there is] distinction as [can be noted in the experience] of the world.*[3]

8. *Air is explained by this.*

From the demonstration given in the previous *sūtra* the origin of the air can also be explained. 'Through it' one can explain the derivation of air from *ākāśa*.

9. *But [there is] no origin of that which is [Brahman], on account of the impossibility [of such an origin].*[4]

10. *Fire [originates] from this [element of air]. Thus in truth [the Śruti] declares.*

āpaḥ // 11 //

āpaḥ: water.

pṛthivyadhikāra rūpa śabda antarebhyaḥ // 12 //

pṛthivī: earth; *adhikāra*: topic; *rūpa*: colour; *śabda*: *Śruti*; *antarebhyaḥ*: of other passages.

tadabhidhyānād eva tu tallingāt saḥ // 13 //

tat-abhidyānāt: on account of His meditative act; *eva*: only; *tu*: but; *tat-liṅgāt*: on account of His distinctive characteristic; *saḥ*: He.

viparyayeṇa tu kṛamo 'ta upapadyate ca // 14 //

viparyayeṇa: by means of the reverse; *tu*: however; *kramaḥ*: order (hierarchy of manifestation); *ataḥ*: from that; *upapadyate*: is reasonable; *ca*: and.

antarā vijñānamanasī krameṇa tal-liṅgād iti cen nāviśeṣāt // 15 //

antarā: between; *vijñāna*: intellect; *manasī*: mind; *krameṇa*: in order; *tat-liṅgāt*: reference; *iti cet*: if so; *na*: not; *aviśeṣāt*: on account of non-difference.

carācaravyapāśrayas tu syāt tad vyapadeśo bhāktas tadbhāvabhāvitvāt // 16 //

cara-acara: moving and unmoving; *vyapāśrayaḥ*: reference; *tu*: but; *syāt*: it may be; *tat-vyapadeśaḥ*: mention of that; *bhāktaḥ*: secondary; *tat-bhāva-bhāvitvāt*: since they depend on the existence of that [body].

11. *Water [takes its origin from fire].*

12. *Earth [referring to anna: food], on account of the topic of colour and further passages in the Śruti.*[5]

13. *But He [is the principle, which irradiates determinations] on account of His mere meditative act and His distinctive characteristic.*[6]

14. *However, the order [of the elements which are re-absorbed] within That is the reverse [of the other, that is, of the process of origination], and [this] is reasonable.*

This *sūtra* may be taken in two ways. The first cause (*Īśvara*, as *saguṇa Brahman* or *Brahmā*) develops, or gives rise to all the unlimited effects, and at the time of return (*pralaya*) the effects go back in reverse order and dissolve in the cause: 'In It all things have their origin and their dissolution.' (*Mā. IV* VI; see also *Tai*. III.I.1).

This can, moreover, be extended to include anyone who, with realisation, goes back to the *Brahmā*, from where he has apparently come forth.

15. *If [it is said that] between [Brahmā and the elements there are mentioned] the intellect and the mind according to an order deduced [from the Śruti, the reply is] no, on account of non-difference.*[7]

16. *The mention of that [birth and death] may be there for moving and unmoving beings; but it is secondary if referred [to the soul] since [the forms] depend on its existence.*[8]

nātmāśruter nityatvāc ca tābhyaḥ // 17 //

na: not; *ātmā*: *jīva*, soul; *aśruteḥ*: according to the *Śruti*; *nityatvāt*: on account of eternity; *ca*: and; *tābhyaḥ*: of those.

jño 'ta eva // 18 //

jñaḥ: intelligence; *ataḥ eva*: for the same reason.

utkrānti gatyāgatīnām // 19 //

utkrānti: leaving the body; *gati*: going, in the sense of transmigrating; *āgatīnām*: returning.

svātmanā cottarayoḥ // 20 //

svaātmanā: natural to the *Ātmā*; *ca*: and; *uttarayoḥ*: of the last two.

nāṇuratacchruter iti cen (na itara: a+i = e) netarādhikārāt // 21 //

na: not; *aṇuḥ*: small, atomic; *atat*: differently; *śruteḥ*: on account of the *Śruti*; *iti cet*: if it is [said]; *na*: not; *itara*: altro (*na itara*: a+i = e); *adhikārāt*: on account of the specific subject.

17. *According to the Śruti, the ātmā [is] not [born]; it is eternal, as [the Śruti] itself maintains.*[9]

18. *For the same reason, [the jīva] is knowledge.*[10]

19. *In leaving the body, it goes and returns.*

Sūtras 19-28 expound the thesis according to which the *jīva* does not have a limitless form; in *sūtras* 29 to 32 the *Brahmasūtra* gives the decisive reply. *Sūtra* 19 propounds the thesis that the *jīva*, being embodied within a form, has a limited form. Having the consistency of an atom which comes and goes, which enters bodies and leaves them, its nature cannot be infinite or unlimited.

20. *And the last ones [are] natural to the Ātmā.*

The last two aspects of coming into bodies and departing from them are related to the *jīva*, and so, since it has limited movement, it cannot be considered to be all-pervasive.

21. *If it [is said that the soul] is not minute because the Śruti [states otherwise], we deny this; the subject [of such reasoning] is another [that is, the Brahman].*

If the *Śruti* mentions the word 'all-pervasiveness', this refers to 'another', according to the objector, that is, it refers to the *Brahman* and not to the manifest *jīva*. This means that there are two different orders of factors: the universal and the particular, the second of which has a limited and minute size in comparison with the other.

svaśabdonmānābhyāṁ ca // 22 //

sva-śabda: direct evidence; *unmānābhyām*: infinitesimal measure; *ca*: also.

avirodhaś candanavat // 23 //

a-virodhaḥ: non-contradiction; *candana*: sandal paste; *vat*: like.

avasthiti vaiśeṣyād iti cen nābhyupagamādhṛdi hi // 24 //

avasthiti: on account of the position; *vaiśeṣyāt*: particular; *iti cet*: if it is [said]; *na*: not; *abhyupagamāt hṛdi hi*: indeed, on account of being admitted in the heart.

guṇād vā lokavat // 25 //

guṇāt: on account of quality; *vā*: or; *loka*: world; *vat*: like, as.

vyatireko gandhavat // 26 //

vyatirekaḥ: being diffused; *gandha*: perfume; *vat*: like.

tathā ca darśayati // 27 //

tathā: thus; *ca*: also; *darśayati*: declares.

22. *Also on account of direct evidence and [its] infinitesimal measure.*[11]

23. *[There is] no contradiction, as [in the case of] sandalwood paste.*

However, the objector continues, this does not contradict our thesis because it can happen, as in the case of a drop of sandalwood essence, which, merely by touching a simple specific organ of the body, expands the sensation it gives throughout the body, so that the *jīva*, even if infinitesimal and lacking physical measure, can have perceptive sensation throughout the body.

24. *If it is [denied in both cases] on account of the particular position, [the reply is that] this is not so, on account of the admission [of being] exactly in the heart.*[12]

25. *Or on account of the quality, as in the world.*[13]

26. *Being diffused, like perfume.*[14]

27. *This is what [the Śruti] also declares.*[15]

pṛthag upadeśāt // 28 //

pṛthak: distinct; *upadeśāt*: on account of the teaching.

tad guṇa sāratvāt tu tad vyapadeśaḥ prājñavat // 29 //

tad-guṇa-sāratvāt: on account of possessing the qualities of that; *tu*: but, however; *tat*: that; *vyapadeśaḥ*: designated; *prājña-vat*: as intelligence.

yāvad ātma bhāvitvāc ca na doṣas tad darśanāt // 30 //

yāvat: as long as; *ātma*: soul; *bhāvitvāt*: on account of the existence; *ca*: and; *na*: not; *doṣaḥ*: error; *tat-darśanāt*: from the observation or verification of that.

puṁstvādivat tvasya sato 'bhivyakti yogāt // 31 //

puṁstvādivat: such as manliness.; *tu*: however; *asya*: its; *sataḥ*: existing; *abhivyakti*: manifestation; *yogāt*: on account of the relationship.

28. *[On account] of the distinct teaching.*

From the teaching of the *Śruti* we learn that the *jīva* is distinct from the intelligence or intellect inasmuch as the latter has a nature which is independent of the former.

From *sūtra* 29 onwards replies are given to the objections that were raised earlier by the interlocutor at *sūtra* 19, where the fundamental question is put. In *sūtras* 20-25 an attempt is made to give proofs of the thesis; the subsequent *sūtras* present the problem of the relationship between the *jīva* and the intellect, that is, between the knower and knowledge.

29. *However, it is [so] designated [because] it possesses the qualities of that [the buddhi] such as intelligence.*[16]

30. *And [there is] no error as long as the soul endures [in its relative] existence; this is stated [in the Śruti].*[17]

31. *However, with the relationship between manifestation and what exists, this [is possible] as [in the case of] manliness, and so on.*[18]

nityopalabdhyanupalabdhi prasaṅgo 'nyatara-niyamovānyathā // 32 //

nityopalabdhi: costant perception; *an-upalabdhi*: non non-perception; *prasaṅgaḥ*: result; *anyatara*: either; *niyamaḥ*: limitation; *vā*: or; *anyathā*: otherwise.

kartā śāstrārthavattvāt // 33 //

kartā: agent, the subject of action; *śāstra*: the Scriptures; *arthavattvāt*: on account of the real meaning.

vihāropadeśāt // 34 //

vihāra: wandering; *upadeśāt*: on account of the teaching.

upādānāt // 35 //

upādānāt: on account of appropriating, acquiring, taking.

vyapadeśāc ca kriyāyāṁ na cen nirdeśa-viparyayaḥ // 36 //

vyapadeśāt: on account of being mentioned; *ca*: also; *kriyāyām*: in referring to the action; *na cet*: if not; *nirdeśa*: the act of indicating; *viparyayaḥ*: opposite, different.

32. *Otherwise [if it did not exist], the result would be either constant perception or [constant] non-perception, or even a limitation upon either of these two.*

On the other hand, if the intellect, as the inner organ (*antaḥkaraṇa*), had to vanish in *suṣupti*, as the opponent's thesis maintains, then there would be either constant perception, since the senses are always in contact with their objects, or an absence of perception, or, as another possibility, one would have to admit a limitation upon either of these two (*jīva* and organs of perception).

33. *The agent [is the soul, and this is how] the Scriptures [can have] meaning.*[19]

34. *[On account of the] wandering, [according to] the teaching.*

35. *On account of taking [the organs].*

36. *Also because [the soul] is mentioned [as agent] with reference to the action; if [it were] not [there would be] an indication of a different [nature].*

The *jīva*, as agent, within the realm of Being (from *Virāṭ* to *Īśvara*) is able to 'wander' on the existential planes, to externalise or internalise itself (*Bṛhadāraṇyaka Upaniṣad*, IV.III.12), and to assume various forms, using the appropriate organs; in other words, it goes where its motives take it. 'If it were not so', there would be an indication of a different nature in the Scriptures. Compare *Bṛhadāraṇyaka Upaniṣad*, II.I.18.

upalabdhivad aniyamaḥ // 37 //

upalabdhivat: like perception; *a-niyamaḥ*: non-limitation.

śakti viparyayāt // 38 //

śakti: power; *viparyayāt*: on account of reversal.

samādhyabhāvāc ca // 39 //

samādhi: meditation; *a-bhāvāt*: on account of the impossibility; *ca*: and.

yathā ca takṣobhayathā // 40 //

yathā: as; *ca*: and; *takṣā*: carpenter, woodworker; *ubhayathā*: in both ways.

parāt tu tac chruteḥ // 41 //

parāt: from the supreme; *tu*: but; *tat*: that; *śruteḥ*: from the *Śruti*.

kṛta prayatnāpekṣas tu vihita pratiṣiddhāvaiyarthyādibhyaḥ // 42 //

kṛta: made; *prayatna*: intentional efforts; *apekṣaḥ*: dependent; *tu*: but, on the contrary; *vihita*: meaning; *pratiṣiddha*: injunctions; *a-vaiyarthya*: not useless; *ādibhyaḥ*: and so forth.

37. *The absence of limitation, as in perception.*[20]

38. *On account of the reversal of power.*

Transferring the reversal of the power of action from the *jīva* to the instrument, for example, to the *buddhi*, does not solve the problem; if the agent and enjoyer were the *buddhi*, there would be no need to acknowledge another agent such as the *jīva*; this would be contrary to the statements of the *Śruti*. Moreover, if the *buddhi* were the agent, to fulfil an action and attain its fruition would require the acknowledgement of another factor which would function as an instrument to take the place of the *buddhi*, which has been placed as the agent and enjoyer.

39. *And on account of the impossibility of meditation.*[21]

40. *And like the carpenter in both ways.*[22]

41. *But according to the Śruti, that [condition of being the agent arises] from the Supreme.*[23]

42. *On the contrary, it depends on the efforts made [by the individual], so that the injunctions and the prohibitions and so forth [can] not [become] devoid of meaning.*

On the contrary, the beings are the ones who, since they are agents, produce merit and demerit. It is through the Supreme that action itself, with its consequent merit and demerit, is able to manifest itself. Hence the injunctions or prohibitions given to the soul by the *Śruti* are pertinent and have precise meaning. It is not the Supreme that dispenses suffering or well-being; it is the beings that, according to the direction that they wish to impress upon their actions, acquire merit or demerit

aṁśo nānāvyapadeśād anyathā cāpi dāśakitavādi-tvam adhīyata eke // 43 //

aṁśaḥ: fragment; *nānā-vyapadeśāt*: on account of the declaration of; *anyathā*: difference; *ca*: and; *api*: also, in another [non-different way]; *dāśakitavāditvam*: having the nature of a fisherman, a juggler; *adhīyata eke*: some teach.

mantravarṇācca // 44 //

mantra: *mantra*; *varṇāt*: from the expression; *ca*: also.

api ca smaryate // 45 //

api: moreover, also; *ca*: and; *smaryate*: [it is stated in the] *Smṛti*.

prakāśādivan naivaṁ paraḥ // 46 //

prakāśa: light, splendour; *ādivat*: like, and so on; *na*: not; *evam*: indeed, as; *paraḥ*: supreme.

smaranti ca // 47 //

smaranti: the *Smṛti*; *ca*: too.

anujñā parihārau deha sambandhāj jyotirādivat // 48 //

anujñā-parihārau: injunctions and prohibitions; *deha*: body; *sambandhāt*: on account of the relationship; *jyotiḥ*: light; *ādi*: and so on; *vat*: as.

43. *[The jīva] is a fragment [a ray of the Lord] according to the declaration of difference and also [of non-difference because] some teach [that that is as] a fisherman, a juggler, and so on.*

44. *Also from the expression of the mantra.*

45. *And [so] also, according to the Smṛti.*[24]

44. *The Supreme [is] not [affected by pleasure and pain], unlike [the jīva], just as light and so on [are not influenced by that with which they come into contact].*

The supreme *Ātman* is not affected by the polarity of the *guṇas* (because it is *nir-guṇa*), just as, on the empirical level, the sun is not affected by the *vṛttis* of the ocean which reflect the sunlight.

47. *The Smṛti, too, [says so].*

Both the *Smṛti* and the *Śruti* confirm the preceding *sūtras*.

'Just as the sun, which is the eye of the entire world, is neither affected by the defects of the [human] eye nor by the external defects, so the inner *ātmā*, which is one and inherent in every being, is not affected by the misery of the world, for it is transcendent.'*

48. *Injunctions and prohibitions [are possible] on account of the relationship [of the jīva] with bodies, as [in the case of] light and so on.*

---

* *Ka*. II.II.11.

asantateś cāvyatikaraḥ // 49 //

a-santateḥ: on account of non-extension; *ca*: and; *a-vyatikaraḥ*: non-confusion.

ābhāsa eva ca // 50 //

ābhāsaḥ: reflection; *eva*: alone, precisely; *ca*: and.

adṛṣṭāniyamāt // 51 //

a-dṛṣṭa: invisible; *a-niyamāt*: on account of non-restriction.

abhisandhyādiṣvapi caivam // 52 //

abhisandhi-ādi-ṣu: in deliberations, decisions, and so on; *api*: also; *ca*: and; *evam*: so.

pradeśād iti cen nāntar-bhāvāt // 53 //

pradeśāt: from the place or position; *iti cet*: if [it is said]; *na*: not; *antar-bhāvāt*: inside, exists, is.

iti tṛtīyaḥ khaṇḍaḥ

dvitīyo 'dhyāyaḥ

49. *And on account of the non-extension [of the jīva towards all bodies, there is] no confusion.*

From the *mantras* of the *Śruti* that were quoted earlier it can be seen that possible injunctions, prohibitions and so on can refer to the subject as agent (the bird of the *Śvetāśvatara* that eats the sweet fruit of the *pippala* or the bitter fruit that can come from it). Moreover, there can be no confusion between the pleasure and pain of an embodied *jīva* and the pleasure and pain of other *jīvas* because it is impeded by *upādhis*, just as the air contained in a pot cannot be confused with the air contained in a different pot or jar and so on.

50. *And [the jīva] alone [is] a reflection [of the Lord].*

51. *In the invisible [it is] not [possible for there to be] restrictions.*[25]

52. *And so [it will be] with decisions, and so on.*

The problem arises likewise with regard to the act of deciding. Given that this can exist in the relationship between the *jīva* and the intellect, there would be the same difficulty that was expounded earlier: the subject of the action is no longer the *jīva* but the vehicle or body (*upādhi*).

53. *If [it is said] that the distinction of pleasure and pain and so on arises from position, [this is] not [so, because the jīva] is within [all bodies].*[26]

End of Chapter Three of Book Two of the Brahmasūtra

NOTES

[1] II.III.3 - The reply given by *sūtra* 3 is that, in fact, there is no contradiction because this process of development that is spoken of by the *Śruti* must be understood in a secondary or figurative sense; it is not a question of a chronological production such as occurs at the level of effects, or sensible plane, but it is a question of an occurrence at the metaphysical level. In fact, *ākāśa* has no parts, it is all-pervading and therefore it is not produced. This is why the *Bṛhadāraṇyaka Upaniṣad* (II.III.3) declares:

> 'And now the subtle, which is air and intermediate space. This is the immortal, this is the mobile, this is the transcendent... .'

On approaching the vision of the *Vedas* and *Upaniṣads* it is important to try to comprehend the essence which underlies the numerous statements; dwelling on the mere literal words, without going beyond, means remaining only on the externalism of the description. Moreover, in ancient times, it has already been said that the teaching was given orally, the written material was only synoptic, at times even of very few words (see the work we are proposing to understand this).

In the *Upaniṣads* one can notice the presence of a teacher and of a disciple to whom the *upadeśa* was bestowed, and the written material we have been left with is only the least part of the entire teaching.

[2] II.III.5 - On the other hand, the 'Vedic word', too, de-

clares this. In some Vedic passages a single word is often used in two senses: both the figurative or allegorical sense and the real sense.

In the *Taittirīya Upaniṣad* (III.II.1) we read:

> '... he knew food as the *Brahman*. In fact, exactly from food indeed these beings come into birth; thanks to food, once born, they live; to food they go back and are absorbed. Having acknowledged it, once more he went to his father Varuṇa: "O venerable sir, teach me the *Brahman*!" Then to him [he] said: "You must ardently wish to know the *Brahman* through meditation... ."

This way of speaking has to be considered in the analogical or figurative sense. By contrast, in the same *Upaniṣad* (III. VI.1) we read: '... he knew bliss as the *Brahman*', which must be interpreted in the direct, real sense. Thus, just as '*Brahman*' is used with multiple meanings, so the term '*ākāśa*' is to be interpreted in the same way. See commentary to *sūtra* 21, Book Two, Chapter One.

[3] II.III.7 - To give a better understanding of the statements in the previous *sūtras*, Bādarāyaṇa makes some distinctions. When data are spoken of in relation to the *Brahman*, we have to recognise that there is no distinction between the two, but when the data are related to each other, there is distinction but not separation in absolute terms. Moreover, *ākāśa* itself can be considered as relatively absolute and primordial in comparison with the other elements, because it is through *ākāśa* that they find their expression, but it does not have the nature of the absolute when compared to the *Brahman*.

[4] II.III.9 - In the *Śruti* (*Śve*. IV.3) we read:

'... Thou that, by coming into existence, takest on the totality of the appearances pertaining to form.'

Referring to the *Brahman*, 'thou' makes us think that even the *Brahman* is born and therefore produced. Here, too, the words need to be understood in a figurative sense. In fact, the same passage (IV.3) says:

'Thou art female and thou art male, thou art boy and thou art girl.'

Clearly, these formulations cannot be taken literally. Later (IV.4) we read,

'Thou art without beginning and exist in thy Plenitude; [Thou] from whom all the worlds draw their origin.'

Here one is raised to a metaphysical dimension, which the mind cannot reach.

These *Śruti* passages, like others, need to be interpreted in the light of supra-rational intuition, rather than with the differentiating empirical mind, in order to avoid finding incongruities and contradictions where there are none. See the commentary to the previous *sūtra* 3.

[5] II.III.12 - In the *Chāndogya Upaniṣad* (VI.II.1-3) there is a description of the production of fire from Being:

'... In the beginning this was just Non-being, one only without a second: on that Non-being is founded the Being... in which way could the Being be born from Non-being? In the beginning this was just Being, one only without a second.
... That considered: May I become manifold! May I manifest myself into existence! That generated fire... .'

On the other hand, the *Taittirīya Upaniṣad* (II.I.3) says that fire is produced from air (*vāyu*: air or wind): '... From that, that is from this *Ātman* alone, space or ether takes its origin, and from space the air, from the air fire... .'

The fact that fire, to express its nature, requires the element of air does not mean that it must necessarily come from air in a rigidly mechanical sequence in time. Water takes its origin from fire, and earth takes its origin from water.

[6] II.III.13 - In so many passages, which have been alluded to in the previous *sūtras*, the *Śruti* posits the *Brahman*, or *That*, as the uncaused Cause of all that exists. It is immanent as the foundation, which always stays in the condition of *akartṛ* with regard to the existential, formal movement, and it is transcendent as the causeless foundation of Being and of non-being, of the manifest and the unmanifest principle.

That allows the first Cause (the state of *Īśvara* or Being) to develop all the seeds or archetypes held within its heart, right down to the formal prototypes.

His is an act like the power to *be* in the eternal present, to be what He is, thus enabling all things to exist without being obliged to be *That*.

In the *Bṛhadāraṇyaka Upaniṣad* we read:

> 'He who dwells in the earth but is other than the earth, whom the earth knows not, whose body is the earth, and who governs the earth from within, this is the inner Ordainer, your immortal *Ātman*.'[1]

And the *Upaniṣad* goes on to mention water, fire, air, sky, sun, all of which, while differing from *That*, continually derive their existence from *That*. Hence *Brahman* is not Being – as cause, time, and space – but is He through whom Being can actually have the possibility of being. *Brahman* is

---

[1] *Bṛ.* III.VII.3.

not knowledge itself, but He through whom knowledge is able to be and to manifest itself in all the varied beings sensible and intelligible.

It is from this perspective that *That* is spoken of as the metaphysical foundation which allows Being and non-being to have their existence.

In the Western Tradition, *That* corresponds to the One: the One Good of Plato, the One of Plotinus, and the Being of Parmenides.

It was said earlier that what exists, what is visible, is not like 'the horns of a hare' or 'the son of a barren woman.' It is not a non-entity, a nothingness. Hence the dialogue between the sensible and the intelligible can take place by means of and on account of the metaphysical One as the founding element. If multiplicity is perceived through the 'Eye' of the *Brahman*, then the many, being generated, necessarily send back to Unity.

'Appearances', the sensible world, and what these present to us as opinion, are merely a reminder of that which transcends opinion itself to grasp *nóesis*. In fact, it is often said that the way to the *Brahman* is by way of *māyā*.

[7] II.III.15 - If it is maintained that between *Brahmā* and the elements are located the intellect (the vehicle of the *jīva*) and the mind (the vehicle of the *ahaṁkāra*) since their origin and dissolution have to be in some position in a sequence inferred from the *Śruti*, the reply is that this is not the case, because dissolution occurs for bodies, the forms which are born and then perish, in a sequence which is the reverse of being born, but not for the *jīva*, or soul, which gives life to the elements, of which the mind and the intellect itself are both attributes.

[8] II.III.16 - As we have been able to see, the *Śruti* works

both with straightforward terms and with analogies, similes, or transferred meanings. It is often said that that person is dead or is alive or has been born, but it is the body which is born, which lives and dies, and not the *jīva* or soul.

In the *Śruti* we read:

> 'When the living self (*jīva*) forsakes a single branch of this [tree], then that [alone] withers; [when] he forsakes a second one, then [only] this withers... But when he forsakes the entire [tree], he withers completely. In the same way, my dear, you must know... In truth, this [body] certainly dies when it is separated from the *jīva*, but the *jīva* does not die. That which is infinitely subtle has That as its foundation. That is the Reality. That is the *Ātman* and "You are That, O Śvetaketu."'[1]

[9] II.III.17 - The *jīva* is a reflection, a ray of sunlight, or a spark of that Fire which does not burn:

> 'This is the truth. Just as from a blazing and radiant [fire] sparks of [its] very same nature shoot out in their thousands, so, my beloved, innumerable existences are generated from the Imperishable and precisely there they will return... The *Puruṣa* is luminous because, in truth, it is formless. It is both without and within [everything], because, in truth it is without birth. It is without *prāṇa*, because, in truth, it is devoid of mind. It is [totally] clear because, in truth, it is superior [also] to the indestructible supreme.'[2]

The *ātmā* (or *jīva*), being the reflection of the *Ātman*, is not born and does not die, because it is consubstantial with

---

[1] *Chā*. VI.XI.2-3.

[2] *Mu*. II.I.1-2.

the eternity of the *Brahman*. That which is born and dies or, more accurately, that which appears and disappears, comprises the forms, the bodies, so that when we say that such and such a person is dead we may say this purely in a figurative sense.

[10] II.III.18 - This *sūtra* seeks to refute the thesis of all those (especially the *Vaiśeṣikas*) who maintain that in deep sleep the *jīva* is non-intelligent and non-conscious, but that it is intelligent and conscious only in the waking state, which is likened to form. If the *jīva* is not produced, the reduction of qualities or attributes can be ascribed only to that which is accidental, and not to the *jīva*, which is aseity. According to the *Śruti*:

> 'Once the bodily [vehicle] has been laid down in the dream state, he, being alert, contemplates those [organs] which have fallen asleep; resuming its glory, the golden *puruṣa*, the sole *haṁsa*, returns once more to its throne.'[1]

Ham at the time of the inward breath or interiorisation, and *saḥ* at the time of the outward breath.

[11] II.III.22 - In the *Śruti* we read:

> 'He who is of the measure of a thumb, has identical nature to the sun, is endowed with determination and with the ego sense, as well as with the quality of the intellect and the quality of the body and his size is comparable to that of the point of a spur [*jīva*], in truth, is perceived as if different [from the *Ātman*]. The *jīva* must be known as [having] the size of the tip of a hair divided into a hundred parts, imagined as divided [yet] a hundred times... .'[2]

---

[1] *Bṛ.* IV.III.11.

[2] *Śve.* V.8-9.

This could lead to the supposition that the *jīva* is as small as an atom; but the *Upaniṣad* ends the same *sūtra* by saying, '... and yet that reaches infinitude.'

What has been stated above implies that the *jīva* is beyond all spatial dimension.

[12] II.III.24 - If it is still maintained that the two situations of the *jīva* and the sandal paste – as the interlocutor always maintains – are not analogous, the reply is that this is not so on account of the fact that the soul, or *jīva*, occupies a position within the heart, according to the *Upaniṣad*. See the *Bṛhadāraṇyaka Upaniṣad* (IV.III.7), according to which

> 'Who is, among all [quoted beings], the *Ātman*?... is the light within the heart.'
>
> 'That, in truth, is the *Ātman* which resides within the heart... . Of that there is this very etymological explanation: this [*Ātman*] is in the heart and, therefore it is [called] heart.'[1]

[13] II.III.25 - Or, again, just as light (quality), though located at a very precise point, pervades the whole ambiance – and there are other similar analogies that are possible – so the soul, though infinitesimal and located at a very precise point (the heart), can fill the whole body with luminosity, as happens in the sensible world.

However the reflection of the embodied *jīva* on the physical plane does not reside within the heart of the physical body (*sthūlasarīra*) but in the vital sheath (*prāṇamayakośa*).

---

[1] *Bṛ*. IV.III.7 and *Chā*. VIII.III.3.

'... similarly this *Ātman* has entered the *ātmā* that is the body [staying hidden] from hair up to the nails... .'[1]

[14] II.III.26 - Being diffused like a perfume indicates that the soul, while being all-pervasive, can resemble the perfume of a flower which endures independently even when the flower is no longer present; this implies that there can be a distinction between the flower and the perfume which endures independently of the flower; in the same way this relationship can take place between the soul and its own intelligence, which can endure independently of the soul or *jīva*.

[15] II.III.27 - The *Śruti* itself states this: that is, considering that the infinitesimal or atomic soul dwells in the heart, the objector concludes that the soul, while being atomic, is able to pervade also the entire body or, while having a limit, is able to transcend its limitation in a relative way.

[16] II.III.29 - This *sūtra* begins the refutation of the opponent's thesis. The designation given by the interlocutor (the *jīva* separated from its intelligence) cannot prevail, because the infinitesimal of which the *Śruti* itself speaks has a figurative meaning, in addition to the fact that the qualities of the intellect are superimposed on the *jīva*.

If the *jīva* or soul is of the same nature as the *Ātman* (*Tat tvam asi*), the conclusion must be that the soul cannot be limited or confined in a well-defined space. This may apply to the vehicle or body, which is mistakenly considered to be the *jīva*. It is *pradhāna* which determines space, not the soul or *jīva*, which is without form.

---

[1] *Kau.* IV.20.

[17] II.III.30 - There is no error in the previous formulation, because the connection of the *jīva* persists until it frees itself from the conditionings of the vehicles or bodies, re-assuming, thus, its nature (*svabhāva*) as the supreme *Ātman* (*Bṛ*. IV.III.7). Thus there is no truthfulness in the opponent's thesis, according to which, since the two natures (that of the *jīva* and that of the intellect) are in mutual opposition, if one (the intellect) were missing the other (the *jīva*) would also disappear; or the *jīva* would no longer have the status of a transmigrating being. The *jīva* deprived of the *buddhi*, according to the opponent's thesis, has no possibility of recognising itself as such, which results in a being devoid of existence, of self-awareness.

[18] II.III.31 - According to the opponent, as the connection with the intellect does not exist in deep sleep or at the end of *pralaya*, how can we speak of an association which lasts as long as the *jīva* assumes a transmigratory body?

The reply given by the *Brahmasūtra* is that in deep sleep (*suṣupti*) the intellect is always connected to the *jīva* but remains in the state of potentiality; this is why it is able to appear again in the waking state (*viśva*). In this way the manliness of a youth can become manifest if he already possesses this quality in potentiality.

[19] II.III.33 - Now that the debate has ended as to whether the *jīva* has to be infinitesimal, limited or unlimited in size, and whether it occupies a space and where its location might be, and so on (*sūtras* 19-32), the next step is to give a better definition of the nature of the manifest soul as the agent (*kartā*) of knowledge. It is only by acknowledging this agent that the Scriptures can have meaning.

Again, when the *Śruti* prescribes sacrificial rites and norms of conduct for the householders or for the various stages of life, there is clearly a need for some one, some agent, to whom the injunctions are directed. See *Muṇḍaka Upaniṣad* (III.II.10-11).

[20] II.III.37 - It is necessary to distinguish between perception as such from its actual implementation.

The manifest *jīva* is capable of independent perception, but to implement this faculty it needs intermediaries or operational instruments, such as a body, to attain a particular objective. Moreover, the *jīva* does not have absolute freedom while it is dependent on instruments that are limited by time and space. Now these instruments, being contingent and imperfect, constrain the *jīva* within definite limits to determine or not conformity with *sattva*.

Having freedom of action, the *jīva* also has freedom of choice.

[21] II.III.39 - Moreover, if the *buddhi* or another instrument made from *prakṛti* were the agent, who should be realised if the *buddhi* is merely a limited instrument which is born and disappears, having the nature of time and space? And the very exhortations of the *Śruti* to realise the *Ātman* would have no meaning.

> '... the *Ātman*, in truth, is what must be realised; it is that of which one must hear, it is that on which one must reflect, it is that on which one must meditate deeply... .'[1]

Now, if the *jīvātman* were not the agent or the subject through which the *buddhi* itself can be and can express itself, on whom should one meditate?

---

[1] *Bṛ.* II.IV.5.

[22] II.III.40 - If the *jīva* possesses the nature of the active agent, it follows that it must be ever in action, and hence the *jīva* is unable to realise itself. Moreover, activity is a sign of dualism, which leads to conflict.

The reply given by the *Brahmasūtra* to this objection is that the *jīva*, being temporarily limited by *upādhis*, experiences polarity, but the nature of the *jīva* is not dual and it is not always the active agent because, being free, it has two possibilities: to act or not to act. Thus, in deep sleep the *jīva*, although being the subject of acting, remains deeply at rest.

The *jīva* is therefore a reflection of the supreme Reality. According to the Scriptures:

> 'The senses are called horses; in relation to them the objects are the roads. When [the reflection of the *Ātman*] is united to the body, to the senses and to the mind, the wise call it: the enjoyer... The sense objects are indeed higher than the senses and the mind is higher than the sense objects; indeed the intellect is higher than mind, and the great *Ātman* is higher than the intellect.'[1]

According to the *sūtra*, the *jīva* is in a state identical to that of the carpenter, who is free to act through his tools or not to act; his ability to act, however, is always accidental, like that of the *jīva*.

[23] II.III.41 - After the exposition given in the previous *sūtras*, stating that the *jīva*, being embodied and therefore determined, is the agent of the activity, Bādarāyaṇa the Teacher now questions whether the *jīva* is the sole agent or whether this possibility comes to it from another source.

Sūtra 41 eliminates this doubt. The *Śruti* always teaches

---

[1] *Ka*. I.III.4,10.

that the *jīva* is not an absolute reality, is not aseity, but it is a reflection of the supreme *Ātman*, which implies that it receives the possibilities of being and of expressing itself from another source, that is, from That.

Hence the *Brahman* is the foundation of all that is, including the *jīva* in its various states of waking, dream, and deep sleep. This also implies that there is no duality, because the 'second' (the world of names and forms), not being an absolute Reality – because there is not sufficient reason within it – vanishes completely, just as the forms produced from the whirling of a blazing firebrand vanish when the whirling stops.[1]

It is worth to keep in mind that the *Ātman* is transcendent, it is *nitya* (eternal), *kūṭastha* (immutable), (*akartṛ*) non-acting (see *Mai*. II.7 and *Bṛ*. II.V.14); its reflection or ray of consciousness (*Mai*. VI.31) enters into manifestation on the intelligible plane, then this ray (*ābhāsa*), see *sūtra* 50, extends itself on the formal individual plane:

Ātman

↓

Jīva

↓

Ahaṁkāra

this last one is '... like an actor who changes garments continuously.' (*Mai*. IV.2).

---

[1] Cp. *Mā. Kā*. IV.47 *et seqq*.

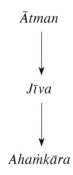

[24] II.III.45 - Once again there is the question as to whether the *jīva* is a fragment, a ray, of the supreme Reality, or the supreme Reality itself.

The preceding *sūtras* clarify this question. The *jīva* is not the supreme Reality (just as a ray of sunlight is not the whole sun), because, limited by the *upādhis*, it considers itself to be non-supreme, and at the same time it is the supreme Reality, because, having the nature of That, it cannot, however conditioned by the *upādhis*, be such as to change its nature.

The *jīva* is thus not like the master with his servant (distinction), but it has the nature of Fire or *Brahman* (identity), just as a ray of sunlight is of the same nature as the sun.

Brahman has no parts, no differences; it is whole in all respects, so that the *jīva* itself is also the supreme Fire according to the *mantra* of the *Upaniṣad*:

> 'This is the truth. Just as from a blazing and radiant [fire] sparks of [its] very same nature shoot out in their thousands, so, my beloved, innumerable existences are generated from the Imperishable and precisely there they go to be reabsorbed.'[1]

Moreover, the *Smṛti*, too, confirms this; witness the *Bhagavadgītā*:

> 'An eternal fragment of Myself, appearing as a living soul in the world of mortals.'[2]

In the *Atharva Veda* there is a hymn addressed to the *Brahman* in which we read: 'The *dāśas* [fishermen] are the *Brahman*, the *dāsas* [servants] are the *Brahman*, and even the

---

[1] *Mu*. II.I.1. See also *Chā*. III.XIII.7.

[2] *Bha*. *Gī*. XV.7. Op. cit.

kitavas [jugglers] are the *Brahman*.' See also the *Śvetāśvatara Upaniṣad* (IV.2 *et seqq*.).

The *essence* of all beings is identical to the *Brahman*, be they *śūdras*, *brāhmaṇas*, or other categories of beings of any order or level.

[25] II.III.51 - Once again it is confirmed that the *jīva* is only a reflection, a spark, a ray, of the supreme Reality. Thus the pleasure and pain or the thoughts of an individual embodied being remain inherent within his potential until they are resolved, and they cannot be confused with those of other beings because all beings are separate on account of their particular *upādhis*.

In *Sāṁkhya*, on the other hand, it is postulated that the agent is *pradhāna*, which is homogeneous and pervades all beings. This presupposes that pain and pleasure, or any mental construct, is related to *pradhāna* either as a cause or as an effect. This way of looking at things also belongs to the *Vaiśeṣika* of Kaṇāda and to Gautama's *Nyāya* itself.

[26] II.III.53 - If it is stated that a distinction such as that of pleasure and pain results from the difference of location or from the position of the vehicle or space, so that there can be no confusion in experiencing pleasure and pain, the answer given by Bādarāyaṇa to the hypothetical interlocutor of the *sūtra* in question (*Nyāya* and *Vaiśeṣika*) is that this is not the case because, if every soul permeates the totality of souls, it cannot possess even one particular body on account of its limitless extension to all souls.

One must therefore acknowledge a single soul or *jīva* which has its own particular experience, distinct from that of all other beings.

All the rays of the sun, even if ontologically they partake of and possess the nature of the sun, the various coulours are yet distinct from each other. If one of the rays simultaneously permeated all the others, the pleasure and pain experienced by the one ray would extend to all the others.

Preliminary Note on Chapter Four of Book Two

In the Fourth Chapter of the Second Book the *Brahmasūtra* examines the various types of *prāṇa*, considered by the *Śruti* both as the origin of the senses, as subtle energy supporting the organs of the physical body, and also as energetic elements permeating the universal condition. But *prāṇa*, as universal energy, is not to be understood in the modern scientific sense; it is that by means of which substance is able to manifest and express itself. Thus the physical organs, with their faculties, are the expression of *prāṇa*, which is also known as 'vital energy' and 'vital breath' inasmuch as it gives life, support, and fulfilment to the organs of all types and levels.

> 'The *Puruṣa* is luminous because, indeed, it is formless. It is at the same time both within and without [all] because, in truth, it is without birth. It is without *prāṇa* because, in truth, it is without mind. It is [wholly] clear because, in truth, it is [even] higher than the supreme indestructible. From this [*Puruṣa*] are born *prāṇa*, mind and all the senses, the cosmos, air, light, water and earth which is the support of the totality.'[1]

> '*Prāṇa*, faith, space, air, fire, water and earth, organs, mind and food; from food vigour, asceticism, the *mantras*, the

[1] *Mu*. II.I.2-3.

rites, the worlds and the name [of every being] in the worlds, all finds its support in That.'[1]

---

[1] *Pra.* VI.4-5.

atha dvitīyo 'dhyāyaḥ

caturthaḥ khaṇḍaḥ

tathā prāṇāḥ // 1 //

tathā: likewise; *prāṇāḥ*: vital breaths.

gauṇyasaṁbhavāt // 2 //

gaunī: derivative; *a-sambhavāt*: on account of impossibility.

tat prāk śruteś ca // 3 //

tat: that; *prāk*: first; *śruteḥ*: on account of the *Śruti*; *ca*: and, again.

tat pūrvakatvāt vācaḥ // 4 //

tat: that; *pūrvakatvāt*: on account of precedence; *vācaḥ*: of the organ of speech.

sapta gater viśeṣitatvāc ca // 5 //

sapta: seven; *gateḥ*: on account of being known; *viśeṣitatvāt*: on account of the specification; *ca*: and.

hastādayas tu sthite 'to naivam // 6 //

hastādayaḥ: the hands, and so on.; *tu*: but, however; *sthite*: being established; *ataḥ*: therefore, for this reason; *na*: not; *evam*: thus.

Book Two

Chapter Four

1. *Likewise the vital breaths.*

2. *It [is] not possible [to explain the origin] in a derivative way.*

This is because it, the principal *prāṇa*, does not have the nature of an organ or of an instrument such as the eye, which is independent of the hands (*Chā*. V.I.7-12). Thus shows the *Śruti*.

3. *Again, according to the Śruti, it [comes] first.*

4. *Because the organ of speech [is] preceded by that [that is, by fire and the other elements].*[1]

5. *Seven: thus they are known [according to the quality] specified.*[2]

6. *But the hands and so on [being mentioned in the texts, are an] established [fact]; this is why [things are] not thus.*

However, according to the same *Śruti*, the hands and so on are joined to the seven, which is why the number gets increased. For this reason it is not so, in the sense that they cannot be considered seven.

aṇavaś ca // 7 //

aṇavaḥ: subtle; *ca*: and.

śreṣṭhaś ca // 8 //

śreṣṭhaḥ: principal; *ca*: and.

na vāyukriye pṛthag upadeśāt // 9 //

na: not; *vāyu*: air; *kriye*: action, function; *pṛthak*: separately; *upadeśāt*: on account of the teaching, taught.

cakṣurādivat tu tat saha śiṣṭyādibhyaḥ // 10 //

cakṣuḥ: sight; *ādi*: and so on; *vat*: like; *tu*: but; *tat*: that; *saha*: with; *śiṣṭi*: prescribed; *ādibhyaḥ*: etcetera, for other reasons.

akaraṇatvāc ca na doṣas tathā hi darśayati // 11 //

a-karaṇatvāt: on account of not having the nature of an organ, or instrument; *ca*: and; *na*: not; *doṣaḥ*: error, defect; *tathā*: thus; *hi*: because; *darśayati*: shows.

7. *And [they are] subtle.*

Moreover, the *prāṇas* have a nature that is not gross but subtle; they can be said to be superphysical because they permeate the structure of the instruments or *upādhis*.

8. *And the principal.*

Apart from the secondary *prāṇas*, the principal one, too, emerges from the first Cause inasmuch as this represents their foundation.

9. *[The vital breath is] not air or function [because it is] taught separately.*

The principal breath is not air, as some schools of thought assert, because it is mentioned separately from the other elements.

> 'From this [*Puruṣa*] draw their origin the *prāṇa*, the mind and all the senses, the cosmos, air, light, water and earth which is the support of the totality.'*

10. *But [prāṇa is dependent on the soul], as [are] sight and so on, [inasmuch as it is] prescribed together with them, and for other reasons.*

Prāṇa, however, is dependent on the *jīva*, which represents its beginning; according to the words of the *Śruti*, this is also true for the other organs.

11. *And because [it does] not [have] the nature of an instrument, [there is] no defect, as [the Śruti] shows.*[3]

---

* *Mu.* II.I.3.

pañcavṛttir manovad vyapadiśyate // 12 //

pañcavṛttiḥ: five modifications; *manovat*: like the mind; *vyapadiśyate*: indicated.

aṇuś ca // 13 //

aṇuḥ: subtle; *ca*: and

jyotirādyadhiṣṭhānaṁ tu tadāmananāt // 14 //

jyotirādyadhiṣṭhānam: the power of fire (light) and so on; *tu*: but; *tat-āmananāt*: on account of the declaration of that.

prāṇavatā śabdāt // 15 //

prāṇavatā: with the possessor of *prāṇa*; *śabdāt*: according to the Scriptures.

tasya ca nityatvāt // 16 //

tasya: of that; *ca*: and; *nityatvāt*: on account of the permanence.

ta indriyāṇi tad vyapadeśāt anyatra śreṣṭhāt // 17 //

te: essi; *indriyāṇi*: organs of sense; *tat*: that; *vyapadeśāt*: on account of the designation; *anyatra*: with the exception; *śreṣṭhāt*: of the principal.

bheda śruteḥ // 18 //

bheda: difference; *śruteḥ*: on account of the *Śruti*.

vailakṣaṇyāc ca // 19 //

vailakṣaṇyāt: on account of the difference of characteristics; *ca*: and.

12. *[Prāṇa] is indicated with five modifications, as [is] the mind.*[4]

13. *And subtle.*[5]

14. *But [there is] the power of fire and so on, as declared [by the Scriptures].*

15. *According to the Scriptures, [the organs are connected] to the possessor of prāṇa.*

16. *And on account of the permanence of that [jīva].*[6]

17. *Except for the principal one, they [are] designated [as] organs of sense.*

The individualised *prāṇas*, or the *prāṇas* which operate in the organic structure, are considered as organs different from the principal *prāṇa*. We shall say that the principal *prāṇa* is the foundation by which the organs of sense, speech, and so on are enabled to exist and to express themselves. The universal *prāṇa* cannot be considered as an organ of sense (Compare *Mu*. II.I.3 and *Bṛ*. I.V.21 *et seqq*.).

18. *[And on account of the] difference [given] by the Śruti.*

19. *And on account of the dissimilarity in characteristics.*[7]

saṁjñā mūrti kḷptis tu trivṛt kurvata upadeśāt //20//

saṁjñā-mūrti: name and form; *kḷptiḥ*: manifesting, shaping; *tu*: but; *trivṛt-kurvataḥ*: tripartite activity; *upadeśāt*: according to the teaching.

māṁsādi bhaumaṁ yathā śabdam itarayoś ca //21//

māṁsa: flesh; *ādi*: and so on; *bhaumam*: produced from earth; *yathā*: as, according to; *śabdam*: Scriptures; *itarayoḥ*: the other; *ca*: so, and.

vaiśeṣyāt tu tad-vādas tad-vādaḥ //22//

vaiśeṣyāt: from the distinction; *tu*: but; *tat*: that; *vādaḥ*: declaration; *tat-vādaḥ*: that declaration.

iti caturthaḥ khaṇḍaḥ

dvitīyo 'dhyāyaḥ

20. *But, [according to] the teaching, the shaping of name and form [belongs to the one who] activated the tripartite division [of the elements].*[8]

21. *According to the Scripture, flesh and so on [are] earthy, and so [are] the other two [water and fire].*

22. *But from the distinction [prevailing between one element and another there arises] the respective designation, the respective designation.*

The threefold differentiation of the elements corresponds to the formation of vehicles both gross and subtle; and their difference can come about only on the basis of greater or less quantity or the prevalence of one over another, from which arises their name. The repetition in the *sūtra* indicates that the Second Book is completed.

End of Chapter Four of Book Two
of the Brahmasūtra

NOTES

[1] II.IV.4 - It is not possible to explain the origin of the *prāṇas*, the senses, and so on as secondary factors, for this would contradict passages in the *Śruti* which state explicitly that the *prāṇas* are not co-existent with the *Brahman*, as if they were two beings, but:

> 'The *Puruṣa* is luminous because, indeed, it is formless... . It is without *prāṇa* because, in truth, it is without mind.'[1]

These explicit statements consider the *prāṇas*, the senses, and so on to come after the supreme Reality inasmuch as they are produced.

[2] II.IV.5 - 'The seven *prāṇas* come into being from That... the *prāṇas* that rest in the cave [of the heart]... .'[2]

And even when the *Śruti* mentions six, seven or more than seven (as in the *Bṛ.* III.IX.26), one still needs to appreciate that the principal *prāṇas* are six: all the others are dependent and secondary in relation to the six.

Moreover, in some contexts the *Smṛti* speaks of six principal *prāṇas* and of 49 focal points which nourish the various minor organs of the human body.

[3] II.IV.11 - And because, being the principal *prāṇa*, it does

---

[1] *Mu.* II.I.2.

[2] *Ibid.* II.I.8 *et seqq.*

not have the nature of an organ or an instrument, like the eye, which is independent of the hands (*Chā.* V.I.7-12).

[4] II.IV.12 - Morover *prāṇa* is indicated with a quintuple function:

> 'To them the principal *prāṇa* said: "Do not fall into error! I alone am, who, being divided into five, support the body by keeping it together." But those remained incredulous.'[1]

[5] II.IV.13 - The principal *prāṇa*, too, is subtle, infinitesimal, and confined within the body or *upādhi* of the *jīva*. When the *Bṛhadāraṇyaka Upaniṣad* (I.III.19) states: '... The *prāṇa*, in fact, is the essence of the limbs. Therefore, since the *prāṇa* is the essence of the limbs, from whichever limb the *prāṇa* strays off, that very [limb] withers away... ,' it is referring to the universal *prāṇa*. Thus the elements of the physical or gross body of the being, however limited they may be, are of the same nature as the universal elements.

Prāṇa nourishes all intelligible and sensible forms; so the very forms of the human being, from the gross physical to *ānanda*, are nourished by *prāṇa*. It is also called vital energy because it gives life, through the *cakras*, to the *nāma-rūpa*. It is a product and, at the same time, producer; because it is pervasive, in many *Upaniṣads*, it is assimilated to the *Brahman*.

In the *Taittirīya Upaniṣad* (II.III.1) we read:

> 'The *devas* breathe following the *prāṇa*, and also those who are human beings and animals. In truth the *prāṇa* is life for [all] beings, this is why it is said, "the life of all." Those who meditate on the *prāṇa* as on the *Brahman* certainly attain the whole length of life... .'

---

[1] *Pra.* II.3.

[6] II.IV.16 - *Prāṇa* is independent by nature, that is, it is its own cause, or is it dependent on something else? *Prāṇa* cannot be taken out of the universal context, being an integral part of it (inasmuch as that which presides over the bodies of the being is restricted and conformable to the various bodies); there can thus be no duality.

And when the *Śruti* declares: 'Fire, having become speech, entered the mouth; wind, having become *prāṇa*, entered the nostrils' (*Ai.* I.II.4), it does not mean that the element of fire, clearly taken as a universal principle, takes the place of the being which governs all the organs, including the individualised *prāṇa* which presides over the individualised state; nor can there be opposition to the governing function of the being within the realm of its own system.

Sūtras 15 and 16 confirm the thesis of *sūtra* 14: the organs are connected to the possessor of the *prāṇas*, because this is in accordance with the Scriptures and also because the *jīva* is permanent in comparison with the organs, which are transient.

[7] II.IV.19 - This lack of identity is corroborated by the *Śruti*: see *sūtra* 9.

The *prāṇa,* confined within form, the *manas*, and all the other sensory faculties are distinct, although not separate or in opposition. On the other hand, it remains obvious that there are differences of qualification, function, and purpose.

The organ of speech is not the organ of hearing, and the organ of hearing is not the organ of sight. Furthermore, the individualised *prāṇa* operates during sleep, while the sensory organs of the physical body are non-operative.

[8] II.IV.20 - It may be thought that the creative act of name and form is something accomplished by the *jīva* or by

the *Ātman* or *Brahman*, but the *Brahmasūtra* considers that name and form, the *guṇas*, the threefold expression of fire, water and food (*trivṛt karaṇa*) are the manifestation of the first cause or *Īśvara-saguṇa*, according to the teaching of the *Śruti*, where it refers to *Ātman* or *Brahman* as the foundation of all that is and to *saguṇa Brahman* as the expression of creative faculties. In order to understand *Advaita Vedānta*, this *sūtra* is of extreme importance. Both the henological and ontological aspects can be acknowledged.

Therefore it is necessary to keep in mind the distinction between what is the foundation – the substratum or founding Cause, by means of which the world of names and forms or the becoming of manifestation stands, giving it unity and order – and what is the principial Cause which gives origin, order and life to the becoming of the forms. We have already seen that both in the *Upaniṣads* and in the *Brahmasūtra*, in some contexts, the *Brahman* is spoken of as the creator of the world. This is done so that the seeming multiplicity of the becoming and the first Cause itself (where multiplicity finds its unity) is overcome and the conclusion is finally that the essential point, substantial and primary, is always the *nirguṇa Brahman*. However, to comprehend these levels of consciousness it suffices to refer to the *Māṇḍūkya Upaniṣad*, *sūtras* VI and VII.

Moreover, it has been said that the *Śruti* provides the metaphysical aspect (*nirguṇa*), the ontological aspect (*saguṇa*), the ritual aspect, *yoga* and so on. This is done to meet the various qualifications of the searchers on the 'way of return', since the *Śruti* does not have a unilateral and absolutist character. However, these diversities of approach to divinity are resolved into the metaphysical state, or in the One without a second (*advaita*), where every duality, polarity and difference find their plenitude.

atha tṛtīyo 'dhyāyaḥ

sādhanā

BOOK THREE

Spiritual Discipline

Some Preliminary Notes on Chapter One of Book Three

The previous Book quashed the various objections to *Vedānta* thought that are put forward by certain schools of thought (*Sāṁkhya*, *Tārkika*).

This First Chapter begins by tracing the journey of the *jīva*, or, rather, the reflection of consciousness of the embodied *jīva* when the gross instrument or body is left. This concerns the problem of the *post mortem* and of the two Ways that are followed.

All the branches of the one Tradition deal with this event, from ancient Egypt to Orphism, Christianity, and the traditional philosophical schools that have arisen over time, right up to our own days. These traditional currents have spoken of the transmigration of souls and hence of the 'Art of Dying.'

What is it that migrates? It is not that individuality, not that same 'actor' who, with that name and that form, has played his part on the great stage of life, but the energies (*guṇas*) qualified and solidified by the repeated tendency towards expression: energies which, being unresolved, lead, or, rather, compel the reflection of the *jīva* to manifest itself and express itself in various ways at the gross physical level, with perspectives that may even be in conflict; this is because the *guṇas* (a passion, for example, is an explosion of energy), belonging to the world of movement, transform and modify themselves.

The whole process of realisation consists in knowing how

to master, direct, and finally transcend this complex which is simultaneously dynamic (*rajas*) and inert (*tamas*), until there is the realisation of the unconditioned state of *nir-guṇa* (absence of *guṇa*).

Here is a synthetic scheme of the threefold aspect of the being in its totality:*

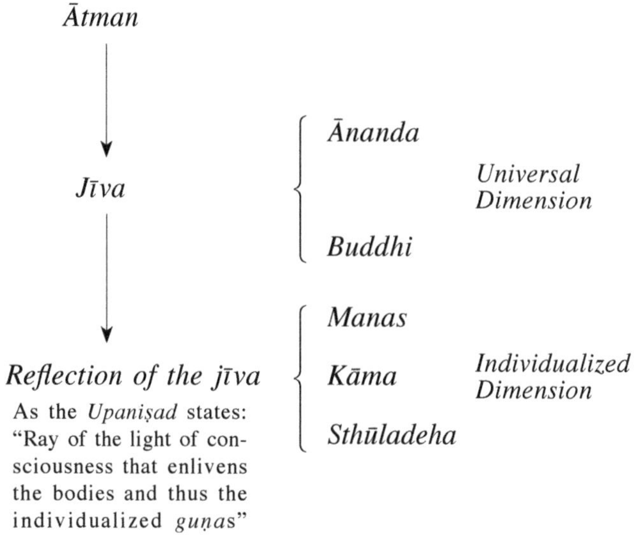

---

* For further consideration on this topic, see 'Final notes to the *Upaniṣad*' in the volume *Upaniṣad*, edited by Raphael. Bompiani, Milan, Italy.

atha tṛtīyo 'dhyāyaḥ
prathamaḥ khandaḥ

tad antara pratipattau raṁhati sampariṣvaktaḥ praśna nirūpaṇābhyām // 1 //

tat: that; *antara*: further; *pratipattau*: in obtaining, acquiring; *raṁhati*: transfers itself, goes from one state to another; *sampariṣvaktaḥ*: enveloped, constrained; *praśna*: question; *nirūpaṇābhyām*: from the explanation and reply.

tryātmakatvāt tu bhūyastvāt // 2 //

tri-ātma-ka-tvāt: on account of being composed of three elements; *tu*: but, on the other hand; *bhūyastvāt*: on account of being abundant, predominant.

prāṇa gateś ca // 3 //

prāṇa: vital breath; *gateḥ*: on account of leaving, transmigrating; *ca*: and.

agnyādi-gatiśruter iti cen na bhāktatvāt // 4 //

agni-ādi-gatiḥ-śruteḥ: according to the *Śruti* there is a movement in the fire, and so on; *iti cet*: if this [is said]; *na*: not; *bhāktatvāt*: on account of having a symbolic sense.

Book Three

Chapter One

1. *[The reflection of the jīva] is compelled [by the subtle part of the elements] to transmigrate with that into a further [body, as] is gathered from the question and explanation [in the texts].*[1]

2. *But [the reflection] of the Ātmā is composed of three elements; however, [only water is mentioned] on account of [its] abundance.*

The reflection of the *jīva* is enveloped by three elements; but only water is mentioned because it is predominant in the human body.

3. *And on account of the departure of the prāṇa.*

When the *prāṇa* departs, all the other elements follow it. In the *Bṛhadāraṇyaka Upaniṣad* (IV.IV.2) it has been seen that '... when the [principal] *prāṇa* leaves the body, all the *prāṇas* follow it.'

4. *If [it is said that the prāṇas and the organs do not follow the jīva] because the Śruti [mentions] going into fire (agni), [the answer is that this is] not [the case] on account of the symbolic meaning [of the statement].*

prathame 'śravaṇād iti cen na tā eva hyupapatteḥ //5//

prathame: in the first [offering]; *a-śravaṇāt*: on account of the non-mentioning, non-hearing; *iti cet*: if this [is said]; *na*: not; *tāḥ*: that; *eva*: indeed; *hi*: because; *upapatteḥ*: on account of being admissible.

aśrutatvād iti cen neṣṭādikāriṇāṁ pratīteḥ //6//

a-śrutatvāt: on account of not being mentioned by the *Śruti*; *iti cet*: if this [is said]; *na*: not; *iṣṭa-ādi-kāriṇm*: of those who fulfil or make sacrifices, and so on; *pratīteḥ*: on account of the mention.

bhāktaṁ vānātmavittvāt tathā hi darśayati //7//

bhāktam: metaphorical, symbolic; *vā*: or; *an-ātma-vittvāt*: through not knowing the *Ātman*; *tathā*: thus; *hi*: because; *darśayati*: [the *Śruti*] demonstrates.

kṛtātyaye 'nuśayavān dṛṣṭasmṛtibhyāṁ yathetam anevaṁ ca //8//

kṛta: that which has been done, made; *atyaye*: at the end of the time, exhaustion; *anuśayavān*: residue of *karma*; *dṛṣṭasmṛtibhyām*: according to inner sight or vision and according to the *Smṛti*; *yathā-itam*: thus gone; *anevam*: different, in a different way; *ca*: and, moreover.

5. *If [it is said that it is] on account of the lack of reference [to water] in the first [sacrificial offering, the answer is that this is] not [the case] because this is indeed [understood] as admissible.*[2]

6. *If [it is said that it is] not mentioned by the Śruti [because the soul does not depart shrouded in water], this is not the case [because the Scripture] implies those who fulfil sacrifices, and so on.*[3]

7. *Or [the statement 'It is the food of the gods' is] symbolic, because [the individualised being] does not know the Ātman, as [the Śruti] demonstrates.*

In the *Chāndogya Upaniṣad* (V.X.4) we read:

> '... the moon: this is King *Soma*. It is the food of the Gods. On it the Gods feed.'

It is natural that the *gods* are not nourished by food, because their bodies, or forms of expression, require no food. In fact, in the same *Upaniṣad* (III.VI.1 and III.V.4) we read:

> 'In truth the *devas* eat not and do not even drink: they are satisfied merely by the sight of this nectar... The *Vedas*, in fact, are nectars, and they are their nectars.'

8. *On the exhaustion of what has been done, [according] to the view [of the Śruti] and Smṛti [the reflection of the jīva] returns, [impelled] by the residue of karma, along the path by which it departed [from this world], or in a different way.*[4]

caraṇād iti cen nopalakṣaṇārtheti kārṣṇājiniḥ // 9 //

caraṇāt: on account of conduct or behaviour; *iti cet*: if [it is said]; *na*: not; *upalakṣaṇa*: indirect; *artha*: meaning, end; *iti*: so; *kārṣṇājiniḥ*: Kārṣṇājini [the Sage].

ānarthakyam iti cen na tad apekṣatvāt // 10 //

ān: not; *artha*: aim, result; *kyam*: that, which; *iti cet*: if [it is said]; *na*: not; *tat*: that; *apekṣatvāt*: on account of derivation or dependence.

sukṛta duṣkṛte eveti tu bādariḥ // 11 //

sukṛta: meritorious action, merit; *duṣkṛte*: demerit, bad action; *eva*: really; *iti*: thus, so; *tu*: but; *bādariḥ*: Bādari.

aniṣṭādikāriṇām api ca śrutam // 12 //

an-iṣṭa-ādi: contrary to the [sacred] law, and so on; *kāriṇām*: of those who act; *api*: even; *ca*: but; *śrutam*: *Śruti*.

saṁyamane tu anubhūyetareṣām ārohāvarohau tad gati darśanāt // 13 //

saṁyamane: in the dwelling of Yama; *tu*: but; *anubhūya*: having enjoyed, experienced; *itareṣām*: of the others; *ārohāvarohau*: ascent and descent; *tat*: this; *gati*: way; *darśanāt*: on account of being declared [by the *Śruti*].

smaranti ca // 14 //

smaranti: the *Smṛti*; *ca*: also, too.

api ca sapta // 15 //

api: moreover; *ca*: and; *sapta*: seven.

9. *If it is said that [the soul descends] on account of its conduct [apart from the residual karma, the reply is that it is] not so because, according to Kārṣṇājini [the Sage, the word 'conduct'] has an indirect meaning.*[5]

10. *If [it is said] that [conduct has] no result, this is not the case because [karma] depends on that [conduct].*[6]

11. *But [the term 'conduct'] really [implies] merit and demerit; this [is what] Bādari [thinks].*

According to Bādari the Teacher, the question does not even arise, because there is no substantial difference between conduct and *karma*. The first is intrinsically related to the second, and *vice versa*. An individual's conduct is the result of action qualified by thc *guṇas*, and these are the effect of previous conditioned conduct or behaviour undertaken by the agent.

12. *But the Śruti [affirms ascent to the moon] even for those who commit acts that are contrary to the [sacred] law, and so on.*[7]

13. *However, for the others [those who have not performed sacrifices], when they have experienced [the fruits of their actions] in the dwelling of Yama, [there are] ascent and descent; this is declared [by the Śruti].*

14. *The Smṛti, too, [affirms it].*

15. *And furthermore, [there are] seven [hells].*

tatrāpi ca tad vyāpārād avirodhaḥ // 16 //

tatra: there; *api*: also; *ca*: and; *tat*: that; *vyāpārāt*: on account of activity or function; *a-virodhaḥ*: non-contradiction.

vidyā-karmaṇor iti tu prakṛtatvāt // 17 //

vidyā: of knowledge; *karmaṇoḥ*: of action; *iti*: this; *tu*: but, however; *prakṛtatvāt*: on account of being under discussion.

na tṛtīye tathopalabdheḥ // 18 //

na: not; *tṛtīye*: in the third; *tathā*: thus, so; *upalabdheḥ*: it being seen or recognised.

smaryate 'pi ca loke // 19 //

smaryate: it is declared by the *Smṛti*; *api*: moreover; *ca*: and; *loke*: in popular opinion.

darśanāc ca // 20 //

darśanāt: from observation; *ca*: and.

tṛtīya śabdāvarodhaḥ saṁśokajasya // 21 //

tṛtīya: terzo; *śabda*: sound, expression; *avarodhaḥ*: contained; *saṁśoka-jasya*: of that which is born from moisture.

sābhāvyāpattir upapatteḥ // 22 //

sābhāvya-āpattiḥ: acquisition of a natural affinity; *upapatteḥ*: being reasonable, conformable to reason.

16. *And on account of the role played by him [who extends] even there [to the seven hells], non-contradiction.*[8]

17. *However, [the expression 'the two paths' indicates the two ways] of knowledge and ritual action (karman): this is the subject under discussion.*[9]

18. *[With reference to the number of oblations] the third does not [apply]: this is what [the Śruti] recognises.*[10]

19. *This is, moreover, declared by the Smṛti and popular belief.*[11]

20. *And from [simple] observation.*

It is a matter of simple and common observation that birth can occur without the five oblations.

21. *That which is born from moisture [is] included in the third expression.*

It may be objected that, although there are four forms of organic reproduction, the *Chāndogya Upaniṣad*, quoted in *sūtra* 19, mentions only three. The fourth, according to the *Śruti*, is included in the third, because reproduction from moisture is included in vegetative reproduction, for both come forth from earth and water.

22. *[When the soul descends from the moon] it acquires an affinity with the nature [of ether, and so on, which is] conformable to reason.*

nāticireṇa viśeṣāt // 23 //

na: not; *aticireṇa*: a long time; *viśeṣāt*: according to a specific statement.

anyādhiṣṭhiteṣu pūrvavad abhilāpāt // 24 //

anya: others; *adhiṣṭhiteṣu*: occupied; *pūrvavat*: as previously; *abhilāpāt*: according to the declaration.

aśuddham iti cen na śabdāt // 25 //

a-śuddham: not pure; *iti cet*: if [it is said]; *na*: not; *śabdāt*: from scriptural authority.

retaḥ sigyogo 'tha // 26 //

retaḥ: the act of generation; *sik-yoga*: joining with him; *atha*: afterwards, then.

yoneḥ śarīram // 27 //

yoneḥ: from the womb; *śarīram*: the body.

iti prathamaḥ khandaḥ

tṛtīyo 'dhyāyaḥ

23. *[The descent of the soul from one level to another occurs] at intervals that are not widely separated, [there being on this matter] a specific declaration.*[12]

24. *[The souls which descend go to those places] occupied by others, as was previously stated [by the Śruti].*[13]

25. *If [it is said] that [the ritual sacrifice of an animal is] impure, [the reply is that] this is not so on the basis of scriptural authority.*[14]

26. *Then, the joining with the one that is fulfilling the act of generation.*

27. *From the womb the [new] body.*

The being that comes down again from the lunar world on account of residual *karma* enters the womb of the woman who is providing a new instrument or body to bring to completion the cycle of the effects of *karma*.

However, there is no kind of *karma* or effect which can produce any modification in the 'constant' or the *Ātman*.

Although the *jīva* may experience intelligible vital expressions and, with its reflection also sensible expressions, its reality and identity always remain beyond all experiential contingency. *Karma* refers to the individualized being governed by the *ahaṁkāra* (ego sense) and can be resolved by proposing a force which is equal and opposite: hate with Love, the various vices, which create disorder to oneself and to others, with virtues and so on. *Karma* is not absolute.

End of Chapter One of Book Three
of the Brahmasūtra

NOTES

[1] III.I.1 - The *Śruti* declares:

'When this *Ātmā* comes to the loss of strength and it seems as fallen into darkness, then these *prāṇas* draw near. By calling to itself these elements of light, it withdraws within its very heart. When the spirit of the eyes withdraws from all parts, then it no longer distinguishes colours. [The function of sight] is then unified [with the subtle vehicle]; therefore they say: 'it no longer sees."

[The function of smell] is then unified [...]; therefore they say: "no longer smells." [The function of taste] is then unified [...]; therefore they say: "no longer tastes." [The function of speech] is then unified [...]; therefore they say: "no longer speaks." [The function of hearing] is then unified; [...] therefore they say: "no longer hears." [The function of the mind] is then unified [...]; therefore they say: "no longer thinks." [The function of touch] is then unified [...]; therefore they say: "no longer touches." [The function of cognition] is then unified [...]; therefore they say: 'it lacks knowledge." In truth, the topmost point of its heart shines and from this the *Ātmā* detaches itself either through the eye or through the top of the head or through other parts of the body and, when that [the *jīva*] goes forth, the *prāṇa* follows it; and when the [prime] *prāṇa* leaves the body, all the *prāṇas* follow it. It [the *jīva*] becomes imbued with the consciousness [of the fruits in the form of latent impressions] and, by identifying itself exactly with this consciousness, it follows it [in acquiring a new body]. Knowledge and action, together with past experience, follow it [after death].'

'This is just as a caterpillar on a blade of grass which, on reaching the blade-top, withdraws within itself to move on to another [blade] and go forward; similarly this *ātmā*, on giving up this body after making it insentient, withdraws within itself to move on to another [body] and go forward.'

'This is just as a goldsmith who, taking some of [the gold] from some jewels, fashions from it a new and more beautiful form, so this *ātmā*, when it has shaken off the body and made it insentient, shapes a new and more beautiful form suited to [the world] of the Fathers, or of the *Gandharvas*, or of the *Devas*, or of *Prajāpati*, or of the *Brahman*, or of other beings.'[1]

[2] III.I.5 - In the *Chāndogya Upaniṣad* (V.III.3) we read:

' "Do you know why the water is called man at the fifth offering?' ' "In truth, O Lord, I do not." '

Later (V.IV.2) it is stated:

'In that, in such fire, the Gods sacrifice faith. From that offering the shining Soma comes forth.'

It would seem that there is a difference between water and faith, but by the term faith the intention is always to signify water.

In the *Taittirīya Saṁhitā* (I.VI.8-9) we read:

'... faith (*śraddhā*) is indeed water.'

In the *Anugītā* we read:

---

[1] *Bṛ.* IV.IV.1-4.

> 'Water indeed generates faith in him to fulfil those ritual acts suited to the earning of merit.'

On the other hand, faith is a conscious attitude and cannot be offered as a sacrificial act.

[3] III.I.6 - The reference is to the *Chāndogya Upaniṣad*, where it is stated:

> '... from the months the year, from the year the sun, from the sun the moon, from the moon the lightning. There a being, non-human by nature, leads them to [the world of] *Brahmā*. This is the way of the Gods.'
>
> 'Then, these who stay in the village, who are devoted to sacrificial rites, to humanitarian acts and to charitable deeds, and so on, they reach the smoke: from the smoke [they reach] the night, from night the other fortnight, from the other fortnight the sixth months [of the descending solar movement that is] the southern one. These do not reach the year.'[1]

By this road they go to the world of the ancestors, *pitṛloka*; this is the road called *pitṛyāna*.

In his commentary Śaṅkara says: 'And "To those who fulfil the sacrifices, and so on," belongs directly the same water in the form of butter, milk, and so on, which are the items required for the celebration of sacrificial rites such as those called *agnihotra*... and so on, by virtue of its prevalence in the natures [of liquids] compared to solid substance. When such substances are placed as offerings into the *āhavanīya* [fire], they become the subtle [vehicles] of the sacrifices which convey merit and by means of which they go and take up their posi-

---

[1] *Chā*. V.X.2-3.

tions within those who fulfil these sacrifices... Thus that same consecrated water, that is, the offerings of liquid substances which form an integral part of the ritual of those sacrifices for the fulfilment of which faith is absolutely indispensable, becomes the vehicle of the power evoked through the actual celebration of those rites and, enveloping the individual selves which have undertaken [in life] the sacrificial acts mentioned below, leads them towards the next existence with the aim of making possible for them the enjoyment of the fruits [of the rites undertaken]... It is thus perfectly legitimate to consider that the individual selves depart [from the body] enveloped by water, that is, by the oblations which have the same nature as water, that they may experience [in another existence] the fruits obtained on the completion of the rites.'[1]

This is the road called *pitṛyāna*.

[4] III.I.8 - Having marked out the pathway called *pitṛyāna*, the second topic explains the reasons for movement along this pathway. Thus, according to the philosophy of the *Śruti* and the *Smṛti*, when the actions which have been fulfilled have run their course the reflection of the embodied *jīva*, after leaving the gross physical body, returns to a new existence under the impulse of the residual unresolved *karma*.

The objector maintains that all beings which follow the way called *pitṛyāna* or the way called *devayāna* resume an embodiment in order to remove the unresolved *karma*.

The *Brahmasūtra* does not agree with this thesis. Those who have followed the path called *devayāna* do not return because, having resolved the residual *karma*, they are on the

---

[1] *Bra. Sū.* III.I.6 with the *bhāṣya* of Śaṅkara. Op. cit.

road which leads to the *Brahman*. See the passage from the *Chāndogya Upaniṣad* (V.X.2) that was quoted earlier.

'*Karma* has a cosmic as well as a psychological aspect. Every deed must produce its natural effect in the world; at the same time it leaves an impression or forms a tendency in the mind of man. It is this tendency or *saṁskāra* or *vasanā* that inclines us to repeat the deed we have once done. So all deeds have their fruits in the world and effects on the mind. So far as the former are concerned, we cannot escape them, however much we may try. But in regard to mental tendencies, we can control them. Our future conduct holds all possibilities.'[1]

The six enemies of the being (*ariṣadvarga*) are: *kāma*: desire, longing; *krodha*: anger, wrath, violence; *moha*: delusion, attachment; *lobha*: greed, cupidity; *mada*: pride, haughtiness; *mātsarya*: envy, jealousy.

Transmigration does not occur because some maleficent God forces us now into one place and now into another; now to suffer and now to enjoy; or anything of the kind. It is we ourselves who produce causes (good or bad, or, rather, harmonious or inharmonious in relation to certain universal laws), and on the plane of becoming it is natural for every cause to produce an effect. Love attracts love, hatred attracts hatred; a thought is something tangible because it is qualified energy with tendencies which the being itself produces; a thought or an emotion (*vṛtti*) can be perceived by an individual and can affect the individual's unconscious.

The potent contents of a solidified thought confine us within subtle levels and make us return to the world ('from

---

[1] S. Radhakrishnan, *La Filosofia Indiana* Vol. 1, Ch. IV, "La filosofia delle *Upaniṣad*" p. 227. Op. cit.

which it departed', as the *sūtra* says). Human beings are the arbiters of their own destinies, according to the direction they wish to give to their thoughts and hence to their actions. A society is the result of the persistence of the thoughts held by a people or by the whole of humanity: 'As ye sow, so shall ye reap', say the Christian Scriptures.[1]

Karma is not the 'law of retaliation', because God does not punish or condemn, give rewards or bestow gifts. It is humanity in its entirety that is responsible for its own evolution. And it is not in a position to condemn any one person exclusively for its own misdeeds, because all beings have contributed to the cultural formation of any such person. If the 'collective unconscious' is characterised by ignorance, violence, envy, and many other such features, it is because all the other individuals in a context of this kind are responsible for the formation of these inharmonious qualities.

No being is absolutely cut off from other beings, for if it were it could not even communicate; this consideration is sufficient to make it clear that each has some responsibility with regard to another, and the two are inter-related by a continuous transference of thoughts, emotions, and acts which influence the collective unconscious in a negative way or in a positive way. Society is the generalised expression of the dominant *culture* of its own particular period of time.

In the sub-human kingdoms there is no self-awareness; there is simply consciousness, and it is the species which directs its own evolution through its own actions. In a human being there is self-awareness, and thus there is born in him the sense of individual responsibility; he is the one who governs his own development, his own progress, and his own acts;

---

[1] Paul, *Letter to the Galatians* VI.7; Luke, VII.18; John, IV.38.

he is responsible for himself, for his own kind, and for the whole of nature. No God punishes or rewards him, but man punishes or rewards himself in accordance with the direction impressed on his own *guṇas*.

All the higher and lower *lokas*, such as the terrestrial world, are 'states of consciousness.' Every being goes therefore to where his heart takes him, to be what he is. A being can raise itself to the glory of Bliss and completeness, just as it can lower itself into the most abominable depths of a *loka*. It has intelligence, feelings, and intuitions. It can create a harmonious world directed by its creative intelligence, just as it can create a world of horrible brutality, darkening its own intelligence and its own positive creative powers and finally losing the dignity of *homo sapiens*.[1]

[5] III.I.9 - In the *Chāndogya Upaniṣad* we read:

'Those who have had a meritorious life conduct, in truth, will, in this way, obtain a favourable birth... On the other hand, those who have performed unworthy deeds here, they will, in truth, obtain an unfavourable birth... .'[2]

Again, in the *Bṛhadāraṇyaka Upaniṣad* we read:

'As one acts and behaves, so one becomes. By doing good, one becomes good. By acting wrongly, one becomes wrong.'[3]

It may be thought from this that present conduct and residual *karma* are two different things, so that it would not seem that the re-birth of a being comes about through the

---

[1] For further consideration on this topic, see 'Final notes to the *Upanisad*' in the volume *Upaniṣad*, by Raphael. Bompiani, Milan, Italy.

[2] *Chā*. V.X.7.

[3] *Bṛ*. IV.IV.5.

operation of a residual *karma* (*saṁcitakarma*); Kārṣṇājini the Sage maintains, on the contrary, that it is current conduct (the present life) that is the cause of future *karma*, which corresponds to the residual *karma* that, in its turn, will be the cause of embodiment in accordance with the nature of the *guṇas* of the being.

[6] III.I.10 - Again, if it is said that, accepting present conduct as the effect of residual *karma*, current behaviour (the present life), even if good, loses its specific meaning, Kārṣṇājini the Sage replies that this does not represent the correct interpretation of the *Śruti*; in fact, an individual's conduct is precisely what determines the *karma*.

This is also expressed in the *Vasiṣṭha Smṛti* (VI.3): 'The *Vedas* do not purify the man who has not observed right conduct.'

Hence the study and contemplation of the *Vedas* depend on a birth that has been predetermined by previous conduct, that is, by residual *karma*.

[7] III.I.12 - The objector declares that all can go to the realm of the moon, even those who commit acts that are contrary to the sacred law.

In the *Kauṣītakī Upaniṣad* (I.2) we read:

'... In truth those who leave this world, all these certainly go [to the sphere of] the Moon (*candramaḥ*)... .'

It would seem from this simple quotation that, after leaving this physical plane, all must go without exception to the realm of the moon, whether they have any merits or not. But the reply given by Bādarāyaṇa is that the same *Upaniṣad* (I.2-3) speaks of two paths: one leading to the celestial world (*devayāna*) and one relating to the world of the ancestors (*pitṛyāna*), from which there is a return to embodiment. These are the two paths which have been mentioned earlier.

There is a third way, which is separate from the two already mentioned, where rebirth is of a decisively lower order.

[8] III.I.16 - According to the *Purānas* (*Smṛti*), there are seven infernal worlds, the first of which is *Raurava*; in these worlds dwell those who have committed acts against others and against universal life.

It was said earlier that those who had not performed sacrifices went to the dwelling of *Yama* (the god of death); the objector now maintains that there are other worlds, such as that of *Raurava*, so that *Yama* has no dominion over these worlds. The *Brahmasūtra*, however, maintains that there is no contradiction, because *Yama* governs these worlds, too, and the *Smṛti* itself shows that *Citragupta*, for example, and the other infernal rulers are dependent on *Yama*.

[9] III.I.17 - The problem, however, is that posed by the 'two ways': *devayāna* and *pitṛyāna*. The third way (a mention was made earlier, in the commentary to *sūtra* 12) is that described also by the *Śruti*.

In the *Chāndogya Upaniṣad* we read:

> '... Do you know where the two ways, the way of the Gods and the way of the ancestors, diverge?... .'[1]

> 'Then, those, who [proceed by] neither of these two ways, become small beings who continuously transmigrate [subject to the divine order]: [now] be born! [now] die! This is the third condition. This is why that world is never filled.'[2]

---

[1] *Chā*. V.III.2.

[2] *Ibid*. V.X.8.

The last statement is in reply to the question (*Chā*. V.III.3): 'Do you know why yonder world is never filled? No, Lord.'

[10] III.I.18 - The reference is to the *Chāndogya Upaniṣad* (V.IX.1), where it is said:

'Thus, truly, at the fifth oblation the water is named man. Enveloped by a membrane, this embryo, after resting within [the mother's womb] for ten months, or nine or however long [it may be needed], it is, hence, born.'[1]

As far as this state of consciousness is concerned, the 'third way' described earlier is inapplicable. Those who have complied with all the sacred rites, all the *dharmas* incumbent upon the benevolent and compassionate person, acquire such merits that the situation of the 'third way' (see the commentary to *sūtra* 17) does not apply.

[11] III.I.19 - The *Smṛti*, moreover, confirms that in some cases the number of oblations has had no importance. For example, Drona, Sītā, and Draupadī, among others, had a human birth without having human parents, and in their case there was no oblation offered in the maternal womb. There are also births by parthenogenesis.

In the *Chāndogya Upaniṣad* (VI.III.1) we also read:

'Of those, who are these very beings, there are only three seeds: birth from an egg, birth from a living matrix, or birth from a sprout.'

In this last type of birth are included those that are born from heat and moisture, and thus from earth and water.

[12] III.I.23 - In the *Chāndogya Upaniṣad* there is the step-

---

[1] *Chā*. V.IX.1.

by-step descent of the soul from the world of the moon to the world of the earth:

> 'From the months [they go] to the world of the Fathers, from the world of the Fathers to the [intermediate] space, from the [intermediate] space to the moon: this is King *Soma*... Having lived in that [world] until the relapse [due to the exhaustion of the fruit], they come back again by the same way by which [they had ascended] to the [intermediate] space; and from the [intermediate] space [each one of them reaches] the air, once he has become air he becomes smoke, once he has become smoke he becomes a clear cloud.'[1]

The objector may think that the soul acquires the specific nature of space or ether, of the wind, or of the rain, and so on.

According to the *Brahmasūtra*, this does not reflect the teaching; the soul does not change its nature to become wind or space and so forth. The value of these references lies in illustrative similarity. It may therefore be said that the physical body is the element of earth, the emotional body is the element of water, the mental body is the element of air, and the *buddhi* is the element of fire.

These correlations are justified; *sūtra* 22 asserts that this is 'conformable to reason.'

[13] III.I.24 - The objector considers that the *Śruti* clearly indicates that the soul becomes smoke, rain, barley, sesame, and so on, in accordance with the description given in the *Chāndogya Upaniṣad* (V.X.6). The reply given by the *Brahmasūtra* is that in this case, too, as has been stated earlier, it is a question

[1] *Chā.* V.X.4-5.

of comparisons, of simple similarity or correlation. Thus it may be said that a being that is completely identified with its own physical body is considered to be 'food' and nothing more. There is, moreover, not a single statement saying that the being must become rain, or anything else, on account of residual *karma*.

[14] III.I.25 - The slaughter of an animal as a sacrificial ritual is not held by the *Śruti* to be impure. The *Śruti* gives us to understand that an action may become pure or impure in relation to the *motive* of the person undertaking it. A sacrifice (*karman*) offered to the gods and conducted by a properly qualified person who sacrifices an animal with all due ritual, at the right time, in circumstances favourable to the animal, and with the correct ceremony given to the animal itself, does not constitute an impure act. Furthermore, this is always an exception which may even benefit the actual animal through the merit which it acquires. In this kind of ceremonial ritual there is no violence, no motive of killing for its own sake, no desire for revenge, and nothing else that might constitute a despicable deed. On the other hand, these aspects, not being invested with a universal nature or anything that constitutes the eternal Truth which transcends contingent actions, can become modified with the passage of time; thus, ritual ceremony itself can undergo modification since it belongs to the realm of the sensible and the relative. Supreme Reality alone is not subject to change or modifications in time and space.

Introductory Considerations on Chapters Two, Three and Four of Book Three

The themes under consideration may be summarised in the following points:

1) The journey of the *jīva* on the plane of manifestation continues to be outlined.

2) The problem of the states of waking, dreaming, and dreamless sleep is raised: the three states of Being.

3) The nature of the *Brahman* (*nirguṇa* and *saguṇa*). Identity of the *jīva* and *Ātman*, the *Ātman* and *Brahman*.

4) *Neti neti* ('Not this, not this').

5) Meditations forming the final act.

6) Observances prescribed by the *Śruti* and *Smṛti*.

I. The *jīva*, which stands for the soul, is the intermediary between the *Ātman* and individuality, between the intelligible and the sensible. The *jīva* holds the key: if it turns its gaze towards the sensible world it enters, with its reflection or ray, the state of individuality; on the other hand, if it looks towards the intelligible it enters into identity with the *Ātman*, its metaphysical source.

Because of the clouding produced by *rajas*, *tamas*, the ray or embodied reflection of the *jīva* is constrained to produce movement, action, causes, and therefore effects. *Karma* is nothing other than the assimilation of the *ahaṁkāra* to cause and effect, to action and result. There is action that conforms to universal principles, and there is also action that conforms to egoistical impulses of a purely individual and separatist nature dominated by the duality of *I* and *you*, subject and object. In accordance with the direction followed by the being, it can find itself in bondage or in freedom. What determines the bondage, therefore, is identification with an idea and with its expression through action and with the subsequent results. As long as one is overburdened with individualised qualities, there will be transmigration through the various levels of consciousness in which these qualities can find expression. The unresolved crystallised qualities (*guṇas*) strive to find expression and fulfilment by dragging in the agent as well. In this way, one is wherever one's own *guṇas* direct the attention; this is a law which is particularly evident in everyday life.

Hence the path called *devayāna* and the path called *pitṛyāna*. The latter leads to the 'sphere of the moon'; it does not lead to liberation but to new states of individuality.

II. *Vedānta* expounds three states: waking, dreaming, and deep sleep or dreamless sleep. These correspond to the three states of Being: *Virāṭ*, *Hiranyagarbha*, and *Īśvara*; and, at the individual level, to *viśva*, *taijasa*, and *prājña*.

According to the *Brahmasūtra*, the waking state is not identical to the dreaming state because they do not coincide in time or space. Dream, however, is not total illusion, for the subject perceives something, and the dream can often even modify the waking state of consciousness.

In his commentary to the *Brahmasūtra*, Śaṅkara agrees with the statement made by Bādarāyaṇa the Teacher. Gauḍapāda, on the other hand, the Teacher of Śaṅkara's Teacher, maintains in his *kārikā* to the *Māṇḍūkya Upaniṣad* that the waking and dreaming states are identical. But in the final analysis there is no contradiction. *Śaṅkara*, for his part, is careful not to identify the waking state with the dreaming state in order to avoid validating the thesis of *Yogācāras*, who assert that the world of waking is a mere projection made by the *subject*, which is exactly what happens in dream.

In this context, however, Gauḍapāda adopts a different perspective. If one compares the three conditions of waking, dreaming, and deep sleep from the state of the *nirguṇa Brahman*, one sees the inconsistency of the three states and therefore of the entire manifestation (quantity and quality).

Adopting the position of this final state, one may say that existence with form is nothing other than a 'dream' of *Īśvara* which has a beginning and an end. One then has a 'waking dream', a 'dream of the dreamer', and a 'dreamless sleep' where the sleeper rests within himself, this being a 'seminal sleep' (*bījanidrā*: seed-sleep).

According to the point of view adopted, there may be diversity among the three states or there may also be uniformity.

The *Śruti* says:

> 'The *Brāhmana*, having recognised that the different worlds are [the result] of [unresolved] *karma*, distances himself from them, [recognising that] it is impossible to attain that which is eternal (*akṛta* = non-produced) through that which is perishable.'

In his *kārikā* Gauḍapāda declares:

> 'Just as in the dreaming state the mind presents the appearance of duality, through the movement of *māyā* [subject

and object], so in the waking state the mind, through the same movement or *māyā*, seems to produce duality.

'There is no doubt that in dream the mind, although single, appears as dual [subject and object]; in the same way, in the waking state the mind, although single, appears as dual.'

'Non-conceptual Knowledge, which is birthless, is not different from the knowable. The knowable *Brahman* is eternal and unborn [therefore] the unborn knows the unborn.'[1]

According to Gauḍapāda, the mind is the cause of differentiation, but this condition is merely apparent because it has no absolute value: in absolute terms, there is only *That*. It may be said that Gauḍapāda, as was previously suggested, assumes the metaphysical standpoint of the Unborn (*ajāti*); Bādarāyaṇa examines the two states (waking and dreaming) from an empirical standpoint.

Furthermore, it is impossible to assert that the philosophy of Gauḍapāda the Teacher, being in conformity with the *Śruti*, can be considered to be a *subjectivist* teaching similar to that of the Buddhist *Vijñānavāda* and opposed to that of the *Brahmasūtra* considered to be objectivist.

The Subject of which Gauḍapāda speaks is not at the psychological level but transcends all psychological expression. Knowledge or Consciousness itself does not stand for a mental empirical concept. The Subject, which is the *Ātman*, is of the same nature as the *Brahman*, so that the sole 'object' of Knowledge remains *That*.

'The non-alterity of the *jīva* with the *Ātman* is taught by means of [their] non-distinction, while what is multiplic-

---

[1] *Mā. Kā.* III.29,30 and 33.

> ity is condemned; this may be understood [only if one considers non-duality].'[1]

With regard to this whole subject, when the *Śruti* states '*Brahman* is pure consciousness' it is good to reflect that such knowledge does not belong to the individualised psychological level, and not even to the universal level, since the *Brahman* transcends all subjectivist and objectivist factors. It may be said that even terms such as 'knowledge' and 'consciousness' are names that are always applied to the *Brahman* from the mental perspective of relationship. *Brahman* is that through which knowledge and consciousness and all other elements are enabled to *be* and to function, but That transcends the knower, the knowledge, and the object of knowledge. Sometimes the *Brahman* is given names such as *ākāśa*, *prāṇa*, and *puruṣa*, but applying a name to the *Brahman* can open the door to ambiguities and can thus be a digression. The *Brahman* is frequently denoted by the single word *That*, which may be more suitable, or by *neti neti*. With regard to this, some words from the *kārikā* of Gauḍapāda are significant:

> 'Those who know the *prāṇa* call *prāṇa* [the reality or *Ātman*]. Those who know the *bhūtas*, call the *bhūtās* reality. Those who know the *guṇas*, call the *guṇas* reality or *Ātman*. Those who know the *tattvas*, call the *tattvas* reality or *Ātman*... Those who know the objects of the senses regard the objects of the senses as *Ātman*. The knowers of the *lokas* consider the *lokas* to be *Ātman*.... And those who do not believe in any form call the formless reality.'[2]

With regard to this whole subject see the commentary of

---

[1] *Mā. Kā.* III.13.

[2] *Ibid.* II.20-23 *et seqq.*

Śaṅkara to *sūtra* 5 of the *Bṛhadāraṇyaka Upaniṣad* II.III.5. See also what has been said in the 'Appendix' of Book Two, Chapter Two.

This suggests that the being seeks to give name and form to *That* in accordance with the mental viewpoint that he has assumed. In these few lines from the *kārikā* (as in others that follow) Gauḍapāda, with extreme simplicity, refers to various conceptions and conceptualisations, such as the hylozoistic theory, the subjectivist or psychological theory (subjective realism), the theory which considers the external world to be real (objective realism), and the theory which considers mere emptiness to be real. This makes it clear that Gauḍapāda, in this context, places himself exclusively in the *nirguṇa* position, where all theoretical dualistic formulations are transcended.

The very term *Ātman* always remains a concept, and Gauḍapāda could have gone on to say, 'Those who believe in the *Ātman* consider the *Ātman* to be reality', so that the theory of the *anātman* (the non-existence of the *Ātman*) which is held by some schools of thought has no meaning when seen from the viewpoint of Gauḍapāda. The *Ātman* is *not* reality as we understand reality, but is that which this word relates to noetic intuition.

> 'It is not conscious-knower of the internal [world], it is not conscious of the external world; nor it is conscious-knower of both of them, it is not a homogeneous unity of consciousness-knowledge, it is not either conscious or non-conscious; it is invisible, not agent, incomprehensible [to the senses], indefinable, inconceivable, indescribable; it is the sole essence of consciousness as *Ātman*; without any trace of manifestation; it is pacified, beneficial, non-dual.

> [The Wise] consider it the Fourth. That is the *Ātman* and as such must be known.'[1]

> 'It is beyond Being. "That which is beyond Being" does not express "something" – because it posits absolutely no determined thing – and it does not even express Its name, but conveys nothing but a negative suggestion: "It is not this... ." And even this name, the One, is nothing but the negation of multiplicity... Only by stripping It of everything, stating nothing about It, nor by saying, untruthfully, that It is something, we are left with nothing but the monosyllable 'is', without giving any evidence of its non-existent attributes... If you are looking for this Principle, do not look for anything outside of It but look for things that come after It; but as for It, leave It in peace!... It is ineffable and indescribable. We are, nevertheless, speaking and writing in order to point towards It, to awake from the sleep of words to the wakefulness of Vision, and, as it were, to show the path to anyone who desires to see something... .'[2]

Thus *Brahman*, *jīva*, *Īśvara* and so on are names which designate that which transcends name itself; it is common to speak of principle as a reference point, as a founding element, or as something which contains within itself something else's reason for existence.

> 'The Tao which can be called Tao
> is not the eternal Tao.
> The name which can be named
> is not the eternal name.

---

[1] *Mā*. VII.

[2] Plotinus, *Enneads* V.5.VI,XIII; VI.8.XVIII; VI.9.IV, edited by G.Faggin. Op. cit.

Nameless, it is the beginning of heaven and earth.'[1]

On the other hand, it is impossible to exclude the Reality which supports the world of phenomena, or appearances, and of knowledge itself, just as it is impossible to exclude the being as the ultimate factor that is conscious of mental dichotomies and so on. To exclude that uncaused Reality which gives *esse* to all that comes after, means to fall into fathomless nihilism. The common statement 'Everything is relative' or everything is impermanent' is never more than a merely relative affirmation.

Gauḍapāda the Teacher, in conformity with the *Śruti*, viewed the whole of manifestation as 'appearance'[2], but behind the appearance is the single Reality which is *That*. The light of a candle is nothing when compared to the light of a thousand suns shining together.

III. Moving to the question of *saguṇa Brahman* and *nirguṇa Brahman*, the *Śruti* presents both aspects, but without professing philosophic dualism. Various views of the supreme Truth are expounded in the *Śruti*, implying that it is not a teaching that is exclusive, unilateral, and absolutist. The *Śruti* addresses all potential disciples, with different qualifications and states of consciousness varying with time and space, and hence there are many ways, giving rise to the six *darśanas*, which are different, but not opposing, interpretative aspects of the same subject (*Brahman*).

From the philosophic viewpoint we thus have dualism, monism, and non-duality. The result is that the *Śruti* embraces the totality of metaphysical Non-Being, ontological Being, and non-being or appearance. The *Śruti* begins from a conviction

---

[1] Lao-Tse, *Tao Tê Ching* 1. Sansoni, Florence, Italy.

[2] Regarding appearace, see what comes later.

which needs no proof. 'I exist, I am, I perceive' constitute evidence which does not require proof, as it is incontrovertible. This statement is therefore correct, but the reference attributed to that 'I am' may be mistaken, because it may, for example, be defined as 'I am the physical body, I am nothing but thought', and so on, which implies reducing the totality of the being's existence and expression.

Thus the *Śruti* represents the indication of an experience which consists first of all in re-discovering unity or wholeness within oneself, resolving the split, and hence integrating that unity with the universal Unity and then with the metaphysical Unity. The philosophy of the *Upaniṣads* thus aims at re-discovering oneself for what one is, then at knowing the Being as one's foundation. And it is good to repeat that this reality is not an object of speculation for the mind, but it can be called, even if the term is improper, an object of *experience* (*anubhava*). If one wishes to know oneself, one cannot objectify a mental image of what one is (duality) and speculate on such an image. Self-knowledge is an experience of direct consciousness in which there is little or no place for the mind (See Book Three II.24).

> 'You cannot see the seer of sight; you cannot hear the listener of hearing; you cannot think the thinker of thought; you cannot know the knower of knowledge. This is your *ātmā*, which is within everything... .'[1]

> 'That, therefore, which provides the truth to known things and the faculty of knowing them to the knower, you should say that it is the Idea of the Good. And since it is the cause of knowledge and truth, hold it as knowable... And while as for the light and sight it is right to hold that

---

[1] *Bṛ.* III.IV.2.

they resemble the sun, but it is not right to hold them as sun, so also here it is right to consider them both similar to the Good, but to think of either of them as the Good is not right, because the condition of the Good must be held as even greater!'[1]

According to some schools of thought, reality is the phenomenal world, the world devoured by time; but according to the *Śruti*, birthless Reality, unmoved, unconditioned (in Plato's expression, ἀνυπόθετον, *Republic* VI.510b), which is and does not become, is the Being which we ourselves are, the Being which is of the same nature as the supreme Being (non-duality), which is the metaphysical foundation by means of which everything can be and without which nothing can be.

IV. The interlocutor may ask whether *neti neti* applies to the *Brahman* or to the sensible world, or to both, and whether it applies absolutely or relatively.

Neti neti cannot be referred to the *Brahman* as if It were not real; on the contrary, it means that no names can be given to the *Brahman* and that the *Brahman* cannot be conceptualised; and if someone declares that the *Brahman* is this or that, the answer can be made: *neti neti*, the *Brahman* is not this. The *Brahman* transcends 'yes' and 'no'; and since the *Brahman* is without form, categories relating to the sensible world are inapplicable. *Neti neti* must thus refer to the manifest world, but must such referral be understood absolutely, with the meaning that the 'second' (*nāma-rūpa*) has no reality at all?

Or is it necessary to accord a certain degree of truth to the 'second'? The *Brahmasūtra* puts forward this last suggestion. But *Brahman* is *not* the 'second', because the 'second' has no

---

[1] Plato, *Republic* VI.508-509. Sansoni, Florence, Italy.

ontological status: it is always related to its foundation, the *Brahman*. The 'snake', to give the classic example, is always related to the 'rope.' The 'second' is the *appearance* viewed from the a-temporal and therefore metaphysical standpoint. 'Appearance' is a frequently used term in both East and West. Parmenides, too, speaks of appearance (τά δοκοῦντα: current opinions, things subject to the process of becoming).

Appearance is everything which *appears* on the plane of manifestation and which, having no independent reason for its existence or any intrinsic reality, disappears. Being, insofar as it is and does not become, is not appearance. Appearances are its instruments or bodies by means of which it may find expression, although it itself transcends all expression. If being, too, were obliged to belong to the nature of appearances, there would be mere nihilism.

Being, the *jīvātman* or *Noûs*, does not emerge from the void or nothingness and does not return to nothingness, because the *Brahman*, and hence the *Ātman*, is the sole metaphysical Reality, around which revolve all appearances, both microcosmic and macrocosmic.

If we have recourse to the Eleatic – as an exponent of the Tradition (Parmenides is considered to be a Pythagorean; in fact, he was very much associated with Ameinias the Pythagorean, who, it is held, was his Teacher) – we find that the Goddess shows him what is to be understood by intelligible truth or reality, but she is able to do this because Parmenides has truth or reality within himself; for if he did not, he could never assimilate something that was not in his nature.[1] Moreover, she also shows what is to be understood by 'opinion' or the world of appearances, that world made of 'name and form' (in *Vedānta*: *nāma* and *rūpa*) which appears and disappears and which human beings confuse with that which is a-temporal Being.

> 'For it [Being] will be names, all of those things that the mortals decided, convinced that they were true.'[2]

In other words, they regard appearances (the snake) as truth, failing to recognise their real foundation, which is supreme Truth (the rope). This leads to the process of making the relative absolute, with the consequent corollary of nihilism. On the other hand, if the Goddess herself imparts to Parmenides also that which represents the world of appearances, this implies that these 'appearances' must have their own degree of truth, because according to the Eleatic himself, 'nothingness is not' (fg. 6.2), and if it is not it cannot even be spoken of. It can be said that the 'appearances' are such when compared to Being. Thus the vision of Parmenides, put forward by the Goddess, is, like that of the Vedic *Ṛṣis*, which was received through the 'supra-sensory eye', not nihilistic, not objective or subjective, not idealistic or pantheistic. The same can be said of Śaṅkara's *Vedānta* and Gauḍapāda's *Asparśavāda*, and thus of the *Brahmasūtra*. Therefore the world, the offspring of time and causality, has its own degree of relative truth (Śaṅkara states that the world is not like 'the horns of a hare or the

---

[1] It may be said that Parmenides, having received the indication of that unique Way (ὁδός) that leads to the recognition of the 'well rounded truth', has seen Truth as the *Ṛṣis* of the *Vedas* have *seen* it. *Veda* comes from the root *vid* = to see with the intelligible eye, just as for Plato ἰδέα comes from ἰδεῖν which means 'to see' in metaphysical terms.

[2] Parmenides, *On the Order of Nature*, fg. 8. Op. cit.

son of a barren woman,' meaning that it is not nothingness or nothing, 'nothingness is not'), and this relativity can be predicated on account of that omnipresent foundation which gives it the possibility of being predicated. And the two terms are not interchangeable: in fact, the *Śruti* maintains that the world of phenomenal appearances seems like a trickle of water, a snake, a stick, and so on (giving rise to the various opinions held by human beings) because it does not have within itself the nature of being absolute or of being a unity.

> 'When the real nature of the rope (*rajjurūpe*) is known, the semblance of the snake (*sarpa*) vanishes (*khandam*), just as the phenomenal world (*prapañcaḥ*) completely vanishes (*gataḥ*) when its substratum (*adhi-ṣṭhāna*: underlying being) is realised.'[1]

That our solar system is being consumed by time is a fact, but the being – not born and not produced – is the eternal witness of time. And the fact that the *Brahman* or *Ātman* has the nature of omnipresence presupposes that the *Brahman*, unborn, is also the substratum of all temporal existence, the substratum for which there is no duality.

V. Now the question of the different *vidyās* (meditations) is addressed.

Various *sūtras* expound questions intrinsic to particular *vidyās* which occur at definite points in the individual's sphere, or meditations of a ritual nature, etc.

The *Brahmasūtra*, however, maintains that although the *vidyās* are different and arise from different promptings, and although the intention may be emotional, devotional, or of some

---

[1] Śaṅkara, *Aparokśānubhūti*, *sūtra* 96, edited by Raphael. Aurea Vidyā, New York.

other kind, they still have a single point of reference, which is the *Brahman* (*nirguṇa* or *saguṇa*), and a single objective, that of realisation, which may be instantaneous or delayed (*kramamukti*). Hence there are no absolute differences or divergent aims; but there are numerous *vidyās* to cater for the needs of the neophyte (See Book III.III.9-11.28). It can be said that the means are many, while the end, or final aim, is one.

This subject is fully dealt with in Chapter Four.

VI. Now, the first *sūtra* of Chapter Four enunciates an ineluctable fact: the aim of human existence, according to the Scriptures, is to pursue that Knowledge which unlocks the 'tragic drama' of duality in which the human being appears. The whole tradition, be it Eastern or Western, has the aim of leading the individual to self-discovery; it is the message of the Pythia spoken of also by Plato.

> 'From non-being lead me to Being;
> From darkness lead me to Light;
> From death lead me to Immortality.'
>
> '*asatomāsadgamaya*
> *tamasomājyotirgamaya*
> *mṛtyormā 'mṛtaṁgamaya*.'[1]

This is the song of the being which, on awakening, turns towards the liberating Wisdom.

The following *sūtras* deal with the question of whether Knowledge by itself can lead to full liberation or whether ritual action is necessary.

The *Brahmasūtra* makes it clear that there is no conflict

---

[1] *Bṛ.* I.III.28.

concerning this question (*sūtra* 26). Thus *Vedānta* does not exclude or oppose ritualism and religious obligations, but it makes it clear that the aim is ever to attain the supreme Reality.

For the seeker of Knowledge, too, certain observances are prescribed, such as mental calm and self-mastery: 'because these are prescribed as aids to that [knowledge, thus] they must necessarily be fulfilled' (*sūtra* 27).

Sūtra 34 states that the duties specific to the various stages of life must be performed both by those who pursue knowledge and by those who follow the practice of Vedic ritual. On this point the *Śruti* and the *Smṛti* are in agreement. Understanding and living the direction of the *Bhagavadgītā* 'to act without acting' would thus be enough to be liberated or realised.

atha tṛtīyo 'dhyāyaḥ

dvitīyaḥ khandaḥ

sandhye śṛṣṭir āha hi //1//

sandhye: in the intermediate state; *śṛṣṭiḥ*: creation, birth; *āha*: it declares; *hi*: because.

nirmātāraṁ caike putrādayaś ca //2//

nirmātāram: he who forms or creates; *ca*: and; *eke*: some; *putraādayaḥ*: sons and so on; *ca*: and.

māyāmātraṁ tu kārtsnyena-ana-bhivyakta svarūpa-tvāt //3//

māyāmātram: pure appearance; *tu*: but, on the other hand; *kārtsnyena*: totally; *ana-bhivyakta*: non-manifestation; *svarūpatvāt*: from essential nature.

sūcakaś ca hi śruter ācakṣate ca tad vidaḥ //4//

sūcakaḥ: indication, sign; *ca*: but; *hi*: because, also; *śruteḥ*: according to the *Śruti*; *ācakṣate*: they declare; *ca*: also; *tat*: that; *vidaḥ*: learned, experienced.

parābhidhyānāt tu tirohitaṁ tato hyasya bandha viparya-yau //5//

para-abhidhyānāt: from meditation on the supreme; *tu*: but; *tirohitam*: unknown, hidden; *tataḥ*: from that; *hi*: because; *asya*: of it, of this; *bandha*: bond, slavery; *viparyayau*: the opposite [that is, liberation].

Book Three

Chapter Two

1. *In the intermediate state [there is effective] creation, for this is what [the Śruti] declares.*[1]

2. *And [according to some], it is he who forms sons and so on.*[2]

3. *But [the intermediate world of dream] is pure appearance; its essential nature is not fully manifested [in the waking state].*[3]

4. *[However, it is not totally illusory] because, according to the Śruti, it is a designation: even those experienced [in dreams] state this.*

On the other hand, if something is perceived in the dream state, it must surely have a certain degree of reality, but one may also have the same condition in the waking state.

Hence one may say that even the dream is not pure illusion: there is something real about it, but it does not have an ontological status within itself and it is not absolute reality.

5. *But [with] the meditation on the Supreme, that which is hidden [is revealed], because from it [arise] bondage and its opposite.*[4]

deha yogād vā so'pi //6//

deha: the body; *yogāt*: from the connection or union; *vā*: or; *saḥ*: that; *api*: also.

tad abhāvo nādīsu tac chruter ātmani ca //7//

tat: that; *a-bhāvaḥ*: non existènce; *nādīsu*: in the *nādī*; *Ātmani*: in the *Ātmā*; *ca*: and; *tat*: that; *śruteḥ*: according to the *Śruti*.

ataḥ prabodho 'smāt //8//

ataḥ: da qui; *prabodhaḥ*: awakening, the act of becoming conscious; *asmāt*: from that.

sa eva tu karmānusmṛti-śabda vidhibhyaḥ //9//

sa eva: that itself; *tu*: but; *karma*: action; *anusmṛti*: recollection, memory; *śabda*: Scripture; *vidhibhyaḥ*: on account of the injunctions.

mugdhe 'rdha sampattiḥ pariśeṣāt //10//

mugdhe: in being deprived of senses; *ardha*: partial; *sampattiḥ*: attainment; *pariśeṣāt*: from what remains or is left.

na sthānato 'pi parasyobhaya liṅgaṁ sarvatra hi //11//

na: not; *sthāna-taḥ*: from place or position; *api*: even; *parasya*: of the Supreme; *ubhaya*: twofold; *liṅgam*: characteristic; *sarvatra*: everywhere; *hi*: because.

6. *Or that [the limitation of the jīva arises] also from union with the body.*

The *jīva*, the reflection of the *Ātman*, is veiled by its direct vehicle, the *buddhi*, which covers its true nature; and thus the reflection, embodied in the three individualised worlds, wanders in conflicting *saṁsāra*, obscured by *kāma*, *manas* and *ahaṁkāra*.

7. *[There is] the non-presence of that in the nāḍīs and in the Ātmā: so the Śruti declares.*[5]

8. *Hence the awakening from That [the Brahman].*[6]

9. *But that same [jīva returns from dreamless sleep] on account of action, recollection, Scripture, and injunctions.*

Unresolved actions of the *jīva*, the recollection of always being a *jīva*, hence a simple reflection of the *Ātman* and not the *Ātman* itself, Scripture, and injunctions: all these produce the understanding that it is a question of the same *jīva* that has practised the observance of Scripture and of ritual injunctions.

10. *[In being] deprived of senses [there is] partial attainment, [this being] what remains.*[7]

11. *Not even on account of a [different] place [can] there be twofold characteristics for the Supreme, for this is the universal [teaching].*[8]

na bhedād iti cen na pratyekam atad vacanāt // 12 //

na: not; *bhedāt*: on account of difference; *iti cet*: if [it is said]; *na*: not; *pratyekam*: each; *a-tad-vacanāt*: on account of the non-declaration of these [differences].

api caivam eke // 13 //

api: moreover; *ca*: and; *evam*: thus; *eke*: some.

arūpavad eva hi tat-pradhānatvāt // 14 //

a-rūpavat: formless, without form; *eva*: indeed; *hi*: because; *tat*: this; *pradhānatvāt*: according to the predominant meaning.

prakāśavac ca-avaiyarthāt // 15 //

prakāśa-vat: like light; *ca*: and; *avaiyarthāt*: on account of not being devoid of meaning or useless.

āha ca tanmātram // 16 //

āha: it declares, affirms; *ca*: and; *tat*: that; *mātram*: state.

12. *If [it is said] that it is not so, on account of the difference [referred to by the Scriptures, the answer is] no, because of the negated declaration of each [difference of quality].*

In some *Śruti* passages there is a mention of difference, but within the same context the difference is then frequently negated.

Some commentators maintain that the duality is admitted by the *Śruti* merely for those who are not yet ready to go beyond individual and universal duality. It is thus an act of comprehension towards those who express religion in terms of worship, adoration, and ritual. (See, for example, the *Bṛhadāraṇyaka Upaniṣad*, II.III.1 *et seqq.*).

This suggests that the *Śruti* offers all its followers the possibility of undertaking the return journey in accordance with their individual qualifications.

13. *And furthermore, some [teach] this.*[9]

14. *Because it is formless: this is the main meaning [of the Śruti].*

Brahman is without form and hence without quality, because it is that by which form has the possibility of existing. The statement in the *sūtra* refers to various scriptural contexts. (See *Chā*. VIII.XIV.1).

15. *And, like light, [the texts are] not devoid of meaning.*[10]

16. *And [the Śruti] declares [that the Brahman is] that state.*

darśayati cātho api smaryate // 17 //

darśayati: it demonstrates, shows; *ca*: and; *athaḥ*: also; *api*: moreover; *smaryate*: the *Smṛti* states.

ata eva copamā sūryakādi-vat // 18 //

ata eva: or this reason, thus; *ca*: also; *upamā*: comparison, likeness; *sūryaka*: sun; *ādi*: and soon; *vat*: like.

ambuvad agrahaṇāt tu na tathātvam // 19 //

ambuvat: like water;; *a-grahaṇāt*: on account of non-perception or non-experience; *tu*: but; *na*: not; *tathātvam*: similarity.

vṛddhi-hrāsa-bhāktvam antar-bhāvād ubhaya sāmañjasyād evam // 20 //

vṛddhi: growth; *hrāsa*: diminution; *bhāktvam*: participating; *antar-bhāvāt*: on account of being within; *ubhaya*: both; *sāmañjasyāt*: on account of similarity; *evam*: thus.

darśanāc ca // 21 //

darśanāt: from the declaration; *ca*: and.

prakṛtaitāvattvaṁ hi pratiṣedhati tato bravīti ca bhūyaḥ // 22 //

prakṛta: said, mentioned; *etāvattvam*: up to this point; *hi*: because; *pratiṣedhati*: denies; *tataḥ*: of this; *bravīti*: says; *ca*: and; *bhūyaḥ*: more.

tadavyaktam āha hi // 23 //

tat: that; *a-vyaktam*: unmanifest; *āha*: afferms; *hi*: because.

17. *[The Śruti], too, and also the Smṛti demonstrate this.*[11]

18. *For this reason [there are] also comparisons, such as the images of the sun [in water], and so on.*

19. *But the similarity [of things being compared is] not [absolute] on account of non-perception [with reference to the Brahman of unseparated substance] as in the case of water.*

20. *[Granted that the Brahman] is within [being the substratum of manifestation into form], it seems to partake of growth and diminution on account of the mutual similarity: [this is indeed] the case.*

In the *Bṛhadāraṇyaka Upaniṣad* (IV.IV.23) we read:

'This [*Ātman*] is the eternal splendour of him who knows the *Brahman*: it is neither increased by any action nor decreased.'

21. *And from the declaration [made by the Scriptures].*[12]

22. *[What has been] said so far [the Śruti] denies, and it says something more about this.*

23. *That [Brahman] is unmanifest, for this is what [the Śruti] states.*[13]

api ca saṁrādhane pratyakṣa anumānābhyām // 24 //

api: also, likewise; *ca*: and; *saṁrādhane*: in deep meditation; *pratyakṣa*: percetion; *anumānābhyām*: deduction.

prakāśādivac cāvaiśeṣyaṁ prakāśaś ca karmaṇi abhyāsāt // 25 //

prakāśa-karmaṇi: light in its activity; *ādi*: and so on; *vat*: like; *ca*: and; *a-vaiśeṣyam*: non differentiation; *abhyāsāt*: from repeated statements.

ato 'nantena tathā hi liṅgam // 26 //

ataḥ: hence, for this reason; *anantena*: with the infinite; *tathā*: thus, so; *hi*: because; *liṅgam*: indication.

ubhaya vyapadeśāt tu ahi-kuṇdalavat // 27 //

ubhaya: double, both; *vyapadeśāt*: from the instruction or designation; *tu*: but; *ahi*: snake; *kuṇdala*: ring, coil; *vat*: like

prakāśāśrayavad vā tejastvāt // 28 //

prakāśa: light; *āśrayavat*: like the substratum or support; *vā*: or; *tejastvāt*: from being luminous.

pūrvavad vā // 29 //

pūrva: preceding; *vat*: like; *vā*: or.

pratiṣedhāc ca // 30 //

pratiṣedhāt: by the denial; *ca*: and.

24. *And also in deep meditation [the Brahman is realised] in accordance with direct perception and deduction.*

The *Brahman*, however, despite being unqualified and unmanifest, can be comprehended and realised through deep meditation or direct recognition, or even through inference, that is, by means of the *Śruti* or the *Smṛti*.

25. *And as [in the case of] light in its activity, and so on, [so within the Brahman there is] non-distinction; [this is confirmed] by repeated statements.*[14]

26. *For this reason [the manifest jīva creates the identity] with the Infinite, because this is what [the Scripture] indicates.*

27. *But [there is] a twofold designation, like [that between] the snake and its coils.*

28. *Or like light and its substratum, since they are [both] luminous.*[15]

29. *Or as previously [expounded].*

Alternatively, the relation must be understood as was previously expounded in *sūtra* 25.

30. *And by the denial.*[16]

Sūtras 31-37 aim at documenting that there is no reality other than the *Brahman*. Hence the *Brahman* is One without a second.

param-ataḥ setūnmāna-sambandha-bheda-vyapade-śebhyaḥ // 31 //

param: beyond, above; *ataḥ*: this; *setu*: embankment; *unmāna*: measure; *sambandha*: connection; *bheda*: separation; *vyapadeśāt*: on account of the designation.

sāmānyāt tu // 32 //

sāmānyāt: by analogy; *tu*: but.

buddhyarthaḥ pādavat // 33 //

buddhyarthaḥ: for comprehension; *pāda*: foot; *vat*: like.

sthāna-viśeṣāt prakāśādivat // 34 //

sthāna: state, condition; *viśeṣāt*: on account of the difference or distinction; *prakāśa*: light; *ādi*: and so on; *vat*: like.

upapatteś ca // 35 //

upapatteḥ: from the reasoning; *ca*: and.

tathānya-pratiṣedhāt // 36 //

tathā: thus; *anya*: other; *pratiṣedhāt*: from the denial or non-acceptance.

anena sarva-gatatvam āyāma śabdādibhyaḥ // 37 //

anena: by means of that; *sarva*: all, entire; *gatatvam*: diffusion, pervasiveness; *āyāma*: extension; *śabdādibhyaḥ*: from the Scriptures, and so on.

31. *Moreover [there is another] on account of the designation of embankment, measure, connection, and separation.*

32. *But [it is only] by analogy.*[17]

33. *[It is solely] for comprehension, like the [four] feet.*

If on occasion something such as a measurement is attributed to the *Brahman*, it is solely to facilitate understanding for the empirical mind that is based on relationship.

Thus the *Chāndogya Upaniṣad* (III.XVIII.2) speaks of *Brahman* as having 'four feet' or parts; it is natural that the *Brahman*, as expounded in the general context of the *Śruti*, cannot possibly have four feet or be divided or measured or contain within itself multiplicity.

34. *[Connection and difference are due] to the difference of state, as in the case of light and so on.*

Again, the relationship of connection and difference refers to the variation in state, as in the case of light that was mentioned previously. Light is always one and undivided, but it appears to be multiple and varied on account of its reflection caused by the different location of the places it is shining upon.

35. *And from the reasoning.*[18]

36. *It is so from the express non-acceptance of [all that is] other [than That].*[19]

37. *By means of that, all-pervasiveness [is declared] in the Scriptures concerning the extension [of the Brahman].*[20]

phalam ata upapatteḥ // 38 //

phalam: fruit, result; *ataḥ*: from Him, from That; *upapatteḥ*: in accordance with reason.

śrutatvāc ca // 39 //

śrutatvāt: from the declaration of the *Śruti*; *ca*: and.

dharmaṁ jaiminir ata eva // 40 //

dharmam: merit, meritorious fruit; *jaiminiḥ*: Jaimini; *ataḥ*: on account of this; *eva*: also.

pūrvaṁ tu bādarāyaṇo hetu vyapadeśāt // 41 //

pūrvam: former, first; *tu*: but, however; *bādarāyaṇaḥ*: Bādarāyaṇa; *hetu*: primary cause; *vyapadeśāt*: on account of the mention.

iti dvitīyaḥ khandaḥ

tṛtīyo 'dhyāyaḥ

38. *From That the fruit: [this is] reasonable.*[21]

39. *And as the Śruti states.*

This is the teaching of the *Śruti*. Hence, not only can we use reasoning and analogies to understand that nothing can subsist without That, but the Scriptures are also there to confirm it.

40. *For this [reason], too, Jaimini [thinks that] religious merit [generates the fruits].*

This is why Jaimini the Teacher thinks that religious merit generates the fruits of action that is in conformity with the Scriptures.

The thesis of Jaimini, according to which the fruit comes *only* from *dharma*, is accepted only inasmuch as this *dharma* is not limited solely to ritual action, which would thus lead to the belief that *dharma* might be the primary and absolute cause of the fruit. Without That there can be neither *dharma* nor fruit.

41. *However, Bādarāyaṇa [thinks that It is] the first [to be] mentioned [as] the cause [of actions].*[22]

End of Chapter Two of Book Three of the Brahmasūtra

NOTES

[1] III.II.1 - From the *Śruti* it may be thought that all objects of the dream state have the same substantial nature as those of the waking state, especially because it is the same being that is the creator of dream:

> 'There are no carts there, no draught animals, no streets; he therefore creates carts, draught animals, and streets... He truly is the creator.'[1]

According to the Teacher Bādarāyaṇa or Vyāsa, this passage is to be interpreted precisely. In the waking state there is a logical and self-conscious succession of causality, time, and space which is lacking in the dream state. If there were identity of nature, there would have to be a reciprocal and identical knowledge between the two states; but in fact the knowledge of one of the states contradicts the knowledge of the other, and *vice versa*. The carts, lakes, or rivers of the waking state cannot be contained within the sleeping body.

It is noteworthy that Gauḍapāda, in the *Māṇḍūkyakārikā*, sees this problem from a completely metaphysical viewpoint (*nirguṇa*); he maintains, as we have seen previously, that the three states of waking, dreaming (or sleep with dreams), and deep sleep are none other than projections or externalisations of the qualities, or *guṇas* both at the universal plane and at the individual plane.

However, there is no contradiction between the proposition

---

[1] *Bṛ*: IV.III.10.

put forward by the *Brahmasūtra* and that put forward by the *Māṇḍūkyakārikā*, for they represent two conscious moments or two aspects of the single Reality which is the *Ātman*. Moreover, the *Brahmasūtra* is replying to a hypothetical interlocutor who maintains that the two states of waking and dreaming are identical in nature and substance; and seen from this perspective, there cannot be said to be a precise identity.

[2] III.II.2 - In the *Kaṭha Upaniṣad* (II.II.8) we read:

> 'This, [the *jīva*], who, [finds its foundation in the *Puruṣa*], when [the senses] lie asleep, is awake and projects endless desires. That [*Puruṣa*] is luminous, That is the *Brahman*. That very one is called the Immortal. In That all the worlds are founded. Nothing truly transcends That. And this, in truth, is That.'

The sons are objects of desire or objectified desires, insofar as they are that which is desired.

Again, the objector states that dream objects are actually created by the *puruṣa*. This is a further confirmation of the first *sūtra*. *Sūtra* 3 answers the objector.

[3] III.II.3 - The objector is trying to support the subjectivist theory, according to which it is the *puruṣa* that is the creator of the worlds. In this context the *sūtra*, on the other hand, maintains the objectivist thesis: if the world of dreams had the same degree of reality as the world of the waking state, it would have to find a place for itself within the space-time dimension already occupied by the world of the waking state. But, in fact, in the dream world one can dream that it is night when in the waking state it is day, and *vice versa*; or one can dream of being dead, while this is not the case in the

waking state. There is therefore no logical link between one world and the other.

[4] III.II.5 - Again, the objector may maintain that, if the *jīva* is of the same nature as the *Brahman*, it possesses all its knowledge and powers, by means of which it is able, in dream, to create things that are real.

It may be said that the *jīva* is limited by the superimpositions of instruments or bodies, and hence by time, space, and causality. A ray of sunlight, although of the nature of the sun, has its own limitation when compared to the sun, so that it is possible to say, 'It is the sun, and it is not the sun.' It is the sun when it removes the qualities which limit it and it is re-absorbed into the sun, but it is not the sun while it is under limitation.

With the meditation on the Supreme, that which is hidden (that is, hidden in the various bodies or instruments) is revealed in its reality as the *Brahman* or *Ātman*. When reality is hidden, by means of the *guṇas*, there is bondage, or limit; when *Brahman* is revealed, there is the opposite, that is, liberation.

[5] III.II.7 - After examining the dream condition, we now move to the condition of deep, or dreamless, sleep. From the *Śruti* we learn that this state is found in the *nādīs* or in the *jīva* itself.

In the *Chāndogya Upaniṣad* (VIII.VI.3) we read:

> 'Thus, when one is asleep, reunified and perfectly pacified, he perceives no dream; then one finds oneself diffused into these *nādīs*; no error touches him. In truth, he becomes then fully enveloped by the light [of the sun].'

Thus, in dreamless sleep, or in the causal principial body, the *jīva* resides in itself, with itself, and for itself; but in this state it could still have some residue of 'qualitative impression' (*vāsanā*) which obliges it on the intelligible plane without allowing it to fly towards the supreme *Brahman* or *Ātman*. See the following *sūtra* and related commentary.

The three states of waking, dreaming, and dreamless sleep are symbols of the manifest: the gross state, the subtle state, and the causal state; *Virāṭ*, *Hiranyagarbha*, and *Īśvara* as the macrocosm, and *viśva*, *taijasa*, and *prājña* as the microcosm.

The causal body is reached through those channels that are called *nādīs*.

Again in the *Chāndogya Upaniṣad* (VIII.VI.6) we read:

> 'The *nādīs* [which lead] from the heart are one hundred and one. Of these, only one ascends through the [top of the] head. Ascending through this *nādī*, one attains immortality. The other *nādīs*, going forth in all directions, take back to death... .'

Above the three states is the Fourth (*Turīya*), that is, the *Brahman*.

Nādī (= channel, passage, artery) is a subtle channel by means of which the stream of *prāṇa* flows. The *nādīs* constitute the energetic luminous structure of the human being. In deep sleep the *jīva* withdraws into the *nādīs* where it lies in a condition of stillness or virtuality.

[6] III.II.8 - From the causal state, which is not distinct from the Fourth or the *Brahman*, one moves directly into the *Brahman*, inasmuch as the being, or the *jīva*, has never been separated from That.

It is always the same *jīva* that re-enters the world of manifestation, and it is the same *jīva* that, once all darkening residue of the *guṇas* has been dissolved, enters into Being, or *Īśvara*, which represents the causal or seed state, the paradigm for the world of *nāma-rūpa*, or sensible world. This principial Unity manifests in the world as the 'norm' (*ṛta*) and 'measure' (*mātra*); and beings, receiving this 'norm' and 'measure', are able to live and express what may be considered as an authentically sattvic way of life. (See *Chāndogya Upaniṣad* VI.X.1-3).

[7] III.II.10 - There is a particular condition in which the senses or consciousness are lacking in the individual, as happens in a swoon; but this condition need not be totally identified with deep sleep or dreamless sleep, even if his state of consciousness, deprived likewise of the residues of *karma*, could take him to that state or beyond.

On the other hand, if we exclude the waking state and the dreaming state because the subject is not conscious of either, what remains is deep sleep.

[8] III.II.11 - Now that the discussion on the embodied *jīva* has been concluded, the question about the nature of the *Brahman* has been broached.

Some parts of the *Śruti* speak of a *Brahman* with attributes, and others speak of a *Brahman* without attributes. An objector could assert that the *Brahman* has two natures.

In the *Chāndogya Upaniṣad* (III.XIV.2) we read:

> '... whose body is composed of *prāṇa*, whose essence is radiance, whose thought is *satya*, whose nature is space.'

In the *Bṛhadāraṇyaka Upaniṣad*, on the other hand, we read:

> 'This in truth is the *Akṣara*. It is neither gross nor subtle, neither short nor long, neither red hot nor liquid, neither shadow nor darkness, neither air nor space... without taste

or smell, devoid of eyes and ears, it is without speech and without mind... .'[1]

In the same *Upaniṣad* (III.IV.2) we also read:

'All that is other than This is perishable.'

The problem that the objector may put forward is this: *Brahman* has two natures, for the texts expound both aspects.

According to the *Brahmasūtra*, there are not two natures within the *Brahman*. Why?

Two natures cannot co-exist within the same Subject, because if that were the case there would be two absolutes, neither of which can change nature (the thing in itself) or be transformed into a different nature, and neither can contradict the other because, since both are absolute, they cannot have any mutual relation or contact. And – following Plato – if two opposed beings are admitted, with neither continuing to remain as it is, it will tend, in time, to be or become the exact opposite; and if this happens to it, either it will go away or it will perish. And supposing a relationship is acknowledged, it will be impossible to express the same possibilities of being, because the result would be a mere identical duplication of the same possibility or the same nature. Now, the question can be put thus: Which of the two is dependent on and subordinate to the other? Is the *Brahman* with attributes, the qualified *Brahman*, necessarily dependent on the *Brahman* without attributes, or is the reverse situation true?

The attributes – quality, quantity, movement, differentiation, and so on – may be considered as accidents, because they are produced, and if they are produced they are also expressly connected to something other which grants them the

---

[1] *Bṛ.* III.VIII.8.

possibility of being what they are. Hence they must depend on an ultimate cause which constitutes their original source.

Motion presupposes motionlessness, just as speech presupposes silence. Thus the *saguṇa Brahman* must depend on the *nirguṇa Brahman* (*nir-guṇa*: without *guṇas*) and represents one of the *infinite* possibilities of the *nirguṇa Brahman*. Being a mere possibility, the *saguṇa* does not represent an absolute necessity, which means that it may be said to be 'something close to non-being' (Aristotle, *Metaphysics*, E 2-4 *et seqq*.).

And the *Brahmasūtra* is primarily interested in the knowledge of the *Brahman*, the supreme Reality, and not in some accidental being; with such presupposition one would have the true aim of metaphysics.[1]

[9] III.II.13 - However, the supreme Truth is not dual, which means that, in accordance with the words of the previous *sūtra*, there is no difference.

In the *Kaṭha Upaniṣad* (II.II.15) we read:

> 'There the sun shines not, nor the moon, nor the stars, neither lightnings flash, and not even this fire. That shining, all consequently shines; all this [universe] shines from the splendour of That.'

Thus in the *Bṛhadāraṇyaka Upaniṣad* it is stated:

> 'He goes from death to death who here sees only multiplicity.'[2]

[10] III.II.15 - This *sūtra* provides an analogy between the *Brahman*, having no form, quality or cause, and light, which is apparently able to assume the forms of the objects it illu-

---

[1] Cp. *Bṛ*. III.VIII.8; *Ka*. I.II.15-16 *et seqq*.; *Mā*. VI and VII.

[2] *Bṛ*. IV.IV.19.

minates. Hence the Scriptures are perfectly justified in speaking of 'light as form', light which possesses attributes, so that there is no contradiction when they speak of the *Brahman* as having form or qualification, too; there are two ways of seeing the sole supreme Reality.

[11] III.II.17 - The *Śruti*, like the *Smṛti*, maintains that the *Brahman* is that state of absolute Reality.

> '... It is perceived as transcending the three times and also without parts'[1]

On the other hand, if the *Brahman* is that foundation or substratum by means of which everything holds out as to permeate the entire universe, formal and formless, meditation without seed on *Brahman* acquires its soundness. (See *sūtra* 20).

Again, in the *Maitry Upaniṣad* (V.1) we read:

> '... Homage to you, the most secretly hidden, inconceivable, non-measurable, without beginning and without cessation!'

[12] III.II.21 - The *Śruti*, too, states that the *Brahman* is within, or, rather, that the substratum is the foundation which governs every expression of life in the process of becoming, while remaining completely uninvolved in it.

In the *Bṛhadāraṇyaka Upaniṣad* (II.V.18) we read:

> 'He is the *Puruṣa* because His dwelling is in all bodies: there is nothing which is not enveloped by Him, there is nothing which is not pervaded by Him.'

And in *śloka* 19 the *Upaniṣad* continues: 'That is this *Brahman*, without antecedent or successor, without inner or outer... This is the teaching.'

---

[1] *Śve*. VI.5.

[13] III.II.23 - These *sūtras* pose the question of the negative formula, that is, *neti neti*. The hypothetical objector may ask: To what does *neti neti* refer? Does it refer to the metaphysical foundation (*Brahman*)? Or to the principial cause from which the effect, or the world, proceeds? Or to the world of names and forms? Or does it refer to all three aspects?

If we rule out the metaphysical foundation (the unborn), we are inferring that some given item within manifestation (the born) would not be able to govern itself, for it would not have its own root from which to discover its reason for existence.

In the same way, a tree without a root cannot come to birth. Nor can a building arise without land, which acts as its foundation.

If we rule out the principial cause (*Īśvara*), which contains all the indefinite manifest qualities and quantities, (multiplicity within unity, the One-many of Plato) then manifestation, having no potential cause, would be unable to emerge as the effect or the world, and there would be no perception of anything. In other words, there would be no subject and object, and no cause and effect.

If we rule out the world of names and forms, there would remain only a principial cause, with no development; a cause, however, which contains potentialities must sooner or later manifest itself or initiate those potentialities; and thus it must pass from power into act.

If we negate all three conditions that have been mentioned, we would reach the point of totally negating the whole of reality itself; but at this point the question may be put: Who is it that is negating? To negate or affirm something there needs be an ultimate subject with the possibility and the ability to negate or affirm. However, if there is no subject who is there that is negating?

What is the position of the *Brahmasūtra*? The following *sūtras* expound the conclusion.

[14] III.II.25 - As we have seen previously, the *Śruti* has confirmed that there is no absolute distinction between the supreme *Ātman* and its manifest reflection.

We consider again the analogy with the sun, whose image is reflected in water: between the image and its source there is no distinction, but nor is there identity; that is, there is no duality, because the reflection in the water has no absolute reality, no aseity.

The world of phenomena is a mere appearance, which indeed appears and disappears on the horizon of the supreme Reality. Between the supreme *Ātman* and the manifest *jīva* there is no duality, because the latter merges into That 'Thou art That: 'thou' is the *jīva*, and 'That' is the *Ātman* or *Brahman*.

Hence, as *sūtra* 26 shows, the ray of sunlight is re-united with the source from which it issued forth.

[15] III.II.28 - There are some *Śruti* passages which speak of difference and lack of difference with regard to the *Ātman* and the *jīva*; but since other passages make explicit statements such as 'Thou art That' (*Chā*. VI.VIII.7), 'I am *Brahman*' (*Bṛ*. I.IV.10), and 'It is your true *Ātman*... which is within all' (*Bṛ*. III.IV.1) and so on, then the statements of 'differences' constitute merely a *pūrvapakṣa*, that is, a thesis which is later refuted (*uttarapakṣa*) in order to finally reach the conclusion (*siddhānta*).

The thesis that there is a distinction between the *jīva* and the *Ātman* is thus refuted by the contrary thesis (I [the *jīva*] am the *Brahman*), to reach the conclusion that there is no distinction between the *jīva* and the *Ātman* or *Brahman*, just as there is no distinction between the sun and a ray of sunlight, with the specifications that were given earlier, and just as, likewise, there is no distinction between the snake and its coils.

[16] III.II.30 - The conclusion that the *jīva* is of the same nature as the *Ātman* or *Brahman* is further reinforced by the fact that the reality of anything distinct from the supreme *Brahman* is denied.

In the *Bṛhadāraṇyaka Upaniṣad* we read:

> 'There is no witness apart from Him, there is no hearer apart from Him, there is no thinker apart from Him, there is no knower apart from Him. This is the inner Ordainer, your own immortal *Ātman*. Whatever is other than Him is doomed to perish.'[1]

[17] III.II.32 - It may seem that above the *Brahman* there is another *Brahman*, even higher still, because, if a literal interpretation is taken, the *Śruti* refers to this possibility on occasion. *Sūtra* 31 puts forward this thesis, which is refuted by *sūtra* 32.

The *Chāndogya Upaniṣad* (VIII.IV.1) puts it like this:

> 'Therefore this *Ātmā* is a dam, a barrier so that these worlds do not disintegrate. Neither day nor night can reach this dam, nor can old age, death or pain, and neither can virtue or vice; all faults recede from that: because, in truth, this *Brahmaloka* is not struck with any flaws.'

But the *Śruti*, in speaking of a dam, an embankment, and so on, has the sole intention of giving an analogy, because, as

---

[1] *Bṛ.* III.VII.23.

we have seen, there is no absolute duality between the *Brahman* and the world; the phenomenal world is not separate and is not in opposition to the *Ātman* or *Brahman*, as if it were a barrier, not having any intrinsic reality of its own in contrast to the supreme Reality.

As has been noted in other contexts, analogy cannot constitute an identity, but it is something which refers to something else.

However, as the *śloka* from the *Chāndogya Upaniṣad* states, all contingent polarities merge into the unity of the *Brahmaloka*, that is, of the principial cause.

[18] III.II.35 - Both this connection and this difference are also resolved by the use of the logical reasoning found where the *Śruti* states 'Thou art That', and so on, from which the logical deduction is made that one can be That only by admitting identity of nature. If an absolute duality had to be maintained, it would be substantially impossible to reconcile the two absolute aspects.

[19] III.II.36 - From the express negation of all that is not the *Brahman* (*neti neti*) it can be deduced that the *Brahman* is One without a second and whatever is other than That is doomed to dissolve.

The negation concerns whatever is not and whatever, in accordance with its particular nature, can have no more than a simple degree of 'appearance' in comparison with that which is: 'The *Brahman* is all this only, this is the Highest.' (*Mu.* II.II.11).

'Nothing is higher or lower than He, smaller or larger than He, who always exists single in [his] radiance, still like a tree, by Him all this [universe] is filled.'[1]

[20] III.II.37 - By the term 'extension' is understood the all-pervasiveness of the *Brahman*, which underlies the causal principial body and, consequently, the world of names and forms.

Sūtras 38 to 41 deal with the fruits of action and whether they arise from ritual action or from the *Brahman* Itself.

[21] III.II.38 - There now arises the question as to whether the fruit of action is comparable to something distinct from the *Brahman* or to the *Brahman* Itself as the foundation of all that exists. In other words, the aspect of *karma* which determines the fruit cannot operate independently of that which constitutes its reason for existence.

Action performed by the earthly being cannot be separated from the same planet which makes human activity possible. We may even say, 'The fruits of the earth', with reference to the trees which bring forth their fruits. Similarly, we may say that the fruits of *karma* for any being cannot be separated from that foundation which constitutes the reason for existence for all that appears on its all-pervading horizon.

[22] III.II.41 - Bādarāyaṇa, however, maintains that That which is prior to all that exists is the origin of every movement that generates causes, actions, and therefore fruits that are meritorious and fruits that are not.

In the *Kauṣītakī Upaniṣad* (III.8) we read:

---

[1] *Śve*. III.9.

'This very *prāṇa* is nothing but the *Ātmā*, [which is] bliss, without age and immortal; he is neither enlarged through good actions nor diminished through bad actions: this very [*ātmā*] in fact makes good actions be performed by the one who intends to rise from these worlds and this very [*ātmā*] makes bad actions be performed by the one who wants to sink into the infernal worlds. This [*Ātman*] is the guardian of the worlds, this is the sovereign of the worlds, and this is the Lord of the universe. That is my *Ātman*. In this way it must be known... .'

The *Ātman* is thus fullness, not bound by old age or death or, therefore, by birth, and not enlarged by good works or diminished by bad works. It is on His bedrock of fullness and immortality that the *jīva* is able to produce movement, then action, and the fruit of action. It is on His eternal reality that merit and demerit can be determined for the *jīva* or *ahaṁkāra*. It is ever in Him that all illusory polarities are resolved, since His is the eternal witness (*sākṣin*).

It is not He who performs actions or movement (remember the two birds in the tree, one of which acts and creates the fruits, while the other remains motionless), but one may say figuratively that He is the founding cause of everything, as has been said previously with the phrase 'the fruits of the earth.' This reflects a figurative way of speaking, because the earth prescinds from any fruits: it is the trees that produce fruits.

In other contexts, too, which have been considered earlier, mention has been made of figurative expressions, analogies, and likenesses... in those passages where a literal meaning of certain expressions in the Scriptures seems to contradict the general meaning of the *Śruti*.

atha tṛtīyo 'dhyāyaḥ

tṛtīyaḥ khandaḥ

sarva-vedānta-pratyayaṁ codanādyaviśeṣāt // 1 //

sarva: all; *vedānta*: *Vedānta*; *pratyayam*: subject-matter; *codana*: injunction; *ādy*: and so on; *a-viśeṣāt*: on account of non-difference.

bhedān neti cen naikasyām api // 2 //

bhedāt: on account of difference or variation in form; *na*: not; *iti cet*: if [it is said]; *na*: not; *ekasyām*: in one; *api*: also, even.

svādhyāyasya tathātvena hi samācāre 'dhikārāc ca savavac ca tan-niyamaḥ // 3 //

svādhyāyasya: of the sacrifice made through the study of the holy Scriptures; *tathātvena*: in such a way, so; *hi*: because; *samācāre*: in *Samācāra*; *adhikārāt*: on account of the qualification; *ca*: and, moreover; *savavat*: as in the case of sacrifice or the rite of consecration; *ca*: and; *tat*: those; *niyamaḥ*: established ordinances.

darśayati ca // 4 //

darśayati: it declares; *ca*: also, and.

Book Three

Chapter Three

In Chapter Two the state of the *Brahman* was expounded. With the present chapter the question of meditation is addressed: Are there different meditations? Even if they are technically different, do they have the same aim? They are meditations inasmuch as they are supports (*prāṇa*, *ākāśa*, *sūrya* and so on), considering that realisation by a direct way may prove difficult for some.

1. *[The methods of meditation] contained in the whole of the Vedānta [are the same] on account of the non-difference of the injunctions and so on.*[1]

2. *If [it is maintained that meditations are] not [the same] on account of variations in form [in secondary cases, this] is denied [because] even in one and the same [vidyā there can be secondary differences].*[2]

3. *The sacrifice through study of the holy Scriptures is such because [it is described] in Samācāra; moreover, it is relevant to those who comply with the [seven] established ordinances.*[3]

4. *[The Śruti] also declares [this].*[4]

upasaṁhāro'rthābhedād vidhiśeṣavat samāne ca // 5 //

upasaṁhāraḥ: combination; *artha*: object; *abhedāt*: on account of non-difference; *vidhi*: precept, rite; *śeṣa*: subsidiary, remainder; *vat*: like; *samāne*: in the same or common; *ca*: and, also.

anyathātvaṁ śabdād iti cen nāviśeṣāt // 6 //

anyathātvam: difference; *śabdāt*: according to the Scriptures; *iti cet*: if [it is said]; *na*: not; *a-viśeṣāt*: on account of non-difference.

navā prakaraṇa bhedāt parovarīyastvādivat // 7 //

na: no; *vā*: or rather; *prakaraṇa*: subject, topic; *bhedāt*: on account of difference; *paraḥ*: high, elevated; *varīyastva*: great; *ādi*: and so on; *vat*: like.

saṁjñātaś cet tad-uktam-asti tu tad api // 8 //

saṁjñātaḥ: on account of the name; *cet*: if [it is said]; *tat*: that; *uktam*: said, spoken; *asti*: is, exists; *tu*: but; *tat*: that; *api*: moreover.

vyāpteś ca samañjasam // 9 //

vyāpteḥ: by permeating; *ca*: and; *samañjasam*: [it is] appropriate.

5. *In the common [vidyā to the various śākhās there must be] combined the particular rituals that are found in each, since [there is] no difference in the object, [just] as in the rite [subsidiary] to the principal ordinance.*[5]

6. *If [it is said that] it is otherwise in the Scriptures, [the reply is] no, on account of the non-difference [of the essential relationship].*

The interlocutor refers to the apparent divergence found in the *vidyā* of the *Udgītha*, that of the *Bṛhadāraṇyaka Upaniṣad* (I.III.1-7), and that of the *Chāndogya Upaniṣad* (I.II.1-7).

7. *Or rather, there is no [equality of the vidyās] on account of the difference of reasoning, just as [meditation on the Udgītha] as the highest and greatest and so on [is different from meditation on the Udgītha which abides in the eye and so on].*

8. *If [it is said that the vidyās are one] on account of [the identity] of the name, that [has already been] discussed; moreover, [within the different vidyās] that [identity of name] exists.*

These *sūtras* show that the different *vidyās* cannot be viewed as identical, but, although they vary in the particular contexts in which they appear, they do belong to a common nomenclature.

9. *And by pervading [the Vedas] it is appropriate.*[6]

sarvābhedād anyatreme // 10 //

sarva: all; *a-bhedāt*: on account of non-difference; *anyatra*: elsewhere; *ime*: those.

ānandādayaḥ pradhānasya // 11 //

ānandādayaḥ: bliss, and so on; *pradhānasya*: of the primordial person.

priyaśirastvādyaprāpti upacayāpacayau hi bhede // 12 //

priya-śiras-tva-ādi: bliss, head, and so on; *a-prāptiḥ*: non-attainment; *upacayāpacayau*: increase and decrease; *hi*: because; *bhede*: in differentiation.

itare tu artha-sāmānyāt // 13 //

itare: others; *tu*: but; *artha*: aim, end; *sāmānyāt*: on account of identity.

ādhyānāya prayojanābhāvāt // 14 //

ādhyānāya: deep meditation; *prayojana*: aim, motive; *a-bhāvāt*: on account of absence.

ātma śabdāc ca // 15 //

ātma: Ātma; *śabdāt*: from the word or term; *ca*: and.

ātmagṛhītir itaravad uttarāt // 16 //

ātma: Ātma; *gṛhītiḥ*: is understood; *itaravat*: as elsewhere; *uttarāt*: from what follows or comes later.

10. *Those [qualities which are found in the various vidyās are] not different from all [the others by means of which they have to be implanted] in other [contexts also].*[7]

11. *Bliss and other [qualities belong] to the primordial person.*[8]

12. *[Qualities such as] 'the bliss [which is] his head' and so on cannot be acquired [in all places] because increase and decrease [belong to] differentiation.*[9]

13. *But the other [qualities are valid for all situations where the Brahman is spoken of] as the basis for the identity of aim.*

On the other hand, other properties which suggest a cohesive reality symbolise a concrete identity of meaning therefore they have as their aim, not the meditation with an object or form (to realise the *saguṇa Brahman*), but an effective metaphysical actualisation of the formless (*nirguṇa*) *Brahman*.

14. *[It is] through deep meditation, through absence of motive.*[10]

15. *And from the word 'Ātma.'*[11]

16. *The Ātma is understood in a different [context], according to what comes later.*[12]

anvayād iti cet syād avadhāraṇāt // 17 //

anvayāt: from the context of the sentence, from the relationship to the sentence; *iti cet*: if [it is said]; *syāt*: [it is] so; *avadhāraṇāt*: on account of the statement.

kāryākhyānād apūrvam // 18 //

kārya: effect, act; *ākhyānād*: come on account of the statement; *apūrvam*: not enjoined elsewhere.

samāna evam cābhedāt // 19 //

samāne: in the same; *evam*: also, thus; *ca*: also; *abhedāt*: on account of non-difference.

sambandhād evam anyatrāpi // 20 //

sambandhāt: on account of the connection or relationship; *evam*: so; *anyatra*: elsewhere, on other occasions; *api*: moreover.

na vā viśeṣāt // 21 //

na vā: or rather, not; *viśeṣāt*: on account of difference.

darśayati ca // 22 //

darśayati: it declares; *ca*: also, too.

17. *If [it is said] that, in relation to the sentence [from the Upaniṣad already quoted, this does not refer to the supreme Ātman, the reply is that, on the contrary, it is] so on account of the affirmation [that only the supreme Ātman existed in the beginning].*[13]

18. *[Mention is made] as affirmation of an act [recognised by the Smṛti, which is] not enjoined elsewhere.*[14]

19. *In the same [śākhā, there is] thus also [equality of vidyās] on account of the non-difference [of the object of meditation].*

If the object of meditation is the same, no difference can be found in the meditations regarding that object; besides, there is no disagreement, among thc characteristics of the meditations, due to such difference.

20. *Moreover, also on other occasions, on account of the relationship.*[15]

21. *Or rather, not on account of difference [of place].*

However, the two meditations, though springing from a single source, are not comparable because they have two distinct functions and two distinct abodes: the sun and the eye. They are two moments of a single process, so that there can be no duality or distinction of form, but simply meditative conditions in relation to the meditator.

22. *[The Śruti] also declares it.*[16]

sambhṛti dyu vyāptyapi cātaḥ // 23 //

sambhṛti: ruling together; *dyu-vyāpti*: pervading the heavens; *api*: also; *ca*: and; *ataḥ*: for this [reason, motive].

puruṣavidyāyām iva cetareṣām anāmnānāt // 24 //

puruṣavidyāyām: in the *puruṣa vidyā*; *iva*: like, as; *ca*: and; *itareṣām*: of others; *anāmnānāt*: on account of not being quoted.

vedhādyartha bhedāt // 25 //

vedhādyartha: perforation and so on; *bhedāt*: on account of difference.

hānau tūpāyana śabda śeṣatvāt kuśāc chandaḥ-stuty upagānavat tad uktam // 26 //

hānau: in elimination; *tu*: but; *upāyana*: acceptance; *śabda*: term, word; *śeṣatvāt*: on account of being complementary; *kuśāt*: from the grass [rods of grass]; *chandaḥ*: poetic metre; *stuti*: hymns; *upagāna*: songs; *vat*: like; *tat*: that; *uktam*: said, spoken.

sāmparāye tartavyābhāvāt tathā hyanye // 27 //

sāmparāye: in crossing or passing to the next world; *tartavya*: to be attained; *abhāvāt*: on account of non-being or non-experience; *tathā*: thus; *hi*: because; *anye*: others.

chandata ubhayāvirodhāt // 28 //

chandataḥ: by preference; *ubhaya*: both, the two; *a-virodhāt*: on account of non-contradiction.

23. *And also for this [reason] ruling together and permeating the heavens.*[17]

24. *And [since the qualities mentioned] in the puruṣa vidyā [of the Chāndogya Upaniṣad are] not quoted, as [in those] of others.*

The two *vidyās* considered in the *Chāndogya Upaniṣad* (III.XVI.1) and in the *Taittirīya Āranyaka* (X.64) are not equal, because they have different aims; the *vidyā* of the *Chāndogya Upaniṣad* cannot be transferred to the *vidyā* of the *Taittirīya Āranyaka*, although they both speak of the same '*puruṣa* as sacrifice.'

25. *Perforation and so on; the object differs.*[18]

26. *But [where] elimination [of merit and demerit is spoken of] the term 'acceptance' is complementary to [the term 'elimination'], as in the case of rods of kuśa grass, metres, hymns, and songs. This is what [has been] said.*[19]

27. *At the time of departure [the knower is liberated] because [there are] no experiences to be attained. In addition, others [declare] the same thing.*[20]

28. *[In accordance with] preference, non-contradiction between the two.*[21]

gater arthavattvam ubhayathā 'nyathā hivirodhaḥ //29//

gateḥ: of the journey; *arthavattvam*: significance, purpose; *ubhayathā*: in two ways; *anyathā*: otherwise; *hi*: because; *virodhaḥ*: contradiction.

upapannas tal-lakṣaṇārtha-upalabdher lokavat //30//

upapannaḥ: reasonable; *tat*: that; *lakṣaṇārtha*: definite purpose; *upalabdheḥ*: in the recognition; *lokavat*: as in the world.

aniyamaḥ sarvāsām avirodhaḥ śabdānumānābhyām //31//

a-niyamaḥ: non-restriction, non-limitation; *sarvāsām*: of all; *a-virodhaḥ*: noncontradiction; *śabda*: the Scriptures; *anumānābhyām*: in inference.

yāvad adhikāram avasthitir ādhikārikāṇām //32//

yāvat: as long as; *adhikāram*: task, function; *avasthitiḥ*: existence; *ādhikārikāṇām*: of those who have a function or task.

akṣaradhiyāṁ tvavarodhaḥ sāmānya tadbhāvābhyāmaupasadavat tad uktam //33//

akṣara: imperishable; *dhiyām*: of conception, meditation; *tu*: but; *avarodhaḥ*: combination; *sāmānya*: similarity, common feature; *tat*: that; *bhāvābhyām*: from the very nature of the object; *aupasadavat*: as in the *upasad* or offering; *tat*: that; *uktam*: said, stated.

29. *The journey [after death has a single] purpose attainable in two ways, but if it were otherwise [there would be] contradiction.*

This *sūtra* raises the question of meditation on *saguṇa Brahman* and meditation on *nirguṇa Brahman*. If this double possibility is not accepted, there will be contradiction within the *Śruti*. Hence, according to the preference of the *jīva* either way may be followed; the *saguṇa* way is conditioned by a journey which is, let us say, in stages, while the *nirguṇa* way is fulfilled immediately after the extinction of the gross body.

30. *This is reasonable [because] a well-defined aim is acknowledged, as [happens in the life] of the world.*[22]

31. *[There are] no restrictions [for the devayāna;] all [the vidyās of saguṇa Brahman apply to this way; and there is] no contradiction between the Scriptures [Śruti] and inference [Smṛti].*[23]

32. *[For those who are undertaking] a function [there is] continuity of existence in order to complete the function.*[24]

33. *The [negative] conceptions of the Imperishable [must be] understood on the basis of the similarity and very nature of the object, as in the [Upaniṣad] offering. This [has been] stated.*[25]

iyad-āmananāt // 34 //

iyat: the same; *āmananāt*: from the description or statement.

antarā bhūta-grāmavat svātmanaḥ // 35 //

antarā: internal, within; *bhūta*: elements; *grāma*: combination; *vat*: like; *svātmanaḥ*: of the same *Ātma*.

anyathā bhedānupapattir iti cen nopadeśāntaravat // 36 //

anyathā: in another way, otherwise; *bheda*: distinction, separation; *anupapattiḥ*: inabmissibility; *iti cet*: if it [is said]; *na*: not; *upadeśa*: declaration, teaching; *antara*: within another; *vat*: like, similar.

vyatihāro viśiṁṣanti hītaravat // 37 //

vyatihāraḥ: reciprocity; *viśiṁṣanti*: they prescribe; *hi*: because; *itara*: others; *vat*: like.

saiva hi satyādayaḥ // 38 //

sā-eva: same, furthermore; *hi*: because; *satya*: truth; *ādayaḥ*: and so on.

kāmādītaratra tatra cāyatanādibhyaḥ // 39 //

kāma: desire; *ādi*: and so on; *itaratra*: elsewhere; *tatra*: here, in that place; *ca*: and; *āyatanādibhyaḥ*: on account of place or position, and so on.

34. *[It is] declared in the same way.*

The *Mundaka Upaniṣad* (III.I.1-2) and the *Kaṭha Upaniṣad* (I.III.1) refer to two *vidyās*, whose object is always the *Brahman*, which is expressed in these contexts as *jīva*; but the *jīva* is nothing but a ray of light from the Imperishable (*Mundaka Upaniṣad*, II.2.1). Thus there is perfect harmony among the various passages of the *Śruti*, both when the qualified or unqualified *Brahman* is spoken of and also when the *Brahman* is referred to as *jīva*, or ether, and so on. All the references, however, point to the single supreme Reality.

35. *[It is stated that] the same Ātman [is] within [everything] as the combination of the elements.*[26]

36. *If it [is said] that the distinction [of the declarations] is otherwise inadmissible, [the reply is] not so; it [is] like other declarations.*[27]

37. *[There is] reciprocity because [the Scriptures] prescribe [this] as in other [cases].*[28]

38. *Furthermore, because the truth and so on [refers] to the same [vidyā].*[29]

39. *[Qualities such as] desire and so on [mentioned in the Chāndogya Upaniṣad and mentioned] here [must be added] there [in the Bṛhadāraṇyaka Upaniṣad] on account of [the uniformity] of the place.*[30]

ādarād alopaḥ // 40 //

ādarāt: on account of respect or regard; *a-lopaḥ*: non-omission, non-loss.

upasthite 'tas tad-vacanāt // 41 //

upasthite: present; *ataḥ*: from this; *tat*: that; *vacanāt*: on account of the declaration.

tan-nirdhāraṇāniyamas tad dṛṣṭeḥ pṛthag hyaprati-bandhaḥ phalam // 42 //

tat: that; *nirdhāraṇa*: specific rules; *a-niyamaḥ*: non-restriction; *tat*: that; *dṛṣṭeḥ*: being seen; *pṛthak*: distinct; *hi*: because; *a-pratibandhaḥ*: non-obstruction; *phalam*: result, fruit.

pradānavad eva tad uktam // 43 //

pradāna: offering, oblation; *vat*: like; *eva*: exactly so; *tat*: that; *uktam*: said, spoken.

liṅgabhūyastvāt taddhi balīyas tad api // 44 //

liṅga: indicatory sign; *bhūyastvāt*: on account of the abundance; *tat*: that; *hi*: because; *balīyaḥ*: more considerable; *tat*: that; *api*: also, moreover.

40. *Out of respect [there must be] non-omission.*

By virtue of the respect shown by the *Upaniṣads* towards the celebration of the *agnihotra* in homage of the *prāṇas*, and hence towards the priests, even in times of exemption, as with the presence of guests or as in periods of fasting, the ritual actions must be observed.

41. *When it [food] is present, this is declared [by the text].*[31]

42. *[There is] no restriction by specific rules upon this, as may be seen [in the texts]; the result [is] distinct, because [there is] no impediment.*[32]

43. *Exactly as [in the case of] the offerings [to vāyu and to prāṇa, they must be kept separate]. This has been stated.*[33]

44. *[And] on account of the numerous indicatory signs [fires do not form part of any rite], because these [signs] are considerable. This also [has been stated].*

The *Agnirahasya* of the *Vājasaneyi Saṁhitā* speaks of fires of the mind, fires of words, and so on, but it says that they do not form part of any ritual sacrifice because the indicatory signs are many when compared to the general context: such fires are mere supports for meditation. This has also been declared by Jaimini the Teacher in the *Pūrvamīmāṁsā* (III.III.14).

pūrva vikalpaḥ prakaraṇāt syāt kriyāmānasavat // 45 //

pūrva: previous, prior; *vikalpaḥ*: formal content, form; *prakaraṇāt*: on account of the specific subject or section; *syāt*: it should be; *kriyā*: part of the sacrifice; *mānasa*: chalice of the mind; *vat*: like.

atideśāc ca // 46 //

atideśāt: on account of analogy or extension; *ca*: and.

vidyaiva tu nirdhāraṇāt // 47 //

vidyā: knowledge, meditation, and so on; *eva*: precisely, indeed; *tu*: but; *nirdhāraṇāt*: on account of being asserted or specified.

darśanāc ca // 48 //

darśanāt: on account of observing or seeing; *ca*: and.

śrutyādi balīyastvāc ca na bādhaḥ // 49 //

śrutyādi: the *Śruti*, ecc.; *balīyastvāt*: on account of the superior nature; *ca*: and; *na*: not; *bādhaḥ*: refutation.

anubandhādibhyaḥ prajñāntara pṛthaktva-vad dṛṣṭaś ca tad uktam // 50 //

anubandha: from the correlation or connection; *ādibhyaḥ*: and so on; *prajñā*: knowledge, cognition; *antara*: further, other; *pṛthaktva*: separate; *vat*: like, as; *dṛṣṭaḥ*: seen; *ca*: and; *tat*: that, this; *uktam*: said, sated.

45. *[The fire of the mind and so on is] a particular form of the previous one [the sacrifice to agni, constructed of bricks] on account of the specific theme; it should be part of the sacrifice, like [that] of the chalice of the mind [mānasa].*

46. *And on account of the analogy [of these fires to the attributes of the first].*[34]

47. *But [the fires are] indeed a vidyā, [as is] asserted [in the texts].*

48. *And [because] there is observation.*[35]

49. *And on account of the superior nature of the Śruti [this cannot] be refuted.*[36]

50. *According to the correlation, and so on, [the fires of the mind, etc., are independent], as the other cognitions [are] separate. And it is seen [that the sacrifices are regarded as independent]. This has been stated [by Jaimini].*

Although the *aveṣṭi* rite is associated with the *rājasūya* sacrifice, it is considered as independent when being spoken of in the *Pūrvamīmāṁsāsūtra* (X.IV.7 and III.V.21).

Thus, while the *rājasūya* can be celebrated only by *kṣatriyas*, the *aveṣṭi* is celebrated by the three orders (*brāhmana*, *kṣatriya*, *vaiśya*), which indicates that the *aveṣṭi* has greater validity than does the *rājasūya*.

na sāmānyād apyupalabdher mṛtyuvan na hi lokāpattiḥ // 51 //

na: not; *sāmānyāt*: on account of the resemblance; *api*: furthermore; *upalabdheḥ*: from the verification; *mṛtyu-vat*: as with death; *na*: not; *hi*: because; *lokāpattiḥ*: the world.

pareṇa ca śabdasya tād vidhyaṁ bhūyastvāttvanubandhaḥ // 52 //

pareṇa: from the following or subsequent; *ca*: and; *śabdasya*: of the teaching or Scripture; *tādvidhyam*: the fact of being so; *bhūyastvāt*: on account of the abundance; *tu*: but; *anubandhaḥ*: the connection.

eka ātmanaḥ śarīre bhāvāt // 53 //

eke: some; *ātmanaḥ*: of the *Ātma*; *śarīre*: in the body; *bhāvāt*: from the existence.

vyatirekas tad bhāvābhāvitvān na tūpalabdhivat // 54 //

vyatirekaḥ: separation; *tadbhāva*: existence of that; *abhāvitvāt*: on account of non-existence; *na*: not; *tu*: but; *upalabdhivat*: comprehension, as in cognitive understanding.

aṅgāvabaddhās tu na śākhāsu hi prativedam // 55 //

aṅga: parte, section; *avabaddhāḥ*: linked, connected; *tu*: but; *na*: not; *śākhāsu*: to branches; *hi*: because; *prati*: concerning the totality; *vedam*: *Veda*.

mantrādivad vā 'virodhaḥ // 56 //

mantra: *mantra*; *ādi*: and so on; *vat*: like; *vā*: or else; *a-virodhaḥ*: non-contradiction.

51. *Furthermore, [the Śruti] verifies [that there is] no similarity as [in the case] of death, for the world does not [become fire].*[37]

52. *And from the following [passage] the teaching prescribes that [separate vidyā]. But the connection [is] on account of the abundance.*[38]

53. *Some [deny] the existence of the Ātmā in the body.*

54. *[There is] separation [because] existence does not [depend] on the existence of this [body], but [there is] no [absolute separation] as in cognitive understanding.*[39]

55. *But [the meditations] which are connected to the parts [of the sacrificial rites are] not [limited] to a single branch of the Vedas, because they are concerned with the totality [of the Vedas].*

56. *Or else, as [in the case of] mantras and so on, [there is] no contradiction.*[40]

bhūmnaḥ kratuvajjyāyastvaṁ tathā hi darśayati // 57 //

bhūmnaḥ: on the whole form; *kratu*: sacrifice, offering; *vat*: like; *jyāyastvam*: pre-eminence, importance; *tathā*: thus; *hi*: because; *darśayati*: verifies, shows.

nānā śabdādibhedāt // 58 //

nānā: distinct, different; *śabda*: word; *ādi*: and so on; *bhedāt*: on account of the difference.

vikalpo 'viśiṣṭa phalatvāt // 59 //

vikalpaḥ: alternative, choice; *a-viśiṣṭa*: non-different; *phalatvāt*: on account of the fruit or effect.

kāmyās tu yathā kāmaṁ samuccīyeran na vā pūrva hetvabhāvāt // 60 //

kāmyāḥ: desires; *tu*: but; *yathā*: thus, as; *kāmam*: desire, will; *samuccīyeran*: combined; *na*: not; *vā*: or; *pūrva*: preceding; *hetu*: motive; *abhāvāt*: on account of the absence.

aṅgeṣu yathāśraya bhāvaḥ // 61 //

aṅgeṣu: with regard to the parts; *yathā*: similar, as; *āśraya*: basis, point of support; *bhāvaḥ*: being.

śiṣṭeś ca // 62 //

śiṣṭeḥ: from the teaching, from what has been taught according to the precepts of the *Śruti*; *ca*: and, moreover.

samāhārāt // 63 //

samāhārāt: on account of the combination.

57. *[The meditation is] pre-eminent on the whole form, as in the sacrifices, because this is what [the Śruti] demonstrates.*

From the *Chāndogya Upaniṣad* (V.XI.1 *et seqq.*) we can see how the meditation on *Vaiśvānara* assumes different forms of meditation; for example, as resplendent light (paradise), as eye, air, vital energy, space, and so on. Now the constant reference point for these meditations with different aspects is *Vaiśvānara* as the sole object of meditation. It is important not to lose sight of the ultimate aim of the meditation or of the ritual sacrifice.

58. *[The vidyās are] distinct on account of the difference of the words and so on.*

59. *[There is] a choice [of vidyā], because the fruit is non-different.*[41]

60. *But [the vidyās] of desires [may] be combined or not combined [in accordance with one's own] will, on account of the absence [of the aim of the] preceding [sūtra].*[42]

61. *With regard [to the vidyās connected with] the parts [of the sacrificial rites, their position] is similar to [their] foundation.*

62. *And on account of the teaching [according to the Sruti].*

63. *On account of the combination.*

guṇa sādhāraṇya śruteś ca //64//

guṇa: quality; *sādhāraṇya*: common to; *śruteḥ*: from the *Śruti*; *ca*: and.

na vā tat-sahabhāvāśruteḥ //65//

na: not; *vā*: or rather, instead; *tat*: that, those; *saha-bhāva*: combination; *aśruteḥ*: not from the *Śruti*.

darśanāc ca //66//

darśanāt: on account of the declaration or teaching; *ca*: and.

iti tṛtīyo khandaḥ

tṛtīyo 'dhyāyaḥ

64. *And because the Śruti [declares that one] quality [of the vidyā is] common [to all the Vedas].*[43]

65. *Instead, according to the Śruti, [the vidyās on the section of the sacrificial rituals] are not [thus because the Śruti excludes] their correlations.*

Instead, according to the *Brahmasūtra*, those *vidyās* that have been expounded previously cannot be considered in a unified way because the *Śruti* does not state that they have to be correlated.

66. *And because [the Śruti] declares it.*

Moreover, the Scriptures confirm what has been said above. In fact, the *Śruti* (*Chā*. IV.XVII.10) speaks of the *brāhmana*, the sacrifice, the sacrificer, and the others who officiate, for each of whom there is assigned a specific office, a particular position, and thus a pre-ordained *vidyā* related to the function that each has to fulfil.

End of Chapter Three of Book Three of the Brahmasūtra

NOTES

[1] III.III.1 - Since perfect *nirguṇa* realisation can be difficult, but not impossible, for some people, the *Śruti* offers a range of means and methods which, if followed, can allow the consciousness of the neophyte to be correctly orientated. The *Śruti* works in two ways, direct and indirect, to accommodate all the different types of people in accordance with their specific *guṇas*. We can therefore speak of Major and Minor Mysteries or of initiatory and religious Vision or, again, of *para* and *aparavidyā*.

By meditating on the *Upaniṣads* we can discover that some of them, for example, prescribe meditation on *prāṇa* or *ākāśa* and so on, so that we might think that there are diverse types of meditation at variance with each other. Bādarāyaṇa, however, does not agree. The current *sūtra* denies this proposition. Although there may be differences in the names given to particular meditations, such meditations do not differ in substance, for all aim at achieving the same end, which is realisation. It may be said that what changes are the means but not the end.

The *Brahman* is given indefinite names, such as *nirguṇa*, *saguṇa*, *ākāśa*, *prāṇa*, knowledge, bliss, and so on, but they all refer to That.

Mokṣasādhanā embraces all the practices, all the disciplines, and all the methods that are capable of leading to *mokṣa*. Moreover, as has been suggested, there are three possible ways of attaining Liberation: *kramamukti*, delayed or step-by-step liberation; *videhamukti*, liberation outside the bodily form, obtained the moment the physical body is relinquished; and *jīvanmukti*, liberation in life while possessing the physical body. All beings are characterised by specific *guṇas*, and, according to their individual make-up, different possibilities of approaching realisation are found to be congenial, and the *Śruti* offers everyone the practical possibility of freeing oneself from error.

It may therefore be said that the *Śruti* works at the individual level, at the universal level, at the principial (ontological) level, and at the supra-ontological or metaphysical level, where all the categories of time, space, and causality disappear.

And this vision or realisation represents that Knowledge, that *Sophia perennis* (the 'well-rounded Truth' of Parmenides), which transcends the differences of time and space.

> 'But life, there, is Wisdom and, moreover, a Wisdom that is not acquired through the processes of reasoning, because it is already fulfilled in eternity and it is not diminished in anything so that it has to be sought; on the contrary, it is the primordial, underived Wisdom; and its very being is Wisdom; be advised that it is not a being which becomes wise at some other time. This is precisely why no wisdom is higher than it.'[1]

> 'This *Ātman* cannot be attained through study, nor with intelligence [alone] and not even by means of much listening [however great]. This [*Ātman*] can be realised through that very [*Ātman*] which [the aspirant] worships... .'

> 'This being is never born and never dies, it did not take its being from anything, nor did anyone [come into be-

---

[1] Plotinus, *Enneads*, V.8.IV, translation of V. Cilento. Op. cit.

ing from It]. It is not born, eternal, always the same and ancient. It is not destroyed when the body is destroyed.'

'That which you know as beyond merit and demerit, as beyond that which is complete and not complete and beyond past and future, That very same expound [to me].'[1]

'Being is ungenerated and imperishable... It was not once, nor will it be one day... Indeed, what beginning will you seek for It? '[2]

Thus the Being presented by Parmenides transcends even ontological Being, time, space, and causation, and hence the world of 'appearances' (time and space).

'The subtle *puruṣa* existed before the sun and the moon.'[3]

The *Ātman* or *Puruṣa* or *Brahman* is unconditioned; in the same way, the supreme Good of Plato, which transcends the state of Being or the world of Ideas, is equally ἀνυπόθεον: unconditioned.

[2] III.III.2 - It may also be thought that within the same *vidyā* (meditation) there may be differences of a secondary nature, but this does not imply any fundamental modification or variation.

Śaṅkarācārya maintains that there cannot be any difference among the various forms of *vidyā* or among the objects of the *vidyā*s, even though there may be the addition or omission of certain elements.

[3] III.III.3 - Given that the followers of the *Atharva Veda*

---

[1] *Ka*. I.II.23, 18 and 14.

[2] Parmenides, *On the Order of Nature*, fg. 8. Op. cit.

[3] *Atharvaśira Upaniṣad* III. In *Cinque Upaniṣad*. Op cit.

refer to the prayerful offering of the fire placed on the head as a fundamental aspect of the attainment of Knowledge, while others make no mention of it, it may seem that there are variations of form within the same knowledge. This ritual *dharma* of the seven offerings belongs only to the study of the *Vedas* and not strictly to Knowledge; In fact, the followers of the *Atharva Veda* interpret the word *tathātvena* to mean 'thus, in such a way': in other words, as a vow ordained in the *Vedas* and referred to in the *Samācāra*, the part which deals particularly with rituals; that is, with reference to the time when the fire rite is performed.

Moreover, we read in the *Śruti*: 'To the one who has not observed the ritual [of the fire] it would be [better] not to read this'[1], which refers only to the person who is predisposed to the study of the *Vedas* which mention the fire ritual; thus, since this duty of the fire on the head (known as *ekarṣi*) refers to the study of the particular *Veda*, it has to be performed only by those who practise such a ritual.

Again, according to other viewpoints (such as that of Baladeva), it can also be acknowledged that the first part of the *sūtra* concerns only those who are followers of the *Atharva Veda*, while the second part is directed at all who follow the realisation of the *Brahman*.

[4] III.III.4 - The *Śruti* also declares what was stated earlier.

'That word which all the *Vedas* witness, to which all ascetic disciplines refer, aiming at which [men] undertake *brahmacarya*, that word in brief I will expound to you: it is *Om*.

---

[1] *Mu*. III.II.11.

'In truth this very syllable is the *Brahmā*; in truth this very syllable is the supreme [*Brahman*].'[1]

In the various sacred formulas and the various *vidyā*s there is a single presupposition: the realisation of the *Brahman*.

[5] III.III.5 - This means that different elements can be observed in the *vidyā*s, even if the aim and the object of meditation are the same. (See *sūtra* 10 of this chapter).

[6] III.III.9 - In the *Chāndogya Upaniṣad* (I.I.1) we read:

'*Om*: this is the syllable which must be meditated as the *udgītha*. Since the *udgītha* is chanted starting with *Om*, [we proceed by giving] an explanation of this [syllable].'

There are different types of meditation which are pertinent to the specific contexts where they are employed, but *oṁkāra* permeates them all; it may be said to constitute the foundation on which are based the various meditative possibilities.

For example, in the *Ṛg Veda* and the *Yajur Veda*, the *udgītha* has a specific connotation for each *Veda*, and it cannot be fully assimilated in the *oṁkāra* because this is its foundation, apart from the fact that the *oṁkāra* extends not only to the *udgītha* but also to other Vedic chants, since it is the all-embracing symbol of all sounds.

[7] III.III.10 - In some *Upaniṣads* (*Bṛ*. VI.I.13-14 and *Chā*. IV.III.1-8) we see that some *vidyā*s, such as that related to *prāṇa*, *ākāśa*, *sūrya* and so on are considered as the most important and highest, while these qualifications are missing in other *vidyā*s. The *sūtra* is of the opinion that these qualifications must be extended to areas where they are not

---

[1] *Ka*. I.II.15-16.

explicitly mentioned, since the same object (*prāṇavidyā*) is always being spoken of.

[8] III.III.11 - There are attributes, such as bliss, fullness, omnipresence and so on, which must be related to the supreme Person, the *Brahman*, which permeates all the other *vidyās* in which particular objects (*pratyaya*) go with specific qualities: for example, *prāṇa* is one of the numerous objects of *vidyā* that has specific attributes. In other words, every differentiation, whatever its nature and level, is related to the sole Reality, which is the attributeless or unqualified *Brahman*.

[9] III.III.12 - On the one hand, happiness and the various sensorial enjoyments belong to what is contingent: they can be or not be, and they can increase or decrease, because they belong to the *upādhis*, which means that they cannot be extended or attributed to all situations, since they belong to the world of differentiation and duality, while the fullness of the *Brahman* must be considered as the only one which is and does not become. (See *Tai.* II.VIII.1-5).

[10] III.III.14 - The *Kaṭha Upaniṣad* (I.III.10) refers to meditation and not to any superiority of the senses and so on:

> 'Indeed, the objects are higher than the senses and the mind is higher than the objects; the intellect is higher than the mind and the great *Ātman* is higher than the intellect.'

This simple sequence in the *Kaṭha Upaniṣad* (taken from the first *Sāṁkhya*, which posits the birth of each from the one before) is not understood to give an ontological status to these faculties, because, in addition, they are merely contingent instruments to make contact with external objects.

In the same *Upaniṣad* (I.III.11) it is said:

> 'Higher than the *Mahat* is the Unmanifest, higher than the Unmanifest is the *Puruṣa*. Nothing is higher than the *Puruṣa*: this is the ultimate goal and the highest abode.'

From the perspective of the *Brahmasūtra* it can be said that there is only one supreme Reality, the *Puruṣa*, non-different in this case from the *Brahman*; everything else is but name superimposed on the unqualified *Ātman* or *Puruṣa*. Again, the *Upaniṣad* continues in verse 15:

> 'Realising That which is without sound, without contact, without form, not subject to decay and similarly, without taste, eternal and without smell, beginningless and endless, greater than the *Mahat* and everlasting, the being is rescued from the jaws of death.'

In this way, the ladder of values given by the verse under consideration acts as a support to meditation; it would have no other aim.

[11] III.III.15 - Moreover, to enable us to understand that that ladder which is being dealt with has the sole purpose of attaining the supreme *Puruṣa*, Bādarāyaṇa returns to verse 12 of the same *Upaniṣad*, which says:

> 'This [*Puruṣa*] is deeply hidden in all beings: it does not appear clearly as *Ātman*, but it is realised thanks to an absorbed and extremely acute intuition by those who perceive the [most] subtle things.'

The *Ātman*, or *Brahman*, fully penetrates and simultaneously transcends all that exists. And when seen from the metaphysical viewpoint, whatever is not *That* turns out to be a mere 'accident' having no essential aspects and thus not being eternal. It is in this way that the world of names and forms can be seen as pure 'appearance.'

'Appearance' is used according to the Greek meaning (τό φαινόμενον = phenomenon).

All that is perceived through the senses is something which appears and disappears in front of the eternal *Ātman*.

The universe (*nāma-rūpa*) is in continuous change: it is born, grows and disappears, so that the very knowledge that one has of the phenomenon is relative to its becoming and to its contradiction. When supreme Knowledge is spoken of, what is meant is that which does not depend on time, space and causality, since It is inherent in the Being or *Ātman* as Witness of the movement of things. On this perspective the knowledge of relation depends and has its possibility of being in supreme Knowledge. *Vedānta* speaks of three orders of truth: supreme (*paramārthika*), empirical or relative (*vyāvahārika*), illusory (*pratibhāsika*).

[12] III.III.16 - In the *Śruti* we read:

> '*Om*. In the beginning the *Ātman* was this (*idam*), that is the One (*eka*). None other than He existed. He thought: "May I, now, create the worlds."'[1]

According to Bādarāyaṇa the Teacher, it is clear that these statements, as those expounded elsewhere in other contexts, lead us to understand that there exists only a supreme Principle, which, although uncaused and hence beyond time, space, and causality, is the origin and foundation of whatever follows It and whatever is subject to birth and death. The *Brahman* is beyond thought and hence beyond evaluations, but for the empirical mind of the being it is necessary to propose things that can be accepted at their own level. The non-acting Pres-

---

[1] *Ai*. I.I.1.

ence itself of the supreme Being ordains that the *manvantaras* proceed from cause to effect, from cause to effect, and so on.

[13] III.III.17 - The *sūtra* referred to confirms that it is always the *Brahman*, or *Ātman*, that is the primordial Source of all that exists; the words from the *Aitareya Upaniṣad* (I.1) are very explicit, even if it may seem in other contexts that it is not the supreme *Ātman* that gives the worlds the possibility to manifest themselves.

[14] III.III.18 - In the *Smṛti* (*kāryākhyānāt*, *sūtra* 18) the act of rinsing one's mouth 'is mentioned as a ritual duty.' Again, the *Chāndogya Upaniṣad* (V.II.2) and the *Bṛhadāraṇyaka Upaniṣad* (VI.I.14) speak of rinsing one's mouth before and after meals; but the *Śruti*, while stating this and without contradicting the *Smṛti*, puts the question as an act of meditation on the *prāṇa*. They are two different aspects propounded by the *Smṛti* and by the *Śruti*.

> 'For this reason the sages, who are versed in the Scriptures, sip water before eating and sip water after eating. By doing so they consider that the vital breath is no longer rendered naked.'[1]

Thinking of water as clothing for the *prāṇa* would be enjoined by the *Śruti* as a meditation on the *prāṇa*, as is clear from the context of the *vidyā* in relation to the *Upaniṣad*.

The *Smṛti* proposes a ritual act as a cause of purification, while the *Śruti* proposes a meditative act on the element of *prāṇa*.

[15] III.III.20 - On other occasions, too, with reference to

---

[1] *Bṛ.* VI.I.14.

the meditations, they have to be considered, as has been said, from the standpoint of the relationship of each one to the same object of meditation.

In the *Bṛhadāraṇyaka Upaniṣad* we read:

> '*Satyam* is the *Brahman*... That which is *satyam*, that is the sun, the being residing in the solar disc, and this being residing in the right eye. These two are founded one upon the other. That is founded upon this by means of the rays, this upon that by means of the *prāṇas*.'[1]

In this context two names considered as 'secret' present themselves as ready to be offered to the 'meditator': the first is *ahar*, referring to the *Brahman*, and the second is *aham*, residing in the eye and referring to the *jīva*. Although their abode is different, there is proof of their identity in the *mahāvākya* '*aham brahmāsmi*: I [as *jīva*] am the *Brahman*.'[2]

[16] III.III.22 - On the other hand, the *Śruti* also states that the two *vidyā*s must be distinct, although they belong to a single process.

In the *Śruti* it is stated:

> 'And again, that being which is seen within the eye is the *ṛc*; it is the *sāma*; it is the *ukhta*; it is the *yajus*; it is the *Brahman*. Its own nature, of this [*Puruṣa* who is in the eye], is also the nature of that [which is in the sun]: the two joints of that are its two joints; the name of that is its name.'[3]

Otherness presupposes unity.

---

[1] *Bṛ*. V.V.1-2.

[2] Cp. *Bṛ*. I.IV.10.

[3] *Chā*. I.VII.5.

[17] III.III.23 - The reference is to the supplementary text of the *Sāma Veda* known as *Rāṇāyanīya-khila*, which states that the *Brahman* is higher than all powers and that in the beginning it held the sensible world and pervaded the heavens or the suprasensible.

This *vidyā* is different from others because it is associated with a particular abode or state. Thus there are *vidyā*s which are relevant to the suprasensible state and there are *vidyā*s which are relevant to the sensible state.

Although *Brahman* is unity, it may serve as an object of meditation in different ways, for its properties and possibilities represent the founding cause of the multiple *vidyās*.

[18] III.III.25 - Some *vidyā*s of the *Śruti* which deal with perforation are not relevant to particular *sādhanās* because their objects have different meanings and aims.

In the *Atharva Veda* (XVI.7.1) we read:

> 'With this [that is, the spell] I pierce it, with an instrument of misfortune I pierce it... by means of *Grāhi* I pierce it, with darkness I pierce it.'[1]

The *Upaniṣads*, by way of principle, are directed to the science of the *Brahman* (*brahmavidyā*), to the knowledge and to the realisation of the *Ātman*, or *Brahman*. However, there may be passages which simply propound ritual acts; now, these passages are not precise injunctions for the realisation of the *Ātman*, and they do not constitute an integral part of the meditation on the *Brahman*. In other words, the *vidyās* on the *Brahman* are not dependent on the ritual act, even if they are a source of preliminary recitation prior to undertaking the Way of Knowledge.

---

[1] *Atharvaveda*, edited by C.Orlandi and S.Sani. Utet, Turin, Italy.

As a matter of fact, some Teachers insist on integrating this phase as a necessary step. Realisation is a precise occurrence of integration of factors, even of religious factors. Compare *Kauṣītakī Upaniṣad* II.13-14.

[19] III.III.26 - Some scriptural passages say that merit (*pu nya*) and demerit (*pāpa*), virtue and vice, are attained by the worthy (merit) and the unworthy (demerit) respectively; other passages, by contrast, teach that there is elimination of both merit and demerit. See the *Chāndogya Upaniṣad* (VIII.IV.1) and the *Kauṣītakī Upaniṣad* (I.4).

The message of the *sūtra* is that the term 'acceptance' is a correlative of the term 'elimination', so that the two terms stand for an operational unity, as happens in the case of rods of *kuśa* grass (to count the hymns), poetic metres, and hymns, as is stated by Jaimini the Teacher in the *Pūrvamīmāṁsā* (X.VIII.15). Where vice is destroyed, there is automatically acquisition of virtue. These terms are correlatives.

[20] III.III.27 - It may be thought that the dissolution of the double effect (virtue and vice, merit and demerit) may be achieved, not when the physical body dies, but after moving from the levels of the subtle world right up to *Brahmaloka*. This implies a delayed realisation (*kramamukti*).

The *sūtra* in question maintains, to the contrary, that at the death of the gross physical body, having acquired knowledge, one is liberated from every effect (merit and demerit), since there is neither desire for any further experiences nor, consequently, any attainment to be achieved, either at the level of the sensible or at the level of the intelligible (*videhamukti*).

[21] III.III.28 - According to the preference of the being, it

can attain to realisation that is immediate or realisation that is delayed; this does not imply any contradiction.

In the *Chāndogya Upaniṣad* (VIII.XIII.1) we read:

> 'From the black I will reach the coloured; from the coloured I will reach the black. As a horse shaking its mane, [shaking away] the error like the moon when it frees itself from the jaws of *Rāhu*, having given up the body and having realised the *ātmā*, I will attain the world of *Brahman* (*Brahmaloka*), I will attain it.'

On the other hand, the *Kauṣītakī Upaniṣad* (I.I.4) maintains that the dissolution of merit and demerit occurs during the journey leading to the gates of *Brahmaloka*. Thus the *Chāndogya Upaniṣad* says that after the death of the gross body, having acquired knowledge, one is born directly in the world of the *Brahman*, which presupposes that the effects of merit and demerit have been dissolved before the departure from the physical level. The *Kauṣītakī Upaniṣad*, on the other hand, states that one moves to the world of the *Brahman* by travelling the way of the gods (*devayāna*) and therefore not immediately on leaving the physical body.

The Teacher Bādarāyaṇa, or Vyāsa, maintains in the *sūtra* under consideration that there is no contradiction between these two possibilities because both ways lead to the *Brahman* in accordance with the will of the being in choosing one way or the other.

[22] III.III.30 - What was said earlier is reasonable, as it prevents contradiction within the *Śruti*. The present *sūtra* may be understood in its essence by paraphrasing an example given by Śaṅkara: to go from one village to the next necessitates movement along a road, and the time taken may be long or

short; but to dissolve our *avidyā* no journey or movement is required, but, rather, being still.

[23] III.III.31 - In the *Chāndogya Upaniṣad* (V.X.1-2) we read:

'There, those who know thus, who meditate with faith and in austerity in the forest, they attain the flame, from the flame [they reach] the daylight, from the daylight the bright fortnight, from the bright fortnight the six months of the ascending [course of the sun]... from the months the year, from the year the sun, from the sun the moon, and from the moon the lightning. There a non-human being makes them move on to [the world of] *Brahmā*. This is the path of the gods.'

In the *Bhagavadgītā* we read:

'The path of Light and the path of Darkness are the eternal paths of the world. By the first, the being goes and never returns; by the second, on the other hand, the being returns [to manifestation].

'The *yogi*, who knows these two paths, O Pārtha, is not led astray. So unyieldingly realise *yoga*, O Arjuna.'[1]

Both the *Śruti* and the *Smṛti* confirm that all these forms of *vidyā* and all the different methods are valid for following the 'Way of the Gods', and thus there are no contradictions. The fruit attained by those who follow this Way is *Brahmaloka*.

[24] III.III.32 - There are beings who, although they have already travelled the 'Way of the Gods' and have therefore been liberated from the *karma* of individuality, nevertheless return to complete or continue to fulfil that function which

---

[1] *Bha. Gī.* VIII.26-27. Op. cit.

they had previously begun. This shows the continuity of a particular *dharma* that a *puruṣa* can unfold in the world of men.

Furthermore, even those who have already realised the supreme Knowledge, while still possessing a physical body (for example, a *jīvanmukta*), if they are pursuing a specific function related to some aspect of the Tradition, remain in life until such a function is fully achieved.

25 III.III.33 - In the *Śruti* there are descriptions of the *Brahman* in negative terms (this is the negative way of symbolising the supreme Reality, a way characteristic not only of the East but also of Western spirituality) and in positive terms as well; these ways need to be considered as making a single reference to the Supreme by virtue of the affinity of the very nature of the object being dealt with, as in the case of the sacrifice.

This has also been stated in the *Pūrvamīmāṁsā* (III.III.8).

In the *Bṛhadāraṇyaka Upaniṣad* we read:

> '... the knowers of the *Brahman* say: in truth this is the *akṣara*. It is neither gross nor subtle, neither short nor long, neither red hot nor liquid... .'[1]

In the *Mundaka Upaniṣad*, too, (I.I.6) the same formula is repeated: 'without eyes or ears, That is without hands or feet, but It is eternal, all-pervading, omnipresent and infinitely subtle... .'

26 III.III.35 - 'This is your *Ātman*, which is within all.' These words from the *Bṛhadāraṇyaka Upaniṣad* (III.I.1) and those contained in III.V.1 of the same *Upaniṣad* may seem like two different *vidyā*s, with divergent aims, but according to the

---

[1] *Bṛ.* III.VIII.8.

Brahmasūtra they always refer to the single *Ātman* within, both when the words speak of the *Ātman* which breathes through the *prāṇa* and when they speak of the *Ātman* which 'transcends hunger and thirst, sorrow and illusion, decay and death.'

It is as the combination of the elements, where we find every element is present in all the others, the understanding being, of course, that the element of water is more internal than the element of earth and more external than the element of fire, and so on. The reference may be more to the *Ātmā* or *jīva* rather than to the transcendent *Ātman*.

[27] III.III.36 - If it is said that the statement about the *Ātmā* in the two previous passages is divergent in nature, so that the repetition of the sentences quoted from the *Śruti* cannot be explained, the reply given by the *Brahmasūtra* is '*Na*: no', because the repeated quotations have a didactic function. Thus, in the *Chāndogya Upaniṣad* (VI.VIII.6-7), although the teaching is expressed on different occasions and even in different ways, this does not imply different *vidyā*s or different aims. What is found in this case is also encountered in other contexts where there is reciprocity in the *vidyā*s.

[28] III.III.37 - In the *Aitareya Āranyaka* (II.II.4-6) we find: 'What I am is That, and That is what I am.'

These two statements must be considered as reciprocal. If we read only 'What I am is That', we may fall into the error of putting the *jīva* before the *Ātman* or above the *Ātman*; on the other hand, if we read only the second part of the Scripture we may consider the infinite nature of the *Brahman* to be within the limited confines of the *jīva*. Now, as with other examples in the Scriptures, there must be reciprocity in the *vidyā*s to avoid errors of interpretation.

[29] III.III.38 - In the *Bṛhadāraṇyaka Upaniṣad* (V.IV.1) there is a meditation called *satya vidyā*, which finds fulfilment when linked to the *vidyā* on the letters of the name; moreover, the same *Upaniṣad* (V.V.2) mentions a *vidyā* whose reference, on the other hand, is: 'That which is *satyam*, that is the sun; the being which dwells in the solar disc and this being which dwells in the right eye. These two are based each upon the other.'

These two *vidyā*s may seem different from each other, just as the result from each would seem different. According to the *Brahmasūtra*, however, the two *vidyā*s are correlated, especially because the reference to *satya* is common to both. In the second case, moreover, the term *satya* (truth or being) is given greater precision.

[30] III.III.39 - Indeed, in the *Chāndogya Upaniṣad* we read:

> 'In this citadel of *Brahman*, there is this small receptacle in the form of a lotus flower. Within it there is a small space (*ākāśa*). That, which is within it, is what must be searched for. That, in truth, is what must be known.'[1]

In the *Bṛhadāraṇyaka Upaniṣad*, on the other hand, we read:

> 'This is He who dwells in that space which is within the heart. He is the Ruler of all, the Lord of all, the Governor of all.'[2]

According to Bādarāyaṇa, these two passages are similar and there is no disharmony, even if one passage is referring

---

[1] *Chā*. VIII.I.1.

[2] *Bṛ*. IV.IV.22.

to *saguṇa Brahman* and the other to *nirguṇa Brahman*; but between the two there is no opposition.

[31] III.III.41 - To what was put forward by the objector in the previous *sūtra*, Bādarāyaṇa replies by observing that when there is no food one is exempt from celebrating the *agnihotra* in homage to the *prāṇas*. The *Śruti* states explicitly that it is obligatory to proceed with the sacrificial rite when food is available. There is thus a relationship between the availability of food and the sacrificial act.

> 'The food which is available first should be offered as the oblation. When the first oblation is being offered, it should be offered with [the *mantra*]: "To the *prāṇa*, *svāhā*!" [In virtue of this] the *prāṇa* is then satisfied.'[1]

[32] III.III.42 - According to the Scriptures, there are no restrictions by specific rules which might make it obligatory to link meditation with sacrificial rituals.

The question is raised as to whether some meditations are correlated to sacrificial rites; the *sūtra* states that meditations do not form an integral part of sacrificial rituals, for the *Śruti* does not lay down any limiting regulation to the effect that meditations must be integral to sacrificial ritual or be accessory to it. Moreover, while the sacrificer, through a particular obstacle in his *karma*, may engender an impediment at the sacrifice, meditation can have the contrary effect of dissolving this impediment.

[33] III.III.43 - The *vidyās* on the *prāṇa* and on *vāyu* must be kept separate. In other words, *prāṇa* (as expressed in the

---

[1] *Chā*. V.XIX.1.

Bṛhadāraṇyaka Upaniṣad, I.V.22) is related to the individual condition, while *vāyu* (in the *Chāndogya Upaniṣad*, IV.III.1) is related to the universal context. *Prāṇa* is considered to be the best among the various functions of the human body, while *vāyu* is the best among the divine principles (*deva*). However, there is no dichotomy between the two *vidyās*, because they are two aspects of a single meditative process inasmuch as the two planes, human and divine, are not separated or divided from the sole Reality. This has been stated by Jaimini the Teacher in the *Pūrvamīmāṁsā*.

[34] III.III.46 - There is still a desire to maintain that the aforementioned fires must be attributed to the ritual sacrifice and not to the meditations, because the *soma* offering, for example, which is made to *Prajāpati*, though having a mental or figurative nature on account of the meditations (the sea is considered to be the *soma*, and the chalice the earth), forms an integral part of the rite and is not an independent meditation. This statement, moreover, is corroborated by the evidence of the extension of these fires, with others of a different order, so that it must be recognised that the attributes which are referred to the first and then to the others must be considered, by analogy, as related to the ritual and are not like mere supports in the meditations.

[35] III.III.48 - With the word *tu* ('but') in *sūtra* 47, the Teacher Bādaṛāyana, or Vyāsa, maintains, in opposition to the previous thesis of *sūtras* 45 and 46, that the fires constitute only a support for the meditation, as is expressly indicated by the Scriptures, which affirm that these fires 'are ignited only by the meditation' inasmuch as they 'are made of knowledge alone' (*Śatapatha Brāhmana*, X.5.3.3). That is to say that they

are acts of meditation which are transposed on the metaphysical plane.

Moreover, all this is clearly verified (*sūtra* 48) in the context of the Scripture.

[36] III.III.49 - Various passages in the Scriptures (such as *Śatapatha Brāhmana*, X.5.3.3) show that the declaration of the *Śruti*, the specific sign (*liṇga*), and the syntactical connection (*vākya*) carry more weight than do other ways of reasoning. From such explicit considerations it can be understood that the fires constitute meditations which are independent of rites but not opposed to them.

On the other hand, the *Śruti*, since it is the essential point of reference, cannot be contradicted or refuted by other contexts which leave aside the *Śruti*.

[37] III.III.51 - Although there may be analogies among the fires, resemblance does not constitute identity. The fires of the mind may be useful symbols in helping meditators to achieve specified ends.

In the *Śruti* we read:

> 'Fire is indeed death... .'[1]

> 'In truth, O Gautama, that world over there is fire. The sun is its fuel, the rays of the sun its smoke, the day its flame, the moon its coals, and the stars its sparks.'[2]

In these passages the *Śruti* presents a particular form of meditation and not a ritual ceremony. The smoke is not the rays of the sun; the coals are not the moon; the flame is not the day; and the fire is not death.

---

[1] *Bṛ*. III.II.10.

[2] *Chā*. V.IV.1.

[38] III.III.52 - In the passages that follow in the *Śruti*, the teaching prescribes a separate *vidyā*, but the connection of the mental fires with objective fires is on account of the abundance of objective attributes that are linked to the mental attributes of the *vidyā*.

In the subsequent passage we learn that there is an exhortation to meditation and not to a ritual ceremony. The reference is to the *Śatapatha Brāhmana* (X.5.2.23), where we read:

> 'By means of Knowledge they ascend to that point where all desires are dissolved. On the other hand, it is not so for those who set out on the southern path nor for those who practise austerities.'

Thus, when the fires are connected with physical fire, they must not be understood to form part of the ritual sacrifice but, by analogy, the attributes of the physical fire are assigned to the attributes of the mind.

[39] III.III.54 - Some materialists deny the existence of the *Ātmā* within the physical body, for they maintain that the *Ātmā*, as consciousness, is nothing but a quality of the physical body itself (*sūtra* 53).

Sūtra 54, on the contrary, refutes such a thesis. It is not possible to consider consciousness as merely a quality of the body, because consciousness persists even when the body is completely inactive, as happens in the dreaming state. Here the senses, mental perception, and consciousness persist, withdrawing from the physical body. In deep, dreamless sleep consciousness remains, although separated from the body, and on waking up it can be said not to have dreamt.

On the other hand, it is impossible to prove absolutely the truth of the non-existence of consciousness, because, at the level of sense-perception, there is no possibility of proof;

otherwise, it would need to be proved objectively that consciousness is extinguished when the coarse body disappears. We can be certain only of the extinction of the body, and not of the part that is conscious, vital, discriminative, and volitional. For the non-proof we must have recourse to a part of the *Śruti* where there are numerous passages which affirm, in different ways, the activity of the *Ātmā* on the various planes of existence, both within the body and outside it. Otherwise, recourse should be had to the direct experience which is available through techniques of *yoga*.

[40] III.III.56 - These *sūtras* deal with the various forms of meditation which, although they may apply to individual parts of the *Vedas*, in fact belong to the totality or unity of the *Vedas* because they have the same aim and meaning. For example, the meditations on *Aum*, *udgītha*, *prāṇa*, *vāyu*, *tejas*, and so on, do not belong to individual or specific parts of the *Vedas* but have the same meditative power and the same object as their aim. The same thing can be related to the various *mantras*.

[41] III.III.59 - The apparently different forms of the meditations, however, are derived from the difference in the verbal expressions, but there is a single objective, even if there are numerous occasions when the meditation and the ceremony express themselves through specific attributes related to the sole object of meditation.

On the other hand, there is the possibility of choice on account of the great number of the meditations, but the fruit or result is always the same.

[42] III.III.60 - Once a meditation has been undertaken, it is proper to pursue it, because it is concerned with the ultimate

aim of realisation, which is the *Brahman*; however, when it is a matter of requests made at the personal and contingent level, then one may practise either isolated meditations or meditations that are combined among themselves.

However, as far as the sphere of the contingent is concerned, there are as many possibilities as there are particular aims in the minds of the meditators. These *vidyās* thus differ from the indications given in the previous *sūtra*.

[43] III.III. 64 - From *sūtra* 61 to *sūtra* 64 there is a series of observations whose overall meaning is: the *Śruti* (*Chā.* IV.XVII.10) proposes various compilations with regard to the ritual sacrifices which must be approached and connected, according to such observations, in a unified way; given that specific meditations are correlated to the various compilations, both the meditations and the compilations must be viewed in a unified way.

According to the *Brahmasūtra*, such observations are not valid; it gives its answer in the following *sūtra*.

Further Introductory Consideration on Chapter Four of Book Three

The first *sūtra* of the Fourth Chapter of the Third Book is extremely important, because it concerns the aim and the 'end of the pathway' which the being follows in accordance with the Tradition of wisdom or initiation.[1]

Traditional East and West both aim to free the human being from the dualistic conflict in which, through its own free choice, it has become imprisoned. The Egyptian Tradition, the Orphic Tradition, and then the successive initiatory, philosophical Schools (from Pythagoras to Parmenides, Plato, Plotinus, and others) have always posed this problem to the human being: assimilation into God. Whether the requirement be ontological or supra-ontological is of little importance; what is important is that the requirement, which the being must necessarily face sooner or later, be made directly and unequivocally. Religions themselves have this aim of bringing the being to *salvation*.

All human actions, whatever their qualitative standing, tend solely to turn 'the wheel of becoming', while those beings which are qualified in this time and space are able to direct

---

[1] Plato, *Republic* VII.532 d-e: 'Tell us what sort of power dialectic has, and what forms of it there are and the paths they follow; for these would seem to lead to our destination, where we shall find rest and reach the end of our journey.' (Sir Desmond Lee, *The Republic*, pag. 282. Penguin Classics, London, England). See also Parmenides, *On the Order of Nature*, fg. 8: 'On this way there are many revealing signs.' Op. cit.

their steps towards a single end: returning to what one really is. All other ends, even those that are noble, are 'diversive' and simply turn 'the wheel of *saṁsāra*.' And since all beings are potentially what they are in reality, they must, sooner or later, at an appointed time and place, face this existential question.

The fact that the operational means to such an end are knowledge, ritual, right action, and so on, is irrelevant because every being, in accordance with its own qualifications, finds a way of moving towards this Path.

In the *sūtras* which follow there are certain indications and clarifications in relation to the means. It is important to realise, however, that in all four Books that which represents 'traditional Society' is also set forth. The *sūtras* briefly set forth the following:

1) The correction of certain doctrinal formulations which do not accord with traditional Philosophy.

2) Realisation both ontological and supra-ontological (*saguṇa* and *nirguṇa*).

3) The operational means of attaining the ultimate end for human beings.

4) The fruits accruing from such means.

5) Conduct for the being, in accordance with a traditional way of life. The stages of life and the four possibilities (*artha*, *dharma*, *kāma*, and *mokṣa*) for a way of life which is coherent and in conformity with the traditional archetype.

In addition to the *Śruti*, the *Smṛti* also aims at the same target: to train the being for transcendence.

Vālmīki's *Rāmāyana*, for example, teaches the 'prisoners of time' the value of detachment and awareness of the Divine which dwells in every being.

With reference to these aspects, Śaṅkara the Teacher, in his *bhāṣya*, set himself on a line of pure knowledge (*paravidyā*), whereas Rāmānuja and others moved along a line that was religious and ontological.

atha tṛtīyo 'dhyāyaḥ

caturthaḥ khandaḥ

puruśārtho 'taḥ śabdāt iti bādarāyaṇaḥ // 1 //

puruṣa: person; *arthaḥ*: aim, end; *ataḥ*: from this; *śabdāt*: according to the Scriptures; *iti*: thus; *bādarāyaṇaḥ*: Bādarāyaṇa.

śeṣatvāt puruśārthavādo yathā 'nyeṣviti jaiminiḥ //2//

śeṣatvāt: on account of being supplementary; *puruṣa*: person, the one who acts; *artha*: object, fruit; *vādaḥ*: explanation; *yathā*: thus; *anyeṣu*: in other cases; *iti*: this, that; *jaiminiḥ*: Jaimini.

ācāra darśanāt //3//

ācāra: practice, conduct; *darśanāt*: from observation.

tac chruteḥ //4//

tat: that, this; *śruteḥ*: according to the *Śruti*.

Book Three

Chapter Four

1. *Hence the aim of the [human] being, according to the Scriptures; this is what bādarāyaṇa [says].*[1]

2. *This [knowledge, being in] supplementary [position], its fruit is the [commendatory] action of the agent, as in other cases; this is what Jaimini says.*[2]

3. *[This] is what is observed in practice.*

What has been said above is observable in relation to current conduct or practice based on the Scriptures. See the *Bṛhadāraṇyaka Upaniṣad* (III.I.1) and the *Chāndogya Upaniṣad* (V.XI.5), where we find the statement, 'O venerable ones, I am now going to make a sacrifice.'

Note that in *sūtras* 2 to 7 the teachings of ritual *Mīmāṁsā* are expounded. In *sūtras* 8 to 17 their refutation is expounded.

4. *This [is] according to the Śruti.*

The above is confirmed by the *Śruti*. In the *Chāndogya Upaniṣad* (I.I.10) we read: 'Only when [the rite] is performed with the help of knowledge, with faith and with the secret teaching, that very same becomes still more efficacious… .' From this it can be understood that knowledge by itself cannot constitute the means of liberation.

samanvārambhaṇāt // 5 //

sam: together; *anvārambhaṇāt*: on account of seizing or following.

tadvato vidhānāt // 6 //

tat-vataḥ: that (action); *vidhānāt*: on account of what they prescribe.

niyamāc ca // 7 //

niyamāt: on account of observances and standards; *ca*: and.

adhikopadeśāt tu bādarāyaṇasyaivam tad darśanāt // 8 //

adhika: higher; *upadeśāt*: according to the teaching; *tu*: but, however; *bādarāyaṇasya*: of Bādarāyaṇa; *evam*: thus; *tat-darśanāt*: because that is verified.

tulyaṁ tu darśanam // 9 //

tulyam: equal; *tu*: but, però; *darśanam*: declaration.

asārvatrikī // 10 //

a-sārvatrikī: not universally valid.

5. *[And] on account of following together.*[3]

6. *On account of the fact that they prescribe that [action].*

The Scriptures, moreover, prescribe ritual even for those who possess Vedic knowledge. This suggests that, according to those who know the *Vedas*, ritual action is not sundered from Vedic knowledge.

7. *And in accordance with observances.*

There is also the consideration of the observances prescribed by the *Śruti*. For example, in the *Īśa Upaniṣad* we read:

> 'One may desire to live for a hundred years, fulfilling one's ritual actions (*karman*) here. For you [who have in mind to live] thus, may *karma* not comply with man.'*

8. *However according to the teaching [the Ātman is] higher [than the transmigrating agent]. This is what Bādarāyaṇa [says], and this is what is established [in the Scriptures].*[4]

9. *However, the declaration [of the Śruti] reconciles [the two points of view].*[5]

10. *[It is] not universally valid.*

The reference made to *sūtra* 4 (III.IV) cannot be taken as an absolute affirmation because in that context the *Śruti* refers to the *udgītha* and not to any other meditation.

---

* *Īśa*. 2.

vibhāgaḥ śatavat // 11 //

vibhāgaḥ: division, separation; *śata*: hundred, hundreds; *vat*: like, as.

adhyayana mātravataḥ // 12 //

adhyayana: reading, study; *mātra-vataḥ*: only he who studies or recites.

nāviśeṣāt // 13 //

na: not; *aviśeṣāt*: on account of the absence of specific mention.

stutaye 'numatirvā // 14 //

stutaye: in the glorification; *anumatiḥ*: consent, approval; *vā*: or.

kāma kāreṇa caike // 15 //

kāma-kāreṇa: by virtue of personal desire; *ca*: and; *eke*: some.

11. *A division, as [into] hundreds.*

There is a fundamental distinction between knowledge and ritual action, like, for example, the division of a hundred coins into two parts, half being given to one person and half to another. In other words, knowledge accompanies particular beings, while ritual action accompanies others, according to the predisposition of the *guṇas* in each one.

12. *Only he who recites [the Vedas].*[6]

13. *[There is] no specific mention.*

The thought expressed in *sūtra* 7 (III.IV) with regard to the *Īśa Upaniṣad* (I.2) is not universally applicable, as it represents a general statement; on the other hand, there is no specific direction that the Knower must follow such a pronouncement.

14. *Or there is agreement to glorify [the Knowledge].*

Or (still with reference to *sūtra* 7) it may come about that the knower of the *Ātman* is able to perform rituals with the sole aim of glorifying Knowledge itself, which is a direct means of eliminating *avidyā*. The *jñāni* may also take part in a ritual sacrifice, but his motive is different from that of the man who makes use of the rites for purificatory purposes; moreover, the *jñāni* is free from the *karman* itself, and hence, not needing to obtain any fruit for himself, has no obligation towards the ritual.

15. *And some by virtue of their own will.*

They have abstained from ritual action for motives inherent in their own choice.

upamardaṁ ca // 16 //

upamardam: solution; *ca*: and.

ūrdhva-retaḥsu ca śabde hi // 17 //

ūrdhva-retaḥsu: to those observing abstinence or sublimation [of the virile seed]; *ca*: and; *śabde*: in the Scritture; *hi*: because.

parāmarśaṁ jaiminir acodanā cāpavadati hi // 18 //

parāmarśam: allusion; *jaiminiḥ*: Jaimini; *a-codanā*: no prescription, no injunction; *ca*: and; *apa-vadati*: does not approve; *hi*: because.

anuṣṭheyaṁ bādarāyaṇaḥ sāmya śruteḥ // 19 //

anu-ṣṭheyam: to be executed, fulfilled, experienced; *bādarāyaṇaḥ*: Bādarāyaṇa; *sāmya*: equally; *śruteḥ*: according to the *Śruti*.

vidhir vā dhāraṇavat // 20 //

vidhiḥ: injunction; *vā*: or; *dhāraṇa*: keeping; *vat*: like.

stuti-mātram upādānāt iti cen nāpūrvatvāt // 21 //

stuti: glorification; *mātram*: simple, alone; *upādānāt*: on account of considering; *iti cet*: if [it is said]; *na*: not; *apūrvatvāt*: on account of the novelty.

bhāva śabdāc ca // 22 //

bhāva: ingiunction; *śabdāt*: on account of the term or expression; *ca*: and, furthermore.

16. *And [hence] the solution.*[7]

17. *And [knowledge makes its way to those who] sublimate [their seed] because [it is so] in the Scriptures.*[8]

18. *[According to] Jaimini [there is] allusion and not prescription because [some passages of the Śruti] do not approve.*

According to Jaimini the Teacher, the texts which speak of the *saṁnyāsin* must be interpreted as mere references or allusions, because other scriptural contexts disapprove of renunciation. Therefore, the texts do not prescribe renunciation.

19. *Bādarāyaṇa [believes that] the Śruti [which enjoins saṁnyāsa is] equally applicable [to the other āśramas].*[9]

20. *Or [there is] an injunction, such as the injunction to keep [fuel for the sacrifice].*[10]

21. *If [it is said that they are] merely praises, being considered [as part of the sacrifices], this is not [so], on account of the novelty [of what they are teaching].*[11]

22. *And also on account of the words of injunction.*

And also on account of precise expressions of injunction. Thus, in the *Chāndogya Upaniṣad* (I.I.1) we read:

> *Om*: this is the syllable which must be meditated as the *udgītha*. Since the *udgītha* is chanted starting with *Om*.'

Here there is a precise injunction without any additional praise.

pāriplavārthā iti cen-na viśeṣitatvāt // 23 //

pāriplavārthāḥ: with the meaning of the *pāriplava*; *iti cet*: if it is [said]; *na*: not; *viśeṣitatvāt*: on account of specification.

tathā caikavākyatā upabandhāt // 24 //

tathā: thus, in such a way; *ca*: and; *eka*: a single whole; *vākyatā*: expressions; *upa-bandhāt*: on account of being gathered together.

ata eva cāgnīndhanādyanapekṣā // 25 //

ataḥevaca: and for this reason; *agni-indhanā*: kindling of the fire; *ādi*: and so on; *an-apekṣā*: disregard.

sarvāpekṣā ca yajñādi śruter aśvavat // 26 //

sarva: all; *apekṣā*: regard, concern; *ca*: and, moreover; *yajña*: ritual sacrifice; *ādi*: and so on; *śruteḥ*: according to the *Śruti*; *aśva*: horse; *vat*: like.

śamadamādyupetaḥ syāt tathāpi tu tad vidhes tad aṅgatayā teṣām avaśyānuṣṭheyatvāt // 27 //

śama: mental calmness; *dama*: self-control; *ādi*: and so on; *upetaḥ*: possession; *syāt*: there should be; *tathā*: thus; *api*: also, moreover; *tu*: but; *tat-vidheḥ*: on account of there being prescription for these; *tat-aṅgatayā*: aids for this; *teṣām*: of these; *avaśyānuṣṭheyatvāt*: on account of the necessary performance.

sarvānnānumatiś ca prāṇātyaye taddarśanāt // 28 //

sarva: all, everykind; *anna*: food; *anumatiḥ*: permission; *ca*: ma; *prāṇātyaye*: when there is harm to life or the vital breath; *taddarśanāt*: from observation of that [in the Scriptures].

23. *If it is [said to be] with the meaning of the pāriplava, [the answer is that] it is not so, [because] there are specifications [only in some accounts].*

The *pāriplava* is a liturgical narration.

24. *And hence [it happens that] the expressions are gathered together into a single whole [with the vidyās].*

25. *And for this reason it does not concern the kindling of the fire, and so on.*[12]

26. *Moreover, [with reference to] ritual action and so on, [there is], according to the Śruti, [an obligation] related to [religious precepts], as [in the case of] the horse.*[13]

27. *But even in this way one should possess mental calmness, self-mastery, and so on, because these are prescribed as aids to that [knowledge, and therefore] they must necessarily be fulfilled.*[14]

28. *But every type of food is permissible, on the [sole] condition that life [is] in danger. This is prescribed [in the Scriptures].*

abādhāc ca // 29 //

a-bādhāt: on account of non-hindrance or non-contradiction; *ca*: and.

api ca smaryate // 30 //

api: moreover, also; *ca*: and; *smaryate*: it is recorded in the *Smṛti*.

śabdaś cāto 'kāmakāre // 31 //

śabdaḥ: the scriptural word, the tradition; *ca*: and; *ataḥ*: da ciò, from that, from this; *a-kāmakāre*: in non-desire, in not acting according to desire.

vihitatvāc cāśrama karmāpi // 32 //

vihitatvāt: on account of prescription or injunction; *ca*: and; *āśrama karma*: duties of the stages of life; *api*: also, as well.

sahakāritvena ca // 33 //

sahakāritvena: through an auxiliary, aid, or means; *ca*: and.

sarvathāpi ta evobhayaliṅgāt // 34 //

sarvathā-api: in any case, moreover; *te eva*: same; *ubhaya*: both; *liṅgāt*: on account of the characteristic or indicatory sign.

29. *And on account of non-contradiction.*[15]

30. *The Smṛti, too [confirms it].*

The *Smṛti*, too, confirms the above.

31. *And hence the scriptural directions not to fulfil [immoderate] desires.*

From what has been said, Scripture proposes to restrain those desires which can lead to a transgression of the fundamental principles of *sādhanā*. It is necessary to make a distinction between desires and necessities.

32. *And the duties of the stages of life [are] also imposed [for the man who does not seek liberation. This is what the Scriptures enjoin].*[16]

33. *And [because there are] means.*

And because there are means, aids, and auxiliaries to assist with the attainment of knowledge.

The *Brahmasūtra* indicates the direct means to attain the supreme Truth, together with the aids and supports that contribute to fostering this knowledge.

Bādarāyaṇa the Teacher is in agreement with the *Śruti*.

34. *In any case, the same [duties must be carried out] on account of possible indicatory signs of both kinds.*

In any case, the duties applicable to the stages of life must be performed both by those who follow knowledge and by those who follow Vedic ritual. On this point the *Śruti* and the *Smṛti* are in agreement.

anabhibhavaṁ ca darśayati // 35 //

an-abhibhavam: not oppressed, not overcome; *ca*: and; *darśayati*: is seen.

antarācāpi tu tad-dṛṣṭeḥ // 36 //

antarā: one in between; *ca*: and; *apitu*: moreover; *tad-dṛṣṭeḥ*: from seeing or observing that.

api ca smaryate // 37 //

api: also; *ca*: and; *smaryate*: it is established in the *Smṛti*.

viśeṣānugrahaś ca // 38 //

viśeṣa: particular, special; *anugrahaḥ*: favour; *ca*: and.

atastvitaraj jyāyo liṅgāc ca // 39 //

ataḥ: than this; *tu*: but; *itarat*: the other; *jyāyaḥ*: better; *liṅgāt*: on account of the indicatory sign; *ca*: and.

tad-bhūtasya tu nātad-bhāvo jaiminer api niyamātad-rūpābhāvebhyaḥ // 40 //

tat: that; *bhūtasya*: of one who has become; *tu*: but; *na*: not; *atat*: from that; *bhāvaḥ*: becoming (return); *jaimineḥ*: Jaimini; *api*: also; *niyama-atat*: on account of restrictions or observances of that; *rūpa*: form; *a-bhāvebhyaḥ*: on account of absence.

35. *And it is seen [from the Scriptures that they are] not overcome.*[17]

36. *And furthermore, [even those who find themselves] between [two stages of life are suitable], as is seen [in the Scriptures].*

37. *And it is also established in the Smṛti.*

Those, too, who are between two stages of life (widows, for instance) can have the right qualifications for knowledge, as is stated in the Scriptures themselves and also corroborated by the *Smṛti*.

38. *And [with] particular [acts, knowledge] is rendered propitious.*[18]

39. *But better than these [sūtras 36-38, is] the other one [that which is more specific], on account of the indicatory signs.*

But the man who belongs to a specific stage of life may find himself in better circumstances, because he is highly favoured.

40. *But for him who has entered that [higher stage of life], and according to Jaimini, [there is] no return from that [stage], on account of the restrictions and because there are no forms of that.*[19]

na cādhikārikam api patana anumānāt tad ayogāt // 41 //

na: not; *ca*: and; *adhikārikam*: qualification; *api*: also; *patana-anumānāt*: on account of the inference of falling; *tat*: that; *ayogāt*: on account of inefficacy.

upapūrvam api tveke bhāvaṃ aśanavat tad uktam // 42 //

upa-pūrvam: minore; *api*: also; *tu*: but; *eke*: some; *bhāvam*: existence; *aśanavat*: like the act of eating; *tat*: this, that; *uktam*: said, stated.

bahistūbhayathāpi smṛter ācārāc ca // 43 //

bahiḥ: excluded; *tu*: moreover, but; *ubhayathā*: in both ways; *api*: furthermore; *smṛteḥ*: according to the *Smṛti*; *ācārāt*: according to custom or habit or current behaviour; *ca*: and.

svāminaḥ phala śruter ityātreyaḥ // 44 //

svāminaḥ: for the one who celebrates the sacrifice; *phala*: fruit, reward; *śruteḥ*: according to the *Śruti*; *iti*: thus, so; *ātreyaḥ*: Ātreya.

ārtvijyam ity audulomis tasmai hi parikrīyate // 45 //

ārtvijyam: the duty of the priest (*ṛtvij*); *iti*: thus; *audulomiḥ*: Audulomi; *tasmai*: for this; *hi*: because; *parikrīyate*: is compensated, rewarded.

41. *And [there is] not even [a mention with regard to] the qualifications [because] the consequence of this [would be] to fall and to become ineffectual.*

According to the interlocutor, the breaking of the *Brahmacārin*'s vow cannot be remedied, because in this particular case, even with the mediation of sacrificial rites, there would be inefficacy in the performance of the expiatory ceremony.

42. *But some [consider this fall to be] minor [and accept] the existence [of expiation, as in the case of] eating [forbidden food]. This is stated [in the Pūrvamīmāṁsā].*[20]

43. *But in both [cases they must be] excluded, according to the Smṛti and also in accordance with custom.*

But those who diverge from the path they have undertaken, whether it be through serious acts of commission or light infringements, would have to be held in suspension, both according to the *Smṛti* and also according to conventional norms of social codification.

44. *[The utterance of the sacrificial act is the responsibility] of the sacrificer; [there is, in fact,] some fruit, according to the Śruti. This is what is said by Ātreya [the Teacher].*[21]

45. *Because [it is] the duty of the priest (ṛtvij), as Audulomi [affirms, he is] rewarded for this.*

According to Audulomi the Teacher, the duty of reciting the ritual formulas falls to the *Brāhmana* (priest) as his specific function.

śruteś ca // 46 //

śruteḥ: in accordance with the *Śruti*; *ca*: and.

sahakāryantara vidhiḥ pakṣena tṛtīyaṁ tadvato vidhyādivat // 47 //

sahakāri: auxiliary aspect or factor; *antara*: further, other; *vidhiḥ*: declaration, injunction; *pakṣeṇa*: alternative; *tṛtīyam*: third; *tat-vataḥ*: the one who possesses; *vidhyā-ādi-vat*: as an injunction, and so on.

kṛtsna bhāvāt tu gṛhiṇopasaṁhāraḥ // 48 //

kṛtsna: all, whole; *bhāvāt*: on account of the existence or state of being; *tu*: however; *gṛhiṇā*: by the householder; *upasaṁhāraḥ*: conclusion, synthesis.

maunavad itareṣām apyupadeśāt // 49 //

mauna-vat: like the *muni*-stage; *itareṣām*: of the others; *api*: also; *upadeśāt*: from the instruction.

anāviṣkurvannanvayāt // 50 //

an-āviṣkurvan: not-manifestation, non-expression; *anvayāt*: in relation.

46. *And [this is also confirmed] by the Śruti.*[22]

47. *[There is] a declaration about a different subsidiary aspect [with regard to knowledge as] the third alternative element [mauna, in addition to the other two: bālya and pāṇḍitya] for the person who possesses this aspect, as [in the case of] injunctions, and so on.*

48. *However, the conclusion [is given with reference] to the stage of the householder, [which] includes everything.*

49. *Just as [there is] instruction about the other [stages of life], so also [about the stage of the] muni.*

If in some contexts the *Śruti* speaks at times of some stages of life and enunciates the duties, injunctions, and aims, this does not mean that the other stages of life are excluded. Instructions are given at times for the *brahmacārin* and at other times for the *gṛhastha*, and so on, but there are also instructions for all the four stages of life taken as a whole.

50. *In relation [to the context, the bālya stage means] the non-expression [of egotism].*

In relation to the context of the *Bṛhadāraṇyaka Upaniṣad* (III.V.1) the stage of *bālya* means being free from the ego, from egotism, from egoism, from maliciousness, and so on; in other words, having 'divine innocence.'

aihikam apyaprastuta pratibandhe tad darśanāt // 51 //

aihikam: in this life; *api*: also, even; *aprastuta*: non-mention; *pratibandhe*: obstruction; *tat-darśanāt*: from what is observed.

evam mukti phalāniyamas tad avasthāvadhṛteḥ tad avasthā avadhṛteḥ // 52 //

evam: thus; *mukti*: liberation; *phala*: fruit; *a-niyamaḥ*: non observances; *tat*: that; *avasthā*: condition; *avadhṛteḥ*: from what has been ascertained.

iti caturthaḥ khandaḥ

tṛtīyo 'dhyāyaḥ

51. *Even in this life [knowledge comes to fruition if there is] no reference to any obstruction. This is declared [in the Scriptures].*

If there are no specific obstacles, the fruition of knowledge can be experienced in the current life of the knower. From the viewpoint of *Advaita* it could even be said that knowledge liberates the consciousness from every qualification of time, space, and causation. Obstacles are inherent in form, or *guṇa*, not in the *Ātman*. The state of the *jīvanmukta* is that of the man who is liberated in this life.

52. *Thus [there are] no observances [in relation to] the fruit [of the knowledge that is] liberation. That is how it is; that is how it is.*[23]

End of Chapter Four of Book Three
of the Brahmasūtra

NOTES

[1] III.IV.1 - The aim of human existence, according to the Scriptures, is the Knowledge, Realisation of the supreme *Brahman*. This first *sūtra* points out that knowledge (*jñāna*), without recourse to other means, can remove the limitations enclosing the being that has fallen into *saṁsāra*. This implies that such knowledge cannot be subordinated or linked to ritual or to other contingent factors.

> 'It is the highest among the sciences, the science which must command the dependent ones, it is the science which knows the aim why everything is made; and the aim, in everything, is the good, and in general in the whole of nature, the aim is the Supreme Good.'[1]

In the *Chāndogya Upaniṣad* (VII.I.3) we read:

> 'I am this, O venerable one, I am a knower of the *mantras* only and not a knower of the *Ātman*... the knower of the *Ātman* goes beyond sorrow... .'

A knower of a metaphysical order goes to the ultimate end of Reality, non-born, eternal, undivided because it is one without a second.

[2] III.IV.2 - The *sūtra* maintáins that, since the knowledge is merely a supplementary aspect of ritual action, action which leads to the *Brahmaloka* (ontological aspect), it has as its fruit

---

[1] Aristotle, *Metaphysics*, A 2.982 b.

nothing but an act of praise on the part of the agent (*puruṣa*), as is confirmed by other cases in which scriptural statements related to the fruit of rituals are made with the sole purpose of exalting the agent. This is what is maintained by Jaimini, the codifier of the *Pūrvamīmāṁsā darśana*.

[3] III.IV.5 - Both knowledge and ritual proceed together; they accompany each other. This shows that knowledge by itself is fruitless.

In the *Bṛhadāraṇyaka Upaniṣad* we read:

> 'Knowledge and action, with his past experience, follow him together [after death].'[1]

[4] III.IV.8 - This *sūtra* introduces the refutation of the *mīmāṁsaka* view expressed in the previous *sūtras*. The *sūtra* in question begins with the conjunction *tu*: 'however' or 'on the other hand', which shows that Jaimini maintains that knowledge is subordinate to, or combined with, ritual action, whereas Bādarāyaṇa holds that Knowledge does not depend on ritual action, for by itself it grants the fruit of the supreme *Brahman*.

If the considerations of Jaimini the Teacher refer to the *jīva*, darkened by the *guṇas*, as is in fact inferred, then we are in agreement with Jaimini. If, on the other hand, he is referring not to the *jīva* but to the *Paramātman* (the supreme *Ātman*), then, as the Scriptures declare, ritual action is secondary because it can have its reason for existing on the manifest level as a preparatory base. See *sūtra* 26 later in this chapter.

It is thus a question of perspective and levels of conscious standpoints.

---

[1] *Bṛ*. IV.IV.2.

In the *Bṛhadāraṇyaka Upaniṣad* we read:

'... it is [the *Ātman*], in truth, that must be realised: it is that which should be heard, reflected upon, and deeply meditated upon.'[1]

Again, in the *Mundaka Upaniṣad* (I.I.9 and I.II.12) we read:

'... he who is omniscient, who knows everything [singly]. For him *tapas* is constituted by Knowledge. From That originates this [qualified] *Brahmā* and also name, warmth and food.'

'The *Brāhmana*, having recognised that the different worlds are [the result] of [unresolved] *karma*, detaches himself from them, [recognising that] it is impossible to attain that which is eternal (*akṛt* = non-agent) through that which is perishable.'

[5] III.IV.9 - As was said previously, Bādarāyaṇa considers that the *Śruti* not only declares the fruit resulting from sacrificial action but also presents knowledge as the means of supreme realisation.

Like other words found in the *Śruti*, those of the *Chāndogya Upaniṣad* (V.XI.5), 'O venerable ones, I am now going to make a sacrifice... .' can be understood with reference to both *saguṇa Brahman* and to the Knower himself (the one liberated in this life), who, though officiating, expects no fruit because he has already obtained the fruit. This is the principle of 'actionless action.'

[6] III.IV.12 - *Sūtra* 6 states that the *Śruti* prescribes ritual action even for those who possess the knowledge, thus ensuring that ritual action is not separated from knowledge. In this

---

[1] *Bṛ.* IV.V.6.

present *sūtra*, on the other hand, it is emphasised that only the man who recites the Vedic *mantras* is fit for ritual action, and not those who are qualified for supreme realisation. In any case, there is no opposition, as one of the two aspects is at the level of purification and is therefore legitimate, while the other is relevant to the total solution of *avidyā*; in this respect, it is presumed that purification through Vedic rites (or those parts of the *Vedas* that expound such rites) has been effectively integrated and transcended. As has often been said, the difference is that between the Minor and the Major Mysteries, or between *vidyā* and *paravidyā*.

[7] III.IV.16 - From what has been explained already it may be seen that knowledge dissolves any action that may be undertaken, that is to say, there is the *solutio* of the threefold superimposition of agent, desire, and the action or fruit.

In the *Mundaka Upaniṣad* (II.II.8) we read:

> 'The knot of the heart is cut, every doubt is resolved, and [the effects of all] actions are destroyed for him when That, supreme and non-supreme, has been realised.'

[8] III.IV.17 - By sublimating the seed, the desire for progeny is resolved, therefore one attains the state of the renouncer person or *saṁnyāsin*. See *sūtra* 19.

Knowledge is a means that raises to the intelligible. True metaphysics is interested in the ultimate Principles of Reality and these Principles, once understood, have to be realised, being these Principles, as *essence*, within the human being. (Reference books: *Chā*. II.XXIII.1-2; *Bṛ*. IV.IV.22; *Mu*. I.II.11).

[9] III.IV.19 - On the other hand, Bādarāyaṇa, having recourse to the *Śruti*, maintains that the reference to the other stages

of life is part of scriptural injunction; and thus austerity and renunciation are also enjoined.

The *Bṛhadāraṇyaka Upaniṣad* says:

> 'It is indeed precisely for this that originally the enlightened sages did not yearn for progeny: "What would we obtain from offspring, we who have realised the *Ātman* and possess this world?" They therefore abandoned desire for progeny, desire for prosperity, and desire with regard to the worlds, and they took up the life of mendicants.'[1]

[10] III.IV.20 - Alternatively, according to Bādarāyaṇa, there is an ordinance for the final stage of life (*saṁnyāsa*), just as there is an injunction to keep fuel for the sacrifice.

In the *Chāndogya Upaniṣad* (II.XXIII.1-2) we read:

> 'Three are the branches of merit. The first branch is sacrifice, study and charitable offering. Austerity alone constitutes the second branch. The third branch is the *brahmacārin* who lives in the house of the Teacher devoting himself totally to the service of the Teacher. All these [who practise the three branches of merit] become [fit to attain] virtuous worlds; [but only] he who is established in the *Brahman* attains immortality.'

This fourth branch represents the one who renounces all that exists.

[11] III.IV.21 - If it were to be maintained that the texts of the *Upaniṣads* referring to *udgītha* and so on are conceived solely to express praise, because they are considered to be part of the sacrifice, the *sūtra* denies this on account of the novelty of what they teach.

---

[1] *Bṛ.* IV.IV.22.

In the *Chāndogya Upaniṣad* (I.I.3) we read:

'This, which is the most essential of essences, is the supreme, it is fit for the highest state and is the eighth, it is the *udgītha*.'

And again, in the same *Upaniṣad* (I.VI.1):

'This [earth] is certainly the *ṛc*, the fire is the *Sāma*. This [fire] which is the *Sāma* is founded on this [earth] which is the *ṛc*. Therefore the *Sāma* is chanted as founded on the *Ṛg*. This very [earth which is the *ṛc*] is [the syllable] *sā*, the fire is *ama*: hence *Sāma*.'

Now, a doubt may arise if these expressions are mere praises of the *udgītha* or mere indications of particular meditations.

According to Bādarāyaṇa, the connotation of an injunction is implicit in the meaning of praise. On the other hand, the condition of praise must pre-suppose a prior injunction to which it must refer; if it is taken in any other way, it declines into meaningless abstraction.

[12] III.IV.25 - If in some passages of the *Upaniṣads* it may seem that their aim is the performance of ritual practices, one of which is named *pāriplava*, the preceding *sūtras* (23-25) deny this. In fact, these passages are integrated with the meditations and their purpose is to focus attention on the *vidyās*. This is why there is no need to kindle the sacrificial fire.

Meditation on the *Brahman* is, of itself, sufficient for supreme realisation. Why is this? Because *Vedānta* starts from the presupposition that the being has 'fallen into generation' through an act of veiling from the *guṇas* and identification with the qualitative object projected by the same *guṇas*. This causes the fall into *avidyā*, so that the being sees itself as what it is not: body, mind and so on.

If *avidyā* has confined the being within *saṁsāra*, then it is by means of *vidyā* or *gnosis* that it can solve its fundamental problem. The recognition of what one is comes about through an act of deep awareness of oneself as ultimate Reality.

Acts of ritual, of purification, of devotion, and so on, are of the utmost importance in relation to time and space, but to 'cross the abyss' it is necessary *to know oneself, to comprehend oneself, to be*. It is appropriate, however, not to omit certain preliminaries of the *sādhanā* (see *sūtra* 26).

[13] III.IV.26 - In the previous *sūtra* it was said that it is only by means of knowledge that one realises one's identity with That. In the present *sūtra* things are put in their places, with the result that a precise value is assigned to ritual action and to religious precepts. *Vedānta* neither excludes nor opposes ritual ceremonies or religious obligations, but it makes it clear that the ultimate aim is to attain the supreme Reality.

Thus ritual sacrifices, religious precepts, and all that the *Śruti* prescribes, must be experienced not only by those who are in the requisite state of consciousness but also by all those who are being borne along the way of knowledge. The *sūtra* thus maintains that a horse serves to pull a cart and not to plough the land, because there are other animals to perform this service. In the same way, ceremonies, observances, and so on, serve to prepare for and facilitate meditation by fostering an appropriate state of mind. On the other hand, as we have seen, if the *Śruti* puts forward the ritual aspect there must be a reason for it.

Ritual by itself does not lead to the supreme Reality, but, equally, knowledge by itself does not lead to that Reality, unless one is profoundly predisposed since birth towards it by a *buddhic, noetic* and *henological* cognitive vision.

In brief, the problem can be expressed in Western terminology as follows: there are the Minor Mysteries and there are the Major Mysteries. The Minor Mysteries are concerned with the whole process that is preparatory to the Major Mysteries, which are relevant to all those who have developed a noetic mind, a mind that is essentially metaphysical.

A fitting metaphysical realisation *integrates* the Minor Mysteries, in order to avoid comprehension that pertains merely to the dianoetic mind. There are some (it may even be agreed that they are the majority) who wish to rise on the wings of *manas* and who have discovered that they are about to fall because their wings, being formed not of the noetic substance but merely of sensory and mental 'wax', have been burnt by the power of the Sun. With regard to the aims of realisation, why does the *Brahmasūtra* posit the problem of knowledge? It is because, as has been said before, *Vedānta* starts from the presupposition that the being 'forgets itself' through an act of *avidyā* or veiling.

It is necessary to distinguish two phases in the act of veiling what one is (*avidyā*). In the first phase the mind thinks itself to be the thought object (an ideal of whatsoever nature, also religious, literary and so on); in the second phase there is the assimilation to the creation or effect thought (this corresponds to *vikṣepa śakti* and *āvarana śakti*).

It is this second phase in particular which causes imprisonment and suffering. It is also from this second phase that there arises the real drama of the being, with all the consequences which can flow from it, including those that ruin social relationships.

On occasions it happens that even a man of knowledge

can become identified with the 'object' of knowledge and turn into an absolutist, a 'fundamentalist.' But the supreme Reality transcends not only *avidyā* but even *vidyā* itself.

> 'Two [things], indeed are in the indestructible, in That which transcends *Brahmā*, in the infinite: there they lie deeply hidden, knowledge and ignorance. Ignorance, in truth, is subject to destruction, whereas knowledge, in truth, is everlasting. But He who controls knowledge and ignorance is other [than them].'[1]

A metaphysical way leads to the resolution of all possible polarities, and the man who is liberated metaphysically is the one who, having integrated Being and non-being, has in fact found total *peace* for himself, and who, in this peace, which is the result of having recovered the 'memory' of himself, is alone able to express that all-pervading Love which has the power to make an offering of itself. In this way, the Knower, having integrated and 'embraced' in their *essence* all manifest beings without exception, realises himself as a true Teacher of Love and Wisdom (*nirvikalpa Samādhi*).

Sūtra 18 of Chapter One of the Fourth Book, where this question is concluded, may also be consulted.

Why the act of 'falling'? (See commentary to *sūtra* 25 of this chapter). It is because the being is free to fall or not, to think or not, and to become identified or not with what has been thought. The being is free to manifest itself in indefinite expressions of life; it can descend or arise through the various levels of existence because this forms part of its nature. It depends on the degree of knowledge and mastery over the *guṇas*.

---

[1] *Śve*. V.1.

[14] III.IV.27 - In the *Bṛhadāraṇyaka Upaniṣad* we read:

'... Therefore he who knows thus, having attained calmness of mind, mastery over the senses, having collected himself, having acquired lasting patience, and having immersed himself in concentration upon himself, he has sure knowledge of himself as the *Ātman* and sees the *Ātman* in everything.'[1]

However, even those who seek total liberation cannot leave aside certain qualifications such as *śama*, *dama*, *uparati*, *titikṣā*, and so on.[2]

[15] III.IV.29 - There is nothing to contradict what is expounded in the *Chāndogya Upaniṣad* (VII.XXVI.2):

'When nourishment is pure, then the mind is purified; when the mind is pure, memory is sound; when memory has been gained, then there is the annulment of all the knots [of the heart].'

Foods which are imbued with *sattva* give rise to purity of both mind and body. This is why the *Śruti* posits precise parameters with regard to the intake of food. At the same time it also indicates that, in case of specific needs, foods may be eaten which are appropriate to those needs. There is therefore no contradiction between the injunctions and the exceptional provisions.

[16] III.IV.32 - In *sūtra* 26 it was seen that the injunctions which are related to ritual and to the stages of life constitute a suitable means for the attainment of knowledge.

---

[1] *Bṛ.* IV.IV.23.

[2] To go deeper into these qualifications see Śaṅkara, *Vivekacūdāmani*, *sūtras* 18-27. Op. cit.

In this *sūtra* further mention is made of the ritual duties applicable also to those who do not seek liberation in this life: to those, for example, who follow *kramamukti*, which is delayed liberation or liberation in stages.

In a traditional society every stage of life has its corresponding function and its appropriate mode of conduct.

[17] III.IV.35 - And from the Scriptures themselves it is seen that those who carry out the prescribed injunctions are not overcome by possible passions.

In philosophical Greek terms all this represents true *paideia* (see Plato, but also Plotinus): *paideia* which, for the disciple, signifies the shaping of the harmonic disposition, the shaping of spiritual perfection, that is, the shaping of the disciple in its highest philosophical expression.[1]

[18] III.IV.38 - Bādarāyaṇa, not wishing to stand in opposition or to present his own viewpoint as exclusive, agrees with those who maintain that for people who do not belong to a specific stage of life knowledge can be rendered propitious by means of specific ritual acts, by means of psychological techniques, or by such means as *japa*, *mantra*, and *yantra*, since these methods are not in conflict with that particular stage of life.

In the *Laws of Manu* (II.87) we read:

'But a *Brāhmana* achieves a perfect outcome by simply chanting: of this there is no doubt.'[2]

Although *Yoga darśana* starts from standpoints held by

---

[1] See G. Reale, *Storia della filosofia antica*, Vol. V, *Paideia*. Vita e Pensiero, Milan, Italy.

[2] Cp. *Laws of Manu* (*Mānavadharmaśāstra*), edited by F. Squarcini and D. Cuneo. Einaudi, Turin, Italy, 2010.

Sāṁkhya, the man who follows *Yoga darśana* equally attains *nirbīja Samādhi*, which corresponds to the *nirvikalpa samādhi* of *Vedānta*.

> 'However, once the [three] *guṇas* have fulfilled their function, the process of modifications [in them] comes to an end.'[1]
>
> '*Kaivalya* follows the re-absorption of the *guṇas* [or the three constituents] when they serve no purpose for the *puruṣa*; [there is *kaivalya*] when consciousness is on its own essence.'
>
> 'For him who has reached the goal, it [all that is visible] becomes non-existent; and yet it is not destroyed, for it is [still] there for others.'[2]

[19] III.IV.40 - It may be asked whether the man who has reached the higher stage (*saṁnyāsa*) can return to an earlier stage, falling from the position that has been attained.

The answer given by the *Brahmasūtra* is that this is not possible for the simple reason that the stage that has been attained is of the same nature as his own being. The *saṁnyāsin* who has reached *paravairāgya* (total detachment) has rediscovered himself within himself, so that he cannot lose his own identity, just as he had not lost it prior to realisation.

This is also confirmed by Jaimini the Teacher.

The perfected *saṁnyāsin* is considered to be *ativarnāśramin*, one who transcends the stages of life and social conventions.

[20] III.IV.42 - But according to some, including Bādarāyaṇa,

---

[1] *nir-guṇa*, in fact, means "without *guṇas*."

[2] Patañjali, *The Regal Way to Realization*, (*Yogadarśana*) IV.32 and 34; II.22, edited by Raphael. Aurea Vidyā, New York, NY.

this breaking of the vow would consist merely in a small defect which can be remedied with an act of purification, as happens, for example, after forbidden food has been eaten. This is also stated by Jaimini the Teacher (*Pūrvamīmāṁsā*, I.3-8). It is therefore necessary to distinguish between motives, or psycho-physical states, and particular existential reasons, before considering a fall from which there is no return. In the light of certain scriptural injunctions there are some events which are serious and some which are less so.

Thus, as we have seen, there are special circumstances in which food that has not been considered by the Scriptures may be eaten.

[21] III.IV.44 - The question that is now asked is whether the various forms of meditation which accompany the sacrificial acts should be performed by the sponsor of the sacrificial rite or by the *Brāhmana* who is presiding at the sacrifice. According to Ātreya the Teacher, it is the one who is performing the rite, and no one else, who is the beneficiary of the fruit.

According to Bādarāyaṇa, on the other hand, this is not the case, because the priest always acts on behalf of others, and he would not concede that the fruit should be given only to him with the exclusion of the other petitioners.

[22] III.IV.46 - In the *Chāndogya Upaniṣad* we read:

'But by this very [*Puruṣa* perceived in the eye] he obtains the worlds which are beneath this [sun], as well as all that men desire. For this reason the cantor of the *udgīta*, who has such knowledge, should ask: What is your aspiration for which I must chant?'[1]

---

[1] *Chā*. I.VII.8,9.

Such questions must be addressed to the sponsor of the sacrifice since the fruits are going to him. However, it is possible for the fruits to be requested by the priest, too. This is stated in the *Śruti.*

[23] III.IV.52 - There is no observance, no rule, no difference with regard to the fruit of knowledge which reveals liberation.

The ultimate aim is the same: to be *That* (*Tat tvam asi*). Just as there is no norm because knowledge manifests in this or a later existence, so there is no norm or difference with regard to the fruit of knowledge itself. *Brahman* admits of no differences with regard to the fruits or effects of knowing.

The repetition at the end of the *sūtra* indicates that the Third Book is concluded.

atha caturthādhyāyaḥ

phalam

BOOK FOUR

The Fruit

atha caturthādhyāyaḥ
prathamaḥ khaṇḍaḥ

āvṛttir asakṛd upadeśāt //1//

āvṛttiḥ: repetition; *asakṛt*: more than once; *upadeśāt*: from the teaching.

liṅgāc ca //2//

liṅgāt: from the distinctive feature; *ca*: and.

ātmeti tūpagacchanti grāhayanti ca //3//

ātmeti: the *Ātman*; *tu*: but; *upagacchanti*: they recognise; *grāhayanti*: they consider; *ca*: and.

na pratīke na hi saḥ //4//

na: not; *pratīke*: a symbol; *na*: not; *hi*: because; *saḥ*: it.

brahma dṛṣṭir utkarṣāt //5//

brahma: *Brahman*; *dṛṣṭiḥ*: seeing, knowing; *utkarṣāt*: raising.

ādityādimatayaś cāṅga upapatteḥ //6//

āditya: the sun; *ādi*: and so on; *matayaḥ*: mental representations; *ca*: and; *aṅge*: imbs, secondary elements; *upapatteḥ*: in accordance with reason.

Book Four

Chapter One

1. *Repetition [is required] by the teaching more than once.*[1]

2. *And from the distinctive feature.*

From the *Śruti* itself there are signs indicative of repetition.

3. *But [the Śruti] recognises the Ātman and considers the Ātman [as Supreme].*[2]

4. *Not [as] a symbol, because it [is] not [so].*[3]

5. *With the raising [of the symbol] the Brahman is recognised.*[4]

6. *And the representations of the sun, and so on, [are] secondary [to the rites; this is] reasonable.*

When the mental representations of the sun, of *Om*, and so on, are attributed and associated with rites such as the *udgītha*, then the rite produces fruits of a higher quality. This implies that it is the *udgītha* that should be seen as the primary element; on the other hand, if it were the sun, it would produce nothing, given that the sun, as such, represents only a symbol that is used by the rite for the ritual ceremony. The sun is the symbol which represents the universal Principle both in the East and in the West.

āsīnaḥ sambhavāt // 7 //

āsīnaḥ: seated; *sambhavāt*: making possible, possibly.

dhyānāc-ca // 8 //

dhyānāt: on account of meditation; *ca*: and.

acalatvaṁ cāpekṣya // 9 //

a-calatvam: motionlessness, still; *ca*: and; *apekṣya*: from the relation or reference.

smaranti ca // 10 //

smaranti: the *Smṛti*; *ca*: and, moreover.

yatraikāgratā tatrāviśeṣāt // 11 //

yatra: where, there where; *ekāgratā*: concentration of the mind on a single point; *tatra*: there; *aviśeṣāt*: on account of non-distinction or non-difference.

āprāyaṇāt tatrāpi hi dṛṣṭam // 12 //

āprāyaṇāt: until the end of being, until death; *tatra*: there; *api*: even; *hi*: because; *dṛṣṭam*: it is seen or affirmed.

tad adhigama uttara pūrvāghayor-aśleṣa-vināśau tad vyapadeśāt // 13 //

tat: that; *adhigame*: obtaining, reaching; *uttara*: successive; *pūrva*: prior, preceding; *aghayoḥ*: errors, impurities; *a-śleṣa*: non-adherence; *vināśau*: distruction, dissolution; *tat*: that; *vyapadeśāt*: according to the indication or declaration.

7. *Possibly seated.*

8. *And [to foster] meditation.*

9. *And with reference to immobility.*

10. *And moreover, the Smṛti [affirms it].*

The best way to meditate is to remain seated and relaxed: this is the way to deep meditation and bodily stillness. Not only does the *Śruti* indicate this position, but so does the *Smṛti* as well. See the *Bhagavadgītā* (VI.11-14) and the various types of *yoga*.

11. *Where [there is] concentration of the mind, there [there is] no difference.*

Where concentration and meditation are possible, they should be practised, provided that there are no specific reasons or scriptural precepts to the contrary. Any place may be useful for the meditator, as long as it is suited to the final aim that is being pursued.

12. *[Meditation should be practised] until death, because even at that point it is affirmed [in the Scriptures].*[5]

13. *On the attainment of That [Brahman, there are] non-adherence and the dissolution of errors past and future, as [the Scriptures] declare.*

The state of the *jīvanmukta* (the one who is liberated in this life) is posited; in this state the effects of *karma*, past and future, have been completely resolved, but there remains the *prārabdhakarma*, the *karma* which has already matured.

itarasyāpyevam asaṁśleṣaḥ pāte tu // 14 //

itarasya: of another; *api*: even, also; *evam*: thus; *a-saṁśleṣaḥ*: non-attachment, non-adherence; *pāte*: in falling, in death; *tu*: but.

anārabdha kārye eva tu pūrve tad-avadheḥ // 15 //

anārabdha: not initiated; *kārye*: the effects; *eva*: alone, only; *tu*: but; *pūrve*: preceding, prior; *tat*: that; *avadheḥ*: end, conclusion.

agnihotrādi tu tat kāryāyaiva tad-darśanāt // 16 //

agnihotra: *agnihotra*; *ādi*: and others.; *tu*: but; *tat*: that; *kāryāya*: to the same effect; *eva*: also; *tat*: that; *darśanāt*: from observation.

Compare *Bṛhadāraṇyaka Upaniṣad* IV.IV.14 and *Muṇḍaka Upaniṣad* II.II.8-9. See also *sūtra* 32 of the Third Chapter of Book Three.

14. *But [there is] also no adherence of the other [merit, or fruit of knowledge]; thus, on the death [of the body, liberation is certain].*[6]

15. *But only the previous [actions], whose effects [are] not initiated [are dissolved by knowledge because] that [death represents] the conclusion.*[7]

16. *But the agnihotra and others [tend] also towards the same effect [as knowledge], as is observed [in the Scriptures].*

The fruit of the *agnihotra* rite, and of other similar rites, to be fulfilled every day throughout life as rites prescribed by the *Vedas*, is declared to produce the same result as that in the previous *sūtra*.

In the *Śruti* we read:

> 'The *brāhmaṇas* aim to know That through the study of the *Vedas* and by means of sacrifice, offerings, ascetic discipline, and fasting... Those who wander about, only hoping to reach that state [the *Brahman*], are mistaken as they are mere itinerants persons.'*

---

* *Bṛ.* IV.IV.22.

ato 'nyāpi hyekeṣām ubhayoḥ // 17 //

ataḥ: from this; *anyā*: different; *api*: moreover, also; *hi*: because; *ekeṣām*: of some; *ubhayoḥ*: of both.

yad eva vidyayeti hi // 18 //

yad eva: that which; *vidyayā*: with the knowledge; *iti*: this, thus; *hi*: in effect, because, so.

bhogena tvitare kṣapayitvā sampadyate // 19 //

bhogena: with the fruition; *tu*: but; *itare*: others; *kṣapayitvā*: having exhausted; *sampadyate*: one realises oneself.

iti prathamaḥ khaṇḍaḥ

caturthādhyāyaḥ

17. *Because for some [there are] also [other good works] different from these. Both [are in agreement].*

There are other rites where the motivation is solely the attainment of specific fruits and thus the intent does not arise from *sattva*; the conditions of the previous *sūtra* obviously cannot apply to those who consider such rites. In this respect there is agreement between Jaimini and Bādarāyaṇa.

18. *In fact, 'that which [is fulfilled] with the knowledge' [means] this.*[8]

19. *But when the other [two types of karma] have been exhausted with their fruition, one realises oneself [as Brahman].*[9]

End of Chapter One of Book Four
of the Brahmasūtra

NOTES

[1] IV.I.1 - Repetition, hearing, reflection, meditation, and so on, are required more than once by the teaching itself.

> 'When the *Ātman* is known, through the grace of hearing, reflection, and deep meditation, all this becomes known.'[1]

In the *Śruti*, and in all traditional teaching, the instructions are repeated frequently because, as they do not constitute a mere process of mental learning, they need to be *absorbed*, contemplated (consider Plotinus, for example), and integrated. The editor of this work has followed the same procedure by repeating some explanatory notes.

The empirical mind can be troubled by certain repetitions, but the Vedic teaching, and the *Brahmasūtra* itself, to which reference is being made, is not a matter of culture. Meditation involves a repetition of intuitive occurrences.

[2] IV.I.3: In the *Śruti* we read:

> 'Now again, whoever knows That as "I am *Brahman*" becomes this [*Brahman*]. Not even the gods can hinder him, because he is, in truth, their own *Ātman*.'[2]

Three aspects of the human being need to be considered: the *Ātman*, which is of the same nature as the *Brahman*; the *jīva*, as a reflection or spark of the *Ātman*; and *ahaṁkāra*, the

---

[1] *Bṛ.* II.IV.5.

[2] *Ibid.* I.IV.10.

sense of I, the psychological and individualised ego, which has no inherent reality.

Let us repeat a passage from the *Muṇḍaka Upaniṣad* (II.I.1):

> 'This is the truth. Just as from a blazing and radiant [fire] sparks of [its] very same nature shoot out in their thousands, so, my beloved, innumerable existences are generated from the Imperishable and precisely there they will return.'

This passage needs to be repeatedly meditated upon, contemplated, absorbed by the consciousness, and thus realised. The empirical mind, being merely an instrument of *ahaṁkāra*, is unable to comprehend that which stands behind it.

The *jīva*, the trans-empirical soul, is of the same nature as the *Ātman* and expresses itself at specific universal levels. The *Ātman* is of the same nature as the supreme *Brahman*.

Our strife-ridden *avidyā* (*a-gnosis*) can be transcended because there is within us a *quid* which pertains to the universal dimension. To exclude this dimension, this state of consciousness, has a limiting effect upon the being, which consequently finds itself facing... nothing, the void. But in spite of 'the will of men' to reduce themselves to 'nothing', they cannot destroy what they really are.

The *ahaṁkāra*, the empirical ego, *is not*, for it does not have the nature *to be*, and it vanishes when seen for what it is. In this way, when the dawn of Knowledge appears above the horizon of our consciousness, ignorance disappears, because, in fact, it is not *substance* and it is not *being*.

[3] IV.I.4 - It is necessary to consider that the *Brahman*, the *Ātman*, and the *jīva* itself are, in themselves, symbols, but they are also realities which need to be directly realised, however,

symbols refer to other as they are the means by which the 'thing symbolised' is to be realised.

Why do the *Śruti* and the various traditions, or rather, the various branches of the single Tradition, use images, symbols, and myths (as Plato does, for example) to designate things of the intelligible world?

It is because certain things cannot be expressed in words, which are the fruit of dianoetic thought. Faced with a symbol, the mind is obliged to be silent. And *sūtra* 5 specifies that the symbol must be merely a means and not an end. Moreover, it is not unrelated to the end itself, which is the *Brahman*, the supreme Reality. In the symbol the *Ātman* is seen, the *Brahman* is seen; but once the Supreme has been realised, the symbol is of no further use and dissolves into the Supreme itself.

[4] IV.I.5 - It is therefore necessary to sce the symbol, the object of contemplative meditation, as the supreme *Brahman* by means of the transposition or sublimation of the symbol itself, and not *vice versa*.

If this is not done, then the symbol, while still a symbol, is given ontological or metaphysical status. In this way, at the religious level, the symbol or body of an *avatāra* is often contemplated as an end in itself, without the transposition of that image or body into what it is intended to represent.

A body is an instrument, a symbol by which to express and manifest a universal reality (such as Love or Knowledge). Identification with form brings with it the individualisation of an intelligible reality or truth, together with the consequences that can be seen in the world in which we live.

[5] IV.I.12 - The repetition of meditation right up to the death of the physical body should be proposed, and, accord-

ing to some references in the *Śruti*, even afterwards, because consciousness transcends the coarse physical level.

In the *Bṛhadāraṇyaka Upaniṣad* we read:

> 'Knowledge and action, together with past experience, follow him [after death].'[1]

Again, in the *Bhagavadgītā*, we read:

> 'He who abandons the body goes whither his thought is directed, O Kaunteya, because he always reaches the spiritual state related [to his thought].'
>
> 'He who devotes himself continuously to meditation without any deviation, O Pārtha, and realises *yoga* through incessant practice attains the supreme Spirit.'[2]

Given that the departure from the physical body is nothing but a transference of one's own consciousness - and of the qualities (*guṇas*) which the being has shaped on the physical level - to another level of existence, it is natural for the practice of meditation to continue even after the dissolution of the body; this implies that the process of realisation continues on the subtle levels, too, unless the identity with That (*Turīya*) has been realised during life or, at least, the overcoming of the individualized state has been realised when one moves onto the intelligible, universal plane.

[6] IV.I.14 - For the person who has obtained the realisation of That in this very life (*jīvanmukta*) the whole of the past and future, and hence all that they contain, is completely dissolved.

The assumption is that, for an effective and total realisation of identity with the Supreme, the *jīva* must have set in motion

---

[1] *Bṛ.* IV.IV.2.

[2] *Bha. Gī.* VIII.6-8. Op.cit.

situations and counter-measures such as to annul not only the demerit but also everything that constitutes merit (*sūtra* 14). The *Śruti* confirms this explicitly:

> '... However, I will tell you about That: just as water does not get attached to the petal of a flower, so wrong action does not get attached to the one who knows thus... .'[1]
>
> Again:
>
> 'When the seer sees the golden Form (*rukmavarṇa*), the *Puruṣa* who is the creator, the Lord and the source which is the *Brahman*, then the knower, having shaken off merit and demerit and freed from any contact, attains supreme identity.'[2]

[7] IV.I.15 - As has been seen, all the works (merit and demerit) of the past which would have had to mature in the present (*saṁcitakarma*) are dissolved at the outset of liberation; there remains only the *prārabdhakarma*, that which has already matured, such as already having a physical body.

When this dies, the *prārabdha*, too, is destroyed. However, for the *jīvanmukta* the physical instrument becomes merely a *shadow* and his consciousness is completely detached from it. It is by means of this *shadow* that the realised person can exercise a particular function of *dharma*.

It is necessary to specify that the various polarities, of whatever nature and degree, concern the embodied 'character' which is '... as an actor who changes garments all the time... .' (*Maitry Upaniṣad* IV.2).

Therefore it is not the *Ātman* that receives merits or demerits because It is *niṣkrya*, non- agent, being devoid of *guṇas*.

---

[1] *Chā*. IV.XIV.3.

[2] *Mu*. III.I.3.

[8] IV.I.18 - In the *Chāndogya Upaniṣad* (I.I.10) we read: '... Only when [the rite] is accomplished with the help of knowledge, faith, and the secret doctrine, it becomes even more efficacious... .'

The fact that a rite accompanied by knowledge is more efficacious than one performed without knowledge is confirmed by various passages in the *Śruti*. However, specific rites such as the *agnihotra* and others, are not inefficacious, because they also contribute, albeit indirectly, to the dissolution of *avidyā*, as has been seen in earlier *sūtras*.

According to the current *sūtra* and the passage quoted from the *Upaniṣad*, the *Brahman* can be realised by means of various 'operative instruments' and different paths, so that, be it with knowledge alone or with the study of the *Vedas*, be it through sacrifice or other means, it is possible to be reintegrated in the *Brahman*.

It may be said – and this was seen when symbols, myths, and so on were spoken of – that if the means, whatever it may be, is considered purely and simply as a means to be ferried across to the further bank, it may be valid for realisation. If the *intention* in the *agnihotra* (the offering to *Agni*) is valued as an offering to the supreme Reality, so that *Agni* acquires the symbol of Reality, this intention may be valid and decisive. If knowledge becomes a mere cultural factor, it does not provide the expected fruits. On the other hand, if the target is the 'fruit', which is *Brahman*, then that fruit is attained. See the *sūtras* which speak of obtaining the fruit through operative means. Thus, the intention is always to dissolve the *avidyā* which the *Vedas* and *Upaniṣads* consider to be the beginning of the 'fall.'

Mention may be made, for example, of three Paths which, by themselves and independently of one another, realise the supreme *Brahman*: *Jñāna mārga*, *Parabhakti mārga*, and *Yogadarśana mārga*.

The first of these realises the Supreme through *nirvikalpa samādhi*, the second through *saṁsakti-samādhi* (cohesive, intimate connection to the Principle), and the third through *nirbīja samādhi*, which corresponds to the *nirvikalpa samādhi*.

Although each of these follows its own route, they merge and unite in the 'Great Silence', the Reality without a second and without a name.

All the Scriptures, and all that derives from them, can be and exist because the *Brahman* exists, which, while being beyond all specification, is the foundation of everything that permeates all the Scriptures.

[9] IV.I.19 - With the fruition of merits and demerits, the other two types of *karma* (*āgāmin* and *saṁcita*), which would still have to take effect, are completely extinguished. It has been said that the dissolution of the two types of *karma* is brought about by the operative means; and, on the other hand, when the *karma* has come to fruition in a specific lifetime and the effects no longer exist, the person aspiring to liberation attains, on the dissolution of the physical body, re-absorption into *Brahman*. This is *videhamukti*, liberation obtained on the death of the physical body, once the fruits of merit and demerit have been exhausted.

atha caturthādhyāyaḥ

dvitīyaḥ khaṇḍaḥ

vāṅ manasi darśanāc chabdācca //1//

vāk: word, speech; *manasi*: in the mind; *darśanāt*: from observation; *śabdāt*: from tradition; *ca*: and.

ata eva ca sarvāṇyanu //2//

ataḥ: from this; *eva*: also; *ca*: and; *sarvāṇi*: all; *anu*: following.

tan manaḥ prāṇa uttarāt //3//

tat: that; *manaḥ*: mind; *prāṇa*: in *prāṇa*; *uttarāt*: according to the later.

so 'dhyakṣe tad upagamādibhyaḥ //4//

saḥ: that; *adhyakṣe*: in the inner ordainer; *tat*: that, he; *upagamādibhyaḥ*: for approaching and so on.

bhūteṣu tac chruteḥ //5//

bhūteṣu: in the elements; *tat*: this, that; *śruteḥ*: from the *Śruti*.

naikasmin darśayato hi //6//

na: not; *ekasmin*: in one, in a single; *darśayataḥ*: it is observed or stated; *hi*: because.

samānā cāsṛtyupakramād amṛtatvaṁ cānupoṣya //7//

samānā: common, equal; *ca*: and; *āsṛti-upakramāt*: [as far as] the beginning of the path; *amṛtatvam*: immortality; *ca*: and; *an-upoṣya*: not having burnt.

Book Four

Chapter Two

1. *Speech [dissolves] into mind: [this is what] is observed and [what is said] in the Scriptures.*[1]

2. *And from this, all the subsequent [functions] also.*[2]

3. *That mind in the prāṇa, according to the later.*[3]

4. *That [the prāṇa] within the inner ordainer for the purpose of approaching it, and so on.*[4]

5. *In the subtle elements: this [is stated] in the Śruti.*

The principle of life (*jīva*), together with the *prāṇa*, organises itself within the very essence of the subtle elements which represent the elementary seeds or nuclei which are used to constitute future organs by means of which the *jīva*, with its reflexion, can express and manifest itself.

6. *Not in a single [element], since [the Śruti and the Smṛti] affirm this.*[5]

7. *[The departure for all is] the same [at the beginning] of the way, [but] the immortality [of the knower who is as yet unqualified is merely relative], since he has not burnt [metaphysical ignorance].*[6]

tad āpīteḥ saṁsāra vyapadeśāt // 8 //

tat: that; *āpīteḥ*: until the attainment; *saṁsāra*: *saṁsāra*; *vyapadeśāt*: on account of the indication.

sūkṣmaṁ pramāṇataś ca tathā upalabdheḥ // 9 //

sūkṣmam: subtle; *pramāṇataḥ*: measure, dimension; *ca*: and; *tathā*: thus, in this way; *upalabdheḥ*: from the perception or understanding.

nopamardenātaḥ // 10 //

na: not; *upamardena*: by means of destruction or dissolution; *ataḥ*: for this reason, thus.

asyaiva copapatter eṣa ūṣmā // 11 //

asya (= *idam*): of this, its; *eva*: only; *ca*: and; *upapatteḥ*: on account of the possibility; *eṣah*: this; *ūṣmā*: heat, warmth.

pratiṣedhāt iti cen na śarīrāt // 12 //

pratiṣedhāt: on account of denial; *iti cet*: if it [is said]; *na*: not; *śarīrāt*: from the embodied being.

8. *That [the subtle body, remains until] the attainment; [this is] the indication [of remaining in] saṁsāra.*[7]

9. *And [that is] subtle in dimension: this is how it is perceived.*

The various bodies, excluding the gross physical body, are subtle and elementary; they are more elusive than light, and they exceed the velocity of light. However, as was hinted at earlier, as long as they persist, one remains at the level of generation. These subtle bodies, with which the *jīva* clothes itself, are, according to *Vedānta*, named *prāṇamayakośa*, *manomayakośa*, and *buddhimayakośa*, and they constitute the *sūkṣmaśarīra*. See the 'Preliminary notes' on the First Chapter of Book Three.

10. *For this reason [it is] not [able to be] destroyed.*

On account of the fact that they are subtle, these bodies cannot be destroyed on the dissolution of the gross body (*sthūlaśarīra*).

11. *And this heat [is] possible only for this [subtle body].*[8]

12. *If it [is said that the vital breaths do not go away], on account of the denial [made by the Scriptures, the answer is that] this is not so [because what is being denied is the detachment of the breaths] from the embodied being [and not the detachment of the breaths from the body].*[9]

spaṣṭo hyekeṣām // 13 //

spaṣṭaḥ: clear, evident; *hi*: in fact, because; *ekeṣām*: of some.

smaryate ca // 14 //

smaryate: it is stated in the *Smṛti*; *ca*: and.

tāni pare tathā hyāha // 15 //

tāni: those; *pare*: in the Supreme; *tathā*: thus; *hi*: because; *āha*: it says.

avibhāgo vacanāt // 16 //

a-vibhāgaḥ: absence of distinction; *vacanāt*: on account of the declaration.

tadoko 'grajvalanaṁ tat prakāśita dvāro vidyā sāmarthyāt tac cheṣagatyanusmṛti yogāc ca hārdānugṛhītaḥ śata-adhikayā // 17 //

tat: that; *okaḥ*: dwelling; *agrajvalanam*: apex, top; *tat*: that; *prakāśita*: shining, luminous, resplendent; *dvāraḥ*: door, opening; *vidyā*: knowledge; *sāmarthyāt*: on account of the strength or power of circumstances; *tat*: that; *śeṣa-gati*: the way of constant practice; *anusmṛti*: knowledge; *yogāt*: on account of meditation, *ca*: and; *hārdānugṛhītaḥ*: favoured by him who resides in the heart; *śata*: one hundred; *adhikayā*: by the one transcending.

raśmyanusārī // 18 //

raśmi: sunbeam; *anusārī*: following.

13. *Indeed, [the denial is] evident, according to some [other schools].*

14. *And [this is also what] the Smṛti states.*[10]

15. *Those in the Supreme, because this is stated [by the Scripture].*[11]

16. *[For this reason, there is] an absence of distinction [from the Supreme]: this has been declared.*

For this reason, there is no distinction between the liberated *jīva* and the *Brahman* itself. Since the breaths are dissolved and the *nāmarūpa* is extinguished (*nirvāṇa*), what is left is only the Being without a second (Compare *Praśna Upaniṣad* VI.5). This is what is declared by the *Śruti*. By the extinction of all desires the *guṇas* return to *prakṛti*, to which they belong.

17. *[When the jīva is about to detach itself from the body, there occurs] the kindling of the top of its dwelling [the heart]; the door [by which it leaves becomes] illuminated through the power of knowledge and of constant meditation [which is part of] that [knowledge, being the jīva] favoured by him [the Lord] who resides in the heart, [and in this way it goes up along that which] surpasses one hundred.*[12]

18. *It follows the rays of the sun.*[13]

niśi neti cen na sambandhasya yāvaddeha-bhāvitvād darśayati ca // 19 //

niśi: at night; *na*: not; *iti cet*: if it [is said]; *na*: not; *sambandhasya*: of the connection or relationship; *yāvat*: until, as long as; *deha*: the body; *bhāvitvāt*: on account of the existence; *darśayati*: it declares; *ca*: and, moreover.

ataś-cāyane 'pi dakṣiṇe // 20 //

ataḥ: for the same reason; *ca*: and; *ayane*: on the path; *api*: also; *dakṣiṇe*: southern.

yoginaḥ prati ca smaryate smārte caite // 21 //

yoginaḥ: for the *yogis*; *prati*: propitious; *ca*: and; *smaryate*: it is stated in the *Smṛti*; *smārte*: belonging to the *Smṛti*; *ca*: and; *ete*: these [two].

iti dvitīyaḥ khaṇḍaḥ

caturthādhyāyaḥ

19. *If it [is said that the jīva] does not [follow the rays] at night, [the reply is] not so [because there is] the connection [of the nāḍīs with the rays] as long as the body exists. Moreover, this is declared [in the Scripture].*[14]

20. *And for the same reason it also follows [the rays] on the southern [course].*

Thus, for the same reason, the *jīva* that follows the rays of the sun can detach itself even during the southern course of the sun, that is, between the summer solstice and the winter solstice.

True realisation is independent of astrological and cosmological circumstances.

21. *[These indications are] in the Smṛti as being propitious for the yogis, and these belong to the Smṛti.*

These indications of time are proposed by the *Smṛti* for those in particular who practise *Yoga* and *Sāṁkhya*. See the *Bhagavadgītā* (VIII.23-27). The indications, however, relate to the two paths called *devayāna* and *pitṛyāna*, which are also mentioned by the *Śruti*.

End of Chapter Two of Book Four
of the Brahmasūtra

NOTES

[1] IV.II.1 - The Second Chapter of the Fourth Book presents the return journey of the *jīva* on the death of the coarse physical body.

The single Tradition (East and West), with variations in verbal expression, points to the same journey that is undertaken after the death of the gross body.

At the moment of the dissolution of the gross physical body, the function of speech ceases to operate, being re-absorbed into the mental function, which persists even after the departure of the physical instrument. This is commonly observable and is also declared by the scriptural Tradition.

[2] IV.II.2 - And following this process, there are also re-absorbed into the mind the functions of the other organs. In this process, what is re-absorbed into the mind is not the physical organ; for example, it is not the physical eye which is re-absorbed, but the vital function which manifests through the physical organ. Thus the reference is not to the vocal chords but to the vital function which manifests through the vocal chords. (*Praśna Upaniṣad* III.9).

On the path of the exteriorisation of the *jīva* at the physical level, the process is reversed.

[3] IV.II.3 - The same mind is re-absorbed into the *prāṇa*, according to the later passage in the *Śruti*. There are various passages from the *Śruti*. See the *Chāndogya Upaniṣad* (VI.

VIII.6), where we read: 'My dear, when man is about to die, his speech withdraws into mind, mind into *prāṇa*... .'

Therefore, as has been seen already, the function of speech is re-absorbed into the mind, and the same function of the mind is re-absorbed into the *prāṇa*. Thus, on the 'way of descent' or exteriorisation, it is the vital function which avails itself of an organ to develop its own specific activity.

[4] IV.II.4 - That – namely, the *prāṇa* – is re-absorbed, in its turn, into the *jīva*, the inner ordainer, which holds all the various functions within itself, as their source and foundation. Once these have been reabsorbed into the *jīva*, the *prāṇa* and the functions are there in potentiality, ready for later descents at the lower levels of manifestation and the appropriation of the corresponding organs.

In the *Śruti* we read:

> 'Just as *ugra* and *sūta* village-heads surround a king who is setting off on a journey, so, at the hour of death, all the *prāṇas* encompass this *ātmā* when the body is about to surrender its last breath.'[1]

[5] IV.II.6 - The *jīva* does not withdraw into a single element, because both the *Śruti* and the *Smṛti* affirm this. The *jīva* dwells in the centre of the subtle essence of all the elements, including the gross elements, because all the elements are required for the constitution of a new body.

The different kinds of *prāṇa* (*apāna, vyāna* and so on) which preside over the various physical organs and the various faculties, which such organs express, withdraw into the *jīva*.

---

[1] *Bṛ.* IV.III.38.

References passages are: *Bṛhadāraṇyaka Upaniṣad* (IV. IV.1-5), *Manu* (I.27), and *Viṣṇu Purāṇa* (I.II.48).

[6] IV.II.7 - The departure from the physical body is identical for both the knower and the non-knower, because death, being the loss of a vehicle or form, applies to the whole of the relative life. (*Bṛhadāraṇyaka Upaniṣad* IV.IV.7; *Kaṭha Upaniṣad* II.II.3 *et seqq.*).

But while the knower, at the time of departure, goes out through the *suṣumṇānāḍī* and reaches the state of immortality (*Brahmaloka*), the non-knower, on the other hand, goes out through one of the many *nāḍīs*, so that the state of *Brahmaloka* is not attained. If the process of death is the same for all, the pathways on the return journey are different. Thus there is the way called *devayāna* and the way called *pitṛyāna*: the way of the gods and the way of the ancestors; or the solar way and the lunar way. (*Kauṣītakī Upaniṣad* I.2-3).

Brahmaloka is the state of *saguṇa Brahman*; for *nirguṇa Brahman* it is necessary to burn all the seeds of *avidyā*, or *māyā*. With *saguṇa* (with *guṇas*) one attains immortality in the world of manifestation (the threefold world); with *nirguṇa* (devoid of *guṇas*) one attains that eternity which transcends time, space, and causality. From the metaphysical perspective there is no death, since the *jīvātman* is non-born.

[7] IV.II.8 - The subtle body, with the various elements, such as fire, and with functions such as hearing, persists until final attainment and identity with the *Brahman* occur. (Compare *Chāndogya Upaniṣad* VI.VIII.6).

Otherwise, as the *Śruti* teaches, one attains the condition of relative immortality in the state of *Brahmaloka*, from which, not having destroyed all the seeds related to *saṁsāra*, one returns; in this case, however, one returns to universal dimensions.

The teaching can be monistic, dualistic, or non-dual, to which there are specific corresponding states of consciousness. As long as the *jīva* is darkened by the *guṇas*, it may find itself in the individualised state with its reflection, or if it has solved the individualized condition, it may find itself in the universal state (*Brahmaloka*), which is its natural abode; when it is freed from the *guṇas* (*sattva*, *rajas*, *tamas*) and hence from the vehicles or bodies by means of which the *guṇas* can express themselves, then it finds itself in the state of *nirguṇa*, without *guṇas*.

[8] IV.II.11 - And the heat (*tejas*) which is noticeable in the gross body belongs to the subtle body; when the subtle body is detached from the gross body, the latter remains cold, deprived of life.

Thus the *Śruti* declares that the gross body is warm in life and cold in death.

[9] IV.II.12 - If it is maintained that the *Śruti* denies that the vital breaths of a knower of *Brahman* do not get detached, the *sūtra* under consideration states that this is not the case, because the *Śruti* denies the detachment of the breaths, and so on, from the embodied soul and not the detachment of the breaths, and so on, from the body. If the vital breaths remained in the gross body, there would be no death at all.

On the other hand, the *Śruti* has two points of reference: one which speaks of the person who, 'departing', *must* return (and hence, he brings the vital breaths along with himself) in order to have a new birth; and one which maintains that:

'He who is desireless, free from desire, having satisfied

desire, and for whom the *Ātman* is the very object of desire: for him, his organs depart not. Being the *Brahman* Itself, he is merged into *Brahman*.'

'When all the desires which lodge in his heart have died away, then the mortal becomes immortal, and in this life he attains *Brahman*.'[1]

This final state of consciousness is specific to the *jīvanmukta* (the one who is liberated in this life).

[10] IV.II.14 - Other schools maintain the same when referring to the *Śruti*.

'"... when this man dies, do his organs detach going back up to him or not?" "They do not," replied Yājñavalkya.'[2]

This condition concerns the state of the 'One liberated in life' mentioned in the previous *sūtra*. On the other hand, if the vital breaths had to depart, drawing the *jīva* with them, there could not be true liberation, because another birth in 'other regions' would be inevitable. This is what the *Smṛti*, too, confirms: see *Mahābhārata* (XII.270.22).

[11] IV.II.15 - Those subtle elements merge into the Supreme, in the sense that they disappear, having no ontological reality.

The result is that the breaths or subtle elements merge into the mental *prakṛti*, to emerge later, making a new body for a future birth at specific levels of existence. For the knower, these elements dissolve and disappear, there being no longer a cause which can support them and nourish them in a coherent fashion. The power of the unresolved *guṇas* imparts attrac-

---

[1] *Bṛ*. IV.IV.6-7.

[2] *Ibid*. III.II.11.

tiveness and coherence to the structure of bodies, in whatever dimension they are to unfold. (See *Muṇḍaka Upaniṣad* III.II.7 *et seqq.*; *Chāndogya Upaniṣad* VI.VIII.6 *et seqq.*).

[12] IV.II.17 - When the *jīva* is about to detach itself from the coarse body, there is released from the centre of the heart (*hṛdayacakra*) a brilliant light, by means of which the way out is illuminated. The *jīva*, favoured by him who resides in the heart, thus takes that path which surpasses the one hundred paths.

The departure – whether it be of the knower or of the one who has not yet realised knowledge in its entirety – occurs in the same way (the way out from the centre of the heart is found by means of the brilliant light), but while for the knower the subsequent movement is along the *nādī suṣumṇā*, through the *cakra* of the head, for the non-knower the movement is diffused along the hundred passage-ways which lead in the different directions of the vital body. (See *Chāndogya Upaniṣad* VIII.VI.6).

The way of return is according to the being's level of consciousness, according to whether the pathway is to the *nirguṇa* or the *saguṇa*, and according to the type of meditation, and so on.

An awakened *jīva* merges with the supreme *Ātman*; a *jīva* not yet awakened follows the law of its own being and goes to occupy that level of existence that is appropriate to its degree of spiritual maturity.

Where the aspiration is, there is one's heart.

The *jīva* is attached to the dense physical body mainly by two luminous 'threads': the one anchored in the head expresses consciousness and all the other faculties, while the one at the centre of the heart gives life to the bodily form.

When the second one is detached, there is that brilliant light which is a sign that the *jīva* has left its point of contact with the physical level.

The consciousness, too, can withdraw, but without total detachment, and the gross body continues to be alive, which is what happens in sleep or in other states of non-awareness, such as a coma.

The *cakras* (= circle, wheel) are accumulators and distributors of the *prāṇa*.

There is now given a brief outline of the seven *cakras* which are located along the spinal column in the *prāṇamayakośa* sheath:

Mūlādhāra which feeds the adrenal glands

Svādhiṣṭhāṇa which feeds the gonads

Maṇipura which feeds the liver and the pancreas

Anāhata which feeds the thymus

Viśuddha which feeds the thyroid and parathyroid

Ājñā which feeds the pituitary gland or hypophysis

Sahasrāra which feeds the pineal gland.

The first three *cakras* are located below the diaphragm, the other three above the diaphragm; the last one combines all the *cakras*. Only a hint has been given because the structure of the *cakras* is complex since it touches the physical, psychological and, mainly, the spiritual sphere leading to realisation.[1]

---

[1] To go deeper into this subject, see Patañjali, *The Regal Way to Realization* (*Yogadarśana*), edited by Raphael. Op. cit.

[13] IV.II.18 - 'But when it separates from the body, then it departs along these rays... The *nāḍīs* [which lead] from the heart are one hundred and one. Of them, only one goes up through [the top of] the head. Rising through that *nāḍī* one gains immortality. The other *nāḍīs*, which lead in all directions... .'[1]

The *jīva*, or better the reflection of the *embodied jīva*, which departs through the *suṣumṇā*, follows the rays of the sun, while the other *jīvas* depart in different directions, thus following the lunar way..

[14] IV.II.19 - On the other hand, the *Śruti* also states that for anyone who is following the rays of the sun this can take place not only by day but also by night. Between the rays of the sun and the *nāḍīs* there also exists a metaphysical connection: whoever follows the rays of the sun is naturally following a metaphysical *sādhanā*.

---

[1] *Chā*. VIII.VI.5-6.

atha caturthādhyāyaḥ

tṛtīyaḥ khaṇḍaḥ

arcirādinā tat-prathiteḥ // 1 //

arciḥ: brilliant flame; *ādinā*: which begins; *tat*: that; *prathiteḥ*: well known.

vāyum abdād aviśeṣa viśeṣābhyām // 2 //

vāyum: the god of the air; *abdāt*: from the year; *a-viśeṣa-viśeṣābhyām*: on account of the absence and presence of specification.

taḍito 'dhi varuṇaḥ sambandhāt // 3 //

taḍitaḥ: lightning, flash; *adhi*: after; *varuṇaḥ*: Varuṇa [the god of the sky and the waters]; *sambandhāt*: on account of the connection or relationship.

ātivāhikāstalliṅgāt // 4 //

ātivāhikāḥ: passing beyond, conveying; *tat*: that; *liṅgāt*: on account of the indicatory sign.

Book Four

Chapter Three

This chapter speaks further of the journey of the *jīva* through the planes of existence as far as *Brahmaloka* and even beyond this.

1. *[The jīva] begins with the brilliant flame; this [is] well-known.*[1]

2. *From [the god of] the year to [the god] Vāyu, on account of non-specification and specification.*

According to the interpretation by Śaṅkara and other commentators (such as Bhāskara), it is a question of putting the year directly after the months, and the world of the gods before that of the air, in accordance with the specification given in the *Bṛhadāraṇyaka Upaniṣad* (VI.II.15). In this context there is a precise specification of the various regions through which the *jīva* passes in order to enter *Brahmaloka*.

3. *From [the god of] lightning to Varuṇa, on account of the connection.*[2]

4. *[The gods are those who] convey beyond; these are the indicatory signs.*[3]

ubhaya vyāmohāt tat siddheḥ // 5 //

ubhaya: both; *vyāmohāt*: from loss of consciousness; *tat*: that; *siddheḥ*: demonstrated.

vaidyutenaiva tatas tac chruteḥ // 6 //

vaidyutena: by the lightning flash; *eva*: only; *tataḥ*: from there; *tat*: that; *śruteḥ*: according to the *Śruti*.

kāryaṁ bādarir asya gatyupapatteḥ // 7 //

kāryam: effect; *bādariḥ*: Bādari; *asya*: its; *gati*: way; *upapatteḥ*: on account of the possibility.

viśeṣitatvācca // 8 //

viśeṣitatvāt: on account of being qualified; *ca*: and.

sāmīpyāt tu tad vyapadeśaḥ // 9 //

sāmīpyāt: on account of nearness, proximity; *tu*: but; *tat*: that; *vyapadeśaḥ*: designation.

kāryātyaye tad adhyakṣeṇa sahātaḥ-param abhidhānāt // 10 //

kārya: effect; *atyaye*: in the extinction or dissolution; *tat*: that; *adhyakṣeṇa*: (with) the ruler, ordainer; *saha*: with; *ataḥ*: than that; *param*: supreme; *abhidhānāt*: on account of the declaration or designation.

5. *This is demonstrated through the unconsciousness of both.*[4]

6. *From there [the jīvas are conducted] only by the one who is related to the lightning flash. This is what the Śruti says.*

From this moment the embodied consciousness is guided by the awakened intelligence to the world of Light, because the intelligence, being itself Light, is related to the lightning flash. This is what the *Śruti* declares.

7. *According to Bādari [the jīvas are conducted] to the qualified Brahman [because there is a] possibility [in relation] to this.*[5]

8. *And on account of being qualified.*[6]

9. *But on account of its proximity [to the nirguṇa] the designation [saguṇa is] as That.*[7]

10. *With the extinction of the effect, together with the Ordainer, [the jīvas merge into] That [which is] the Supreme, according to the declaration.*

With the extinction of the causal body and thus of the manifestation, together with its ruler, the *jīvas* which have attained perfect knowledge reach the Supreme, which transcends the non-Supreme (*Brahmaloka*), in accordance with the declaration made by the *Śruti*. (See the previous *sūtra*).

smṛteś ca // 11 //

smṛteḥ: according to the *Smṛti*; *ca*: and.

paraṁ jaiminir mukhyatvāt // 12 //

param: supreme; *jaiminiḥ*: Jaimini; *mukhyatvāt*: in accordance with the chief or pre-eminent.

darśanāc ca // 13 //

darśanāt: from observation; *ca*: and.

na ca kārye pratipattyabhisandhiḥ // 14 //

na: not; *ca*: and; *kārye*: in the effect *pratipatti*: the act of obtaining; *abhisandhiḥ*: intent, intention.

apratīkālambanāt nayatīti bādarāyaṇa ubhayathā 'doṣāt tat kratuś ca // 15 //

apratīka-ālambanāt: those who do not rely on symbols; *nayati*: leads, guides; *iti*: this; *bādarāyaṇaḥ*: Bādarāyaṇa; *ubhayathā*: in two ways, in both cases; *adoṣāt*: through no defect; *tat*: that; *kratuḥ*: purpose; *ca*: and.

11. *This is [confirmed] by the Smṛti.*

The above is confirmed by both the Śruti and the Smṛti. In the Kurma Purāṇa (I.XII.269) we read:

> 'When it is the time of dissolution (*pralaya*), all those [who have acquired perfect knowledge] go to the supreme abode.'

This confirms that, when the time of dissolution comes, the *jīvas* that have the requisite qualifications go back to the Supreme.

12. *Jaimini [maintains that the jīvas are led] to the Supreme, [in accordance with] the principal [meaning].*

Jaimini the Teacher maintains that the *jīvas* are led to the Supreme (*param*), because this expression must be understood as the primary element, in contrast to the secondary element. (See the *Chāndogya Upaniṣad*, IV.XV.5).

13. *And this is stated.*

And the above is stated in the *Śruti*.

14. *And the intent to obtain [That can] not [be in relation to] the effect.*[8]

15. *Bādarāyaṇa [maintains that the universal being] leads [to Brahmaloka alone] those who do not rely on symbols [in their meditations], and because there is no defect in this twofold division [which is a result of this, each achieves] the purpose of that [on which he meditates].*

viśeṣaṁ ca darśayati // 16 //

viśeṣam: the difference; *ca*: and; *darśayati*: it is verified [in the Scriptures].

iti tṛtīyaḥ khaṇḍaḥ

caturthādhyāyaḥ

16. *And [in the Scriptures] the difference of meditations on symbols is verified.*[9]

End of Chapter Three of Book Four
of the Brahmasūtra

NOTES

[1] IV.III.1 - The *jīva* proceeds towards *Brahmaloka*, beginning with the brilliant flame. In the *Śruti* there are some differences with regard to the return journey. Thus we can read:

> 'There, those who know thus, those who meditate with faith and in austerity in the forest, they attain the flame, from the flame [they attain] the daylight, from the daylight the bright fortnight, from the bright fortnight the six months of the ascending [course of the sun]... from the months the year, from the year the sun, from the sun the moon, and from the moon the lightning. There a non-human being makes them move on to [the world of] *Brahmā*. This is the path of the gods.'[1]

There is another part of the *Śruti* in which we read:

> 'When a man departs from this world, he reaches the air: there, the air opens, making a passage for him [as wide] as the axle-hole in a cart-wheel. Through this he proceeds upwards and reaches the sun... .'[2]

The first quotation associates the process of return with fire, while the second associates it with air in order to go upwards and reach the sun. Thus there seem to be some discrepancies.

According to the *Brahmasūtra*, there are no substantial differences, because the *Bṛhadāraṇyaka Upaniṣad* (VI.II.15)

---

[1] *Chā*. V.X.1-2.

[2] *Bṛ*. V.X.1.

also has the same sequence as the *Chāndogya Upaniṣad*. The paths may be different but the destination is the same.

[2] IV.III.3 - After the lightning there is *Varuṇa*, on account of the connection which he has with lightning. *Varuṇa* represents the god of rain and is placed after the lightning: rain is released after the lightning and thunder.

In the *Chāndogya Upaniṣad* (VII.XI.1) we read:

> 'It is hot; it burns; it will surely rain... Fire, which has revealed itself previously, later generates water. When, among the rumbles of thunder, that propagates upwards and crosswise like the flashes of lightning, then everyone says, "There is lightning and thunder. It will surely rain."'

[3] IV.III.4 - These divinities are those which convey the *jīva* along the return path called *devayāna*. This is the path which leads to *Brahmaloka* or *Satyaloka*, from which one must not return to the plane of individuality. Symbolically, it is also the northward course of the sun from the Tropic of Capricorn to the Tropic of Cancer, which is the time intervening between the winter solstice and the summer solstice.

These passages, with their symbols and their Gods, should be interpreted as states of consciousness. On its journey to *Brahmaloka* the *jīva* experiences states of consciousness which can be defined symbolically as earth, water, air, fire, and ether.[1]

The Hermetic Tradition, too, speaks of these elements as states of consciousness.

[4] IV.III.5 - On the withdrawal of the individualised being, the organs of the sensory principles fail, being thus in a state

---

[1] Cp. *Chā*. IV.XV.5.

of unconsciousness and darkness, as happens when someone faints, so that the intervention of an external intelligent agent is required to lead and guide the embodied reflection of consciousness. Thus the one who is making the return journey and the pathway itself are both darkened.

[5] IV.III.7 - According to Bādari the Teacher, the *jīvas* are conducted to *kārya-Brahmā*, that is, to *saguṇa Brahman*, because there is a possibility that may be admitted in relation to this way.

From the passage in question, which deals with the return journey of the *jīva*, it is to be understood that the destination is always *Brahmaloka*. It is only with reference to this way that one can speak of states of consciousness that are experienced, with the additional possibility of giving specific positions of consciousness. The *nirguṇa Brahman*, having no connection, no relationship (*asparśa*), with anything since it is the root of all that exists (Being and non-being), cannot be an object of rational explanation or of states of objective experience, and it does not have any relationship with the sensory principles. The 'experience-less' *nirguṇa* is realised when the *Kevala* within us reveals itself as the supreme Reality devoid of everything that is 'second.'

[6] IV.III.8 - In the *Śruti* we read:

'There, a being generated by the mind [of *Hiraṇyagarbha*, that is *Brahmā* or *Íśvara*] leads to the worlds of *Brahmā* those who have reached the lightning flash. They dwell in those worlds of *Brahmā* like divinities and for a long time. For them, there is no more returning.'[1]

---

[1] *Bṛ.* VI.II.15.

That is, there is no more returning to the world of men. This *Śruti* passage, like others, speaks of worlds in the plural (in this particular case the word is *lokān*, the accusative plural), these being the states of consciousness of indefinite numbers of *jīvas* who take up their positions according to their level of realisation.

Sometimes the *Śruti* speaks of the 'World of *Brahmā*' as being *nirguṇa*, but it is clear that, from the actual context in which these words occur, this phrase can be understood to refer to a figurative or allegorical symbol.

In the *nirguṇa* there are neither innumerable worlds nor many *jīvas*, for these belong to the world perceived by the senses and to the intelligible world.

[7] IV.III.9 - The designation concerns the realisation of *saguṇa*, which is also attained on account of its proximity to *That*, that is, the *nirguṇa Brahman*. The *saguṇa* is nothing other than the principial cause, so that there are not two distinct *Brahmans*; there is only *That*, because the *saguṇa*, as the cause of manifestation, depends on, and receives its reason for existence from the *nirguṇa Brahman*.

On the dissolution of manifestation (*pralaya*) those who have attained perfect Knowledge through proximity to the *nirguṇa* merge into the *nirguṇa*. This is what the *Śruti* calls *kramamukti*, delayed liberation or liberation in stages; it is the ascent of the *jīva* in the course of successive lives on different levels of existence (*loka*), until final liberation. We are still on the way known as *devayāna*.

[8] IV.III.14 - And the intent, or aspiration, to attain the supreme *Brahman* cannot be understood as a *Brahman* that is not supreme.

According to Śaṅkara the Teacher, *sūtras* 12-14 may be considered by a theoretical objector, according to whom the realisation of the supreme *Brahman* is attained by following the path of determinations, differences, the end, and so on.

Śaṅkara, on the other hand, agrees with the proposition of Bādari the Teacher, whose interpretation is that the *jīvas* are led to the *kārya-Brahmā*, that is, to the *saguṇa Brahman* and not to the *nirguṇa Brahman.*[1]

[9] IV.III.16 - Bādarāyaṇa maintains that one becomes that on which one meditates, but this cannot be valid, of course, if the only support to meditation is a mere symbol. Only those whose object of meditation is the *saguṇa Brahman* (*Brahmaloka*) go to the *saguṇa Brahman.*

There is no fault in the twofold division of those who do not rely on symbols and those who meditate on that which one must be, which is *nirguṇa Brahman.*

On the other hand, the *Śruti* witnesses to the differences relating to the fruits that are obtained from meditating on symbols, symbols of varying nature: sounds, lights, *maṇḍalas*, and so on. The *Śruti* shows which fruits are yielded by specific meditations.

> "“He who meditates on name as *Brahman* there he achieves freedom of movement as far as the range of the name extends. He who meditates on name as *Brahman.*” “O venerable sir, is there anything higher than name?” “There is certainly something higher than name.” “O venerable sir, teach me it.”"[2]

The *Upaniṣad* begins with the ‘name’ of the Lord and

---

[1] Cp. *Bra. Sū.* IV.III.7-8 with the *bhāṣya* of Śaṅkara. Op. cit.

[2] *Chā.* VII.I.5; VII.II.1-2 *et seqq.*

continues with an ascending series: word (*vāc*) is higher than names, mind (*manas*) is higher than word, and so on, until we reach the *Ātman*, the *Brahman*, which is Infiniteness.

In accordance with the seed of meditation, that seed is realised, but there is meditation without seed (*nirbīja*) too.

atha caturthādhyāyaḥ
caturthaḥ khaṇḍaḥ

sampadyāvirbhāvaḥ svena śabdāt // 1 //

sampadya: having obtained, having realised; *āvirbhāvaḥ*: revelation; *svena*: its own; *śabdāt*: from the scriptural word.

muktaḥ pratijñānāt // 2 //

muktaḥ: liberated; *pratijñānāt*: according to the promise.

ātmā prakaraṇāt // 3 //

ātmā: *Ātman*; *prakaraṇāt*: from the explanation of a doctrinal context.

avibhāgena dṛṣṭatvāt // 4 //

a-vibhāgena: through non-separation; *dṛṣṭatvāt*: on account of the verification.

brāhmeṇa jaiminir upanyāsādibhyaḥ // 5 //

brāhmeṇa: through the nature or state of the *Brahman*; *jaiminiḥ*: Jaimini; *upanyāsādibhyaḥ*: according to the reference, exposition, declaration, and so on.

citi tanmātreṇa tad-ātmakatvād ityauḍulomiḥ // 6 //

citi-tanmātreṇa: through essential intelligence alone; *tat*: this, that; *ātmakatvāt*: from the nature of the *Ātman*; *vāt*: how; *iti*: thus; *auḍulomiḥ*: Auḍulomi.

Book Four

Chapter Four

1. *Having realised [That], it reveals itself [in its own nature, as is made clear] from the word 'its own.'*[1]

2. *[It is] liberated, in accordance with the promise [of the Scriptures].*

3. *[That Light is] the Ātman, in accordance with a contextual explanation.*

4. *[The jīva] is not separate [from the Brahman], as is verified [in the Scriptures].*[2]

5. *Jaimini maintains that [there is possession] of the state of the Brahman, in accordance with the declaration and so on [made in the Scriptures].*

According to Jaimini the Teacher, on express reference made in the Scriptures, one who is liberated possesses the state of the *Brahman*.

For the specific aphorisms see Note 2.

6. *[The liberated jīva exists] only as essential Intelligence, which [is the nature of] the Ātmā. This is what Auḍulomi says.*[3]

evam apyupanyāsāt pūrva bhāvād avirodhaṁ bāda-rāyaṇaḥ // 7 //

evam: thus, in this way; *api*: also, even; *upanyāsāt*: from scriptural reference; *pūrva*: previous, preceding; *bhāvāt*: on account of existence; *avirodham*: non-contradiction; *bādarāyaṇaḥ*: Bādarāyaṇa.

saṁkalpād eva tu tac chruteḥ // 8 //

saṁkalpāt: on account of determination; *eva*: only; *tu*: but; *tat*: that; *śruteḥ*: from the *Śruti*.

ata eva cānanyādhipatiḥ // 9 //

ataḥ eva: for this reason; *ca*: and; *an*: not; *anya*: other; *adhipatiḥ*: lord, sovereign.

abhāvaṁ bādarir āha hyevam // 10 //

a-bhāvam: non-existence; *bādariḥ*: Bādari; *āha*: says, affirms; *hi*: because; *evam*: thus.

bhāvaṁ jaiminir vikalpāmananāt // 11 //

bhāvam: existence; *jaiminiḥ*: Jaimini; *vikalpa*: difference; *āmananāt*: on account of the declaration.

dvādaśāhavad ubhaya vidhaṁ bādarāyaṇo 'taḥ // 12 //

dvādaśa-aha-vat: like the time of the twelve-day ceremony; *ubhaya*: twofold, both; *vidham*: aspects; *bādarāyaṇaḥ*: Bādarāyaṇa; *ataḥ*: hence, for this reason.

7. *According to Bādarāyaṇa, even on account of the existence of anterior qualities [admitted] from scriptural references [there is] non-contradiction.*

Even admitting the existence of anterior qualities, to which Jaimini the Teacher has referred, this does not, in the view of Bādarāyaṇa, constitute any contradiction, because Jaimini is referring to anterior qualities of the *saguṇa Brahman*, the qualified *Brahman*.

8. *But it is only through determination [that the jīva achieves its aim]. This is what the Śruti declares.*[4]

9. *And for this reason [the liberated jīva has] no other lord.*[5]

10. *According to Bādari, [there is] no existence, because this is what [the Śruti] affirms.*[6]

11. *According to Jaimini [on the other hand, there is] existence [of bodies and of organs therefore] different [forms can be assumed], in accordance with the declaration.*[7]

12. *For this reason Bādarāyaṇa [believes that the liberated jīva can assume] both aspects, as in the case of the twelve-day ceremony.*

According to Bādarāyaṇa, there is no contradiction: there can be a *jīva* that assumes a form, just as there can be a *jīva* that does not assume a form; thus the twelve-day sacrifice can consist of *sattra* (conducted by a number of officiants) or of *ahīna* (conducted by a single officiant). That is, it presents itself in two different ways. This is also affirmed by the *Śruti*.

tanvabhāve sandhyavad upapatteḥ // 13 //

tanu: the body; *a-bhāve*: in the absence; *sandhya-vat*: as in dream; *upapatteḥ*: on account of the possibility or reasonableness.

bhāve jāgradvat // 14 //

bhāve: in being, in existing; *jāgrat*: the waking state; *vat*: like, as.

pradīpavad āveśas tathā hi darśayati // 15 //

pradīpa-vat: like a lamp or flame or lamplight; *āveśaḥ*: the act of entering; *tathā*: thus; *hi*: because; *darśayati*: it is verified [in the Scripture].

svāpyaya sampattyor anyatarāpekṣam āviṣkṛtaṁ hi // 16 //

svāpyaya: deep sleep; *sampattyoḥ*: in uniting with each other; *anyatara*: one (of two); *apekṣam*: reference; *āviṣkṛtam*: known, evident; *hi*: because.

jagad vyāpāra varjam prakaraṇād asannihitatvāc ca // 17 //

jagat: world; *vyāpāra*: function, activity; *varjam*: except, apart from; *prakaraṇāt*: from the doctrinal treatise; *a-sannihitatvāt*: from non-relationship, from non-contiguity; *ca*: and.

pratyakṣopadeśād iti cen nādhikārika maṇḍalasthokteḥ // 18 //

pratyakṣa: direct perception; *upadeśāt*: on account of the teaching; *iti cet*: if [it is said]; *na*: not; *adhikārika*: with reference to the qualified; *maṇḍalastha*: the [solar] disk; *ukteḥ*: from what is said.

13. *In the absence of the body [the fulfilment of the will is] possible, as it is during dream.*

14. *[On the other hand], when [the body] exists [it is] as if in the waking state.*

Whether a body or vehicle of expression exists or not is of little importance to the liberated *saguṇa*, inasmuch as its will remains ever free.

15. *The entry [of the jīva into various bodies is] similar [to the diversification of] the flame of a lamp, because this is what is verified.*[8]

16. *[The mention by the Scriptures of the absence of every distinctive cognition is] with reference to one or the other of the [following] two: deep sleep or union [with the Brahman], because this [is] evident [in the Śruti].*[9]

17. *Apart from the activity of the world [this is affirmed] in the doctrinal treatises and on account of non-contiguity.*[10]

18. *If [it is said that the one who is liberated has unlimited powers] from direct teaching, [the reply is] that this is not so, on account of the statement [with reference to] the Qualified [which dwells in] the disk [of the sun].*[11]

vikārāvarti ca tathā hi sthitim āha // 19 //

vikāra: changeable; *a-varti*: without location, beyond; *ca*: and; *tathā*: thus; *hi*: because; *sthitim*: state of being or existence; *āha*: has said.

darśayataś caivam pratyakṣa anumāne // 20 //

darśayataḥ: they show; *ca*: and; *evam*: also, thus; *pratyakṣa*: direct perception (*Śruti*); *anumāne*: inference, deduction.

bhoga mātra sāmya liṅgāc ca // 21 //

bhoga: enjoyment; *mātra*: measure; *sāmya*: sameness, equality; *liṅgāt*: from the reason or characteristic; *ca*: and.

anāvṛttiśabdāt anāvṛttiḥ śabdāt // 22 //

anāvṛttiḥ: not subject to restriction, free; *śabdāt*: according to the word; *anāvṛttiḥ*: free, and hence no longer on the return journey; *śabdāt*: according to the scriptural word.

iti caturthaḥ khaṇḍaḥ

caturthādhyāyaḥ

iti brahmasūtra

Oṁ śāntiḥ śāntiḥ śāntiḥ

19. *And [there is a form of the Lord which] transcends the changeable, because this is how [the Scriptures] describe the state [of His] being.*

Beyond the *saguṇa* form, the *Śruti* mentions another aspect of being which is beyond movement and beyond effects: that is *nirguṇa* (*Chā.* III.XII.5-6-7).

20. *And in this way they show [both] direct perception [Śruti] and deduction [Smṛti].*[12]

21. *And by reason of equality in the measure of the enjoyment.*[13]

22. *[For the liberated jīva] there is no return, according to the Scriptures. There is no return, according to the Scriptures.*[14]

End of Chapter Four of Book Four

of the Brahmasūtra

End of the Brahmasūtra

Om śāntiḥ śāntiḥ śāntiḥ

NOTES

[1] IV.IV.1 - Having attained the supreme Light, the *jīva* reveals "its real nature", the nature of the *Ātman* or *Brahman*.

The *jīva* does not have to reach anything, does not have to acquire what it does not have, does not have to import anything new into its being. *Sādhanā* consists in dissolving the *avidyā* that has been superimposed over its real nature.

The being is immortal. If it did not have the nature of immortality, it could never realise this nature.

In the *Śruti* we read:

> '... in the same way it, perfectly still, emerging from this body, having attained the supreme Light, is established in its own nature. That is the supreme *Puruṣa*.'
>
> 'That which is infinitely subtle: it has That as essence. That is the Reality. That is the *Ātman* and 'That thou art', o Śvetaketu.' 'O Venerable sir, speak to me about it once more! 'May it be so, my dear, answered [the father].'[1]
>
> 'On this side of That, the Year, with its days, revolves. On That, which is the light of lights, the *devas* indeed meditate, as on life immortal.'[2]

The light spoken of is the *Ātman*, for this is what the *Śruti* declares.

'Having realised [the *Ātman*], after the separation from

---

[1] *Chā*. VIII.XII.3; VI.IX.4.

[2] *Bṛ*. IV.IV.16.

the body, he ascends into That and, having satisfied all desires, in the world of the heavens he becomes immortal: becomes [immortal].'[1]

[2] IV.IV.4 - He who has realised himself is in identity with the supreme *Brahman*. This is confirmed by the *Śruti*. The *essence* which permeates the bodies or *guṇas* of the living being is of the same nature as the *nirguṇa* Reality, that metaphysical Foundation which underlies the whole manifestation. In the Western Tradition it corresponds to the One Good of Plato, the One of Plotinus, the *Ain soph* of Qabbālāh, and so on.

The *Śruti* contains various clear statements which show the identity of the *jīva* with the *Ātman* or *Brahman*.

'That thou art.'[2]

'This *Ātman* is *Brahman*.'[3]

'That knew only itself as "I am *Brahman*", and so It became all. Whoever among the gods knows That, he himself becomes That. The same is true for the sages; the same is true for [other] human beings.'[4]

Of course what is meant is the *jīva* and not the *ahaṁkāra* which changes all the time. (*Mai*. IV.2).

[3] IV.IV.6 - According to Auḍulomi the Teacher, on the other hand, once the *jīva* is liberated, it exists only as essential nature. Although Auḍulomi maintains that one is pure Intelligence only when one has realised oneself in the *Brahman*, Bādarāyaṇa does not contradict this assertion, because all the

---

[1] *Ai*. II.6.

[2] *Chā*. VI.VIII.7.

[3] *Mā*. II.

[4] *Bṛ*. I.IV.10.

time that the *jīva* turns its gaze towards the 'second' it can be considered as such. This a state is illusory, however, because the *jīva* has always been *Ātman*. It is simply that, darkened by *tamas*, by superimposing particular qualitative conditions upon itself, it has qualified itself. The supreme *Ātman* cannot have a double nature. See *Brahmasūtra* III.II.11 with related commentary and *Bṛhadāraṇyaka Upaniṣad* IV.V.13-14.

[4] IV.IV.8 - In the *Śruti* we read:

> 'If he aspires to the world of the Fathers as object of enjoyment, the Fathers present themselves only by virtue of his deliberation and, since he is associated with this world of the Fathers, he attains the glory.'[1]

This means that the determination of one who has transcended the empirical ego needs no other support or collateral acts, as happens for one who puts mere individual desire in place of the determination exercised by the *buddhi*. The *Śruti* is clear on this subject.

[5] IV.IV.9 - And for this reason the Knower has no other lord different from himself.

In the *Śruti* we read:

> '... Thus, those who depart without having realised the *Ātman* and the true aspirations here, they will not be free to move in all the worlds. On the other hand, those who depart having realised the *Ātman* and the true aspirations here, they will be free to move in all the worlds.'[2]

---

[1] *Chā*. VIII.II.1.

[2] *Ibid*. VIII.I.6.

> 'By doing *saṁyama* on the relationship between body and *ākāśa*, similar to a cotton strand, one travels in space.'[1]

[6] IV.IV.10 - According to Bādari the Teacher, the body and the physical senses no longer exist for one who has realised the *Brahmaloka*; there exists only the noetic mind with which to deliberate and by means of which every aspiration can be realised.

In the *Śruti* we read:

> 'Then, he who has the consciousness: "may I think!", that is the *Ātmā*. Mind is his divine eye. That very same, in truth, by seeing them through this divine eye, which is the mind, he delights in these objects of desire which are in *Brahmaloka*.'[2]

[7] IV.IV.11 - According to Jaimini, on the other hand, there is existence of the body and the senses insofar as the liberated *saguṇa* can assume various forms or vehicles at will. At the subtle levels the 'matter' or essence of bodily substance, being by nature simpler, is lighter and can be shaped by the strength of thought. We can notice this in the dream state where the body or vehicle is the mental one (*manas*), freed by the physical body.

We are still in the realm of the three worlds: gross, subtle, and causal. Beyond these worlds there is the root of all that exists: the supreme *Brahman*, without quality or form.

[8] IV.IV.15 - The *jīva*, while remaining a unity, can manifest

---

[1] Patañjali, *The Regal Way to Realization* (*Yogadarśana*) III.42, edited by Raphael. Op. cit.

[2] *Chā*. VIII.XII.5.

itself through numerous vehicles, just as a single flame can feed numerous lamps. This reflects the teaching of the *Śruti*: 'He, which is single, he becomes triple, and then fivefold, sevenfold and ninefold... .'[1]

Even at the gross physical level there can be an action of bi-location, and with a yogic discipline it is possible to reach the point of being able to multiply oneself into several forms or bodies. This phenomenon is a qualification for many *yogis*: 'A single mind directs the activity of the different minds.'[2]

[9] IV.IV.16 - In the two states of *saguṇa* and *nirguṇa* there is no distinctive or dualistic knowledge; but while in deep or dreamless sleep the distinctive qualities (qualities which are nonetheless of the order of *sattva* at this level) remain latent, in the *nirguṇa* state all that is quality, distinctiveness, and self-otherness is completely dissolved. Compare *Bṛhadāraṇyaka Upaniṣad* II.IV.14, IV.III.30 and *Chāndogya Upaniṣad* VI.XV.1-3.

[10] IV.IV.17 - In the *Brahmaloka* the *jīva* holds in potentiality all the possibilities inherent in such a state, but it cannot have the power to create or destroy the worlds. And nowhere are there contiguous or similar arguments affirming that these powers can be exercised.

A *manvantara* is nothing other than an unresolved seed from an earlier *manvantara*, just as the embodiment of a *jīva* at the threefold individualised level is nothing other than an unresolved seed from an earlier embodiment. It may be said that when cause and effect, time and space, are not resolved,

---

[1] *Chā*. VII.XXVI.2.

[2] Patañjali, *The Regal Way to Realization* (*Yogadarśana*) IV.5, edited by Raphael. Op. cit.

these factors must perpetuate themselves, and this constitutes *saṁsāra*. *Saṁsāra* cannot be destroyed because all the *jīvas* at the universal level, and with their reflections or rays at the formal level, must conclude their cycle of manifestation and of solution of their qualifications.

However a *manvantara* does not concern only the human being or *jīva*. The principial causal Body (*Íśvara*) contains indefinite archetypes, 'seeds', or paradigms and, only one of them is the human *jīva*. Therefore, on an ontological level there exist archetypes, intelligible and sensible, which will become prototypes on the manifest level, and this represents the world of names and forms in its qualitative and quantitative unfolding. All this is an orderly process because the principial causal Body, with its manifold content, remains always fixed in itself or rotates on itself, as long as the *manvantara* lasts and this implies that each being, whatever dimension it belongs to, is the result of what must be and nothing else. The *saguṇa Brahman* represents this principial ontological state, but being multiplicity, although unity, in its whole, it must find its reason for existence in the *nirguṇa Brahman*. The *nirguṇa Brahman* represents its ultimate foundation, non-born. It is the infinite in its purest connotation, beyond time, space and causality. This, moreover, causes *Íśvara*, with its indefinite forms and names, to vanish into the *mahāpralaya* - the great cosmic dissolution - while *nirguṇa Brahman* remains unaltered, since it has no beginning and no end. *Íśvara* (One-many) could not even exist and manifest without the support of *nirguṇa Brahman*.

> 'The *Brāhmaṇa*, having recognised that the different worlds are [the result] of [unresolved] *karma* (*karma-citāh*), detaches himself from them, [recognising that] it is impossible to attain that which is eternal (*akṛta* = non-produced) through that which is perishable. In order to realise the

knowledge of That, he should go with fuel in his hands to a teacher versed in the *Śruti* and founded in the *Brahman*.'[1]

[11] IV.IV.18 - If it is believed that, on the basis of the Scriptures (*Tai.* I.VI.2) the liberated *saguṇa jīva* can have unlimited powers, the *Brahmasūtra* replies that this is not so, because this cannot be a reasonable possibility inasmuch as that which is in particular locations, such as the solar disk, is clearly qualified and determined and therefore cannot have such powers. Hence limit, time, and so on, refer to something standing behind them, namely, the *nirguṇa Brahman*.

Bādarāyaṇa is not opposed to the Scripture, but he gives an extensive interpretative value to it. Although the Scripture speaks of the supreme Lord, this always refers to the *saguṇa* condition, according to the evidence of the specific text.

[12] IV.IV.20 - On the other hand, both the *Śruti* and the *Smṛti* demonstrate the existence of the Supreme, which transcends every form and attribute.

In the *Śruti* we read:

'There the sun shines not, the moon shines not, the stars shine not, nor do these lightnings flash.'[2].

See also the *Śvetāśvatara Upaniṣad* (VI.14), which conveys the same *vidyā*.

In the *Smṛti* we read:

'Neither the sun nor the moon nor fire illuminates it. It is my supreme abode, from which those who attain it will no longer return.'[3]

---

[1] *Mu.* I.II.12.

[2] *Ibid.* II.II.10.

[3] *Bha. Gī.* XV.6. Op. cit.

In the *Śruti*, however, there are many other passages which point to this 'fourth condition', which is *nirguṇa Brahman* or *Turīya*.

[13] IV.IV.21 - According to the scriptural indications, it is through the equality of enjoyment alone, such as bliss, and therefore of experience, that the *jīvas* have the same value, but in the reality of the *nirguṇa Brahman* there is no experience and no enjoyment of any degree or kind. Where there is enjoyment of something the *guṇas* still exist, and so do subject and object, but there are no *guṇas* in the *Brahman*, because it is *nir-guṇa*, that is, devoid of the *guṇas*.

[14] IV.IV.22 - Having reached *Brahmaloka*, the *jīva*, as has already been hinted at, no longer makes the return journey to the individualised condition (the way of the *pitṛ*). It dwells in the universal principial condition (the way of the *devas*) and is not subject to any restriction, which means that it is free from lunar reincarnations.

> 'This is the way of the gods, the Way of *Brahman*. Those who follow this Way return no more to this human condition. They return no more.'[1]

Having exhausted the reasons or seeds which impel it into the manifest, the *jīva* is totally freed from all impediment, thus assuming the condition of 'supreme *Sākṣin*', by which it discovers itself to be like the actor who, having fulfilled his manifold parts on the stage, takes his seat in the stalls as a mere spectator, free from all formal action.

The repetition of the words in the *sūtra* indicates that the work is completed.

---

[1] *Chā*. IV.XV.5.

Some Final Notes

Some observations may be useful to elucidate an aspect of the teaching which is present both in the East, including this work, as well as in the West.

What is it about? It is to posit a reflection on two fundamental principles which concern philosophy; that is, the principle of Being and the principle of supra-Being. As far as the East is concerned, we have the *saguṇa Brahman* (= Being) and the *nirguṇa Brahman* (*eka* = the One without a second); while for the West we have Being (ὄν) and the transcendent One (ἕν), or the One Good. In other words, it is possible to speak of two data: the ontological datum and the henological datum.

Let us examine these two dialectical aspects:

1) In the *Bṛhadāranyaka Upaniṣad* (II.I.1) we read:

> '*Om*! The haughty Bālāki, descendant of the Gārgya race, in truth, was proud of speaking. Once he told Ajātaśatru, [king] of Kāśi: "I will speak to you of the *Brahman*... ."'

Then Gārgya set forth many names for the *Brahman*: *Brahman* which is in the sun, in the moon, in the thunderbolt, in the space and so on. He indicated the qualified (*saguṇa*) *Brahman* and not the metaphysical (*nirguṇa*) *Brahman*. When the haughty Bālāki-Gārgya had finished putting forward his knowledge of the *Brahman*, Ajātaśatru told him: 'Is this all?.' Gārgya answered: 'Yes, this is all.' And Ajātaśatru replied: 'But only with this, in truth, nothing is known.'

In the same *Upaniṣad* (II.III.1) we read:

'In truth, two are the aspects of the *Brahman*: the aspect with form (*rūpa*) and the subtle aspect, the mortal and the immortal, the moving and the steady, the existing and the transcendent.'

Again in the *Upaniṣad* (II.III.6) we read:

'... therefore, after this, there is the description [of the *Brahman*] as 'not this, not this' (*neti, neti*), because, in truth, there is no other [indication] better than 'not this.'

The *Bṛhadāranyaka*, one of the most ancient *Upaniṣads*, speaks of the unqualified *Brahman*, that is, of the foundation which holds everything, and of the qualified *Brahman* as principial cause from which the movement and the development of the multiple manifestation (*nāma-rūpa*), that is to say, the ontological state, start.

'Then [the father] told him: "My dear, you cannot perceive this subtle foundation; my dear, in truth, the great *nyagrodha* lives on this subtle foundation... That which is infinitely subtle has That as foundation. That is the only Reality, it is the *Ātman* and "That thou art" O Śvetaketu... .' (*Chā*. VI.XII.2-3).

2) The metaphysical state is posited as the state which transcends the ontological level and consequently the entire manifestation. One may attain the ontological state, hence the Being (*saguṇa*), by means of the dianoetic thought, with mental reasoning and rationality. We are at the level of concepts. However, the being, by making this sphere exclusive, can consider the supra-ontological as pure abstraction, as an indecipherable void, as something which, lying outside the realm of thought, is difficult to accept.

It is interesting to see the dialectic of Bādarāyaṇa with

the *bhedābhedavāda* schools: the doctrine of distinction non-distinction, the theist doctrine, the dualist doctrine, the ritual doctrine and so on.

The *saguṇa Brahman* (Being) is already multiplicity; it is movement. And thought, which is movement and differentiation, finds its reason for existence in engaging discursively with multiplicity and within multiplicity. However, it must be acknowledged that, despite everything, Plato, Plotinus, Sankara, Badarayana, and others speak of the One without a second and of Being as a paradigm of manifest Being.

> 'And just as in the sensible world light and sight resemble the sun, although it is not right to put them in place of the sun, so in the intelligible world it is right to consider that knowledge and truth are both similar to the Good, but it is not right to consider that either of them is the Good, whose naturc, in fact, is to be regarded as of much greater value.'[1]

A faculty is needed to raise oneself to the One, a faculty which is higher than dianoetic thought, which everyone has but very few use (Plato, Plotinus, Śaṅkara and so on). A faculty which offers the possibility to catch and comprehend the One with immediacy.

> '... Whoever has contemplated, knows what I am saying... .'[2]

As far as the being *thinks* of himself only as thought (the Being is thought of thought, νόησις νοήσεως, Aristotle) it is inevitable, and also natural, not to allow the henological or 'One without a second' perspective.

However, this way of thinking is not wrong, and there is

---

[1] Plato, *Politéia* VI.508e-509a, in G. Reale, *Tutti gli scritti*. Op. cit.

[2] Plotinus, *Enneads* VI.9.9, translated by G. Faggin. Op. cit.

nothing to say or to question. It represents a way of philosophising which is acceptable and logical.

On the other hand, the problem may be posited, in our view, thus: though accepting that One, the tendency is to want to confine it within the 'measure of man', that is, to evaluate it with the faculty of the *diànoia*, or empirical thinking, since the purpose of philosophising, for such minds is to seek, to know and to understand the 'other' (subject and object). However, since there is no object, no *other* or second, on what can one philosophise? This, too, is quite right, even if it is a particular way of seeing things.

> 'That he, in truth, does not think there, it is because, although in reality he may think, still, there, he thinks [nothing]. In fact there is no cessation for the thought of the thinker, since [this] is indestructible, but there is no second apart from him [being undivided unity], such that he may think of him as another'[1]

> 'In fact in which way, could the news be given of Him as someone different, when he who saw Him did not see Him as different during the contemplation, but he saw Him as one with himself?'[2]

The two quotations given above are explicit: when the subject and the object merge themselves into the *Ātman* or *Noûs* there is no other of whom to think, hence the *One without a second*. At this point philosophical knowledge is no longer an end in itself but it is a means, the highest, which raises us '... from darkness to light, from the unreal to the Real.'

From what has been said above one can understand that the

---

[1] *Bṛ.* IV.III.28 *et seqq.*

[2] Plotinus, *Enneads* VI.9.X, translated by G. Faggin. Cp. also VI.7.XXXVII *et seqq.*, where it is stated that the One is beyond thought.

dianoetic function is based on the 'other.' This has been mainly put forward by Aristotle, and it is since his time that in the West this problem has been faced, discussed and perpetuated without finding any conclusion which, for obvious reasons, cannot be found, however long one may philosophise. In the East this problem, of ontology and henology, has been posited for millennia.

And yet it is possible to reach the metaphysical One, better still one must reach it, by means of the Being, because That integrates, comprehends (takes with Itself), completes and gives *raison d'être* to the Being. Therefore It offers unity, gives order to multiplicity (Being), supports Being and allows things to be what they must be (*ṛta*).

In fact, in the process of realisation they speak of two movements (even if the two are realised in the immediacy of pure contemplation): the first is *neti neti* to acknowledge that the entire world (*nāma-rūpa*) is not the unqualified Supreme, which transcends what is born. Once this acknowledgement has been actuated, there is: *iti iti*, this too - that is to say, Being and whatever originates from it - has to be integrated and resolved into the Supreme. Hence everything is realised in the ἕν-*eka* without the second, because the second in comparison to the ἕν-*eka* is only appearance, that is, it appears and disappears on the horizon of the *eka* (One).

3) However, for Plato, and for *Advaita Vedānta*, the 'highest knowledge' is that which leads to the Idea of the Good, or of *nirguṇa* (whence the text under consideration draws its inspiration and paradigm), and on which the philosophers must philosophise. According to Plato and to *Advaita Vedānta*, the true philosopher is he who goes in search of what is Immutable.

> 'Since philosophers are those who have the capacity to reach realities which are always the same and identical

> to themselves, while those who have not this capacity go wandering among the many realities which are different in many ways and for this reason they are not philosophers... .'[1]

The philosopher has always the Immutable and the uncaused as a reference point; this is expressed as we have seen, by the answer of Ajātaśatru: 'But only with this, in truth, nothing is known', that is, by standing by the multiple, one does not reach the 'end of the journey.'

> 'First of all a firm point which we will adopt concerning the nature of the philosophers is that they will have to prefer all the time the science which reveals the substance, which is and never changes as far as generation and corruption are concerned.'[2]

The *Upaniṣads* and the *Brahmasūtra*, in fact, speak of concentrating and meditating on the *nirguṇa Brahman*, or on the One without a second, which is and does not become, because it is *amātra* (= without measure, or supreme measure to which everything must refer).

> 'But friend - I said - a measure of things of this kind, which leaves behind whatsoever part of the being, does not prove to be, really, a right measure. In fact nothing, which is incomplete, can be the measure for anything. And yet, at times, it seems to someone that this is enough and that it is not necessary to seek further.'[3]

This statement from Plato is emblematic as well as sig-

---

[1] Plato, *Republic* VI.484 b, in G. Reale, *Tutti gli scritti*. Op. cit.

[2] *Ibid*. VI.485 b.

[3] *Ibid*. VI.504 c.

nificative. See the answer of Ajātaśatru which corresponds to the one given by Plato.

4) With the metaphysical path (ὁδός-*mārga*) one arrives at the 'end of the journey' (Plato, Plotinus, Śaṅkara, Bādarāyaṇa and so on), so that the being 'fallen into generation' can find its existential solution (*tat tvam asi*: You, *jīva* or Soul, are That).

> 'That same, O Gārgī, is this Indestructible who sees but is not seen, hears but is not heard, thinks but is not thought, knows but is not known. Besides Him, no other seer exists, no other hearer exists, no other thinker exists, no other knower exists. And, in truth, it is on this Indestructible, O Gārgī, that space is designed and woven.'[1]

> 'What, then, should we think - he said - if someone should happen to see absolute Beauty in itself, pure, unmingled, not corrupted by human flesh, by colours or by any other mortal meanness, but he could contemplate, as unique form, the divine Beauty in itself?.' 'Or rather do you think - he said - that it would be a worthless life, the life of a man who looked there and who contemplated that Beauty, with what it must be contemplated, and would remain united to It?'[2]

Supreme truth cannot be but one, indestructible, immutable and realisable, and hence beyond time, space and causality, since logic itself suggests that there cannot be multiple truths, or else anyone could create his own personal truth up to the point of reaching a cognisable confusion, a 'tower of Babel', and this would imply the dissolution of thought itself and of Intellect, and hence the 'death' of σοφία, or of *philo-sophia*.

---

[1] *Bṛ.* III.VIII.11.

[2] Plato, *Symposium* 211 e - 212 a, in G. Reale, *Tutti gli scritti*. Op.cit.

A Brief Outline of
Pūrva Mīmāṁsā and Uttara Mīmāṁsā

1) In the various *sūtras* of the Four Books, Jaimini, the codifier of the *Pūrva Mīmāṁsā*, is often cited. His main treatise is the *Saṁakarṣaṇakāṇḍa Kāṇda*, or *Devatākāṇḍa*, whose content is of *upāsana* (act of ritual, of sacrifice) order. The *darśana* is of a realistic order, the world of becoming is real, it is polytheist, initially atheistic but it becomes theistic with Kumārila; it may be said that by putting its attention solely on rite or sacrifice this *darśana* becomes, one may say, a liturgical pragmatism by subordinating knowledge to ritual. Why is this? It is because the *Mīmāṁsā* does not start from a philosophical enquiry, but from the assumption that the being acts only through *karma* = action, acting, that is, by means of cause and effect, so that in his acting he produces merit (*puṇya*) and demerit (*pāpa*), and therefore he can create his prisons or his liberation.

This is not wrong, quite the reverse: it is also shared by the *Vedānta darśana*. However, with such an exclusive point of view it is obvious that knowledge (*jñānamārga*) becomes something accessory, secondary and, ultimately, it is good for nothing.

2) With such pragmatic vision (cause and effect, effect and cause and so on, *kāryakāraṇa*) one is obviously left with rendering the ritual act exclusive, so that for knowledge, faith, meditation and so on *Pūrva Mīmāṁsā* substitutes the *kar-*

man, the liturgical sacrifice, in order for the being to break the cause-and-effect, effect-and-cause chain and attain bliss.

The *prastotṛ*, he who chants the *prastāva*, the *udgātṛ*, another officiating priest who chants the *sāman*, and so on (the rite is very complex and also complicated), and with the benefit of the *karman* the postulant is led to liberation, even though this liberation is of a relative order because it attains only the Heaven, the universal.

Pūrva Mīmāṁsā includes several renowned commentators, later than Jaimini, with profound *bhāṣyas*. See the *bhāṣya* of Śabara which represents the main foundation of *Mīmāṁsā* and of the subsequent commentators. Kumārila has given a remarkable contribution to the development of the *darśana*, as has Prabhākara. According to Prabhākara, liberation still consists in the solution of the *dharma* and of the *adharma* but with considerable doctrinal discussions.

3) *Uttara Mīmāṁsā* (which corresponds to this fundamental work of *Vedānta*) puts itself at a different initial perspective. The questions which it puts are: Why have I fallen into *saṁsāra*? Who am I while I am on the plane of manifestation? From this inquiry *Vedānta* has understood that the human mind is qualified by the *guṇas* (*rajas-tamas* for the individual), causing the being to lose discrimination and the recollection of what is. And this condition begins from *avidyā*, which is not ignorance of contingent things, but is a kind of 'ignorance', which may be called metaphysical. The superimposition (*adhyāropa*) of the *avidyā* upon the *jīvātman* makes real (*sat*) the non-real (*asat*), because of ignorance itself or *avidyā* (*ajñāna*).

And if *avidyā* has led us into the world of becoming, then its opposite, which is *vidyā* (knowledge-*gnosis*), makes us free from all conditioning, to the point of allowing us to comprehend and assimilate the *mahāvākya* of the *Bṛhadārṇyaka Upaniṣad* (I.IV.10) '*ahaṁ brahmāsmi*': I, *jīva*, am the *Brahman*, and this represents integral liberation.

Thus, *Vedānta* deals with knowledge and with what one really is (*Brahmajñāna*). *Karma Mīmāṁsā* deals with *dharma*, *adharma* and ritual *karman* for their dissolution. One may say, free from prejudices and bias, that the two *Mīmāṁsās* complete each other, because *Karma Mīmāṁsā* corresponds to a level of truth which to be complete needs something more: something that the *Vedāntasūtra* has.[1]

---

[1] For the various *darśanas* see R. Radhakrishnan, *La filosofia indiana* Vol. 2. Op. cit.

PUBLICATIONS

Books by Raphael
published in English

At the Source of Life, *Questions and Answers Concerning the Ultimate Reality.*
Aurea Vidyā, New York.

Beyond the illusion of the ego, *Synthesis of a Realizative Process*
Aurea Vidyā, New York.

Essence and purpose of Yoga, *The Initiatory Pathways to the Transcendent.*
Element Books, Shaftesbury, U.K.

Initiation into the Philosophy of Plato.
Aurea Vidyā, New York.

Orphism and the Initiatory Tradition.
Aurea Vidyā, New York.

The Pathway of Fire according to the Qabbālāh, *'Ehjeh 'Ašer 'Ehjeh (I am What I am).*
Aurea Vidyā, New York.

The Pathway of Non-duality, *Advaitavāda.*
Motilal Banarsidass, New Delhi.

The Science of Love, *From the desire of the senses to the Intellect of Love.*
Aurea Vidyā, New York.

Tat tvam asi, *That thou art, The Path of Fire According to the Asparśavāda.*
Aurea Vidyā, New York.

The Threefold Pathway of Fire, *Thoughts that Vibrate.*
Aurea Vidyā, New York.

Traditional Classics
in English

Śaṅkara, ***Ātmabodha****, *Self-knowledge.*
Aurea Vidyā, New York.

Bhagavadgītā*, *The Celestial Song.*
Aurea Vidyā, New York.

Bādarāyaṇa, ***Brahmasūtra***.*
Aurea Vidyà, New York.

Drigdriśyaviveka*, *Discernment between Ātman and Non-Ātman.*
Aurea Vidyā, New York.

Gauḍapāda, ***Māṇḍūkyakārikā****, *The Metaphysical Path of Vedānta.*
Aurea Vidyā, New York.

Parmenides, ***On the Order of Nature*****, *Περί φύσεως, For a Philosophical Ascesis.*
Aurea Vidyā, New York.

Patañjali, ***The Regal Way to Realization**** (*Yogadarśana*). Aurea Vidyā, New York.

Śaṅkara, ***Vivekacūḍāmaṇi****, *The Crest Jewel of Discernment*. Aurea Vidyā, New York.

Forthcoming Publications
in English

Śaṅkara, ***Aparokṣānubhūti****, *Self-realization*.

Śaṅkara, ***Brief Works****, *Treatises and Hymns*.

Five Upaniṣads*, *Īśa, Kaivalya, Sarvasāra, Amṛtabindu, Atharvaśira*.

Raphael, ***Fire of Ascesis***.

Raphael, ***Fire of Awakening***.

Raphael, ***Fire of the Philosophers***.

Raphael, ***The Path of Non-duality***, *Advaitavāda*.

* Translated from the Sanskrit, and Commented, by Raphael.
** Edited and Commented by Raphael.

Aurea Vidyā is the Publishing House of the Parmenides Traditional Philosophy Foundation, a Not-for-Profit Organization whose purpose is to make Perennial Philosophy accessible.

The Foundation goes about its purpose in a number of ways: by publishing and distributing Traditional Philosophy texts with Aurea Vidyā, by offering individual and group encounters and by providing a Reading Room and daily Meditations at its Center.

* * *

Those readers who have an interest in Traditional Philosophy are welcome to contact the Foundation at: parmenides.foundation@earthlink.net.

The *Brahmasūtra* or *Vedāntasūtra* of Bādarāyaṇa represents the fundamental text of exegesis of *Vedānta*.

The intent of Bādarāyaṇa – the sage that for authority and realization of consciousness has been identified with Vyāsa, the *Ṛṣi* who ordered the texts of the *Vedas* – is that of providing the right perspective in the interpretation of the most profound and meaningful contents of the *Upaniṣads*. This had proven necessary in order to rectify some unilateral aspects propounded by several schools of thought, both orthodox and non-orthodox.

The *Brahmasūtra* presents, in their simplicity and incisiveness, the assertions of the *Śruti* and of the *Smṛti*, showing their concordance in the recognition of the *Nirguṇa Brahman* as the ultimate Realty.

The *Brahmasūtra* contains 555 *sūtras*, arranged in four Books, each of which is divided into four Chapters.

In Book One, "Harmony", the vision of the *Brahman*, as the Foundation of all that exists, is expounded; the purpose being that of reconciling different Vedic statements on the subject.

In Book Two, "Absence of Contradiction", the objections raised against this vision are examined and refuted. Moreover, there are some notes regarding the nature of the *jīva*, its attributes, and its relationship with the *Brahman*, the body and its actions.

In Book Three, "Spiritual Discipline", the ways and the means (*sādhana*) necessary to realize the *brahmavidyā*, the knowledge of the supreme *Brahman* are expounded. The state of consciousness of the *jīva* is also dealt with in this Book.

In Book Four, "The Fruit", the fruits (*phala*) of the *brahmavidyā* are reviewed. There is also the description of the departure of the *jīva* after the death of the physical body, along the two paths, that of the gods and that of the ancestors (*devayaṇa* and *pitṛyaṇa* ways), and of the nature of the final liberation.

In his notes, Raphael underlines the fact that Bādarāyaṇa does not oppose the various philosophical schools, but the *Ṛṣi* allows us to comprehend that their postulates cannot represent the ultimate Truth as expounded in the *Vedas* and in the *Upaniṣads*. Moreover, at times Raphael focuses on certain aspects of the *Advaita* Doctrine with references to the Western Tradition, and – making the relevant parallels to the philosophy of Parmenides, Plato, Plotinus, and so on – highlights the unity of the sole universal Tradition at the metaphysical level.

Lastly, Raphael clarifies an aspect which is of special importance in the *Advaita* view: that is, that between the perspectives of Gauḍapāda and Śaṅkara there is neither opposition nor contradiction. They are just two modes of approach which, all the same, reach supreme *nirguṇa* Truth. In fact, Gauḍapāda puts himself from an exclusively *pāramārthika* perspective (ultimate and supreme Truth), while Śaṅkara begins with the *vyāvaharika* knowledge (empirical, phenomenal and relative reality) to then lead the seeker to the dimension of the pure *pāramārthika* knowledge.

ghtning Source UK Ltd.
Keynes UK
W011906271021
2933UK00002B/435

9 781931 406178